ATTRIBUTION
Basic Issues and Applications

ATTRIBUTION
Basic Issues and Applications

Edited by

JOHN H. HARVEY

Department of Psychology
Texas Tech University
Lubbock, Texas

GIFFORD WEARY

Department of Psychology
Ohio State University
Columbus, Ohio

ACADEMIC PRESS, INC.
Harcourt Brace Jovanovich, Publishers
San Diego   New York   Berkeley   Boston
London   Sydney   Tokyo   Toronto

ACADEMIC PRESS, INC.
1250 Sixth Avenue, San Diego, California 92101

United Kingdom Edition published by
ACADEMIC PRESS INC. (LONDON) LTD.
24–28 Oval Road, London NW1 7DX

LIBRARY OF CONGRESS CATALOGING IN PUBLICATION DATA

Attribution : basic issues and applications.

Includes index.
1. Attribution (Social psychology) — Addresses, essays,
lectures. I. Harvey, John H.,   II. Weary,
Gifford,
HM291.A87   1985   302'.12   84-18557
ISBN 0-12-329960-8 (alk. paper)

PRINTED IN THE UNITED STATES OF AMERICA

87 88   9 8 7 6 5 4 3 2

To our parents

Contents

3. Cognitive Economy and Commonsense Attribution Processing

RANALD D. HANSEN

4. Implicit Relations Between Dispositions and Behaviors: Effects on Dispositional Attribution

GLENN D. REEDER

5. Motivation and Attribution: The Effects of Control Deprivation on Subsequent Information Processing

THANE S. PITTMAN and PAUL R. D'AGOSTINO

9. Attributional Models of Depression, Loneliness, and Shyness

CRAIG A. ANDERSON and LYNN H. ARNOULT

III
CONCLUDING COMMENTS   281

10. Attribution Research: Past Contributions, Current Trends, and Future Prospects

JAMES M. OLSON and MICHAEL ROSS

Contributors

Numbers in parentheses indicate the pages on which the authors' contributions begin.

Craig A. Anderson[1] (235), Department of Psychology, Rice University, Houston, Texas 77251

Robert M. Arkin (169), Department of Psychology, University of Missouri, Columbia, Missouri 65211

Lynn H. Arnoult (235), Department of Psychology, Rice University, Houston, Texas 77251

Reuben M. Baron (37), Department of Psychology, University of Connecticut, Storrs, Connecticut 06268

Ann H. Baumgardner (169), Department of Psychology, University of Missouri, Columbia, Missouri 65211

Paul R. D'Agostino (117), Department of Psychology, Gettysburg College, Gettysburg, Pennsylvania 17325-1486

Susan D. Elbin (143), Department of Psychology, Ohio State University, Columbus, Ohio 43210

Frank D. Fincham (203), Department of Psychology, University of Illinois, Champaign–Urbana, Illinois 61801

Ranald D. Hansen (65), Department of Psychology, Oakland University, Rochester, Michigan 48063

John H. Harvey (1), Department of Psychology, Texas Tech University, Lubbock, Texas 79409

Lorraine Hildebrand-Saints (143), Department of Psychology, Ohio State University, Columbus, Ohio 43210

Martha G. Hill (143), Department of Psychology, Ohio State University, Columbus, Ohio 43210

Saul M. Kassin[2] (37), Department of Psychology, Williams College, Williamstown, Massachusetts 01267

James M. Olson (283), Department of Psychology, University of Western Ontario, London, Ontario N6A 5C2, Canada

[1] Present address: Department of Psychology, Ohio State University, Columbus, Ohio 43210.

[2] Temporary address: Federal Judicial Center, Dolley Madison House, 1520 H Street, N.W., Washington, D.C. 20005.

Thane S. Pittman (117), Department of Psychology, Gettysburg College, Gettysburg, Pennsylvania 17325-1486

Glenn D. Reeder (87), Department of Psychology, Illinois State University, Normal, Illinois 61761

Michael Ross (283), Department of Psychology, University of Waterloo, Waterloo, Ontario N2L 3G1, Canada

Melinda A. Stanley (1), Department of Psychology, Texas Tech University, Lubbock, Texas 79409

Gifford Weary (1, 143), Department of Psychology, Ohio State University, Columbus, Ohio 43210

Timothy D. Wilson (9), Department of Psychology, University of Virginia, Charlottesville, Virginia 22901

Preface

We began the planning of this volume in a most tentative fashion. There have been, after all, a string of edited volumes on attributional processes produced during the 1970s and early 1980s, starting with the 1972 volume that arose from the 1969 UCLA conference on attribution (*Attribution: Perceiving the Causes of Behavior*, edited by Jones, Kanouse, Kelley, Nisbett, Valins, and Weiner). As we discuss in an introductory commentary, however, the field of attribution work has continued to expand and attract scholars from throughout the discipline of psychology. In fact, this breadth is such that the continued publication of volumes at regular intervals may be useful to the integration of ideas, data, strands of work, and even major schools of thought in psychology and related disciplines (e.g., the attributional perspective and Piagetian ideas, symbolic interactionism, Freudian conceptions, or Meadian social behaviorism).

We believe, though, that the integrative task is imposing because attribution's tentacles now spread far beyond issues that traditionally were the focus of research programs in the field. One will not, for instance, find much attention centered on the traditional topics of attribution of responsibility, attitude or trait attribution, or attributions for achievement-related behavior in the present volume. Rather, as is evident, attributional analysis has been applied to disparate phenomena that increasingly include all the human conditions of our time that occupy counselors and therapists in their practice—depression, loneliness, social ineptitude, relationship breakdown, and so on. It is a field that is virtually a potpourri of many of the concepts and research problems of what is endearingly referred to as "soft psychology." We do not despair about this amalgam and would even argue that it reflects the acumen of Heider's (1976, p. 18) expansive definition of attribution, namely: "Attribution is part of our cognition of the environment. Whenever you cognize your environment you will find attribution occurring" ("A Conversation with Fritz Heider." In *New Directions in Attribution Research*, Vol. 1, edited by J. H. Harvey, W. Ickes, and R. F. Kidd, Hillsdale, NJ:

Erlbaum). Indeed, the general scholar and especially advanced seminar students should find this volume useful. And we hope that as the need arises, we and other ''interested purveyors'' of this perspective will be able and willing to offer future volumes on interesting features of the attribution landscape.

Introduction: Attribution Theory and Research—Still Vital in the 1980s

John H. Harvey, Gifford Weary, and Melinda A. Stanley

BACKGROUND

The present volume represents a contribution to an emerging set of edited volumes on attributional processes published in the 1970s and early 1980s. It is a direct descendant of the series, *New Directions in Attribution Research*, edited by Harvey, Ickes, and Kidd and published in 1976, 1978, and 1981. Those volumes showcased the work on attribution of many senior scholars, as well as that of many young scholars who were beginning to develop their research programs. The aim of the present volume is to continue that tradition by publishing chapters representing some of the new and most promising lines of work in the attribution area. Again, we are emphasizing the work of several younger scholars—writers who no doubt will influence the field in the 1980s in the same fashion that other writers in the Harvey et al. series influenced the field in the 1970s and continue to influence it today.

We believe that the present collection of writings makes clear the continued vitality of attribution in contemporary work in psychology. As evidence that attributional ideas remain prominent in contemporary psychology, Kelley and Michela (1980) report that between 1970 and 1980, over 900 references relevant to attribution were revealed in a computer-assisted search. More recently, Harvey and Weary (1984) counted between 400 and 500 relevant works published between 1978 and 1982. This volume of production and its solid intellectual basis and promise suggest that it would be untenable to regard attribution research as simply faddish and likely to fade from the scene, as have so many topics in social psychology. As Kelley (1978) suggested, the area naturally emerged out of numerous phenomena that social psychologists have

1

examined and tried to interpret, and it is likely that some such type of attributional analysis will remain with us indefinitely because of the inexorable link between many phenomena and this type of conception.

At the same time, the current attribution scholar is well aware that there is no grand, coherent theory of attribution. As is true in other areas, there now exists a sea of mini-theories or general ideas and hypotheses that are not clearly interrelated in a logical manner. This state of affairs is likely to remain, given the breadth of the field. As long as the ideas in their more isolated state have the explanatory merit Kelley imputed to them, the need to develop an overarching theory is not as urgent. The fertility and durability of Heider's ideas and mini-theories of attributional processes are ever remarkable, and that fertility hardly has been exhausted since the publication of his 1958 book, *The Psychology of Interpersonal Relations*.

Another mark of the vitality of attributional ideas is their breadth of influence in contemporary psychology. Attribution was born and nurtured for at least a decade in the general domain of social and person perception work in social psychology. Now, however, as has been true since the early 1970s, attributional ideas and research have generated interest among workers in other fields such as clinical, cognitive, counseling, developmental, and industrial psychology, and even sociology (see Crittenden, 1983). In any field where scholars are interested in how people understand their world, including themselves, there is considerable potential for contribution by the attribution literature and perspective.

BASIC TENETS

It is possible to discern certain basic tenets of attributional processes in the chapters in this volume and in other works in the field in the 1980s. Among these tenets are the following:

1. As a phenomenal state, attribution is a pervasive activity. It may occur spontaneously, as one cognizes the environment (Heider, 1976), or it may involve more deliberate inferential or deductive activities (Kelley, 1967). Further, the fact that people may not be able to report (or are not willing to report) attributional activity does not necessarily mean that it is not occurring. It may occur subtly or quickly without conscious recognition. Or, people may not readily have the words or constructions with which to report the process. Also, attributional processes may be posited as a hypothetical construct without necessary reference to people's actual cognitive activity.

2. Because of the complexity of many real world events, attributions

often will not be completely accurate. In recent years, there has been "much ado" regarding the so-called "fundamental attribution error" (Ross, 1977) that refers to people's tendency to over-attribute events and behavior to others' personalities (see Reeder, 1982; Harvey & McGlynn, 1982). At present, the idea that any one attributional bias is any more prevalent than other such biases is far from established empirically or logically. Not only does the complexity of events always mitigate against perfectly accurate attribution, but also attributors often attempt to meet conflicting goals (e.g., self-esteem protection, self-presentation concerns, desire to be honest and sincere).

3. As Jones (1984) suggests, people, by and large, behave according to their perceptions and their understandings. This view probably represents as fundamental a position as could be entertained by attribution theorists. If true, it means that people usually do not become "lost in thought" with little or no relationship developing between their attributions about people or events and some action vis-à-vis those people (including self) or events (Yarkin, Harvey, & Bloxom, 1981).

4. Another quite basic tenet of attributional activity is that it often serves the needs of human adaptation. In this sense, attribution may involve a relatively unbiased search for the causal sequence in some phenomenon (e.g., who and/or what was responsible for an airplane crash). Or it may be highly biased (e.g., the type of inquiry frequently conducted by persons for whom close relationships recently have ended; see Harvey, Wells, & Alvarez, 1978). Even in the latter case, biased interpretations may be adaptive because of their tranquilizing function (Weiss, 1975). As Jones (1984) suggests, the social order typically produces its own predictability whether or not participants' attributions are accurate. Further, as has been shown in an intriguing fashion, people sometimes seek out attributional ambiguity (Snyder & Wicklund, 1981), presumably in the interest of preserving a sense of personal control. In general, then, and as a classic premise in attribution work, attributional processes are assumed to facilitate people's feelings of control. (Olson and Ross in their commentary in Chapter 10 on the chapters in this volume identify a number of additional themes. Interested readers are referred to their discussion.)

Finally, in showing problems and issues workers must address to refine both theory and method of study in the field, this volume reflects the current status of attribution work quite well. As expressed clearly by Kelley and Michela (1980), a transcending issue in the study of attribution is that there are "too few researchers spread too thinly over too many problems. Each question has received far less attention, in terms of number of paradigms and replications, than its definitely and undoubtedly complex answer requires. Conceptually . . . the theories are piecemeal and greatly in need of synthesis'' (p. 494). Kelley and Michela's points still ring true in the mid-1980s.

REFERENCES

Crittenden, K. S. (1983). Sociological aspects of attribution. *Annual Review of Sociology, 9,* 425–446.

Harvey, J. H., Ickes, W., & Kidd, R. F. (Eds.) (1976). *New directions in attribution research* (Vol. 1). Hillsdale, NJ: Erlbaum.

Harvey, J. H., Ickes, W., & Kidd, R. F. (Eds.). (1978). *New directions in attribution research* (Vol. 2). Hillsdale, NJ: Erlbaum.

Harvey, J. H., Ickes, W., & Kidd, R. F. (Eds.). (1981). *New directions in attribution research* (Vol. 3). Hillsdale, NJ: Erlbaum.

Harvey, J. H., & McGlynn, R. P. (1982). Matching words to phenomena: The case of the fundamental attribution error. *Journal of Personality and Social Psychology, 432,* 345–346.

Harvey, J. H., & Weary, G. (1984). Current issues in attribution theory and research. *Annual Review of Psychology, 35,* 427–459.

Harvey, J. H., Wells, G. L., & Alvarez M. W. (1978). Attribution in the context of conflict and separation in close relationships. In J. H. Harvey, W. Ickes, & R. F. Kidd (Eds.), *New directions in attribution research* (Vol. 2). Hillsdale, NJ: Erlbaum.

Heider, F. (1958). *The psychology of interpersonal relations.* New York: Wiley.

Heider, F. (1976). A conversation with Fritz Heider. In J. H. Harvey, W. Ickes, & R. F. Kidd (Eds), *New directions in attribution research* (Vol. 1). Hillsdale, NJ: Erlbaum.

Jones, E. E. (1984). ''Attributional context of interpersonal relations.'' National Science Foundation Grant Proposal.

Kelley, H. H. (1978). A conversation with Edward E. Jones and Harold H. Kelley. In J. H. Harvey, W. Ickes, & R. F. Kidd (Eds.), *New directions in attribution research* (Vol 2). Hillsdale, NJ: Erlbaum.

Kelley, H. H. (1967). Attribution theory in social psychology. *Nebraska Symposium on Motivation, 15,* 192–238.

Kelley, H. H., & Michela, J. L. (1980). Attribution theory and research. *Annual Review of Psychology, 31,* 457–501.

Reeder, G. W. (1982). Let's give the fundamental attribution error another chance. *Journal of Personality and Social Psychology, 43,* 341–344.

Ross, L. (1977). The intuitive psychologist and his shortcomings. *Advances in Experimental Social Psychology, 10,* 174–220.

Snyder, M. L., & Wicklund, R. A. (1981). Attribute ambiguity. In J. H. Harvey, W. Ickes, & R. F. Kidd (Eds) *New directions in attribution research* (Vol 3). Hillsdale, NJ: Erlbaum.

Weiss, R. S. (1975). *Marital separation.* New York: Basic Books.

Yarkin, K. L., Harvey, J. H., & Bloxom, B. M. (1981). Cognitive sets, attribution, and social interaction. *Journal of Personality and Social Psychology, 41,* 243–252.

PART I

BASIC ISSUES IN ATTRIBUTION THEORY AND RESEARCH

The first six chapters are concerned with basic psychological processes—both antecedent and consequent—involved in attributional activities. Wilson (Chapter 1) focuses on the question of whether individuals can have knowledge of the psychological dispositions that causally influence their behaviors. That is, can individuals really know their attitudes, traits, moods, and evaluations? Wilson proposes a cognitive process model that involves two mental systems: one that mediates behavior and is largely nonconscious and one that is conscious and functions to verbalize and explain behavior. Wilson cogently argues that people often do have access to their mental states, and in these cases the verbal system can make direct and accurate reports. When there is limited access, however, the verbal system makes inferences about what these states might be. Such inferences may be incorrect and may conflict with unregulated behavioral indices of the psychological disposition. The implications of this analysis for attribution research are examined.

Kassin and Baron (Chapter 2) argue that since Heider (1958), attribution theory and research has emerged within a zeitgeist that has favored an information-processing model. They argue that the time has come to return to basics. According to Kassin and Baron, the basic determinants of attribution are those characteristics of stimulus events that appear to activate automatic, perceptual processes rather than those that are more controlled and inferential. In reviewing research from several different domains of inquiry, these authors make a compelling case for their position.

In Chapter 3, Hansen embraces the more traditional information-processing metaphor and proposes a model of attribution compatible with current approaches to social cognition. Hansen contends that attribution theories for the most part are theories of content (e.g., distinctiveness, consensus, and consistency of information) and logic (e.g., common sense and principles such as covariation, discounting, and augmentation). Moreover, he argues that translation of these theories into cognitive processing terms has not been fruitful to date because

ATTRIBUTION
Basic Issues and Applications

psychological theories of attribution have not taken into account important concepts of cognitive processing theory. Important among these is cognitive economy. Hansen presents a reformulation of Kelley's (1967) ANOVA model into a psychological model of attribution reflecting the commonsense goal of reasonable accuracy of causal understanding through inference economy. In the final sections of this chapter, an attempt is made to translate this psychological model into a cognitive processing model of attribution. Future research will need to determine the utility of this ambitious translation.

Kelley's influence on the study of basic attribution processes is also evident in the chapter by Reeder (4). According to Kelley (1972), attributors generally will tend to give less weight to a particular cause if additional plausible causes of an event are present. This tendency has been termed the discounting principle. However, Reeder notes that there may be important limits to discounting. Several researchers, for example, have found evidence of insufficient discounting: observers have been found to attribute an individual's behavior to his or her dispositions, even when the situational demands provide a sufficient explanation for the behavior. Reeder outlines and extends a schematic model of dispositional attribution (Reeder & Brewer, 1979) in an attempt to explain such insufficient discounting. Specifically, he examines implicit links between dispositions and the behaviors these dispositions are assumed to imply as well as factors that influence these implicational relations. Recent research findings consistent with this schematic model also are reviewed by Reeder.

What instigates causal inference processes? Pittman and D'Agostino (Chapter 5) review a number of studies designed to explore the motivational antecedents of attributional analyses. These authors begin with Kelley's (1967) suggestion that we make attributions in order to render the world predictable and controllable. Pittman and D'Agostino then review evidence suggesting that when control motivation is strong, individuals are more likely to engage in attributional activity. This increased attributional activity, in turn, appears to be associated with an increased need for diagnostic information and with careful and deliberate processing of the available information.

In the final chapter (6) of this part, Hill, Weary, Hildebrand-Saints, and Elbin focus on a possible, neglected motivational consequence of attributional analyses. These authors argue that causal judgments often are made in complex, ambiguous social situations. Consequently, an individual who has evaluated and made causal attributions for an event may experience a sense of uncertainty regarding the quality or accuracy of his or her judgments. This uncertainty may motivate the search for social comparison information. In their chapter, Hill et al. describe how social comparison of causal judgments may provide a perceiver with self-evaluative feedback. They also present the results of two laboratory studies that evaluated the affective consequences of social comparison of causal judgment.

CHAPTER 1

Strangers to Ourselves: The Origins and Accuracy of Beliefs about One's Own Mental States*

Timothy D. Wilson

INTRODUCTION

> We are confused about consciousness because of an almost irresistable urge to overestimate the extent of our incorrigibility. Our incorrigibility is real; we feel it in our bones, and being real it is, of course, undeniable, but when we come to characterize it, we generously endow ourselves with capacities for infallibility beyond anything we have, or could possibly have.
>
> (Dennett, 1978, p. 33)

It is generally assumed that people have direct, accurate access to their own mental states, such as their attitudes, evaluations, and affects. When we ask someone "How did you like the movie?" or "How do you feel about Jane?", we believe that the person has the ability to answer accurately. We recognize that people sometimes lie about or try to hide their feelings, but we assume that people usually know their own internal states.

It is undoubtedly true that people have direct access to many (if not most) mental states. It would be extremely maladaptive to be confused about whether or not we feel pain when touching a hot stove, or fear when confronted by a mugger in a dark alley. There may be times, however, when we have imperfect access to our own mental states and make erroneous reports about them, even when trying to be accurate. In this chapter I describe a preliminary model explaining why a lack of access

*The writing of this chapter and the research described were supported by National Science Foundation Grant BNS79-21155. I thank Edward Deci, Bella DePaulo, G. Daniel Lassiter, Richard Nisbett, Christopher Wetzel, Robert Wicklund, and Robert Wyer for valuable comments on an earlier draft.

can occur and outline several conditions specifying when a lack of access is to be expected.

The states with which I am concerned are psychological dispositions that exert a causal influence on behavior. Examples include attitudes, desires, moods, traits, affects, and evaluations. This definition corresponds closely to what philosophers refer to as intentional states (e.g., Dennett, 1969; Searle, 1979). These states can exist in relation to a specific stimulus ("I like the movie") or as a more general disposition ("I feel happy"), with the assumption that they usually guide behavior in some way.[1]

DEFINING ACCURACY: BEHAVIORAL MEASURES OF MENTAL STATES

It is not a simple matter to demonstrate that a belief about a mental state is inaccurate. Indeed, such beliefs are often said to be incorrigible precisely because there is no means of verifying their accuracy. This presents a major difficulty that will leave a cloud of ambiguity over all attempts to investigate access to mental states. In this section I discuss ways of cutting through this fog as much as possible, although it cannot be completely dispelled.

Virtually all mental states have behavioral indicants that can be publicly observed. As argued by Rorty (1970),

> Our subsequent behavior may provide sufficient evidence for overriding contemporaneous reports of [mental states]. If I say that I believe that p, or desire X, or am afraid, or am intending to do A, what I go on to do may lead others to say that I couldn't *really* have believed p, or desired X, or been afraid, or intended to do A. . . . Statements about beliefs, desires, emotions, and intentions are implicit predictions of future behavior, predictions which may be falsified. (pp. 419–420)

For example, suppose Jones sincerely states that he likes Smith. On what grounds could we call into question the accuracy of Jones's statement? The best criterion is Jones's behavior. If Jones greets Smith with a sneer each time they meet and always speaks to him in a spiteful tone of voice, we might doubt Jones's belief that he likes Smith.

This is not, of course, a perfect solution to the question of accuracy. As noted by many researchers, a belief about an internal state could

[1]This is not to say that it is wise to consider such disparate mental states as pain and beliefs under the same rubric (Rorty, 1982). Though some attempt will be made to specify which types of mental states are most accessible, considerably more effort is needed in this direction. The present strategy is to begin with a very broad discussion of mental states, until such time as more specific classifications can be made.

conflict with behavior for a number of reasons besides the fact that the belief is false. For example, behavior is often more a function of social norms and pressures than internal states (e.g., Ajzen & Fishbein, 1977). Further, people may suppress any overt sign of their feelings. An employee might loathe her boss, but behave as if they were long-lost friends. There is evidence, however, that even when people try to disguise their feelings, their true feelings "leak" through some nonverbal channels (DePaulo, Zuckerman, & Rosenthal, 1980; Ekman & Friesen, 1969, 1974; Wilson, Lassiter, & Stone, 1984; Zuckerman, DePaulo, & Rosenthal, 1981; Zuckerman, Larrance, Spiegel, & Klorman, 1981). This raises an important issue concerning behavioral indicants of mental states. Since verbal reports are themselves a form of behavior, it is necessary to become more specific about which kinds of behaviors are the best indicants of mental states. To do so, a distinction is made here between behaviors that are consciously regulated versus those that are not. Verbal reports and many other behaviors (such as facial expressions) are usually under conscious control and typically reflect people's beliefs about how they feel (barring attempts to be deceptive). To test the accuracy of these beliefs, behaviors should be measured that are not under conscious control and therefore have the potential to reveal quite different feelings. Thus, the behaviors must not be those that people deliberately control to correspond with their verbal reports, but those that are indicative of other, hidden feelings.

At present there are few good behavioral measures of mental states that cannot be controlled. The next best course is to choose behaviors that can be regulated if the person attends to them but are not normally regulated, and to reduce the motivation for people to attend to and control their overt behavior. For example, in social interaction people are much more apt to regulate their facial expressions than their body cues or tone of voice (Ekman & Friesen, 1974; Zuckerman et al., 1981). Thus, the latter responses are better measures of feelings of which the person may be unaware than are facial expressions. The accuracy of beliefs about mental states is best defined as the correspondence between beliefs and unregulated behaviors.

Of course, one cannot use just any unregulated behavior as a criterion for accuracy. If my beliefs about how much I like different individuals were uncorrelated with my skin temperature in their presence, we could not conclude that my beliefs were inaccurate. Unregulated behaviors must be chosen that have been demonstrated to be diagnostic of the feeling in question. Diagnosticity is not easy to establish; nevertheless, considerable evidence in support of the diagnosticity of a behavior can be gathered by seeing how the behavior varies under different stimulus conditions. For example, several researchers have used the amount of time people spend on an activity (e.g., a game or puzzle) in an unconstrained, "free-time" period to test predictions on intrinsic interest derived from self-attribution and other theories (Deci & Ryan, 1980; Fazio & Zanna, 1981; Lepper & Greene, 1978; Ross, 1976). One hypothesis that has been heavily researched is that people who engage in interesting activities for extrinsic reasons will experience lower interest in those activities. This hypothesis has received substantial support, as indicated by the fact that people given extrinsic reasons to do something subsequently spend less time pursuing those activities in a free-time period than people not given extrinsic reasons. Interestingly, a different conclusion would be reached if only self-report measures of liking for the activity were used, as we will see shortly in a review of research in this area. However, since the amount-of-time behavioral measure has been shown to be very sensitive to experimental manipulations and has generally responded as predicted by major theoretical positions, it is generally accepted as a valid measure of people's liking for the activity.

It is possible, of course, that the theories are wrong and that free-time activity reflects something other than liking. This is the residual fog of ambiguity that is impossible to eliminate from any behavioral measure. I will plunge forward, however, and assume that free-time activity and other well-established behavioral measures are valid reflections of mental states. In virtually all of the research reviewed and reported here, well-established behavioral measures were used. As we will see, these measures often conflict with beliefs about the mental states that the behaviors are said to measure. This will lead to one of two conclusions: Either the behavioral measures are invalid, which will necessitate a major reinterpretation of several social psychological literatures that have relied on these measures (e.g., self-attribution, attitude, and nonverbal communication research), or, as I will argue, people's beliefs about their mental states are not always completely correct.

EVIDENCE FOR LIMITED ACCESS TO MENTAL STATES

A striking finding in social psychological research over the past several decades has been the tendency for people to behave inconsistently with their attitudes, emotions, and evaluations. This finding has occurred regularly in two of the major areas of the field, attitude and self-attribution research. For example, in a review of research on attitudes and behavior, Wicker concluded that "it is considerably more likely that attitudes will be unrelated or only slightly related to overt behaviors than that attitudes will be closely related to actions'' (1969, p. 65).

A similar lack of correspondence between verbally reported mental states and behavior is often found in dissonance and self-attribution research. Both of these formulations argue that experimental manipulations (typically the amount of justification offered for behavior) lead to causal inferences resulting in new internal states (e.g., attitudes, emotions) that produce behaviors consistent with these new internal states. In the dissonance paradigm, for example, numerous studies have found that people who are induced to perform an undesirable activity for inadequate external justification infer that they performed the behavior because they liked it and subsequently perform the activity at a superior level than control subjects (Weick, 1967). In the attribution paradigm, it has been demonstrated that people's inferences about the causes of many other types of responses, such as autonomic activity and proattitudinal behaviors, have lead to changes in internal states and to behavior consistent with these changes (e.g., Schachter & Singer, 1962; Lepper & Greene, 1978).

As research on dissonance and attribution blossomed, a curious pattern of results emerged that was at odds with the shared model of causal inference ⟶ internal state change ⟶ new behavior. Researchers increasingly included measures of behavioral change, hypothesized to come at the end of the cognitive chain of events, as well as self-report measures of the internal states supposedly mediating the behavior. As noted by several investigators, however (Bem, 1972; Nisbett & Valins, 1971; Nisbett & Wilson, 1977; Weick, 1967), the behavioral measures produced effects ''more easily, more strongly, more reliably, and more persuasively than the attribution changes [i.e., self-report effects] that are, theoretically, supposed to be mediating them'' (Bem, 1972, p. 50).

If these failures to find self-report effects were isolated occurrences, they could be explained away as due to random error or experimental flaws. Nisbett and Wilson (1977), however, found that this result is typical. They reviewed all dissonance and attribution studies that included both self-report and behavioral measures of internal state change, and found that (1) the majority of studies found significant behavioral effects in the absence of differences on self-report measures; (2) the remainder found significant self-report effects, but in most cases they were weaker than the differences on the behavioral measures; and (3) though not often reported, the available correlations between the two types of measures were all close to zero.

Nisbett and Wilson's (1977) review of dissonance and attribution research is by now several years old. Subsequently, the majority of research in this area has been on the overjustification effect. To update the Nisbett and Wilson (1977) review, the overjustification literature was surveyed. The criteria for inclusion in this review were that (1) the study manipulated external reasons for behavior in an attempt to change intrinsic interest in an activity; (2) significant changes in intrinsic interest were found, as indicated by the behavioral measures; (3) self-report measures of intrinsic interest were obtained at the same time as the behavioral measures. This review revealed a pattern of results very similar to those in the Nisbett and Wilson (1977) survey. Most of the studies found either significant behavioral results in the absence of self-report effects (Berman, 1977; Deci, 1971; Dollinger & Thelen, 1978; Fazio, 1981; Folger, Rosenfeld, & Hays, 1978; Gersch, 1978; E. Goldstein, 1978; Lauridsen, 1978; Lee, Syrnyk, & Hallschmid, 1977; McLoyd, 1979; Morgan, 1981, Studies 1 and 2; Reader & Dollinger, 1982; Ross, 1975, Study 2; Ryan, 1982; Ryan, Mims, & Koestner, 1983; R. Smith & Pittman, 1978; W. Smith, 1976; Weiner & Mander, 1977, 1978; Wells & Shultz, 1980; Williams, 1980; Wilson, Hull, & Johnson, 1981, Study 2) or significant self-report and behavioral effects but in different directions (Cusella, 1978; Farr, Vance, & McIntyre, 1977, Study 1; L. Goldstein, 1978; New, 1979). Of the remaining studies several found self-report effects weaker than behavioral effects (Boggiano, 1981; Kruglanski, Riter, Amitai, Margolin, Shabtai, & Zaksh, 1975, Study 2; Pritchard, K. M. Campbell, & D. J. Campbell, 1977; Ross, 1975, Study 1; Scott & Yalch, 1978). The remaining studies found the reverse—self-report effects stronger than behavioral effects (Amabile, DeJong, & Lepper, 1976; Blanck, Reis, & Jackson, 1979, Study 1; Daniel & Esser, 1980; Harackiewicz, 1979; Mossholder, 1980; Rosenfield, Folger, & Adelman, 1980; Wimperis & Farr, 1979.[2] Correlations between self-report and behavioral measures typically were not reported, but in the 13 studies where they were noted, they tended to be low (mean $r = .21$).

There are several possible reasons why self-report effects have been so elusive in attribution research.[3] Perhaps there were methodological problems with the self-report measures, such as self-presentational or positivity biases, or perhaps the scales were poorly-constructed or insensitive. It is also possible that subjects were reluctant to admit the

---

[2]When possible, the strength of the effects were computed using Cohen's (1977) d statistic. When d could not be computed from the reported data, the p-levels were used.
[3]The present review has been selective, considering only those studies that included both self-report and behavioral dependent measures. Dissonance and attribution studies that included only self-report measures will be discussed shortly.

existence of some internal states, such as fear or anger. However, the self-presentational view does not explain why subjects would have been reluctant to admit having experienced states that are more socially acceptable than fear or anger, such as liking a film or puzzle, especially since the self-report measures were usually private and anonymous. It is also unlikely that scaling problems can account completely for the failure to find self-report effects, since virtually every type of self-report measure has been used in one or more studies that failed to find such effects.

Another possible explanation for the failure to find self-report effects was offered by Nisbett and Valins (1971). The dissonance and attribution manipulations in some studies may have succeeded in producing only weak changes in internal states, they argued, which is why self-report measures were often nonsignificant. This weak effect might have existed in the form of a hypothesis about a state, and the behavioral measures were indicative of an attempt to test this hypothesis to ''see how it feels.'' The hypothesis testing view essentially challenges the validity of the behavioral measures used in attribution research, arguing that they are not indicative of internal state change but of attempts to test one's feelings. Nisbett and Valins (1971) acknowledged that this interpretation did not apply to all such studies, however. It should apply only to studies that measured regulated behaviors, that is, those that people have the ability to monitor and control. Many studies have not used behavioral measures which lend themselves readily to hypothesis testing (e.g., GSR in a study by Zimbardo, Cohen, Weisenberg, Dworkin, & Firestone, 1969), yet behavioral effects were still found in the absence of self-report results. Thus, as later argued by Nisbett and Wilson (1977), the hypothesis-testing view can explain at best only a limited range of the failures to find self-report effects.

I certainly do not deny that these or other interpretations account for some of the inconsistency between reported mental states and behavior that has been observed (cf. Leventhal, 1980; Quattrone, 1984). This is particularly true in the attitude literature, where considerable advances have been made of late in demonstrating the conditions under which attitudes are consistent with behavior (Fazio & Zanna, 1981). What I would like to suggest is that the vast amount of inconsistency that has been found is not fully explicable by such problems as measurement error or hypothesis testing. It is proposed that a contributing factor may be inadequate access to mental states. Reasons for poor access are discussed in the next two sections, as are some of the conditions under which access is apt to be limited.

TWO MENTAL SYSTEMS

If it is true that access to mental states can be limited, the question arises as to what people are doing when attempting to report their attitudes, beliefs, and evaluations. A preliminary model will be offered to explain the origins of beliefs about mental states. Issues involving consciousness are exceedingly complex, thus this model is presented more as a heuristic for generating research than as a theory with firm empirical underpinnings.

Following Bem (1972) and Nisbett and Wilson (1977), it is argued that people often attempt to infer their internal states with the use of a conscious, verbal, explanatory system. This verbal system involves conscious attempts to estimate one's feelings, independently of cognitive processes mediating behavior. This position can be understood best by making a distinction between conscious attempts to examine one's thoughts and feelings and cognitive processes that typically do not occur in consciousness. As stated cogently by Mandler (1975), "Cognition and conscious thought are two different concepts" (p. 13). Many cognitive processes appear to be unavailable to conscious scrutiny (Nisbett & Wilson, 1977). When asked to report these processes people are unable to examine them directly; thus they rely on a conscious explanatory system. The present analysis extends this argument to reports about mental states. Cognitive processes and resulting changes in internal states can occur unnoticed. This appears to be what sometimes happens in dissonance and attribution studies. Processes are triggered which lead to changes in attitudes, yet people are unable to report either the cognitive processes or the resulting internal states. When asked to report these states, people rely on the conscious, verbal system to do so.

In essence the argument is that there are two mental systems: One which mediates behavior (especially unregulated behavior), is largely nonconscious, and is, perhaps, the older of the two systems in evolutionary terms (Jaynes, 1976). The other, perhaps newer system, is largely conscious and attempts to verbalize, explain, and communicate mental states. As argued earlier, people often have direct access to their mental states, and in these cases the verbal system can make direct and accurate reports. When there is limited access, however, the verbal system makes inferences about what these processes and states might be.

This position is very similar to what Wason and Evans (1975), in a somewhat different context, have called Type 1 and Type 2 cognitive processes. The first process underlies behavior and is generally nonconscious and thus can be deduced only by observing people's behavior in response to different stimulus conditions. The second is described as a "conscious thought process" (Evans, 1976, p. 517), which involves the "tendency for the subject to construct a justification for his own behavior consistent with his knowledge of the situation" (Wason & Evans, 1975, p. 149).

THE VERBAL EXPLANATORY SYSTEM

It is possible to outline how the verbal explanatory system operates when trying to describe and justify one's responses. As discussed by Nisbett and Wilson (1977), the verbal system relies heavily on representativeness and availability heuristics (Tversky & Kahneman, 1974) and utilizes a priori causal theories. Thus, when trying to decide why they performed a certain action, people call upon reasons that are available in memory and representative of (or similar to) the response, and use their culturally-learned and idiosyncratic theories about "why I perform behavior X." Similarly, if access to internal states is sometimes limited, people may call upon the explanatory system to infer how they feel. These conscious inferences are influenced by theories about oneself and about what feelings seem like plausible reactions to a stimulus.

This view bears some similarity to the sociologist Hochschild's (1979) discussion of what she terms "emotion work." She argues that people often engage in an active attempt to evoke a new emotion or suppress an existing one. People make such attempts according to "feeling rules," namely what the culture and situation demand we should feel. For example, a person feeling happy at a funeral or sad at a wedding will attempt to change his or her feelings in a more appropriate direction. In my view, emotion work may often occur only at a conscious level; that is, it may involve attempts by the verbal explanatory system to change a belief about how one feels. Thus, a bride who feels sad on her wedding day may convince herself that it is really the happiest day of her life, and genuinely believe that she is happy since it is very difficult to change the actual feeling. The bride's sadness is apt to remain and be expressed behaviorally, even though she has convinced herself she is not sad.

A further example comes from the following excerpt from a story by Mary Kierstead, where two people, when children, consciously adopted the "feeling rule" that children love their pony. It was not until much later that they realized their true feelings were quite different:

> "You know, it wasn't until I was about thirty that I realized that I'd always hated that goddamn pony. He had a mean disposition, and he was fat and spoiled. He would roll on me, and then step on my foot before I could get up."

"And he bit you when you tried to give him lumps of sugar," Kate added. It wasn't until Blake said it that Kate realized that she, too, had always hated Topper. For years they had been conned into loving him, because children love their pony, and their dog, and their parents, and picnics, and the ocean, and the lovely chocolate cake. (Kierstead, 1981, p. 48)[4]

If beliefs about feelings are often inferences generated by an explanatory system, they may be incorrect. A child may assume that he loves his pony, for example, when he actually hates it. If so, the child's report of liking should conflict with his unregulated behaviors towards the pony, which would leak his true feelings. Inferences about feelings may also be accurate, however, producing spuriously correct reports, spurious because the accuracy is not the result of direct access to the feeling but to the coincidental correspondence between the feeling and the inference made by the explanatory system. Thus, the characters in Kierstead's stories eventually realized that their theory about their liking for Topper was incorrect, and made what were presumably more accurate inferences about their feelings.

PRIMING THE EXPLANATORY SYSTEM

This analysis suggests that the origins of how we feel and how we think we feel can be quite different. For example, the fact that a pony steps on our feet and bites us may produce genuine dislike, but due to the cultural theory that children love their ponies, we overlook this data and infer that we love him. If so, one ought to be able to manipulate self-reports independently of actual feelings by altering what theories and data are salient to people.

Such a hypothesis may explain why some experiments in dissonance and attribution have found self-report effects. The earlier review of these areas was selective, in that only those studies that included both self-report and behavioral measures of internal state change were included. Though it is true that these studies often find behavioral effects in the absence of self-report effects, this ignores the large numbers of studies which included only self-report measures. It is common to find that subjects who are induced to perform a counterattitudinal activity (e.g., write an essay against their beliefs), in the absence of a strong external reason for doing so, report attitudes that are more in line with their behavior. It is difficult to assess how accurate subjects in these studies were, since no behavioral measures were included. However, since most of these studies have found self-report effects, perhaps subjects did have direct

---

[4]Reprinted by permission; © 1981 Mary D. Kierstead. Originally in *The New Yorker*.

access to their attitudes and did not have to rely on an explanatory system.

If a rough distinction is made, it has typically been dissonance research on counterattitudinal activities that has found self-report effects (e.g., Festinger & Carlsmith, 1959), while it has been attribution research on proattitudinal or autonomic responses that has not (e.g., Davison & Valins, 1969). One of the chief differences between counterattitudinal dissonance and attribution studies is that in the former, subjects become aroused. In a clever series of studies, Zanna and Cooper (1976) have demonstrated that the dissonance produced by performing a counterattitudinal behavior involves physiological arousal. One function of arousal, according to Mandler (1975), is to signal the individual consciously to search for its causes, that is, to "inquire either about the sources of autonomic arousal or generally about the present state of the environment and the organism" (p. 67). In the present terminology, arousal might trigger the verbal explanatory system, making it more likely that people would infer the existence of a new attitude.

There is no direct evidence for this hypothesis, but there have been some dissonance studies that manipulated subjects' attention to their behavior, which might be viewed as a way of priming the explanatory system. This manipulation has been found to increase the magnitude of self-report effects above and beyond the effects normally found (Zanna, Lepper, & Abelson, 1973). Thus, self-report effects in dissonance research may not be the result of direct access to internal states, but due to inferences by the verbal explanatory system, which have been primed by the arousal these studies produce.

This suggests that self-report effects might be produced in non-arousing attribution experiments by priming the verbal system. Three experiments have been conducted to test this hypothesis (two studies by Wilson, Hull, & Johnson, 1981; Wilson & Linville, 1982). Each study used attributional manipulations to produce changes in internal states and included both self-report and behavioral measures of change. The major purpose of the studies was to see if priming the verbal explanatory system produced new self-reports independently of the manipulations influencing behavior. Crosscutting the attributional manipulations, some subjects were asked to reflect consciously upon the reasons for their behavior. By making people take a closer look at themselves and the situation, inferences about how they felt were expected to change. The "reasons analysis" manipulation was not expected to influence behavioral measures of internal states, since the verbal explanatory system is hypothesized to be relatively independent of the feelings mediating behavior.

For example, in Wilson et al.'s (1981) Study 2, college students were either paid $1 or not paid to work on an interesting puzzle. Their subsequent interest in the puzzle was assessed with standard self-report measures, as well as with a behavioral measure, namely, the amount of time subjects played with the puzzle in an unrewarded, free-time period. A reasons analysis manipulation crosscut the attribution manipulation (in this case, the reward). Just before the dependent measures were administered, some subjects were asked to think about why they had initially played with the puzzle. This reasons manipulation was administered in different forms; for example, some subjects were asked to think only about internal reasons for having played with the puzzle; others were asked to think only about external reasons. For present purposes the different forms of the reasons manipulation will be considered together and compared to a control, no-reasons analysis condition.

The results were generally as predicted. In the absence of a reasons analysis, subjects behaved as if their internal states had changed, but did not report these new states. That is, subjects who were rewarded played with the puzzle significantly less in the free-time period than did subjects in the no-reward condition, but rewarded subjects did not report that they liked the puzzle significantly less than did nonrewarded subjects (see top of Figure 1.1). As seen in the bottom half of Figure 1.1, however, a different pattern of results occurred in the reasons analysis condition. When people were induced to reflect on the reasons for their behavior, behavioral evidence for changes in attitudes towards the puzzle were still found, but now significant self-reported differences were found as well. Similar results were found in Wilson et al.'s (1981) Study 1.

DIRECT ACCESS OR INDIRECT INFERENCE?

The two Wilson et al. (1981) experiments showed that when subjects reflected on reasons for their behavior they reported internal state changes that were consistent with their behavior (see the lower half of Figure 1.1). It is important to consider in detail why this pattern of results occurred. One possibility is that subjects normally do not exert much effort in discovering what their current internal state is, but when made to look more carefully, as in the reasons analysis conditions, they are able to examine their internal states directly. According to this view, the reasons analysis manipulation caused subjects to introspect more carefully, leading to direct access to internal states. This view is very similar to a self-awareness theory position, which argues that focusing

NO REASONS ANALYSIS

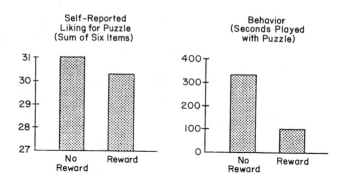

REASONS ANALYSIS

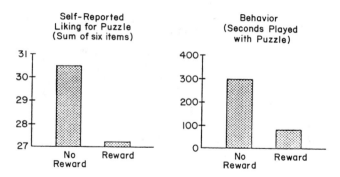

Figure 1.1 The effects of reasons analysis and reward on self-reports and behavior. Adapted from Wilson, Hull, Johnson (1981). © 1981 by the American Psychological Association. Adapted by permission.

attention on the self produces more valid reports about mental states (Carver & Scheier, 1981; Wicklund, 1982).

In contrast, the reasons analysis variable in the Wilson et al. (1981) studies was conceived not as a manipulation of self-awareness, but as a means of priming the verbal explanatory system, which then made spuriously correct inferences about internal states. There are several sources of evidence in support of this view. In Wilson et al.'s (1981) Study 2, scores were available for subjects on the private self-conscious-ness inventory (Fenigstein, Scheier, & Buss, 1975), which measures the dispositional tendency to focus on the self. If analyzing reasons were a self-awareness manipulation, then its effects on self-reports should have mimicked differences found between people high and low in private self-consciousness (e.g., Scheier, A. H. Buss, & D. M. Buss, 1978). This was not the case; in fact, there were no significant differences in self-reported liking for the puzzle between highs and lows, nor were the self-report–behavior correlations significantly greater for highs than lows (contrary to a self-awareness theory prediction). Furthermore, a reasons analysis manipulation in a study by Wilson and Linville (1982) significantly changed subjects' mood reports, but not in a more accurate direction. That is, subjects who analyzed reasons made different inferences about their mood, but their average mood reports did not become uniformly more consistent with behavioral measures of their internal states, as would be expected if the reasons analysis were increasing the accuracy of their reports.

Finally, if analyzing reasons increases access to one's mental states, then the correlation between self-reports and behavior should be higher in the reasons analysis conditions. Correlational differences in the Wilson et al. (1981) and Wilson and Linville (1982) studies were difficult to interpret since there were differences in means across conditions that could influence correlations for artifactual reasons. Nonetheless, it should be noted that there were no significant differences in correlations between the reasons analysis and no-reasons analysis conditions in any of the three studies. In fact, averaging across studies, the self-report–behavior correlations were slightly lower in the reasons analysis conditions. More convincingly, three of our subsequent studies, discussed in the next section, found significantly lower correlations when subjects analyzed reasons.

CONDITIONS FOSTERING IMPERFECT ACCESS TO MENTAL STATES

It is very unlikely that people always or even usually have imperfect access to their mental states. It is thus important to specify the conditions fostering good versus imperfect access. Four such conditions, some speculative, have been identified.

MOTIVATED SELF-DECEPTION

The idea that people possess a mistaken belief about how they feel is usually thought of in motivational terms, that is, as an instance of self-deception. A mental state that is anxiety-producing or threatening to one's self-esteem might lead to a denial that the state exists. This view dates back at least to Freud, who spoke of unconscious ideas as akin to "the legendary Titans, weighed down since primaeval ages by the massive bulk of the mountains which were once hurled upon them by the victorious gods" (1900/1972, p. 592). Freud's position remains controversial to this day, although the concept of motivated self-deception continues to receive a good deal of attention by both psychologists and philosophers (Fingarette, 1969; Gur & Sackeim, 1979; Martin, in press; Sackeim, 1983).

The present model acknowledges that motivated self-deception can occur. The presence of a motive to self-deceive, however, is not viewed as a necessary condition for poor access to mental states. As already discussed, under some conditions the verbal, conscious system may possess mistaken beliefs about one's attitudes and evaluations, even in the absence of a motive for self-deception. The remaining three conditions promoting poor access do not necessarily involve a self-deception motive.

EFFECTS OF SELF-ANALYSIS

Self-reflection is often considered to be a beneficial exercise, leading to greater insight about one's feelings. We have obtained evidence, however, that analyzing the reasons for one's feelings can, under some conditions, actually lower the correspondence between reported feelings and behavior. In the words of Theodore Roethke, perhaps "Self-contemplation is a curse/That makes an old confusion worse" (1975, p. 249).

Wilson et al. (1981) and Wilson and Linville (1982) found that inducing subjects to analyze reasons changed their reported mental states more than their behavior, though it was not entirely clear whether this change was in a more accurate direction. Two of the studies found greater consistency between mean reported feelings and mean behavior in the reasons analysis conditions, but given that there was no increase in self-report–behavior correlations in these conditions, the correspondence between means could have been fortuitous.

Fortunately this ambiguity regarding accuracy has been cleared considerably by three studies by Wilson, Dunn, Bybee, Hyman, and Rotondo (1984). The first study was a replication of a within-subjects design utilized by Regan and Fazio (1977). Subjects were given several minutes to familiarize themselves with five different types of puzzles (e.g., a letter series task where people guessed the next letter that logically followed a given progression and a Gestalt completion task, where people guessed what object was depicted from an incomplete portrayal of the object). In the reasons analysis condition, subjects were instructed to think about why they felt the way they did about each puzzle while working on it. After working on the puzzles, they wrote down reasons why they found each one interesting or boring. They then rated how interesting they thought each puzzle was and were left alone with several examples of each puzzle during a "free play" period. Subjects in the control condition were treated identically except that they completed a filler task after initially working on the puzzles and were not instructed to analyze reasons.

Spearman rank-order correlations were computed for each subject between his or her interest ratings and the time spent in the free play period working on each of the five puzzles. For the control group, the average correlation was .54, demonstrating a fair degree of correspondence between the interest ratings and behavior. For the reasons analysis subjects, however, the average correlation was only .17, which was significantly lower than the control group's mean, $t(24) = 2.23$, $p <$ .05. Artifactual reasons for the lower correlation in the analyze condition were tested and ruled out. There were no significant differences between conditions in mean interest ratings, mean times spent working on the puzzles, mean variances of interest ratings, or mean variances of time spent with the puzzles (see Table 1.1). Interestingly, subjects who analyzed reasons compared to control subjects did report a different ordering of puzzles considered the most interesting, but showed an ordering nearly identical to that of the control group on those played with in the free-time period.

Two other studies by Wilson, Dunn, Bybee, Hyman, and Rotondo (1984) replicated the finding that analyzing reasons reduces self-report–behavior correlations. These studies utilized very different situations than the puzzle experiment. In one, subjects watched a slide show of scenery (e.g., mountains, an ocean) and were asked either to analyze why they liked each picture while watching it or to watch the slides as they would a film in a theater. The correlation between subjects' reported enjoyment of the slide show and coders' ratings of the pleasantness of their facial expression during the show was .55 in the control condition (averaging across one study and a replication), but only − .01 for subjects who analyzed reasons ($z = 2.71$, $p < .01$). There were no significant differences across conditions in the means or variances of facial pleasantness.[5]

---

[5]It was stated earlier that facial expression is a regulated behavior and thus not a good indicant of mental states that may be inaccessible. This tends to be true only when people are aware they are being observed, however. When they are alone, as in our slide show study, people tend not to regulate their facial expressions (Krauss, 1981).

Table 1.1

RESULTS OF WILSON, DUNN, BYBEE, HYMAN, AND ROTONDO (1984) PUZZLE STUDY[a]

Dependent measure	Control condition	Analyze condition	t (24)
Mean self-report–behavior correlation	.54*	.17	2.23*
Mean reported interest in puzzles	4.25	4.46	1.18
Mean variance of interest ratings	2.71	3.22	1.19
Mean time played with puzzles (seconds)	882	863	.48
Mean variance of time played with puzzles	69,772	80,017	.81

[a]The interest ratings were made on 7-point scales, with higher ratings reflecting more interest. Adapted from Wilson et al. (1984). © 1984 by the American Psychological Association. Adapted by permission.
*p < .05

In Wilson, Dunn, Bybee, Hyman, and Rotondo's (1984) third study, heterosexual couples who had been dating for an average of seven months were brought into the laboratory where each member of the couple, separately and privately, filled out Spanier's (1976) Dyadic Adjustment Scale, modified to make it suitable for dating couples (including, for example, an item where they rated how happy they were with their relationship). In the control condition the couples filled out this questionnaire only. In the analyze condition the couples were first asked to list all the reasons they could think of why their relationship with their dating partner was good or bad, and then were asked to fill out the adjustment scale. As a behavioral measure of the couples' adjustment, they were contacted several months later and asked whether or not they were still dating each other. The correlation between self-reported adjustment and whether or not they broke up was .56 (df = 38, p < .01) in the control condition. Among subjects who first analyzed reasons, however, the self-report–break-up correlation was significantly lower (r = .08). As with the slide show and puzzle studies, the difference in correlation across conditions was not due to a statistical artifact, since the means and variances of the measures were very similar across conditions.

Three studies, conducted in rather different situations, have thus found that analyzing reasons reduces the consistency between reported attitudes and behavior. There are several possible interpretations of this finding, many of which were ruled out by Wilson, Dunn, Bybee, Hyman, and Rotondo (1984). One possibility is that analyzing reasons causes people to bring to mind a sample of reasons that are not representative of the attitude which is driving their behavior. When subsequently asked how they feel, people may report an attitude that is not "accurate" in the sense of predicting their behavior.

INCORRECT ADOPTION OF FEELING RULES

The verbal explanatory system may sometimes operate according to feeling rules independently of one's actual feelings, as in the earlier example of the bride who convinces herself that her wedding day is the happiest day of her life when in fact she is miserable, or the child who adopts the rule that "children love their pony" when in fact he can't stand it. If by consciously adopting a feeling rule people become convinced that they feel something they do not, then their self-reported feelings and their regulated behaviors should be consistent with the feeling rule, while a different feeling should be expressed with unregulated nonverbal behaviors.

Evidence consistent with this view has been obtained by Snyder and Endelman (1979) and Wilson, Lassiter, and Stone (1984). The feeling rule investigated in both studies is one that has been well-studied in social psychology, namely that similarity causes attraction. Dozens of studies have found that people like others who have similar attitudes (Byrne, 1971). Interestingly, by far the majority of research in this area has relied on self-report dependent measures of liking. In the standard paradigm, developed by Byrne (1971), subjects fill out a series of attitude scales, are shown responses on the same scales supposedly made by another subject, then report their liking for this subject. The larger the overlap between the subject's attitude responses and those of the other person, the greater the liking reported by the subject for this person.

Occasionally researchers have included behavioral measures of liking, typically how close the subject places his or her chair to the other person's chair (e.g., Allgeier & Byrne, 1973; Byrne, Baskett, & Hodges, 1971; Byrne, Ervin, & Lamberth, 1970; Snyder & Endelman, 1979; Tesch, Huston, & Indenbaum, 1973). The results on these measures have been mixed, though they are often at odds with self-report measures of liking. For example, Snyder and Endelman (1979) manipulated three levels of similarity (slight, moderate, and extreme), and found that as similarity increased, so did self-reported liking. A curvilinear relationship was found between similarity and interpersonal distance, however, such that subjects placed their chairs closest to the moderately similar other, but kept their distance from both the slightly and extremely similar other.

Consistent with the present viewpoint, Snyder and Endelman (1979) argued that self-reported liking is "susceptible to the expectations placed upon [people] as members of a society that make certain assumptions about the merits of similarity" (p. 494). Interpersonal distance revealed people's actual feelings, they argued, which reflected concerns about uniqueness. That is, people may actually prefer moderately similar others the most, since they are rewarding but do not challenge one's sense of uniqueness (Snyder & Fromkin, 1977).

Wilson, Lassiter, and Stone (1984) first established more definitively which nonverbal behaviors are regulated in social interaction. In the first study subjects were instructed either to hide or reveal their feelings toward a likable confederate while interacting with him. Three behaviors were much more positive in the reveal than the hide condition (facial expression, body inclination, and talking time), suggesting that these are regulated channels. Three other behaviors did not differ across condition (interpersonal distance, body orientation, and eye contact). Since each of these channels has been identified as a measure of attraction (e.g., Byrne et al., 1971; Exline, 1971; Mehrabian, 1972), but was not controlled by subjects in our first study, we labeled them as unregulated indicants of attraction.

In Wilson, Lassiter, and Stone's (1984) second study the similarity–attraction feeling rule was investigated from an individual difference perspective. Subjects reported whether they preferred moderately or extremely similar others. They then came to the laboratory several weeks later, where they met a confederate whose attitudes were either moderately or extremely similar to their own. As hypothesized, subjects' reported preferences for moderate versus extremely similar others predicted their self-reported liking for the confederate several weeks later, as well as their regulated behaviors in her presence (facial expression, body inclination, talking time). Consistent with the idea that the reported preferences reflected a conscious feeling rule that may not have corresponded to actual preferences, subjects' initial reports did not predict their unregulated behaviors in the presence of the confederate (interpersonal distance, eye contact, body orientation). The unregulated behaviors were unaffected by either initial preferences or the similarity of the confederate to subjects.

Despite the fact that the unregulated behaviors we assessed have been shown to be sensitive to situational manipulations of attraction in other studies (e.g., Rubin, 1970; Word, Zanna, & Cooper, 1974), the possibility that they were invalid measures in our experiment, rather than signs of inaccessible feelings, cannot be completely ruled out. A conservative summary of the results of the Wilson, Lassiter, and Stone (1984) and Snyder and Endelman (1979) studies is that there are two possible interpretations, both very interesting. First, the unregulated behaviors may have been invalid measures of attraction, in which case a substantial part of the literature on nonverbal communication will have to be revised (e.g., Exline, 1971; Mehrabian, 1972). What we view as a more compelling interpretation is that people sometimes adopt feeling rules at a conscious level (e.g., "I like extremely similar others."; "I love my pony.") which do not correspond to their actual reactions. When this occurs, self-reports and regulated behaviors will reflect the feeling rule, but be at odds with unregulated behaviors.

This interpretation may help explain why self-reported internal states are so often discrepant from behavioral results in dissonance and attribution research. It has long been argued that the predictions made by these theories are counterintuitive, which is another way of saying they violate our feeling rules. Perhaps subjects base their self-reported states on these cultural feeling rules, while the behavioral measures are the result of less verbalizable, more implicit attributional processes. For example, many of Wilson et al.'s (1981) subjects said in debriefing that receiving money did not affect their liking for the puzzle, yet they behaved as if their liking had decreased.

AMOUNT AND ACCESSIBILITY OF PROCESSING PRECEDING ATTITUDES

The attitudes usually studied by social psychologists are the result of substantial information processing by subjects, such as the inferences made by people in self-attribution studies, or the processing of persuasive communications in attitude change experiments (e.g., Hovland, Janis, & Kelley, 1953; McGuire, 1969). In contrast, many affective states appear to be preceded by minimal processing of stimulus information (Zajonc, 1980). It is interesting to note that it is the former type of states—those that are the result of substantial processing—that have been found to be poor predictors of behavior.

Perhaps there is something about the processing preceding attitudes in attribution and attitude change experiments that reduces the accessibility of the attitudes. For example, the processes themselves are often unavailable to conscious scrutiny (Mandler, 1975; Nisbett & Wilson, 1977), which might reduce the accessibility of the resulting mental states. In contrast, states that are more immediate, and not the result of complex, inaccessible processing, may be much more accessible.

Such a hypothesis is tentative; in fact I can offer only a thought experiment to support it. Suppose subjects were introduced to a confederate, who preceded to punch them in the nose. Subjects would then be given a questionnaire asking how much they like the confederate. Several behavioral measures of their liking would also be gathered, including their tone of voice while talking with the confederate, their aggressiveness toward the confederate, and the likelihood of their initiating future interactions with him. All of these measures would be compared to a different group of subjects to whom the confederate was warm and friendly.

There seems to be little doubt that the subjects who were punched in the nose would have immediate, negative reactions to the confederate, and that they would have good access to this reaction. Both their reported liking and their behavioral reactions to the confederate should be very negative, compared to the group to whom the confederate was warm and friendly. In addition, compared to self-attribution and attitude change studies, the self-report–behavior correlations in our punch-in-the-nose study would probably be high. Why? One possibility is that the more processing subjects have to do to form an attitude the more apt they are to lose tract of what that attitude is, especially if the processes themselves are inaccessible. (Other possible interpretations of the thought experiment are of course possible, i.e., that the more extreme or more negative the attitude is the more accessible it will be.)

CONCLUSIONS AND IMPLICATIONS

There are several theoretical and practical implications of the present arguments concerning access to mental states. Theoretically, they may help to organize the self-attribution literature. Some of the conflicting results in this area may be understood by looking at whether behavioral or self-report dependent measures were used. For example, there has been some controversy over when and how children learn the discounting principle, the tendency to downplay the significance of a causal agent when other plausible causal agents are present (Jones & Davis, 1965; Kelley, 1972). There have been two chief paradigms to study the discounting principle in children. In one, children of various ages are read a story describing people who perform an activity either in the presence or absence of an external causal agent (e.g., playing with a toy with or without receiving an ice cream cone for doing so), and are asked how much the people liked the activity. It has generally been found that children do not use the discounting principle (i.e., inferring that people who played with the toy without receiving ice cream liked it more) until approximately age 9 (Cohen, Gelfand, & Hartmann, 1981; DiVitto & McArthur, 1978; Karniol & Ross, 1976; Kun, 1977; Morgan, 1981; Shultz, Butkowsky, Pearce, & Shanfield, 1975; M. Smith, 1975).

In the other paradigm (overjustification), children are either rewarded or not for performing an attractive activity, following which interest in the activity is assessed by seeing how much time they continue with it in a "free-play" period. If children use the discounting principle, they should downplay their interest in the activity when another plausible reason for doing it, the reward, is present. This result has been repeatedly found in children as young as 3 to 5 years of age (e.g., Lepper, Greene, & Nisbett, 1973). Thus, children do not give verbal responses that reflect the discounting principle until approximately age 9, but behave as if they were utilizing it as young as age 3.

There are many differences between the two paradigms that might account for this conflicting pattern of results, such as the fact that one involves other-perception and the other self-perception (Guttentag & Longfellow, 1977). One possibility, however, is that the two types of studies were tapping different systems. The story reading paradigm, by using self-reports as dependent measures, may have been investigating the development of the verbal explanatory system. The overjustification paradigm, by using behavioral measures, may have been investigating processes that are less verbal and, perhaps, nonconscious. If so, the two systems may well develop at different rates, accounting for the discrepancy between the ages at which discounting effects are found in the different types of studies (see also Kassin & Lepper, 1984; Wells & Shultz, 1980).

Another implication of the present analysis is a distressing one: It is even more difficult to investigate cognitive processes than generally believed. Though it is recognized by cognitive psychologists that many mental processes cannot be accurately reported and must be studied indirectly with the use of converging operations (Garner, Hake, & Eriksen, 1956), social psychologists rely heavily on self-report measures of attributions, attitudes, and moods. If it is true that people sometimes lack access to higher order mental phenomena, then social psychologists should be more inclined to study them with the use of behavioral dependent measures.

This is distressing because behavioral measures themselves are often ambiguous, making it difficult to rule out competing interpretations of one's data. For example, the exact interpretation of the overjustification effect is still controversial, despite ten years of voluminous research. Imagine how much easier it would be to explore this issue if people could verbalize their exact cognitive processes as well as their feelings towads the task. Since it appears that people cannot verbalize their thoughts or feelings very well, it is all the more difficult to infer the nature of the mediating processes of the overjustification effect.

I am not suggesting that social psychologists abandon the long-trusted self-report questionnaire. People often can make very accurate reports about their attitudes, moods, motives, and evaluations. Often they can not, however, and it is under these conditions that behavioral measures of internal states are useful. Though I have outlined several possible conditions under which reports will be inaccurate, it is clear that considerably more work is necessary to confirm and add to an understanding of these conditions. In the meantime, researchers should adopt the safe course of including both self-report and behavioral dependent measures. If it is established that the two measures correlate (particularly if self-report measures correlate with both regulated and unregulated behaviors), then the self-report measures can be trusted. If such correlations are not found, and one has reason to believe that the behavioral variables are valid measures of the mental phenomena under study, faith in people's access to these phenomena should be reduced.

REFERENCES

Ajzen, I., & Fishbein, M. (1977). Attitude–behavior relations: A theoretical analysis and review of empirical research. *Psychological Bulletin, 84,* 888–918.

Allgeier, A. R., & Byrne, D. (1973). Attraction toward the opposite sex as a determinant of physical proximity. *Journal of Social Psychology, 90,* 213–219.

Amabile, T. M., DeJong, W., & Lepper, M. R. (1976). Effects of externally imposed deadlines on subsequent intrinsic motivation. *Journal of Personality and Social Psychology, 34,* 92–98.

Bem, D. J. (1972). Self-perception theory. In L. Berkowitz (Ed.), *Advances in experimental social psychology* (Vol. 6). New York: Academic Press.

Berman, L. N. (1977). Contingency, probability of success, ability feedback, and knowledge of reward attainment as factors affecting intrinsic motivation. *Dissertation Abstracts International, 37,* 4211B. (University Microfilms No. 7702000).

Blanck, P., Reis, H. T., & Jackson, L. (1979, September). *The effects of verbal reinforcement on intrinsic motivation for sex-linked tasks.* Paper presented at the meeting of the American Psychological Association, New York, NY.

Boggiano, A. (1981). Self-perception vs. cued-expectancy: Analyses of overjustification. *Dissertation Abstracts International, 41,* 4738B. (University Microfilms No. 8108085).

Byrne, D. (1971). *The attraction paradigm.* New York: Academic Press.

Byrne, D., Baskett, G. D., & Hodges, L. (1971). Behavioral indicators of interpersonal attraction. *Journal of Applied Social Psychology, 1,* 137–149.

Byrne, D., Ervin, C. R., & Lamberth, J. (1970). Continuity between the experimental study of attraction and real-life computer dating. *Journal of Personality and Social Psychology, 16,* 157–165.

Carver, C. S., & Scheier, M. F. (1981). *Attention and self-regulation: A control-theory approach to human behavior.* New York: Springer-Verlag.

Cohen, E. A., Gelfand, D. N., & Hartmann, D. P. (1981). Causal reasoning as a function of behavioral consequences. *Child Development, 52,* 514–522.

Cohen, J. (1977). *Statistical power analysis for the behavioral sciences* (rev. ed.). New York: Academic Press.

Cusella, L. P. (1978). Variations in verbal feedback messages following task performance as related to intrinsic motivation. *Dissertation Abstracts International, 39,* 2616A–2617A. (University Microfilms No. 7821431)

Daniel, T. L., & Esser, J. K. (1980). Intrinsic motivation as influenced by rewards, task interest, and task structure. *Journal of Applied Psychology, 65,* 566–574.

Davison, G. C., & Valins, S. (1969). Maintenance of self-attributed and drug-attributed behavior change. *Journal of Personality and Social Psychology, 11,* 25–33.

Deci, E. L. (1971). Effects of externally mediated rewards on intrinsic motivation. *Journal of Personality and Social Psychology, 18,* 105–115.

Deci, E. L., & Ryan, R. M. (1980). The empirical exploration of intrinsic motivational processes. In L. Berkowitz (Ed.), *Advances in experimental social psychology* (Vol. 13). New York: Academic Press.

Dennett, D. C. (1969). *Content and consciousness.* London: Routledge & Kegan Paul.

Dennett, D. C. (1978). *Brainstorms: Philosophical essays on mind and psychology.* Montgomery, VT: Bradford.

DePaulo, B. M., Zuckerman, M., & Rosenthal, R. (1980). Modality effects in the detection of deception. In L. Wheeler (Ed.), *Review of personality and social psychology* (Vol. 1). Beverly Hills, CA: Sage.

DiVitto, B., & McArthur, L. Z. (1978). Developmental differences in the use of distinctiveness, consensus, and consistency information for making causal attributions. *Developmental Psychology, 14,* 474–482.

Dollinger, S. J., & Thelen, M. H. (1978). Overjustification and children's intrinsic motivation: Comparative effects of four rewards. *Journal of Personality and Social Psychology, 36,* 1259–1269.

Ekman, P., & Friesen, W. V. (1969). Nonverbal leakage and clues to deception. *Psychiatry, 32,* 88–106.

Ekman, P., & Friesen, W. V. (1974). Detecting deception from the body or face. *Journal of Personality and Social Psychology, 29,* 288–298.

Evans, J. St. B. T. (1976). A critical note on Quinton and Fellows' observation of reasoning strategies. *British Journal of Psychology, 67,* 517–518.

Exline, R. V. (1971). Visual interaction: The glances of power and preference. In J. K. Cole (Ed.), *Nebraska Symposium on Motivation* (Vol. 19). Lincoln: University of Nebraska Press.

Farr, J. L., Vance, R. J., & McIntyre, R. M. (1977). Further examination of the relationship between reward contingency and intrinsic motivation. *Organizational Behavior and Human Performance, 20,* 31–53.

Fazio, R. H. (1981). On the self-perception explanation of the overjustification effect: The role of the salience of initial attitude. *Journal of Experimental Social Psychology, 17,* 417–426.

Fazio, R. H., & Zanna, M. P. (1981). Direct experience and attitude–behavior consistency. In L. Berkowitz (Ed.), *Advances in experimental social psychology* (Vol. 14). New York: Academic Press.

Fenigstein, A., Scheier, M. F., & Buss, A. H. (1975). Public and private self-consciousness: Assessment and theory. *Journal of Consulting and Clinical Psychology, 43,* 522–527.

Festinger, L., & Carlsmith, J. M. (1959). Cognitive consequences of forced compliance. *Journal of Abnormal and Social Psychology, 58,* 203–210.

Fingarette, H. (1969). *Self-deception.* London: Routledge & Kegan Paul.

Folger, R., Rosenfield, D., & Hays, R. P. (1978). Equity and intrinsic motivation: The role of choice. *Journal of Personality and Social Psychology, 36,* 557–564.

Freud, S. (1972). *The interpretation of dreams* (J. Strachey, Ed. and Trans.). New York: Avon. (Original work published 1900)

Garner, W. R., Hake, H. W., & Eriksen, C. W. (1956). Operationism and the concept of perception. *Psychological Review, 63,* 149–159.

Gersch, W. D. (1978). Differential effects of initial interest, reward schedule and performance feedback upon intrinsic interest. *Dissertation Abstracts International, 38,* 3467B–3468B. (University Microfilms No. 7730032)

Goldstein, E. A. (1978). The effects of extrinsic rewards, evaluation, and feedback on intrinsic motivation and learning from instruction. *Dissertation Abstracts International, 39,* 2830A–2831A. (University Microfilms No. 7820226)

Goldstein, L. W. (1978). Intrinsic motivation: The role of reward and feedback on quality of performance and subsequent interest in photography. *Dissertation Abstracts International, 38,* 5646B–5647B (University Microfilms No. 7805721)

Gur, R. C., & Sackeim, H. A. (1979). Self-deception: A concept in search of a phenomenon. *Journal of Personality and Social Psychology, 37,* 147–169.

Guttentag, M., & Longfellow, C. (1977). Children's social attributions: Development and change. In C. B. Keasey (Ed.), *Nebraska Symposium on Motivation,* (Vol. 25). Lincoln: University of Nebraska Press.

Harackiewicz, J. M. (1979). The effects of reward contingency and performance feedback on intrinsic motivation. *Journal of Personality and Social Psychology, 37,* 1352–1363.

Hochschild, A. R. (1979). Emotion work, feeling rules, and social structure. *American Journal of Sociology, 85,* 551–575.

Hovland, C. I., Janis, I. L., & Kelley, H. H. (1953). *Communication and persuasion.* New Haven, CT: Yale University Press.

Jaynes, J. (1976). *The origin of consciousness in the breakdown of the bicameral mind.* Boston: Houghton Mifflin.

Jones, E. E., & Davis, K. E (1965). From acts to dispositions. In L. Berkowitz (Ed.), *Advances in experimental social psychology* (Vol. 2). New York: Academic Press.

Karniol, R., & Ross, M. (1976). The development of causal attributions in social perception. *Journal of Personality and Social Psychology, 34,* 455–464.

Kassin, S. M., & Lepper, M. R. (1984). Oversufficient and insufficient justification effects: Cognitive and behavioral development. In J. Nicholls (Ed.), *The development of achievement motivation.* Greenwich, CT: JAI Press.

Kelley, H. H. (1972). Causal schemata and the attribution process. In E. E. Jones, D. Kanouse, H. H. Kelley, R. E. Nisbett, S. Valins, & B. Weiner (Eds.), *Attribution: Perceiving the causes of behavior.* Morristown, NJ: General Learning Press.

Kierstead, M. D. (1981, April 6). The Shetland pony. *The New Yorker,* pp. 40–48.

Krauss, R. M. (1981). Impression formation, impression management, and nonverbal behaviors. In E. T. Higgins, C. P. Herman, & M. P. Zanna (Eds.), *Social Cognition: The Ontario Symposium* (Vol. 1). Hillsdale, NJ: Erlbaum.

Kruglanski, A. W., Riter, A., Amitai, A., Margolin, B., Shabtai, L., & Zaksh, D. (1975). Can money enhance intrinsic motivation? A test of the content-consequence hypothesis. *Journal of Personality and Social Psychology, 31,* 744–750.

Kun, A. (1977). Development of the magnitude-covariation and compensation schemata in ability and effort attribution of performance. *Child Development, 48,* 862–873.

Lauridsen, R. W. (1978). The effects of verbal cueing on second grade students' subsequent intrinsic motivation. *Dissertation Abstracts International, 38,* 4689A. (University of Southern California Microfilm No. 2484A)

Lee, D. Y., Syrnyk, R., & Hallschmid, C. (1977). Self-perception of intrinsic and extrinsic motivation: Effects on institutionalized mentally retarded adolescents. *American Journal of Mental Deficiency, 81,* 331–337.

Lepper, M. R., & Greene, D. (Eds.). (1978). *The hidden costs of reward.* Hillsdale, NJ: Erlbaum.

Lepper, M. R., Greene, D., & Nisbett, R. E. (1973). Undermining children's intrinsic interest with extrinsic reward. A test of the "overjustification" hypothesis. *Journal of Personality and Social Psychology, 28,* 129–137.

Leventhal, H. (1980). Toward a comprehensive theory of emotion. In L. Berkowitz (Ed.), *Advances in experimental social psychology* (Vol. 13). New York: Academic Press.

Mandler, G. (1975). *Mind and emotion.* New York: Wiley.

Martin, M. W. (in press). *Self-deception and self-understanding: Essays in philosophy and psychology.* Lawrence, KS: University Press of Kansas.

McGuire, W. J. (1969). The nature of attitudes and attitude change. In G. Lindzey & E. Aronson (Eds.), *The Handbook of Social Psychology* (2nd ed.) (Vol. 3). Reading MA: Addison-Wesley.

McLoyd, V. C. (1979). The effects of extrinsic rewards on differential value of high and low intrinsic interest. *Child Development, 50,* 1010–1019.

Mehrabian, A. (1972). *Nonverbal communication.* Chicago: Aldine-Atherton.

Morgan, M. (1981). The overjustification effect: A developmental test of self-perception interpretations. *Journal of Personality and Social Psychology, 40,* 809–821.

Mossholder, V. W. (1980). Effects of externally mediated goal setting on intrinsic motivation: A laboratory experiment. *Journal of Applied Psychology, 65,* 202–210.

New, J. R. (1979). Rewards as perceived external pressure in the undermining of intrinsic motivation. *Dissertation Abstracts International, 39,* 5034A. (University Microfilms No. 7902566)

Nisbett, R. E., & Valins, S. (1971). *Perceiving the causes of one's own behavior.* New York: General Learning Press.

Nisbett, R. E., & Wilson, T. D. (1977). Telling more than we can know: Verbal reports on mental processes. *Psychological Review, 84,* 231–259.

Pritchard, R. D., Campbell, K. M., & Campbell, D. J. (1977). Effects of extrinsic financial rewards on intrinsic motivation. *Journal of Applied Psychology, 62,* 9–15.

Quattrone, G. (1984). *On the congruity between attributions and action.* Unpublished manuscript, Stanford University, Stanford, CA.

Reader, M. J., & Dollinger, S. J. (1982). Deadlines, self-perceptions, and intrinsic motivation. *Personality and Social Psychology Bulletin, 8,* 742–747.

Regan, D. T., & Fazio, R. H. (1977). On the consistency between attitudes and behavior: Look to the method of attitude formation. *Journal of Experimental Social Psychology, 13,* 38–45.

Roethke, T. (1975). *The collected poems of Theodore Roethke.* Garden City, NY: Anchor.

Rorty, R. (1970). Incorrigibility as the mark of the mental. *The Journal of Philosophy, 67,* 399–424.

Rorty, R. (1982). Contemporary philosophy of mind. *Synthese, 53,* 323–348.

Rosenfield, D., Folger, R., & Adelman, H. F. (1980). When rewards reflect competence: A qualification of the overjustification effect. *Journal of Personality and Social Psychology, 39,* 368–376.

Ross, M. (1975). Salience of reward and intrinsic motivation. *Journal of Personality and Social Psychology, 32,* 245–254.

Ross, M. (1976). The self-perception of intrinsic motivation. In J. H. Harvey, W. J. Ickes, & R. F. Kidd (Eds.), *New Directions in Attribution Research* (Vol. 1). Hillsdale, NJ: Erlbaum.

Rubin, Z. (1970). Measurement of romantic love. *Journal of Personality and Social Psychology, 16,* 265–273.

Ryan, R. M. (1982). Control and information in the intrapersonal sphere: An extension of cognitive evaluation theory. *Journal of Personality and Social Psychology, 43,* 450–461.

Ryan, R. M., Mims, V., & Koestner, R. (1983). Relationship of reward contingency and interpersonal content to intrinsic motivation: A review and test using cognitive evaluation theory. *Journal of Personality and Social Psychology, 45,* 736–750.

Sackeim, H. (1983). Self-deception, self-esteem, and depression: The adaptive value of lying to oneself. In J. Masling (Ed.), *Empirical studies of psychoanalytic theory.* Hillsdale, NJ: Erlbaum.

Schachter, S., & Singer, J. E. (1962). Cognitive, social and physiological determinants of emotional state. *Psychological Review, 69,* 379–399.

Scheier, M. F., Buss, A. H., & Buss, D. M. (1978). Self-consciousness, self-report of aggressiveness, and aggression. *Journal of Research in Personality, 12,* 133–140.

Scott, C. A., & Yalch, R. F. (1978). A test of the self-perception explanation of the effects of rewards on intrinsic interest. *Journal of Experimental Social Psychology, 14,* 180–192.

Searle, J. R. (1979). Intentionality and the use of language. In A. Margalit (Ed.), *Meaning and use* (pp. 149–162). Dordrecht, Netherlands: Reidel.

Shultz, T. R., Butkowsky, I., Pearce, J. W., & Shanfield, H. (1975). Development of schemes for the attribution of multiple psychological causes. *Developmental Psychology, 11,* 502–510.

Smith, M. C. (1975). Children's use of the multiple sufficient scheme in social perception. *Journal of Personality and Social Psychology, 32,* 737–747.

Smith, R. W., & Pittman, T. S. (1978). Reward, distraction, and the overjustification effect. *Journal of Experimental Social Psychology, 36,* 565–572.

Smith, W. E. (1976). The effects of anticipated vs. unanticipated social reward on subsequent intrinsic motivation. *Dissertation Abstracts International, 37,* 1043B–1044B. (University Microfilms No. 7618209)

Snyder, C. R., & Endelman, J. R. (1979). Effects of degree of interpersonal similarity on physical distance and self-reported attraction: A comparison of uniqueness and reinforcement theory predictions. *Journal of Personality, 47,* 492–505.

Snyder, C. R., & Fromkin, H. L. (1977). Abnormality as a positive characteristic: The development and validation of a scale measuring need for uniqueness. *Journal of Abnormal Psychology, 86,* 518–527.

Spanier, G. B. (1976). Measuring dyadic adjustment: New scales for assessing the quality of marriage and similar dyads. *Journal of Marriage and the Family, 38,* 15–28.

Tesch, F. E., Huston, T. L., & Indenbaum, E. A. (1973). Attitude similarity, attraction, and physical proximity in a dynamic space. *Journal of Applied Social Psychology, 3,* 63–72.

Tversky, A., & Kahneman, D. (1974). Judgment under uncertainty: Heuristics and biases. *Science, 184,* 1124–1131.

Wason, P. C., & Evans, J. St. B. T. (1975). Dual processes in reasoning? *Cognition, 3,* 141–154.

Weick, K. E. (1967). Dissonance and task enhancement: A problem for compensation theory? *Organizational Behavior and Human Performance, 2,* 175–216.

Weiner, M. J., & Mander, A. M. (1977). The effect of aversive consequences upon persistent behavior. *Motivation and Emotion, 1,* 367–377.

Weiner, M. J., & Mander, A. M. (1978). The effects of reward and perception of competency upon intrinsic motivation. *Motivation and Emotion, 2,* 67–73.

Wells, D., & Shultz, T. R. (1980). Developmental distinctions between behavior and judgment in the operation of the discounting principle. *Child Development, 51,* 1307–1310.

Wicker, A. W. (1969). Attitudes versus actions: The relationship of verbal and overt behavior responses to attitude objects. *Journal of Social Issues, 25,* 41–78.

Wicklund, R. (1982). Self-focused attention and the validity of self-reports. In M. P. Zanna, E. T. Higgins, & C. P. Herman (Eds.), *Consistency in Social Behavior: The Ontario Symposium* (Vol. 2). Hillsdale, NJ: Erlbaum.

Williams, B. W. (1980). Reinforcement, behavior constraint and the overjustification effect. *Journal of Personality and Social Psychology, 39,* 599–614.

Wilson, T. D., Dunn, D. S., Bybee, J. A., Hyman, D. B., & Rotondo, J. A. (1984). Effects of analyzing reasons on attitude–behavior consistency. *Journal of Personality and Social Psychology, 47,* 5–16.

Wilson, T. D., Hull, J. G., & Johnson, J. (1981). Awareness and self-perception: Verbal reports on internal states. *Journal of Personality and Social Psychology, 40,* 53–71.

Wilson, T. D., Lassiter, G. D., & Stone, J. I. (1984). *Regulated versus unregulated nonverbal behavior in social interaction: Evidence for limited access to mental states.* Unpublished manuscript, University of Virginia.

Wilson, T. D., & Linville, P. W. (1982). Improving the academic performance of college freshmen: Attribution therapy revisited. *Journal of Personality and Social Psychology, 42,* 367–376.

Wimperis, B. R., & Farr, J. L. (1979). The effects of task content and reward contingency upon task performance and satisfaction. *Journal of Applied Social Psychology, 9,* 229–249.

Word, C. H., Zanna, M. P., & Cooper, J. (1974). The nonverbal mediation of self-fulfilling hypotheses in interracial interaction. *Journal of Experimental Social Psychology, 10,* 109–120.

Zajonc, R. B. (1980). Feeling and thinking: Preferences need no inferences. *American Psychologist, 35,* 151–175.

Zanna, M. P., & Cooper, J. (1976). Dissonance and the attribution process. In J. H. Harvey, W. J. Ickes, & R. F. Kidd (Eds.), *New directions in attribution research* (Vol. 1). Hillsdale, NJ: Erlbaum.

Zanna, M. P., Lepper, M. R., & Abelson, R. P. (1973). Attentional mechanisms in children's devaluation of forbidden activity in a forced-compliance situation. *Journal of Personality and Social Psychology, 28,* 355–359.

Zimbardo, P. G., Cohen, A., Weisenberg, M., Dworkin, L., & Firestone, I. (1969). The control of experimental pain. In P. G. Zimbardo (Ed.), *The cognitive control of motivation.* Glenview, IL: Scott, Foresman.

Zuckerman, M., DePaulo, B. M., & Rosenthal, R. (1981). Verbal and nonverbal communication of deception. In L. Berkowitz (Ed.), *Advances in experimental social psychology* (Vol. 14). New York: Academic Press.

Zuckerman, M., Larrance, D. T., Spiegel, N. H., & Klorman, R. (1981). Controlling nonverbal cues: Facial expressions and tone of voice. *Journal of Experimental Social Psychology, 17,* 506–524.

CHAPTER **2**

Basic Determinants of Attribution and Social Perception

Saul M. Kassin and Reuben M. Baron

INTRODUCTION: THE MANY DIRECTIONS OF ATTRIBUTION THEORY

It has now been over 25 years since the publication of Fritz Heider's *The Psychology of Interpersonal Relations* (1958). Although unaccompanied by groundbreaking ceremonies, this book marked the formal beginning of ideas that collectively have come to be known as attribution theory. Heider's (1958) theory is really an amalgam of two rather disparate approaches to social knowing in general and the process of attribution in particular, as he explicitly distinguished between what he called *phenomenal* and *causal* description. In the former, the person or object in an observer's field is directly experienced; in the latter, the observer experiences a person or object as the result of a constructive process often represented by a series of cognitive operations. Heider has referred to these modes of social knowing with the more familiar terms *perception* and *inference*, respectively.

Chapter 3 of Heider's book is entitled "Perceiving the Other Person." In it, he describes attributional processes in social perception as essentially similar to those that characterize inanimate object perception. As such, several basic problems and phenomena discovered by the Gestalt psychologists (e.g., apparent movement, figure-ground relations, perceptual constancies, unit formation) were deemed relevant in the interpersonal domain. This emphasis was apparent in Heider's early writings (1939, 1944). In fact, in what can be considered the first empirical study of attribution in a social context, Heider and Simmel (1944) sought to explore how the dynamics of motion, factors such as temporal contiguity, spatial proximity, range, direction, and velocity of movement, convey impressions about human behavior and its causes. Accordingly, they created and showed subjects a brief animated film depicting the movements of geometrical objects and found that certain impressions naturally followed from specific configurational patterns. For example, when two objects move successively in time and make momentary contact, the first object is perceived to have energized or propelled the second, causing it to move forward.

In contrast to this work on phenomenal causality, Chapter 4 of Heider's (1958) book is devoted to "The Naive Analysis of Action." In this chapter, attribution is viewed within Brunswik's (1952) lens model wherein the perceptual process is conceived as an arc encompassing two endpoints—the distal stimulus (i.e., the actual object in the environment toward which attention is directed) and the perceptual judgment. This distinction is drawn and a non-isomorphic relationship between the distal and proximal stimulus (i.e., the object as it is perceived or imagined) is assumed because the former must be obtained through some form of mediation (e.g., light and sound waves, videotape, language) and also acted upon by constructive, interpretive processes within the observer (e.g., specific expectancies and cultural stereotypes). This approach encourages an emphasis on factors that are extraneous to the focal event and on cognitive activities that reside within the perceiver. As such, the attributional principle of covariation was articulated, as were the commonsense determinants of such causal factors as ability, effort, task demands, and luck.

Although Heider clearly emphasized both the processes of perception and inference of causality, subsequent theories focused almost exclusively on the latter. As the zeitgeist favored an information-processing metaphor replete with prescriptive models, cubes, and flow charts, this historical trend, in retrospect, is not surprising. Jones and Davis (1965), for example, presented their theory of correspondent inferences which asserted that people perform a two-pronged analysis of observed behavior, inferring the presence of personal dispositions from acts that produce unique and socially undesirable effects. Kelley (1967) then introduced his ANOVA model of attribution in which people were said to analyze and compare an observed act to variations across the causal dimensions of persons, stimuli, time and modality. In so doing, causal attribution for behavioral events was said to follow from information about their consensus, distinctiveness, and consistency.

Several attempts were made over the next few years to extend, integrate, and reconceptualize the constructs of attribution within broader theoretical frameworks. As before, the emphasis in attribution was on mental structures (e.g., Jones & McGillis's content-specific expectancies, 1976; Kelley's more generalized causal schemas, 1971) and constructive processes (e.g., Anderson's information integration approach, 1974; Ajzen & Fishbein's Bayesian analysis, 1975). In fact, in a recent *New Directions* chapter, Ostrom (1981) essentially defined attribution as causal inference.

Today, there are two good answers to the question, "What's new in attribution theory?" Kelley and Michela (1980) distinguished between *attribution* research, aimed at discovering the antecedents of causal beliefs, and *attributional* research, directed at the behavioral consequences of these beliefs. The field has always been characterized by these dual interests. Currently, state-of-the-art research conducted within the antecedents tradition, through the use of rather sophisticated cognitive methodologies, is aimed at "getting inside the head" (Taylor & Fiske, 1981) and tracing the mental activity across a sequence of information-processing states from which causality may be inferred (Hastie, 1983; Wyer & Carlson, 1979). Smith and Miller's (1979) use of reaction time data to provide support for a subtractive process of causal attribution is a prime example. In the meantime, research following within the behavioral consequences tradition, through the use of field-based methodologies in natural contexts and real-world subject populations, has taken on a very applied focus. Attributional accounts have thus been advanced for such problems and phenomena as depression, alcoholism, crowding, teacher–pupil interactions, intrinsic motivation, and bias in jury decision-making (Frieze, Bar-Tal, & Carroll, 1979). Kassin and Wrightsman's (1985) attributional analysis of coerced confession evidence in criminal law is a case in point.

What is left? Hasn't attribution theory and research covered all bases? Hasn't it all been said before? As the title of this chapter suggests, we believe it has not. Emerging within a zeitgeist that favored an information-processing motif and a concern for (or the necessity of) clinical and societal application, the rapid growth and expansion of the attribution paradigm has not proceeded without cost. In a chapter partially entitled "Back to Basics," Shaver (1981) suggests that the time has come to pull back and sharpen the guiding theory with an eye toward the concept of causality and its philosophical underpinnings. In a related vein, Shultz and Schleifer (1983) argue for the need to disambiguate such distinct concepts as causality, responsibility, and reward–punishment, drawing on the philosophies of science, mind, law, and ethics.

In spirit and in tone, the present chapter may also be viewed as a back to basics call. In substance and in direction, however, the emphasis is on a class of relatively neglected informational antecedents in social perception, the raw material contained in Heider's Chapter 3—"The Basic Determinants of Attribution."

WHAT DO WE MEAN BY "BASIC"?

What constitutes a fundamental or basic determinant of attribution? The answer to this question probably depends on who you ask. Several reasonable, partially overlapping definitions are worth considering. Perhaps the most obvious possibility is what may be called the *developmental priority* definition. Simply put, the basicity of a causal rule or informational cue may be defined by the age at which it is reliably used. As a rough guideline, a marked shift in causal reasoning seems to accompany the transition from Piaget's preoperational to concrete-operational stages of cognitive development. As such, it might tentatively be suggested that those cues that are reliably used at the preoperational level be considered basic. The logic of this developmental definition is straightforward—without the intellectual and logical abilities needed for sophisticated inference processes and with relatively little in the way of schema-generating experiences, young children's attributions must be compelled in large part by environmental cues. In broader terms, we would suggest that evidence for basicity is to be found in the behavioral effects of an attributional cue on organisms that are limited in cognitive capacity. Though attributionally consistent behavior is an admittedly imperfect criterion, it will be seen that such effects can be gleaned from the vast empirical literature on animal learning.

DiVitto and McArthur (1978) have proposed that the extent to which information influences children's attributions depends on the number of cognitive steps required to make the linkage. This hypothesis quite naturally suggests a second possible definition of basic—the *stimulus sufficiency* definition. By this account, the basicity of information is a function of its ability to reliably convey a causal impression to observers who need not, in turn, supply knowledge from other sources (e.g., schemata, extraneous data) in order to make sense of it. This definition is consistent with a Gibsonian or ecological approach to social knowing which takes as a starting point the task of specifying the physical stimulus properties upon which perceptual judgments are based (Baron, 1980b; McArthur & Baron, 1983). As such, it essentially assumes that basic determinants are those that produce causal attributions via a process of direct rather than mediated perception. It also suggests that basic determinants correspond to Buss' (1978) causal as opposed to reason types of attributional data. That is, from a direct-perception perspective, the information is rooted in the ability of the perceptual apparatus to discover in the environment naturally existing organizations of events that induce a causal reading in a lawlike manner (e.g., the operation of perceptual salience). Reasons, on the other hand, are optional constructions that typically have the character of post hoc rationalizations designed to fit social rule systems (cf. Baron, 1984, for a broader discussion of rules and laws in the operation of cognitive and perceptual processes).

Closely related to stimulus sufficiency is what might be termed the *response immediacy* definition. It is often assumed that compared to complex, higher order processes which take time, the more primitive, noninferential processes are relatively instantaneous, or, as described by the Gestalt psychologists, the work of "insight" (e.g., Koffka, 1935). This assumption is widely shared among cognitive psychologists (e.g., Julesz', 1981, notion of effortless perception, operationally defined as the sufficiency of brief exposure to a stimulus) and forms the basis for Schneider, Hastorf, and Ellsworth's (1979) discussion of "snap judgments" in person perception. The adaptive role of immediacy is evident in regard to both skilled performance and social interaction. Consider, for example, how in tennis or baseball the player is able to spontaneously adjust his or her racket or bat to meet the trajectory of a speeding ball. While the precise nature of how such on-line coordination occurs is unknown, it is clear that the visual–motor system, in order to function under stringent temporal constraints, makes direct use of higher order sources of information for which the organism must be prepared or trained to detect. Similarly, in the realm of interpersonal interaction, there are on-line situations in which people spontaneously adjust their nonverbal responses to rapid changes in social indicators such as a smile or a raised eyebrow (Eibl-Eibesfeldt, 1975). In any event, reaction time is an operational criterion often invoked as evidence for the simplicity or directness of an information-processing path (e.g., Taylor, 1976), or the organism's level of preparedness to receive and react to an environmental cue (e.g., Michotte, 1946/1963).[1]

The foregoing criteria are, at best, piecemeal attempts to define what is meant by the term "basic determinants." At this point, we believe it is worthwhile to conceptualize these criteria within a larger framework that defines basicity in operational terms, by the apparent ease (i.e., a minimum of attention and effort) with which a stimulus event suggests an attribution.

In recent years, several cognitive psychologists have distinguished mental processes along a continuum ranging from those that are automatic, requiring only minimal allocations of attention to occur, to those that are more controlled and effortful, demanding considerable attentional capacity for their occurrence (Hasher & Zacks, 1979; LaBerge, 1973;

---

[1]In view of the possibility that slowly changing events such as aging may be perceived directly (Pittenger & Shaw, 1975), response immediacy might be considered a sufficient but perhaps not a necessary criterion.

Posner & Snyder, 1975; Schneider & Shiffrin, 1977: Shiffrin & Schneider, 1977). When coupled with Kahneman's (1973) thesis that people are limited in their capacity for performing mental operations, this distinction suggests several testable implications. First, automatic processes may be activated almost reflexively, without awareness or intention (e.g., incidental learning). Second, because they drain minimal amounts of energy from the attentional system, automatic processes do not interfere with other ongoing cognitive activity, nor are they disrupted by circumstances that place high demands on the organism's limited capacity (e.g., acute stress or arousal). Finally, although it is possible for nonautomatic processes to become automatized through extensive practice and overlearning (Langer, 1978; Shiffrin & Schneider, 1977), it appears that when such processes deal with information of high adaptive value, they may be innately based—that is, there is a "preparedness" to receive certain types of information and to perceive and learn certain relationships. As such, automatic processes should develop early in life and exhibit little individual-difference variability as a function of age, education, motivation, experience, culture or intelligence. It is interesting to note that, in a discussion of affective reactions to environmental stimulation, Zajonc (1984) has argued that there is a physiological basis for the concept of an automatic, nonmediated mental process. In contrast to all this, of course, controlled processes are often consciously initiated, they limit one's ability to simultaneously engage in other effortful activities, they are disrupted by conditions that reduce attentional capacity, and they are subject to a wide range of individual differences.

In view of the foregoing comparison as well as the duality that characterizes Heider's work, *basic determinants of attribution are defined as those that appear to activate automatic, perceptual processes rather than those that are more controlled and inferential.* At the very least, this definition should encompass portions of the criteria described earlier. As such, it presumes the primary importance of stimulus-based information, the direct relevance of animal-learning and early developmental research, and the need to investigate attributional processes in the context of spontaneous, on-line interaction.

THE BASICS OF SOCIAL PERCEPTION

IDENTIFYING HUMAN ACTIONS

A primary task in the realm of social perception is to detect and accurately identify an actor's thoughts, feelings, and behavior. Several classes of cues have attracted scientific attention, two of which will be considered here—facial expression and gross motoric behavior. Because the literature on these cues has traditionally presumed the basicity of their phenomena and because the approach taken has proved successful, it provides a firm starting point from which lessons can be drawn by attribution theorists.

FACIAL CONFIGURATION AND EXPRESSION

Perhaps the strongest case to make for automatic processes in social perception is in the relationship between specifiable configurations of the face and attributions of emotion. Beginning with Darwin's (1872) analysis of the adaptive value of emotional expression and communication, several theorists have argued for the basicity of facial cues and an ecological approach to their perception (McArthur & Baron, 1983). Three lines of converging evidence have been cited in support of this position. First, there is reason to believe that the automatic perception of emotion in the face is innate. Sackett (1966), for example, showed that infant rhesus monkeys raised since birth in isolation react with appropriate fear to a photograph of a large male engaging in a threat display. Equally as relevant is the impressive array of demonstrations of cross-cultural constancy among human perceivers. It has been reported, for example, that posed expressions of certain primary affects (happiness, sadness, anger, disgust, and surprise–fear) are similarly interpreted across a diversity of cultures, Western and non-Western alike (Ekman, Sorenson, & Friesen, 1969; Izard, 1969). Finally, it appears that although preschool children cannot readily attach the correct verbal labels, they do display significant ability to extract the emotional content from facial expression (Alper, Buck, & Dryer, 1978). In fact, even 4-month-old infants react differentially to faces expressing happiness, anger, and surprise (e.g., Young-Browne, Rosenfeld, & Horowitz, 1977).

A second line of support for the basicity of facial-expressive cues is the evidence suggestive of stimulus sufficiency. Ekman and Friesen (1975), using a posed-photograph methodology, discussed in detail the kinds of facial configurations that are associated with various primary affects. More recently, in response to the notion that affect is revealed in the *dynamics* of expression, techniques have been developed to analyze the components of facial anatomy and muscular movement that seem to be universally associated with specific emotions (Ekman & Friesen, 1976; Izard, Huebner, Riser, McGinnes, & Dougherty, 1980) and their perception (Bassili, 1978). The importance of this research is that it suggests that, at least for spontaneous expressions of emotion, the overt facial display is largely isomorphic with the individual's true in-

ternal state. These data thus enhance the viability of a stimulus sufficiency hypothesis and, consequently, the relative unimportance of
constructive, elaborative processes.

In sum, the empirical literature appears to corroborate the Darwinian
claim that perhaps for reasons of adaptability, facial expression is a basic
determinant of emotion perception. This position rests on evidence
which suggests organismic preparedness, cross-cultural consistency, developmental priority, and stimulus sufficiency.

GROSS MOTORIC BEHAVIOR

Paralleling the work on the perception of facial features is the relatively recent research on the physical parameters or biomechanics of
human movement that give rise to the identification of various activities.

In a series of experiments, Johansson (1973, 1976) had subjects watch
films in which human actors moved about in a darkened room with
flashlight bulbs attached to their shoulders, elbows, wrists, knees, and
ankles. When actors sat motionless in a chair, subjects perceived nothing more than a random constellation of disconnected elements. As soon
as they began moving, however, subjects immediately perceived that
the lights were attached to otherwise invisible people. Through the use
of this point-light display, Johansson found that perceivers were readily
able to identify and distinguish such complex categories of motion as
walking, running, jumping, dancing, falling, and exercising. In addition, the findings collectively suggested the operation of automatic processing—subjects exhibited extraordinarily high rates of accuracy, they
made their judgments almost instantaneously, they were not conscious
of the cues they had used, and they required little pretraining or practice
to achieve their level of proficiency (Johansson, von Hofsten, & Jansson,
1980).

As with facial expression and emotion recognition, the literature on
biological motion perception strongly suggests that there are transfor-
mational invariants in animate motion and that, as perceivers, we need
only to discover—not construct—these biomechanical laws. Thus, Pearson (1976) reported that the kinematic cues that characterize running or
walking hold whether the actor is a man, a cat, or a roach. Further, the
stimulus parameters that naturally distinguish different types of physical activity can be specified mathematically (e.g., Restle, 1979) and simulated via computer-animation techniques (e.g., Todd, 1983).

PERCEIVING CAUSALITY

It could be argued that people are so prepared to perceive causal relationships that experience teaches us when *not* to make attributions.

Beginning with Piaget's (1930) observations, the developmental litera-ture has thus shown that, as a general rule, preoperational children over-attribute causality (i.e., in instances of coincidental event pairings). Among adults, there are times when causal relationships are so com-pelling that they are apprehended via automatic, effortless processes. Taylor and Fiske (1978) recently introduced the term "top-of-the-head" response to describe the phenomenon that people often express an at-tribution after having "spent little time on the matter, gathered little or no data beyond that of the immediate situation, and responded with an opinion nevertheless" (p. 252). What environmental cues activate a top-of-the-head response set? At least two types of stimulus events and con-figurational patterns clearly emerge, by our definition, as basic deter-minants of attribution.

SPATIOTEMPORAL CUES

When two events co-occur, we naturally perceive the first event as the cause, and the second as its effect. The strongest support for the basicity of ordinal priority resides within the behavioral literature on classical conditioning, where it has been repeatedly demonstrated that infrahumans, infants and young children can be classically conditioned through traditional procedures (i.e., where the conditioned stimulus [CS] precedes the unconditioned stimulus [US]) but not through the procedure of backward conditioning (Reese & Lipsitt, 1970). Current de-velopmental evidence also favors this notion. Bullock and Gelman (1979), for example, had subjects make attributions for a mechanical ef-fect and found that even three-year-old children were receptive to or-dinal priority cues. In fact, they continued to respond as such even when the antecedent event was spatially removed from the effect while the consequent event was spatially proximal (also see Kun, 1978).

In a related vein, perhaps the cornerstone rule guiding attribution is that causes and effects coincide in time and space. Indeed even Hume (1740/1960) and other philosophers within the empiricist tradition who were skeptical about the ontological status of causation conceded that despite its questionable basis in reality, the condition of spatio-temporal contiguity produces the inescapable perception of a causal link. Thus, according to Duncker (1945), when a gust of wind blows a door shut and, at the same time, an electric light happens to go on at the other end of a corridor, the impression of causality is immediately forced upon us.

As before, the animal conditioning literature provides strong, indirect support for the basicity of temporal contiguity. Pavlov (1927) and others have consistently found that the absolute time interval between successive stimuli is a critical determiner of their effect on subsequent behavior, as classical conditioning proceeds most rapidly if the CS–US interval does not exceed a fraction of a second. Likewise, instrumental learning is consistently facilitated by the use of immediate- as opposed to delayed-consequence procedures (Renner, 1964; Terrell & Ware, 1961). When we turn to peoples' perceptions of causality, we encounter the same phenomenon with Michotte's (1946/1963) report that human observers perceive a causal relation between successive events if the second follows the first within 100 ms.

Employing the classic case of one object striking another, Michotte conducted a series of studies wherein subjects watched and described sequences in which one object (A) moves toward a second, stationary object (B) and stops when it has reached it, after which B moves away in the same direction at the same or slower speed (the launching effect) or with an increase in velocity (the triggering effect). For the vast majority of subjects, temporal contiguity consistently induced the perception of causality, and the presence of even a brief delay between events 1 and 2 could erase this impression.

Michotte's work has drawn criticism on methodological grounds, such as the imprecision of the disc method for generating displays and the use of trained observers and suggestive procedures (Joynson, 1971; Montpellier & Nuttin, 1973; Runeson, 1977; Weir, 1978). And, other investigators have reported somewhat lower rates of perceived causality within the same paradigm (Beasley, 1968; Boyle, 1960). Yet, despite these drawbacks, there is reason to believe that Michotte and others had spuriously underestimated the perception of a causal link between contiguous events. In an insightful analysis of the kinematics of Michotte's displays, Runeson (1977) concluded that, in several respects, the sample of stimulus events employed was mechanically and ecologically nonrepresentative of real linear collision events. Of course, Michotte was impressed with precisely those paradoxical cases in which causal impressions were obtained despite the use of inadequate and, hence, novel simulations of real, dynamic events. For him, this problem provided evidence for a nativistic position rather than one based on acquired knowledge structures. In part, we agree. From our standpoint, the data suggest that because we assume such determinants of attribution are based in the laws of mechanics and because Michotte's simulation events violated these realities, the effects of contiguity had not been fully realized.

The most persuasive evidence for temporal-contiguity effects on attribution is developmental in nature. Piaget (1930) believed that young, preoperational children based their attributions exclusively on contiguity and, in fact, are overly seduced by this cue, often linking events that happen to co-occur by chance. Although young children do not spontaneously describe Michotte-like events in causal terms (Lesser, 1977; Olum, 1956), research employing more sensitive measures of attribution has revealed a strong receptivity to such information. Siegler and Liebert (1974) devised an ingenious mechanical event in which subjects were shown a "computer" equipped with various sounds and flashing lights (Cause 1) and a "card programmer" containing a slot for IBM cards (Cause 2), both attached by wires to a large electric light bulb (effect). A card was inserted and a light went on either immediately or after a 5-second delay. As it turned out, kindergarteners were strongly influenced by the contiguity factor, choosing the card programmer as the cause of the illumination more often in the immediate than in the delayed condition. This finding has proven to be extremely robust. Others have found that 3- and 4-year-olds attribute an effect to a temporally contiguous event even when the two (1) do not covary across trials (Mendelson & Shultz, 1976; Siegler, 1975; Siegler & Liebert, 1974), (2) lack spatial contact (Bullock, 1979), and (3) conflict with physical similarity cues (Shultz & Ravinsky, 1977). Moreover, this perceived link persists even when the antecedent event is not intuitively related to the effect (Ausubel & Schiff, 1954).

Finally, in a highly persuasive study, Leslie (1982) found that 4–8-month-old infants exhibited a sensitivity to the causal implications of temporal contiguity. Through the measurement of visual fixation, subjects were habituated to a Michotte-like launching sequence in which Object B reacted either immediately upon contact (40 ms) or after a brief (580 ms) delay. They were then shown test films in which either Object A or B moves in isolation, again as visual tracking time was recorded. It was reasoned that if the infants had perceived the initial contiguous launching events as causally connected, they should dishabituate more rapidly (i.e., attend to for a longer period of time) to the test films than if they had already been exposed to a delayed, discontinuous sequence. The results of this and another conceptually analogous experiment were consistent with this hypothesis and the more general view "that perception of causality is *direct* and *immediate* implying no specific basis in action" (Gibson, 1979; Leslie, 1982, p. 185). Similar results have been reported for infants' sensitivity to spatial-contiguity information (Borton, 1979).

To sum up: Animal behavioral evidence and research with human infants, children, and adults implicate spatiotemporality as a basic determinant of attribution. So compelling are the data that we might speculate about a prewired tendency to perceive contiguous events in causal terms. It is, after all, likely that the contiguity mechanism is a reflection of corresponding ecological regularities in various species' evolutionary history. Other things being equal, the probability that an effect is—in reality—caused by some antecedent event must be related to the amount of time separating the two events. The longer the delay, the greater is the chance that other, intervening events will have contributed to the effect and, as such, the less likely it is that the earlier event was ultimately causal. Of course, this temporal function need not be monotonic and it may even differ for different classes of events. For example, research on the classical conditioning of skeletal responses has shown a downturn in the response probability function at very brief CS–US intervals (Kimble, 1947). Instrumental conditioning experiments have likewise revealed a nonmonotonic relationship between response and reinforcement (Landauer, 1969). Yet in taste-aversion learning situations, even long delays between cause and effect are tolerated (Garcia, Ervin, & Koelling, 1966). In short, we would suggest that the spatiotemporal contiguity of causes and effects is based in ecological reality and that the apparent automaticity with which such cues determine causal attribution reflects a biological preparedness.

PERCEPTUAL SALIENCE

Psychologists of the Gestalt tradition had observed that "fixation of one of two equivalent objects tended to make it the carrier of motion whether it moved objectively or not" (Koffka, 1935). Recent research has provided an impressive array of evidence that supports the importance of figural emphasis or salience cues in attribution. On a behavioral level, studies of animal learning have demonstrated stronger conditioning to salient than nonsalient components of a complex pattern of stimulation (Rescorla & Wagner, 1972). More recent investigations of the attribution processes of adults contributes several additional and unique lines of support.

In one experiment, Taylor and Fiske (1975) manipulated visual salience via subjects' seating position as they observed a live conversation between two individuals. Consistent with the salience hypothesis, subjects rated the actor upon whom their attention was focused as the more causal of the two. In a subsequent series of studies, McArthur and Post (1977) manipulated the salience of an actor via physical attributes that spontaneously attract visual attention. Subjects thus observed videotapes of two individuals engaged in conversation. In each instance, one of the two was highlighted either by being seated under a bright light, by rocking in a rocking chair, or by wearing a boldly patterned shirt.

Overall, the salient actors' behaviors were rated as less situationally determined than those of their counterparts.[2]

Of relevance to the basicity question, Taylor, Fiske, and their colleagues made several follow-up attempts to identify the link in the chain of inferential activities that is responsible for this salience–causality relationship. This line of inquiry, however, has generally failed to locate a reliable mediating process, as the effect is not necessarily dependent upon either the differential volume or the availability of visual or verbal recall (Fiske, Kenny, & Taylor, 1982).[3]

At this point, rather than declare salience a basic determinant by default, let us consider several sources of affirmative support for an alternative notion that people automatically attribute causality to salient objects and events. First, significant salience effects on attribution have been obtained even when additional information processing demands are imposed on subjects. Within the paradigm established earlier, Taylor, Crocker, Fiske, Sprinzen, and Winkler (1979) distracted half of their subjects as they watched the dyadic interaction by asking them to keep a running count on the number of pronouns used in their conversation. In addition, half of the subjects were distracted by an irrelevant audiovisual presentation as they filled out the postobservation attribution questionnaire. Self-report and information-recall data confirmed the efficacy of these manipulations. Still, the salience effect on perceived causality remained. In similar fashion, Taylor et al. (1979) reported that the effect persisted despite alterations in subjects' observational goals, personal involvement with the topic of discussion, or level of caffeine-induced arousal.

Second, the salience phenomenon is unaffected by whether people are encouraged to give minimal or extensive thought to their attributional responses. Thus, the phenomenon appears even when subjects are instructed, prior to answering the closed-ended attribution measure, to think of and write several possible explanations for a series of events, to consider them all carefully, and to indicate the best one (Smith & Miller, 1979).

Third, developmental research has revealed that young children exhibit a pronounced tendency to attribute effects to salient antecedent events (Dix & Herzberger, 1983), even when the latter conflict with in-

---

[2]It is interesting to note that a parallel effect has been demonstrated repeatedly in the area of self-perception (Duval & Hensley, 1976).

[3]There is some support for the idea that people preferentially recall causally *relevant* information as a function of salience (Fiske et al., 1982), but there are, as McArthur (1980) noted, plausible competing explanations for these data that do not presume a relevant recall-attribution process model.

formation that is logically more appropriate (e.g., covariation; for reviews of this literature, see Kassin, 1981; Sedlak & Kurtz, 1981). In fact, in the overjustification literature it has been shown that perceptual salience manipulations can be employed to reduce the adverse impact of rewards on the intrinsic motivation of preschoolers (Fazio, 1981; Ross, 1975).

To sum up: Salience appears to qualify as a basic determinant of attribution. As with contiguity, we ask, Is this an innate phenomenon, one that has evolved as a result of its adaptational importance? McArthur and Baron (1983) have suggested that it is—that perhaps perceptually salient stimuli are *in nature* more likely than nonsalient stimuli to exert causal influences in the environment, and that survival pressures have necessitated the development of a perceptual apparatus that is sensitive to this reality. As examples, they note that

> bright lights, such as lightening or fires, and loud sounds, such as thunder, a roaring animal, or a screaming baby, are most apt to exert causal influence than their less intense counterparts. Similarly, moving stimuli, such as a charging bull, and unit-forming stimuli, such as a herd of buffalo, are more apt to exert causal influence than a stationary or unrelated collection of animals. (McArthur & Baron, 1983, p. 232)

TRAIT ATTRIBUTION

Within the predominant information-processing models of social cognition, the process of trait attribution is viewed as indirect, mediated by prior judgments of intention and causality. Nevertheless, there is a small but growing body of literature which is devoted to articulating the snap judgments we so frequently and naturally make about others about whom we have relatively little information. Two classes of basic determinants are considered here—static physical-appearance cues and the kinematics of action.

PHYSICAL APPEARANCE

It has long been recognized that people readily make judgments about others on the basis of structural physiognomic cues. The empirical literature is rather sparse, however, consisting primarily of isolated reports of physical feature-trait attribution relationships (for reviews, see Livesley & Bromley, 1973; McArthur, 1982; Schneider et al., 1979).

In the most extensive study of "personalities in faces," Secord, Dukes, and Bevan (1954) had subjects look at a set of photographed faces and rate them either on 23 physiognomic characteristics (e.g., width of face, fullness of lips, distance between eyes, complexion) or on 35 trait dimensions (e.g., honest, aggressive, intelligent). Overall, several strong relationships emerged between the two sets of ratings (e.g., thin lips are associated with the perception of conscientiousness). More germane to the present discussion, the following additional results suggested the possible operation of an automatic process. First, there was a high level of consensus on impressions of personality—in fact, the rate of inter-subject agreement was approximately as high for personality judgments as it was for physiognomic ratings. Second, trait attributions were made in a rapid, unhesitating manner, several traits frequently being rated after a single glance at the photograph. Third, even though subjects felt confident about their attributions, they were generally unaware of (i.e., unable to articulate) the cues that guided their judgments. On the basis of these findings, it appears that the information conveyed by physiognomy is often sufficient to produce reliable, immediate, and nonconscious trait attributions. The authors thus concluded that "these schemata would indeed appear to be well learned" and that "one possible explanation is that such stereotypes have some validity" (p. 271).

One outcome of Secord et al.'s (1954) study was the finding that relationships were stronger between clusters than between single features and traits. Indeed a promising new line of research is focused on physiognomic *configurations* as basic determinants of trait attribution. Keating, Mazur, and Segall (1981), for example, have obtained cross-cultural evidence that broad faces and receding hairlines are perceived as relatively dominant. Similarly, consistent with ethological observations concerning the cross-species stimulus characteristics of infants, McArthur and her colleagues have found that adult males with "babyish" features such as large eyes, short noses and ears, or low vertical placement of all features, are perceived as less strong and assertive than those with the reverse, more "mature" appearance (Berry & McArthur, in press; McArthur & Apatow, in press). Along similar lines, Alley (1981) found that subjects report a greater desire to protect and cuddle stimulus persons whose head shape or bodily proportion is babyish rather than mature.

The most persuasive evidence for the basicity of such cues can be gleaned from recent research on the relationship between craniofacial morphology, body proportion, and perceptions of age. Specifically, it has been shown that the actual physical aging process can be modeled by a group of topological geometric transformations called cardioidal strain, and that subjects' estimates of age from computer-generated human profiles are largely determined by these transformations (Pittenger & Shaw, 1975). Subsequent studies have revealed that these ecologically valid cues are so fundamental that they affect people's perceptions of age in dogs, birds, monkeys, VW's, and chairs (Pittenger, Shaw, & Mark, 1979; for a review, see Todd, Mark, Shaw, & Pittenger, 1980).

KINEMATIC CUES

We have seen that people can quite readily identify biomechanical motions such as walking and running strictly on the basis of kinematic patterns provided in point-light displays. Recent research has likewise uncovered specific kinematic cues that convery information that is of direct relevance to person perception.

As an example, Runeson and Frykholm (1981) demonstrated that subjects could accurately judge the weight of a box by watching another person lifting and carrying it. Moreover, their level of accuracy remained high when, through the use of Johansson's point-light technique, only the actors' main joints and the corners of the box were visible. The authors concluded that actual variations in the weight of the box introduced specifiable changes in the kinematic patterns of the actor-box system and that human observers had the perceptual sophistication to pick up this information. In a similar vein, it has been found that point-light displays involving gait are sufficient for the perception of gender (e.g., Kozlowski & Cutting, 1977) and the identity of a friend (Cutting & Kozlowski, 1977).

In an elegant series of studies, Runeson and Frykholm (1982) found that even psychological characteristics such as expectations, intentions, and attempted deception can be perceived from simple kinematic displays. In one study, for example, actors were asked to lift boxes they knew to be of varying weights. Throught the light-patch technique, subjects watched only the actors' prelift movements. On the basis of these cues, observers accurately discriminated the weight of the boxes. Apparently, actors unknowingly convey their task expectations via bodily cues such as preparatory postural adjustments, cues to which perceivers are receptive.

A second type of kinematic cue that specifies the perception of trait-like characteristics in an object's path of motion. Koffka (1935) suggested that one can actually see moods such as depression in "slow dragging movements" and irritability in "discontinuous movements" (p. 658). In a relevant study, Tagiuri (1960) had subjects watch films of dots traveling from one point to another, varying the angle of their movement. He found that an object that travels a straight, linear path was seen as alert, well-reasoned, persevering, determined, logical, and ambitious; a more erratic path elicited impressions such as drunk, confused, immature, emotional, undependable, and careless: in contrast, an arched path was seen as nonchalant, leisurely, relaxed, and even complacent. Complementing Taigiuri's work, Michotte (1950) focused on the information conveyed by the speed of movement. He found, for example, that rapid movement gives the impression of violence, slow movement is characterized by gentleness, a sudden reduction in speed is interpreted as hesitation, and sudden, repeated variations in speed elicit impressions of nervousness and agitation. Finally, Bassili (1976) has reported that the spatially contiguous movements of two objects are sufficient to elicit perceptions of the nature of their interaction and relationship.

COVARIATION: A MIXED CASE

In reviewing what appear to be basic determinants of social perception, we have excluded a host of factors that are, at least for now, left to be considered nonbasic. The reason for this distinction is that, by the definition we adopted and the criteria that follow, the experimental evidence suggests that these remaining sources of information activate effortful rather than automatic processes. The most noticeable omission here is temporally extended information about the covariation of causes and effects.

Covariation is a principle that is widely regarded as a critical component of attribution in particular and adaptive personal and social functioning in general. Moreover, the voluminous literature on conditioning and contingency learning reveals rather striking parallels between animals and humans, suggesting the operation of a common and fundamental process (Alloy & Tabachnik, 1984). And yet, reviews of the human covariation-judgment literature have yielded the conclusions that "statistically naive individuals have a tenuous grasp of the concept of covariation" (Crocker, 1981, p. 272) and that "perception of covariation in the social domain is largely a function of preexisting theories and only secondarily a function of true covariation" (Nisbett & Ross, 1980, p. 111). In a developmental context, covariation has proven to be considerably less basic in attribution than spatiotemporal contiguity and perceptual salience cues (Kassin, 1981). In short, the evidence for the basicity of covariation is mixed.[4]

---

[4]As is discussed in a later section, it is conceivable that conclusions about covariation usage rest largely on the response criteria that are employed (i.e., behavior vs. verbal report). Also, Shultz (1982) has argued for the basicity and adaptive value of "generative transmission" cues in attribution (i.e., that real-world properties that transmit energy, such as sound, wind, and light, tend to be perceived as causal). In a series of interesting experiments, he obtained strong developmental and crosscultural support for this position. Space limitations preclude an extensive discussion of this research. The interested reader should therefore consult this monograph.

THE ATTRIBUTION PARADIGM: HOW CAN
SOMETHING SO BASIC BE SO OVERLOOKED?

The research reviewed herein accounts for only a small portion of the literature on attribution and social perception. Why, we ask, has mainstream social psychology largely overlooked these basic determinants? We noted earlier that because the zeitgeist has favored the information-processing metaphor, attribution has been placed squarely in the chain of intrapersonal processes that characterize the broader domains of "social cognition" (Taylor & Fiske, 1984) and "human inference" (Nisbett & Ross, 1980) rather than having been conceptualized as a special instance of event perception. This emphasis has quietly but dramatically guided the attribution research paradigm and, in turn, the state of our knowledge.

THE STIMULUS EVENT

To begin with, attribution experiments have generally denied subjects access to the dynamic, temporally extended raw material that we have termed basic determinants. The most extensively employed method for conveying information has been the questionnaire in which subjects are presented with experimenters' written descriptions of behavioral events. These prepackaged, second-hand descriptions are often contained in a single sentence to which attributionally relevant information is appended, or they may consist of more embellished vignettes in which the data about an actor and situation are embedded. To be sure, this paper-and-pencil technique, as exemplified by Asch's (1946) classical use of trait words and McArthur's (1972) introductory test of Kelley's (1967) ANOVA model, is quite efficient. We could even speculate about linguistic mediation as a basic determinant of attribution (Brown & Fish, 1983). A reliance on such impoverished stimulus events, however, has precluded the study of behavioral and kinematic cues (Kassin, 1982; Lowe & Kassin, 1980), and has forced subjects into an inferential, non-automatic response set (Baron, 1980). The limitations of a questionnaire technique are especially notable in developmental research, where we have consistently found that children can perceive causal principles such as discounting and augmentation at an earlier age when they are illustrated in animated films than when conveyed through verbal stories (Kassin & Gibbons, 1980, 1981; Kassin & Lowe, 1979; Kassin, Lowe, & Gibbons, 1980). A review of this literature thus led Kassin (1981) to conclude that "young children are better able to utilize causally relevant information when it is concretized through the use of pictures, dynamic displays, and live events, than when presented through verbal descriptions that make excessive linguistic, memorial, and conceptual demands on the perceiver" (p. 37).

In contrast to the questionnaire are those methods that provide perceivers with visual, dynamic information. Toward this end, four techniques, each with their own strengths and limitations, can be distinguished: (1) behavioral observation, as used in research on perceptual organization (Newton, 1976) and salience (e.g., McArthur & Post, 1977; Taylor & Fiske, 1975), (2) point-light displays, as employed in research on the kinematics of human action (e.g., Johansson, 1973; Runeson & Frykholm, 1982), (3) animated films, as developed by Heider and Simmel (1944) and Michotte (1946/1963) for the manipulation of spatiotemporal information (for a review, see Kassin, 1982), and (4) live mechanical events, as typically employed in research with young children (e.g., Bullock & Gelman, 1979; Siegler & Liebert, 1974). In each case, "new" higher order sources of information have been made available to the perceiver. And in each case, basic determinants of social perception have been revealed.

THE ATTRIBUTIONAL RESPONSE

On the response side, attribution psychology has suffered from the trappings of phenomenology and a reliance on verbal self-report data. As we noted earlier, it is our belief that peoples' responses to the basic determinants of social perception are often manifested in spontaneous, on-line action, and not necessarily in a symbolic mode. As such, we would argue that two important consequences follow from an exclusive reliance on verbal response measures of attribution.

First, it could be argued that by requiring subjects to engage in symbolic, intentional communication, we fundamentally modify a naturally occurring automatic process. That is, having to transmit a direct perceptual experience into terms that can be understood by others requires the adoption of a more categorical mode of processing that is easier to communicate than are the complexities of an idiosyncratic sensory experience. Support for this argument can be found in Zajonc's (1960) concept of cognitive tuning and the distinction between perceivers who expect to communicate and those who expect merely to receive their observations. Zajonc hypothesized that compared to receivers, transmitters activate cognitive structures that are more differentiated and unified. Indeed, research has shown that subjects who are provided with a transmission set tend to suppress inconsistent information and polarize their impressions of a stimulus person (Leventhal, 1962). In an interesting study, Harkins, Harvey, Keithly, and Rich (1977) obtained a comparable effect on causal attributions, but only when this perceptual set manipulation was introduced prior to subjects' observations. These data suggest that cognitive tuning affects the manner in which events are encoded, and thereby modifies the process of social perception. In the context of our discussion of basic determinants, it is conceivable that forcing subjects to engage a verbal response mode leads them to invent rationalizations, and produces the Nisbett and Wilson (1977) effect.

A second consequence of the phenomenological paradigm is that because subjects' responses to perceptual cues are often exhibited in behavior, verbal measures of attribution may be relatively insensitive and likely to result in a general underestimation of people's competencies to extract meaning from the social environment. Simply put, the question is, What must a subject do to convince a psychologist that he or she is responsive to a basic determinant? In a discussion of response criteria in research with children, Kassin (1981) distinguished three broad classes of response: (1) *overt behaviors* that are presumed to be manifestations of an underlying causal attribution, (2) *judgments*, involving a prediction, choice, or rating, and (3) *explanations* that require subjects to articulate the reasons for their behavior or judgment (cf. Brainerd, 1973, and Reese & Schack, 1974, for a controversy about these criteria). A review of the developmental attribution literature reveals unambiguously that children behave as if they are sensitive to causal cues before they can make the appropriate judgments which, in turn, precede their ability to articulate the basis for that knowledge. Thus, there appears to exist three levels of competent functioning in social perception, ranging from the most automatic (behavioral) to the most effortful (explanatory).

As an illustration of this principle, consider the literature on the overjustification effect. Beginning with Lepper, Greene, and Nisbett's (1973) study, research with preschool children has consistently demonstrated the phenomenon on a behavioral level despite these young subjects' apparent inability to employ the presumed underlying principle of discounting in their social judgments. In a review of this developmental paradox, Kassin and Lepper (1984) concluded that there is no evidence for alternative, nonattributional mediators of the behavioral effect and, in fact, that there is affirmative support for the attribution–behavior link. Young children thus behave *as if* they are operating by a causal principle that does not emerge in their verbal measures of attribution. Interestingly, a comparable pattern characterizes the adult literature, where overjustification effects on behavior often appear in the absence of self-report effects. Wilson, Hull, and Johnson (1981), however, have found that when subjects are induced to think about the reasons for their behavior, the corresponding attribution effects do then appear. These results suggest that even among adults, verbal response measures are less sensitive than behavioral indices of attribution, often needing to be primed in order to surface.

An obvious and important implication of the foregoing discussion is that in order to uncover basic determinants, we need to devise and cultivate sensitive, nonverbal indices of social perception. Our use of the animal conditioning literature in this context is a case in point. Several other techniques, originally developed for research with infants and preschool children, are also of potential significance. For example, there is a class of measures that might be referred to as the "effect-reproduction technique." Bullock (1979) thus reported research in which young children observed a mechanical effect (e.g., a jumping jack-in-the-box) along with other possibly causal events (e.g., inserting a marble into a runway) that varied on dimensions such as temporal or spatial contiguity. As a measure of attribution, subjects were given the opportunity to reproduce the effect by initiating what they believed to be its causal agent. Indeed a similar behavioral methodology has been employed in studies of "intuitive physics" (cf. McCloskey, 1983). Another possibility worth exploring is Keil's (1979) assessment of facial "surprise" reactions to events that violate intuitive, ecological laws. Thus, subjects who have knowledge of physical laws such as balance and support should exhibit greater surprise than those who do not when confronted with "trick" events that violate these principles. Finally, Leslie's (1982) use of a dishabituation-of-looking technique with infants, as described earlier, represents yet another potentially applicable device.

CONCLUSIONS

In this chapter, we have attempted to advance a conceptual and operational perspective on attribution and social perception that challenges the mainstream for its customary emphasis on nonbasic determinants and centrally mediated, effortful processes. Having done so, it can be seen that there is strong evidence for automatic processes and the perceptual system's sensitivity to such cues as facial expression, physical appearance, the kinematics of motoric behavior, spatiotemporal contiguity, and perceptual salience. Moreover, this view assumes (1) an increased role for stimulus-based as opposed to internally generated social knowledge, (2) the direct relevance of crosscultural, animal learning, and early developmental research, and (3) the need to investigate attributional processes that are characterized by the immediacy of response via non-verbal indices, as in the context of spontaneous, on-line interaction.

In addition to offering an alternative perspective, the present analysis generally raises the problem of the relationship between basic and higher-order processes as they determine complex phenomena such as causal attribution. For example, to what extent was Heider (1958) justified in assuming a two-staged process whereby the primitive, perceptual meaning extracted at the first stage serves as the source of input for more controlled, constructive processes? Is it not possible that in certain instances the processes are parallel, or even that we sometimes begin with inferences that are than adjusted by perceptual input in an accommodative mode (for a discussion, see Baron, 1980b; Newtson, 1980)?

Finally, it is apparent that the search for basic determinants encourages a worthwhile shift in emphasis on a methodological level, toward the use of dynamic stimulus displays and nonverbal indices of attribution. The time has come, we believe, to investigate attribution and social perception from the perspective initially espoused by Heider and readily accepted by others—that these processes are driven by an adaptive function, the regulation of on-line behavior vis-à-vis an informative physical and interpersonal environment.

REFERENCES

Ajzen, I., & Fishbein, M (1975). A Bayesian analysis of attribution processes. *Psychological Bulletin, 82*, 261–267.

Alley, T. R. (1981). Head shape and the perception of cuteness. *Developmental Psychology, 17*, 650–654.

Alloy, L. B., & Tabachnik, N. (1984). Assessment of covariation by humans and animals: The joint influence of prior expectations and current situational information. *Psychological Review, 91*, 112–149.

Alper, S., Buck, R., & Dryer, A. (1978). Nonverbal sending accuracy and receiving ability in preschool children. *Research Relating to Children, 41*, 89.

Anderson, N. H. (1974). Cognitive algebra: Integration theory applied to social attribution. In L. Berkowitz (Ed.), *Advances in experimental social psychology* (Vol. 7). New York: Academic Press.

Asch, S. E. (1946). Forming impressions of personality. *Journal of Abnormal and Social Psychology, 41*, 258–290.

Ausubel, D. P., & Schiff, H. M. (1954). The effect of incidental and experimentally induced experience in the learning of relevant and irrelevant causal relationships by children. *Journal of Genetic Psychology, 84*, 109–123.

Baron, R. M. (1980a). Contrasting approaches to social knowing: An ecological perspective. *Personality and Social Psychology Bulletin, 6*, 590–600.

Baron, R. M. (1980b). Social knowing from an ecological event perspective: A consideration of the relative domains of power for cognitive and perceptual modes of knowing. In J. H. Harvey (Ed.), *Cognition, social behavior and the environment*. Hillsdale, NJ: Erlbaum.

Baron, R. M. (1984). Distinguishing between perceptual and cognitive "groundings" for consistency theories: Epistemological implications. *Personality and Social Psychology Bulletin, 10,* 165–174.

Bassili, N. J. (1976). Temporal and spatial contingencies in the perception of social events. *Journal of Personality and Social Psychology, 33,* 680–685.

Bassili, J. N. (1978). Facial motion in the perception of faces and of emotional expression. *Journal of Experimental Psychology: Human Perception and Performance, 4,* 373–379.

Beasley, N. E. (1968). The extent of individual differences in the perception of causality. *Canadian Journal of Psychology, 22,* 399–407.

Berry, D., & McArthur, L. Z. (in press). Some components and consequences of a baby face. *Journal of Personality and Social Psychology.*

Borton, R. W. (1979, April). *The perception of causality in infants.* Paper presented at the Society for Research in Child Development, San Francisco, CA.

Boyle, D. G. (1960). A contribution to the study of phenomenal causation. *Quarterly Journal of Experimental Psychology, 12,* 171–179.

Brainerd, C. J. (1973). Judgments and explanations as critera for the presence of cognitive structures. *Psychological Bulletin, 79,* 172–179.

Brown, R., & Fish, D. (1983). The psychological causality implicit in language. *Cognition, 14,* 237–273.

Brunswik, E. (1952). *The conceptual framework of psychology.* Chicago: University of Chicago Press.

Bullock, M. (1979). *Aspects of the young child's theory of causation.* Unpublished doctoral dissertation, University of Pennsylvania.

Bullock, M., & Gelman, R. (1979). Children's assumptions about cause and effect: temporal ordering. *Child Development, 50,* 89–96.

Buss, A. R. (1978). Causes and reasons in attribution theory: A conceptual critique. *Journal of Personality and Social Psychology, 36,* 1311–1321.

Crocker, J. (1981). Judgment of covariation by social perceivers. *Psychological Bulletin, 90,* 272–292.

Cutting, J. E., & Kozlowski, L. T. (1977). Recognizing friends by their walk: gait perception without familiarity cues. *Bulletin of the Psychonomic Society, 9,* 353–356.

Darwin, C. (1872). *Expression of the emotions in man and animals.* London: Murray.

DiVitto, B., & McArthur, L. Z. (1978). Developmental differences in the use of distinctiveness, consensus, and consistency information for making causal attributions. *Developmental Psychology, 14,* 474–482.

Dix, T., & Herzberger, S. (1983). The role of logic and salience in the development of causal attribution. *Child Development, 54,* 960–967.

Duncker, K. (1945). On problem solving. *Psychological Monographs, 58,* (Whole No. 270).

Duval, S., & Hensley, V. (1976). Extensions of objective self awareness theory: the focus of attention-causal attribution hypothesis. In J. Harvey, W. Ickes, & R. Kidd (Eds.), *New directions in attribution research* (Vol. 1). Hillsdale, NJ: Erlbaum.

Eibl-Eibesfeldt, I. (1975). *Ethology: The biology of behavior.* New York: Holt, Rinehart, and Winston.

Ekman, P., & Friesen, W. V. (1975). *Unmasking the face.* Englewood Cliffs, NJ: Prentice-Hall.

Ekman, P., & Friesen, W. V. (1976). Measuring facial movement. *Environmental Psychology and Nonverbal Behavior, 1,* 56–75.

Ekman, P., Sorenson, E. R., & Friesen, W. V. (1969). Pan cultural elements in facial displays of emotions. *Science, 164,* 86–88.

Fazio, R. H. (1981). On the self-perception explanation of the overjustification effect: the role of salience of initial attitude. *Journal of Experimental Social Psychology, 17,* 417–426.

Fiske, S. T., Kenny, D. A., & Taylor, S. E. (1982). Structural models for the mediation of salience effects on attribution. *Journal of Experimental Social Psychology, 18,* 105–127.

Fiske, S. T., & Taylor, S. E. (1984). *Social cognition.* Reading, MA: Addison-Wesley.

Frieze, I. H., Bar-Tal, D., & Carroll, J. S. (1979). *New approaches to social problems.* San Francisco: Jossey-Bass.

Garcia, J., Ervin, F. R., & Koelling, R. A. (1966). Learning with prolonged delay of reinforcement. *Science, 5,* 121–122.

Gibson, J. J. (1979). *The ecological approach to visual perception.* Boston, MA: Houghton-Mifflin.

Harkins, S. G., Harvey, J. H., Keithly, L., & Rich, M. (1977). Cognitive tuning, encoding, and the attribution of causality. *Memory and Cognition, 5,* 561–565.

Hasher, L., & Zacks, R. T. (1979). Automatic and effortful processes in memory. *Journal of Experimental Psychology: General, 108,* 356–388.

Hastie, R. Social inference. (1983). *Annual Review of Psychology, 34,* 511–542.

Heider, F. (1939). Environmental determinants in psychological theories. *Psychological Review, 46,* 383–410.

Heider, F. (1944). Social perception and phenomenal causality. *Psychological Review, 51,* 358–374.

Heider, F. (1958). *The psychology of interpersonal relations.* New York: Wiley.

Heider, F., & Simmel, M. (1944). An experimental study of apparent behavior. *American Journal of Psychology, 57,* 243–259.

Hume, D. (1960). *A treatise of human nature.* Oxford, England: Clarendon. (Original work published 1740)

Izard, C. E. (1969). Emotions and emotion constructs in personality and cultural research. In R. Cattell (Ed.), *Handbook of modern personality theory.* Chicago: Aldine.

Izard, C. E., Huebner, R. R., Riser, D., McGinnes, G., & Dougherty, L. (1980). The young infant's ability to produce discrete emotion expressions. *Developmental Psychology, 16,* 132–140.

Johansson, G. (1973). Visual perception of biological motion and a model for its analysis. *Perception and Psychophysics, 14,* 201–211.

Johansson, G. (1976). Spatio–temporal differentiation and integration in visual motion perception. *Psychological Research, 38,* 379–393.

Johansson, G., von Hofsten, C., & Jansson, G. (1980). Event perception. *Annual Review of Psychology, 31,* 27–53.

Jones, E. E., & Davis, K. E. (1965). From acts to dispositions: the attribution process in person perception. In L. Berkowitz (Ed.), *Advances in experimental social psychology* (Vol. 2). New York: Academic Press.

Jones, E. E., & McGillis, D. (1976). Correspondent inferences and the attribution cube: a comparative reappraisal. In J. H. Harvey, W. J. Ickes, & R. F. Kidd (Eds.), *New directions in attribution research* (Vol. 1). Hillsdale, NJ: Erlbaum.

Joynson, R. B. (1971). Michotte's experimental methods. *British Journal of Psychology, 62,* 293–302.

Julesz, B. (1981). Figure and ground perception in briefly presented isodipole textures. In M. Kubovy & J. Pomerantz (Eds.), *Perceptual organization.* Hillsdale, NJ: Erlbaum.

Kahneman, D. (1973). *Attention and effort.* Englewood Cliffs, NJ: Prentice-Hall.

Kassin, S. M. (1981). From laychild to "layman": Developmental causal attribution. In S. Brehm, S. Kassin, & F. Gibbons (Eds.), *Developmental social psychology: Theory and research.* New York: Oxford University Press.

Kassin, S. M. (1982). Heider and Simmel (1944) revisited: Causal attribution and the an-imated-film technique. In L. Wheeler (Ed.), *Review of personality and social psychology* (Vol. 3). Beverly Hills, CA: Sage.

Kassin, S. M., & Gibbons, F. X. (1980, September). *The augmentation principle in MR persons: perceptual versus verbal approaches.* Paper presented at the American Psychological Association, Montreal, Canada.

Kassin, S. M., & Gibbons, F. X. (1981). Children's use of the discounting principle in their perceptions of exertion. *Child Development, 52,* 741–744.

Kassin, S. M., & Lepper, M. R. (1984). Oversufficient and insufficient justification effects: Cognitive and behavioral development. In J. Nicholls (Ed.), *The development of achievement motivation.* Greenwich, CT: JAI Press.

Kassin, S. M., & Lowe, C. A. (1979). On the development of the augmentation principle: A perceptual approach. *Child Development, 50,* 728–734.

Kassin, S. M., Lowe, C. A., & Gibbons, F. X. (1980). Children's use of the discounting principle: A perceptual approach. *Journal of Personality and Social Psychology, 30,* 718–728.

Kassin, S. M., & Wrightsman, L. S. (1985). Confession evidence. In S. Kassin & L. Wrightsman (Eds.), *The Psychology of evidence and trial procedure.* Beverly Hills, CA: Sage.

Keating, C. F., Mazur, A., & Segall, M. H. (1981). A cross-cultural exploration of physiognomic traits of dominance and happiness. *Ethology and Sociobiology, 2,* 41–48.

Keil, F. (1979). The development of the young child's ability to anticipate the outcomes of simple causal events. *Child Development, 50,* 455–462.

Kelley, H. H. (1967). Attribution theory in social psychology. In D. Levine (Ed.), *Nebraska symposium on motivation.* Lincoln, NE: University of Nebraska Press.

Kelley, H. H. (1971). *Causal schemata and the attribution process.* Morristown, NJ: General Learning Press.

Kelley, H. H., & Michela, J. L. (1980). Attribution theory and research. *Annual Review of Psychology, 31,* 457–501.

Kimble, G. A. (1947). Conditioning as a function of the time between conditioned and unconditioned stimulus. *Journal of Experimental Psychology, 37,* 1–15.

Koffka, K. (1935). *Principles of gestalt psychology.* New York: Harcourt Brace.

Kozlowski, L. T., & Cutting, J. E. (1977). Recognizing the sex of a walker from a dynamic point-light display. *Perception and Psychophysics, 21,* 575–580.

Kun, A. (1978). Evidence for preschoolers' understanding of causal direction in extended causal sequences. *Child Development, 49,* 218–222.

LaBerge. D. (1973). Attention and the measurement of perceptual learning. *Memory and Cognition, 1,* 268–276.

Landauer, T. K. (1969). Reinforcement as consolidation. *Psychological Review, 76,* 82–96.

Langer, E. J. Rethinking the role thought in social interaction. In J. Harvey, W. Ickes, & R. Kidd (Eds.), (1978). *New directions in attribution theory* (Vol. 2). Hillsdale, NJ: Erlbaum.

Lepper, M. R., Greene, D., & Nisbett, R. E. (1973). Undermining children's intrinsic interest with extrinsic rewards: a test of the "overjustification" hypothesis. *Journal of Personality and Social Psychology, 28,* 129–137.

Leslie, A. M. (1982). The perception of causality in infants. *Perception, 11,* 173–186.

Lesser, H. (1977). The growth of perceived causality in children. *Journal of Genetic Psychology, 130,* 145–152.

Leventhal, H. (1962). The effects of set and discrepancy on impression change. *Journal of Personality, 30,* 1–15.

Livesley, W., & Bromley, D. (1973). *Person perception in childhood and adolescence.* London: Wiley.

Lowe, C. A., & Kassin, S. M. (1980). A perceptual view of attribution: Theoretical and methodological implications. *Personality and Social Psychology Bulletin, 6,* 532–542.

McArthur, L. A. (1972). The how and what of why: Some determinants and consequences of causal attribution. *Journal of Personality and Social Psychology, 22,* 171–193.

McArthur, L. Z. (1980). Illusory causation and illusory correlation: Two epistemological accounts. *Personality and Social Psychology Bulletin, 6,* 507–519.

McArthur, L. Z. (1982). Judging a book by its cover: A cognitive analysis of the relationship between physical appearance and stereotyping. In A. Hastorf & A. Isen (Eds.), *Cognitive social psychology.* New York: Elsevier.

McArthur, L. Z., & Apatow, K. (in press). Impressions of baby-faced adults. *Social Cognition.*

McArthur, L. Z., & Baron, R. M. (1983). Toward an ecological theory of social perception. *Psychological Review, 90,* 215–238.

McArthur, L. Z., & Post, D. L. (1977). Figural emphasis and person perception. *Journal of Experimental Social Psychology, 13,* 520–535.

McCloskey, M. (1983). Intuitive physics. *Scientific American, 248,* 122–130.

Mendelson, R., & Shultz, T. R. (1976) Covariation and temporal contiguity as principles of causal inference in young children. *Journal of Experimental Child Psychology, 33,* 408–412.

Michotte, A. E. (1950). The emotions regarded as functional connections. In M. L. Reymert (Ed.), *Feelings and emotions.* New York: McGraw Hill.

Michotte, A. (1963). *The perception of causality.* London: Methuen. (Original work published 1946)

Montpellier, G., & Nuttin, J. (1973). A note on Michotte's experimental methods and Michotte's ideas. *British Journal of Psychology, 64,* 287–289.

Newtson, D. (1976). Foundations of attribution: The perception of ongoing behavior. In J. H. Harvey, W. J. Ickes, & R. F. Kidd (Eds.), *New directions in attribution research* (Vol. 1). Hillsdale, NJ: Erlbaum.

Newtson, D. (1980). An interactionist perspective on social knowing. *Personality and Social Psychology Bulletin, 6,* 520–531.

Nisbett, R. E., & Ross, L. (1980). *Human inference: strategies and shortcomings of social judgment.* Englewood Cliffs, NJ: Prentice-Hall.

Nisbett, R. E., & Wilson, T. D. (1977). Telling more than we can know: verbal reports on mental processes. *Psychological Review, 84,* 231–259.

Olum, V. (1956). Developmental differences in the perception of causality. *American Journal of Psychology, 69,* 417–428.

Ostrom, T. M., (1981). Attribution theory: whence and wither. In J. Harvey, W. Ickes, & R. Kidd (Eds.), *New directions in attribution research* (Vol. 3). Hillsdale, NJ: Erlbaum.

Pavlov, I. P. (1927). *Conditioned reflexes.* Oxford, England: Oxford University Press.

Pearson, K. (1976). Control of walking. *Scientific American,* 82–86.

Piaget, J. (1930). *The child's conception of physcial causality.* London: Kegan Paul.

Pittenger, J., & Shaw, R. E. (1975). Aging faces as viscal-elastic events: implications for a theory of non-rigid shape perception: *Journal of Experimental Psychology: Human Perception and Performance, 1,* 377–382.

Pittenger, J., Shaw, R. E., & Mark, L. S. (1979). Perceptual information for the age level of faces as a higher-order invariant of growth. *Journal of Experimental Psychology: Human Perception and Performance, 5,* 478–493.

Posner, M. I., & Snyder, C. R. (1975). Attention and cognitive control. In R. L. Solso (Ed.), *Information processing and cognition: the Loyola symposium.* Hillsdale, NJ: Erlbaum.

Reese, H. W., & Lipsitt, L. P. (1970). *Experimental child psychology.* New York: Academic Press.

Reese, H. W., & Schack, M. L. (1974). Comment on Brainerd's criteria for cognitive structures. *Psychological Bulletin, 81,* 67–69.

Renner, K. E. (1964). Delay of reinforcement: a historical overview. *Psychological Bulletin, 61,* 341–361.

Rescorla, R. A., & Wagner, A. R. (1972). A theory of Pavlovian conditioning: variations in the effectiveness of reinforcement and nonreinforcement. In A. M. Black & W. Prokasy (Eds.), *Classical conditioning II: current research and theory.* New York: Appleton-Century-Crofts.

Restle, F. (1979). Coding theory of the perception of motion configurations. *Psychological Review, 86,* 1–24.

Ross, M. (1975). Salience of reward and intrinsic motivation. *Journal of Personality and Social Psychology, 32,* 245–254.

Runeson, S. (1977). *On visual perception of dynamic events.* Unpublished doctoral dissertation, University of Uppsala, Uppsala, Sweden.

Runeson, S., & Frykholm, G. (1981). Visual perception of lifted weight. *Journal of Experimental Psychology: Human Perception and Performance, 7,* 733–740.

Runeson, S., & Frykholm, G. (1982). Kinematic specification of dynamics as an informational basis for person and action perception: expectation, gender recognition, and deceptive intention, *Uppsala Psychological Reports* (No. 324). University of Uppsala, Uppsala, Sweden.

Sackett, G. P. (1966). Monkeys reared in isolation with pictures as visual input: evidence for an innate releasing mechanism. *Science, 154,* 1468–1473.

Schneider, D. J., Hastorf, A. H., & Ellsworth, P. C. (1979). *Person perception.* Reading, MA: Addison-Wesley.

Schneider, W., & Shiffrin, R. M. (1977). Controlled and automatic human information processing: I. detection, search, and attention. *Psychological Review, 84,* 1–66.

Secord, P. F., Dukes, W. F., & Bevan, W. (1954). Personalities in faces: I. an experiment in social perceiving. *Genetic Psychology Monographs, 49,* 231–279.

Sedlak, A. J., & Kurtz, S. T. (1981). A review of children's use of causal inference principles. *Child Development, 52,* 759–784.

Shaver, K. G. (1981). Back to basics: On the role of theory in the attribution of causality. In J. Harvey, W. Ickes, & R. Kidd (Eds.), *New directions in attribution research* (Vol. 3). Hillsdale, NJ: Erlbaum.

Shiffrin, R. M., & Schneider, W. (1977). Controlled and automatic human information processing: II. perceptual learning, automatic attending, and a general theory. *Psychological Review, 84,* 127–190.

Shultz, T. R. (1982). Rules of causal attribution. *Monographs of the Society for Research in Child Development, 47,*(1).

Shultz, T. R., & Ravinsky, F. B. (1977). Similarity as a principle of causal inference. *Child Development, 48,* 1552–1558.

Shultz, T. R., & Schleifer, M. (1983). Towards a refinement of attribution concepts. In J. Jaspars, F. Finchman, & M. Hewstone (Eds.), *Attribution theory and research: conceptual, developmental, and social dimensions.* New York: Academic Press.

Siegler, R. S. (1975). Defining the locus of developmental differences in children's causal reasoning. *Journal of Experimental Child Psychology, 20,* 512–525.

Siegler, R. S., & Liebert, R. M. (1974). Effects of contiguity, regularity, and age on children's causal inferences. *Developmental Psychology, 10,* 574–579.

Smith, E. R., & Miller, F. D. (1979). Salience and the cognitive mediation of attribution. *Journal of Personality and Social Psychology, 37,* 2240–2252.

Tagiuri, R. (1960). Movement as a cue in person perception. In H. P. David & J. C. Brengelmann (Eds.), *Perspective in personality research.* New York: Springer.

Taylor, D. A. (1976). Stage analysis of reaction time. *Psychological Bulletin, 83,* 161–191.

Taylor, S. E., Crocker, J., Fiske, S. T., Sprinzen, M., & Winkler, J. D. (1979). The generalizability of salience effects. *Journal of Personality and Social Psychology, 37,* 357–368.

Taylor, S. E., & Fiske, S. T. (1975). Point of view and perceptions of causality. *Journal of Personality and Social Psychology, 32,* 439–445.

Taylor, S. E., & Fiske, S. T. (1978). Salience, attention, and attribution: Top of the head phenomena. In L. Berkowitz (Ed.), *Advances in experimental social psychology* (Vol. 11). New York: Academic Press.

Taylor, S. E., & Fiske, S. T. (1981). Getting inside the head: methodologies for process analysis in attribution and social cognition. In J. Harvey, W. Ickes, & R. Kidd (Eds.), *New directions in attribution research* (Vol. 3). Hillsdale, NJ: Erlbaum.

Terrell, G., & Ware, R. (1961). The role of delay of reward in speed of size and form discrimination learning in childhood. *Child Development, 32,* 409–415.

Todd, J. T. (1983). Perception of gait. *Journal of Experimental Psychology: Human Perception and Performance, 9,* 31–42.

Todd, J. T., Mark, L., Shaw, R., & Pittenger, J. (1980). The perception of growth. *Scientific American, 242,* 132–144.

Weir, S. (1978). The perception of motion: Michotte revisited. *Perception, 7,* 247–260.

Wilson, T. D., Hull, J. G., & Johnson, J. (1981). Awareness and self perception: verbal reports on internal states. *Journal of Personality and Social Psychology, 40,* 53–71.

Wyer, R. S., & Carlston, D. E. (1979). *Social cognition, inference, and attribution.* Hillsdale, NJ: Erlbaum.

Young-Browne, G., Rosenfeld, H. M., & Horowitz, F. D. (1977). Infant discrimination of facial expressions. *Child Development, 48,* 555–562.

Zajonc, R. (1960). The process of cognitive tuning in communications. *Journal of Abnormal and Social Psychology, 61* 159–167.

Zajonc, R. (1984). On the primacy of affect. *American Psychologist, 39,* 117–123.

CHAPTER 3

Cognitive Economy and Commonsense Attribution Processing

Ranald D. Hansen

INTRODUCTION

Thought is efficient. Within the domain of causal thought, efficiency can be described as the coming to a reasonable view of causal reality through the most economic inference strategy. Perhaps the best evidence that the goal of causal thought is a reasonable rather than an accurate view of causal reality is that people commonly have a less than accurate or even erroneous understanding of cause (Kahneman, Slovic, & Tversky, 1982; Nisbett & Ross, 1980) and yet have the capacity to communicate causal understanding to one another; indeed, to use it without undue problem as a basis for interaction. Leaving aside the issue of whether people would be better off with an accurate rather than a reasonable view of causal reality, it would seem that partial and/or erroneous causal understanding can suffice in a social world where others share a similar view. It would seem obvious, then, that theories of causal thought embracing the goal of causal precision for the perceiver could not capture the commonsense causal logic used by perceivers to arrive at an adequate, but imprecise, view of causal reality. Most major attribution theories fall into this category (Jones & Davis, 1965; Jones & McGillis, 1976; Kelley, 1967; Shaver, 1981). Short of discarding this substantial body of theory or of relegating it to the obscurity of those few instances (science and gambling among them) in which the individual acknowledges the goal of causal precision is the possibility of translating these theories into models of commonsense causal understanding reflecting the goal of reasonable accuracy through inference economy. In this chapter I shall attempt to make a case for this translation by focusing on the attribution theory most foreign to this commonsense goal: Kelley's (1967) ANOVA theory.

ATTRIBUTION
Basic Issues and Applications

FROM COGNITIVE ECONOMY
TO INFERENCE ECONOMY

Social perception has given way to special cognition as a predominant fashion of conceptualizing naive social understanding (Bargh, 1984; Hamilton, 1981; Hastie, 1981). Two of the most elegant concepts within this framework are *automatic processing* and *schema*. Both are statements of cognitive economics. The first acknowledges the need of the individual to process vast amounts of information rapidly without loading up capacity-limited, attention-directed conscious processing (Bargh, 1984). The efficiency of automaticity is defined by the trade-off of processing economy for accuracy (Langer, Blank, & Chanowitz, 1978). Schema refers to a cognitive structure for the representation in memory of information about a particular category of objects, persons, or events (Taylor & Crocker, 1981). As such, schemas can be viewed as closely related to the organization and recognition of incoming data (Hastie & Kumar, 1979) and as providing theories or hypotheses (Jennings, Amabile, & Ross, 1982; Neisser, 1976) to guide the search for and use of information (Darley & Gross, 1983; Rothbart, Evans, & Fulero, 1979; Snyder, 1981). It is this latter function, in particular, that seems to imply a principle of cognitive economics. Information is screened, highlighted, or stored on the basis of schematic congruity (Hastie, 1981) or its capacity to confirm schematically generated hypotheses (Snyder, 1981; Snyder & Swann, 1978a, 1978b). Aside from reducing the amount of data with which the processor must come to grips and store, the cognitive economy of a confirmatory or consistency "bias" is made explicit in formal information-processing models (Trabaso, Rollins, & Shaughnessy, 1971) arguing that conceptual disconfirmation requires additional processing operations beyond those required for verification.

The imposition of these concepts on attribution theories has produced a discouraging meld (Kelley, 1972b). Greatly contributing to this has been the conceptual confusion in the attribution literature surrounding the use of terms such as process, schema, content, and logic. Examples would include Jones and Davis' (1965) use of "attribution process" to describe their model of attribution logic applied to specific content, Ross' (1977) use of "process" to describe errors of logic, and Kelley's (1972b) use of the terms "schema" and "process" to bring the ANOVA model into the cognitive domain. With the exceptions of "cognitive subtraction" offered by Smith and Miller (1979) and the "template-matching-plus-correction" approach offered by Orvis, Cunningham, and Kelley (1975), the attribution literature has little to say about process. Most centers on causal logic and/or content. Given that the direct translation of attribution theory—largely a theory of logic and content—into cognitive processing terms has not been fruitful, another approach should be taken.

The first step in the direction of a new approach is to recognize the distinctions among content, logic, and process (Nisbett & Ross, 1980; Smith & Miller, 1979). As I shall use them, causal content refers to the information potentially available and/or used by the individual coming to a causal understanding of an event as well as the causal understanding itself. Commonsense principles such as covariation, discounting, and augmentation are the causal (psycho-) logic applied to information resulting in causal understanding. The second step in this approach, then, is the construction of a psychological theory of attribution portraying the individual's use of causal logic to arrive at causal understanding. This would be a theory of attribution inferencing not of attribution processing. Processing is represented in the final step in the approach; the translation of this psychological theory into a process theory of attribution.

Mindful of the goal to develop a process theory of attribution, it is important that a psychological theory of attribution reflect the important concepts of cognitive processing theory. Chief among these is cognitive economy and all that this implies. In short, the translation of Kelley's (1967) ANOVA theory of attribution into a psychological theory of attribution has at its base the assumption that economy of the information processing level is manifest in economy of inference at the psychologic level.

A PSYCHOLOGICAL MODEL OF ATTRIBUTION

Kelley's (1967) theory of attribution evolved as an analysis of variance analog. The model had the individual identifying three sources of potential behavioral variance and then assessing the amount of variance associated with each factor entered. Factor(s) identified as substantially covarying with behavior were seen as the cause(s) to which the behavior could be attributed. The model had a number of drawbacks. First, the model appeared to specify a "data-driven" rather than a "theory-driven" operation (Jennings et al., 1982). Individuals approached each causal quandry without expectation or theory and applied a quasi-statistic to accumulated data to obtain an attribution. Such an analog to statistical procedure is unlikely in view of current research (Nisbett & Ross, 1980). Second, the model required the individual to represent behavioral effects in multidimensional space and to necessarily account for all dimensions when assessing the reliability of a covariation of behavioral effect with any one dimension. This again seems unlikely in view

of contemporary research (Kahneman et al., 1982). Third, the output of
the analysis was an attribution to dimension (i.e., person, stimulus, circumstance) rather than a specific cause (e.g., a specific attribute of the
person). Specific causation seems to characterize most naive explanations (Weiner, Russell, & Lerman, 1978).

Nevertheless, some strengths of the model can be identified. First,
the model singled out covariation as a preeminent psychologic principle
used to associate cause with effect. Second, the model noted that mul-
tiply caused effects are frequently encountered by the attributor and
must be dealt with. Third, a most important innovation, the model
structurally acknowledged the intimate commonsense relationship between potential causes for effects with the use and search of specific
categories of information that seem to allow for a commonsense assessment of the strength of cause–effect covariation.

The strengths and weaknesses formed a partial basis for the reformulation of the ANOVA model into a psychological model of attribution
which follows. Unlike the ANOVA model, the psychological model of
attribution explicitly distinguishes between the logic and content of inference. What follows, then, is (1) the explication of the psychologic
principles—covariation, discounting and augmentation—underlying the
inferences described by the model and (2) the content of the inferences
reflecting the operation of the psychologic principles. As a result of this
distinction, the psychological model of attribution makes it clear that
content is epiphenomenal of attributional psychologic. An outcome of
the model is the inference of a specific attribute which bears witness to
an underlying attribution, not the attribution itself. That is, John's running from a dog might result in an inference of John's fear which reflects
an underlying attribution: John's running was caused by (i.e., covaried
with) his fear. The content and psychologic have been portrayed in Figure 3.1. A quick inspection of the table will indicate that the model is
constructed of two inference steps. In the first, covariation is described
as making commonsense of base-rate information. In the second, covariation, discounting, and augmentation are described as being applied
to the inferential outcome of the first step to make commonsense of a
single instance of behavior. Although these two steps are described in
sequence, it will become clear that they might be carried out by the attributor at two, quite distant, points in time.

COVARIATION PSYCHOLOGIC

Simple covariation of effect magnitude with causal force strength
makes sense to people and they use it to estimate the strength of a force
from the size of the effect it produces (Hansen & Hall, 1984, Exp. 3).

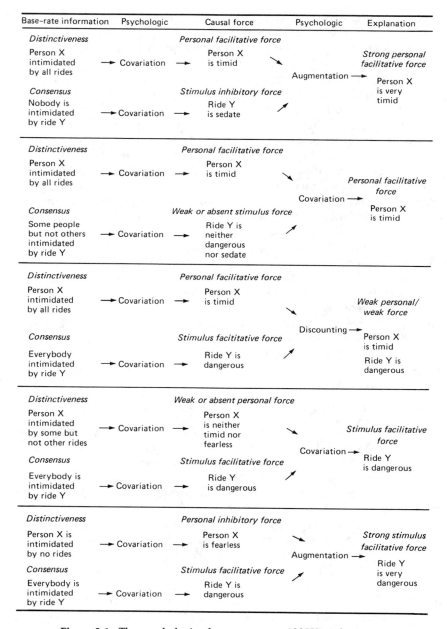

Figure 3.1 The psychologic of commonsense ANOVA inferences.

This, apparently theory-driven operation, renders the unknown strength of a force knowable from an observable effect. Hansen and Hall, for example, demonstrated that persons and objects producing outcomes of greater magnitude (e.g., beating opponents by wider margins of victory) resulted in their being judged more potent than persons and objects producing outcomes of lesser magnitude. However, there seem to be definable bounds to the covariation theories driving inferences of force strength from effects. Notably, the covariation of effect magnitude with facilitative force strength (Kelley, 1972a) would seem more obvious to the observer than the covariation with inhibitory force weakness.

Hansen and Hall (1984) found that effect magnitude had a substantial effect on estimates of facilitative force strength and an almost negligible effect on estimates of inhibitory force weakness; wide-margin winners being much stronger than narrow-margin winners, but wide-margin losers not being appreciably weaker than narrow-margin losers. This suggests that the psychologic of covariation is bounded by a resemblance criterion (Nisbett & Wilson, 1977). Forces with which effects covary, and whose strength can be inferred from the effect, resemble the effect; a wide margin of victory resembles more a strong winner than a weak loser. Consistent overlooking of the contribution of weak inhibitory forces would result, as implied by Nisbett and Ross (1980), in both inferential overconfidence—the effect is seen as an instance of simple rather than multiple causation—and over-estimation of facilitative force strength.

DISCOUNTING AND AUGMENTATION PSYCHOLOGIC

Effect magnitude is not seen as covarying with individual force strength when multiple forces plausibly could have entered into producing the effect (Hansen & Hall, 1984; Hull & West, 1982; Kelley, 1972a; Wells & Ronis, 1982). Multiple facilitative forces coacting to produce an effect render the effect an overestimate of individual force strength. For example, if two persons together lift two 100-pound weights one foot, each will be judged weaker than another person who can produce the same effect alone. The *effect is discounted* as diagnostic of either of the former individual's strength. In commonsense terms, if either was removed, the effect produced by the remaining person would be diminished below that produced by the lone lifter. On the other hand, multiple inhibitory forces in opposition to a facilitative force render the effect produced an underestimate of facilitative force strength. The presence of multiple inhibitory forces *augments the effect* from which facilitative force strength is inferred.

It should be noted that this description of discounting and augmentation differs from that prevailing in the attribution literature (Shaver, 1981) which holds that discounting and augmentation are "substitutes" for covariation. The current description reflects the position (Hansen & Hall, 1984) that discounting and augmentation are special cases of covariation. Indeed, covariation would seem to play a role in the operation of these two psychologic priniciples in two ways. First, the observer must recognize that the magnitude of an effect covaries with the strength of all forces interacting to influence it. As a result, in order to infer the strength of an individual force, the effect must be diminished (discounted) or enhanced (augmented). The subsequent individual force strength inference, then, reflects the covariation of the discounted or augmented effect with individual force strength.

CONTENT: FROM BASE-RATE INFORMATION TO COVARYING CAUSAL FORCES

Distinctiveness is base-rate informative of an individual's behavior in the presence of different stimuli within a given stimulus category (Kelley, 1967, 1972b; Jones & McGillis, 1976; McArthur, 1972, 1976; Shaver, 1981). The proportion of stimuli within a given stimulus category in the presence of which the individual behaves similarly naively is seen as estimating the strength of a covarying force within the individual predisposing the behavior (Hansen, 1980; McArthur, 1972, 1976). A person's modal behavior across many stimuli is a behavioral effect from which the observer infers the covarying strength of a person force facilitating the effect. For example, an individual observed to be intimidated by all rides in an amusement park is judged timid, whereas a person intimidated by none is judged fearless.

Consensus is base-rate informative of many individuals' behavior in the presence of a particular stimulus (Hansen, 1980; Kelley, 1967, 1972b; McArthur, 1972, 1976; Nisbett & Borgida, 1975; Nisbett & Ross, 1980; Shaver, 1981). The proportion of people who, in the presence of a stimulus, behave similarly is naively seen as estimating the strength of a covarying force within the stimulus provoking the behavior (Hansen, 1980; McArthur, 1972, 1976). A stimulus modal behavior is a behavioral effect from which the observer infers the covarying strength of a stimulus force facilitating the effect. For example, an amusement park ride initimidating all people is judged dangerous while one which intimidates no one is judged sedate.

Consistency is base-rate informative of an individual's behavior in the presence of a particular stimulus under different circumstances (Kelley,

1967; Mitchell, Hyde, & Friedman, 1983). The proportion of circumstances in which the individual behaves similarly in the presence of a particular stimulus potentially can be construed as estimating the strength of a covarying facilitative force in the person, the stimulus, or both. For example, an amusement park ride intimidating a person frequently could be indicative of a dangerous ride, a timid person, or a moderately intimidating ride and a slightly timid person. Available attribution theory (Kelley, 1972a) would suggest that a stimulus X person modal behavior would be discounted as diagnostic of both: The behavioral effect is an overestimate of both the person's timidity and the scariness of the ride. Indeed, some research supports this view (Mitchell et al. 1983). This is a data-driven inference wherein the observer is attempting to make best covariation sense of the available data. But, to foreshadow what is to come, in a theory-driven context (for example, when an observer trying to discover whether this person is timid), a modal person X stimulus behavior may be construed very differently.

CONTENT: MULTIPLE FORCES TO SINGLE INSTANCE INFERENCE

The product of the naive ANOVA described by Kelley (1967, 1972b) was an explanation of a single instance of behavior. That product requires the application of additional psychologic to the force strength inferences derived from base-rate information. Recall that covariation applied to distinctiveness can result in an inference of personal force strength. Covariation applied to consensus can result in an inference of stimulus force strength. These forces can be construed as facilitative or inhibitory of a behavior observed in a specific instance. For example, a personal force (person is timid) making commonsense of distinctiveness information (person is intimidated by all amusement park rides) would be facilitative of some behaviors (person refuses to go on a specific ride) and inhibitory of others (person enthusiastically goes on a specific ride). Likewise, a stimulus force (ride is dangerous) making commonsense of consensus information (everyone is intimidated by a specific ride) would be facilitative of some behaviors (person refuses to go on the ride) and inhibitory of others (person enthusiastically goes on the ride). If exemplars of weak person forces (person is neither timid nor fearless) making commonsense out of weak distinctiveness effects (person is intimidated by some rides but not others) and weak stimulus forces making commonsense out of weak consensus effects are incorporated, the full pattern of inferences making commonsense out of specific instances of behavior emerges (see Figure 3.1).

Both consensus and distinctiveness can result in an attribute of the person (timidity), the stimulus (dangerous), or both being seen as the cause of an event. However, the psychologic used to arrive at these conclusions differ. A personal attribute can become viewed as causal through the application of covariation psychologic to a distinctiveness-based (person-facilitative) attribute inference, or of augmentation to a consensus-based (stimulus-inhibitory) attribute inference. A stimulus attribute can become viewed as causal through the application of augmentation psychologic to a distinctiveness-based (person-inhibitory) attribute inference or covariation to a consensus-based (stimulus-facilitative) attribute inference. Given the possibility of using both types of information, a personal facilitative attribute inferred from distinctiveness potentially can be either discounted (presence of stimulus-facilitative force) or augmented (presence of stimulus-inhibitory force) by consensus. A stimulus facilitative attribute inferred from consensus potentially can be either discounted (presence of personal facilitative force) or augmented (presence of personal inhibitory force) by distinctiveness.

COMMONSENSE INFERENCE ECONOMY

This model requires less of the inference than does the ANOVA model (for example, it does not require behavioral effects to be represented in multidimensional space). However, it is far from simple and remains rigorous—namely, the commonsense goal of reasonable accuracy. Much of the remaining complexity is a remnant of the ANOVA model within which understanding of a single behavioral instance required the integration of multiple base rates. Commonsense understanding, being less precise, probably requires less information. The reasonableness of this suggestion is indicated by research demonstrating that attributors overlook or don't use relevant base-rate information (Nisbett & Ross, 1980) and that inferences derived from multiple base rates are not more extreme or more confidently held than those derived from single base-rate categories (Hansen, 1980; Orvis et al., 1975). Two assertions would suggest the form of simplifying heuristic (Ajzen, 1977). First, commonsense inferences are theory-driven rather than data-driven as implied by the ANOVA model. Second, the theory drives or guides a search for information and this search proceeds toward the end of confirming the theory with the least complex inferencing (Hansen, 1980).

CAUSAL GUESSES

That people approach causal understanding by advancing a causal hypothesis and then fitting information to the hypothesis has been suggested previously (Ajzen, 1977; Hansen, 1980; Snyder & Gangestad, 1981). This causal guess, I propose, takes the form of a specific attribute of the person or of the stimulus *sufficient* to have produced the observed effect (Jones & Davis, 1965; Kelley, 1972b). Consistent with inference economy, I would argue that this causal guess tends to be a simple–single-force rather than a complex–multiple forces explanation, although, as effect magnitude increases, a tendency toward more complex causation might be evidenced (Kelley, 1972b). The particular category guess—person or stimulus—advanced may derive from a number of factors including point-of-view (Taylor & Fiske, 1975, 1978), resemblance of force to effect (Jennings et al., 1982), sex of the person (O'Leary & Hansen, 1984), or the motivation of the inferencer. Although the generation of these hypotheses is not the focus of this chapter and has been discussed at length elsewhere (Wyer, 1981), it is pivotal in that they are described as triggering the subsequent inferences and as theories guiding information search. I will return to this trigger process later in the chapter.

Confirming Information

A primary manifestation of inference economy is the tendency for information search to be directed toward the detection of data confirming advanced causal guesses. A "confirmatory bias" has been demonstrated in both acquisition of new information (Snyder, 1981; Snyder & Campbell, 1980; Snyder & Swann, 1978a, 1978b) and retrieval of previously acquired information (Darley & Gross, 1983; Snyder & Cantor, 1979). Although the confirmatory tendency would seem well documented, two questions relevant to the current approach need to be addressed. First, can a confirmatory bias plausibly be associated with the economy of underlying psychological principles? Second, does a confirmatory bias predict the content of the information search related to commonsense understanding of a single instance of behavior?

Psychological Economy

The principles of psychologic are described here (inference step two in the model) as being used to determine whether an observed single instance of behavior is associated with an effect that is indicative of a facilitative force naively hypothesized as causing the behavior. A causal guess can be confirmed by the discovery of an effect that either plausibly covaries with the hypothesized facilitative force or implies the existence of an opponent inhibitory force augmenting the effect. A causal guess can be disconfirmed by information connoting an effect plausibly covarying with an alternative facilitative force, discounting the observed behavioral instance as indicative of the hypothesized facilitative force. Disconfirmation of a causal guess, then, results from the application of discounting psychologic. Confirmation results from the application of either covariation or augmentation psychologic. As described, discounting and augmentation psychologic is more complex than covariation. Both are adjustments to effect magnitude, resulting in a psychological identity of effect magnitude with individual force strengths. This would imply (1) disconfirmation generally involves more complex psychologic than confirmation, and (2) confirmation of a causal guess with information requiring only the use of covariation is less complex than confirmation with information requiring augmentation.

SEARCH ECONOMY

This reasoning predicts that person attributes as causal guesses would lead to a search for distinctiveness information while stimulus attributes as causal guesses would lead to a search for consensus information (Hansen, 1980). This reasoning also would predict that the use of consensus to confirm a person-attribute hypothesis and of distinctiveness to confirm a stimulus-attribute hypothesis would not be efficient. Both of these confirmations require augmentation. Augmentation is more complex than covariation and has been shown to be less powerful than logically predicted (Hansen & Hall, 1984; Orvis et al., 1975). This could partially explain previous findings of the insensitivity of person-attribute inferences to consensus information (Nisbett & Borgida, 1975). Returning to the first point, a preference for acquiring distinctiveness information when holding a person-attribute hypothesis and for consensus when holding a stimulus-attribute hypothesis has been documented (Hansen, 1980; Hardy, Garland, & Stephenson, 1975; Major, 1980). Further, this was explicitly tested in a recent experiment (Hansen & Ronis, 1984). Subjects testing person-attribute hypotheses tended to conduct searches clustered by persons but not stimuli. Subjects testing stimulus-attribute hypotheses tended to conduct searches clustered by stimuli not persons. Thus, the psychological model of attribution, at least as far as predicting search for causal information, would seem consistent with available data. But, does it help in the production of a process theory of attribution?

TOWARD A THEORY
OF ATTRIBUTION PROCESSING

In the previous sections I have developed a view of the ANOVA model based on three principles of psychologic and argued that these principles were commonsense rules used to make judgments about the properties of persons and stimuli by virtue of rendering them causes to which effects are attributable. The answer to the question "Why did this happen?" then, is presumed by the outcome: the answer to the question "What have I learned from this?" This approach comes close to the position that attribute ascription from behavior is prima facie evidence of antecedent causal attribution. Two observers watch a child's voracious attack on an ice-cream cone. One concludes that the child is an ice cream lover; the other that the ice cream is particularly good. The conclusion of the first reflects an assumption that voracity of ice cream consumption is covaried with (caused by) love of ice cream. The conclusion of the second reflects the assumption that voracity is covaried with ice cream quality. In such instances attributions are represented by the operation of causal psychologic per se without an "overt" attributional response. Further, it would seem that the observers have not consciously sought a causal solution but implicitly understood why the behavior occurred.

Such circumstances presumably constitute minimal causation. Yet, in many instances, observers both make an overt attribution and consciously seek causal solutions. The balance of this chapter is an attempt, by way of developing a process model of attribution, to specify (1) when attributions remain at minimal causation and when conscious causal solutions are sought, (2) a mechanism triggering person or stimulus attributions, and (3) the implications of these processes for information memory.

MINIMAL CAUSAL PROCESSING

Early in the processing of observed behavior it is represented in the context of previous experience as stored in schematic memory (Wyer, 1981; Wyer & Srull, 1981). This process, often suggested as automatic, has been discussed at length by many theorists (Graesser, 1981; Smith, 1984; Hastie, 1981). Much of this discussion implies that early encoding is accomplished through the use of "scripts" (Schank & Abelson, 1977) or event schemas (Taylor & Fiske, 1981). These schemas bring the observed event into the lexicon of behavior-event memory allowing for initial interpretation of incoming data (Wyer & Srull, 1980, 1981) as well as more elaborated comprehension of behavior, objects, and persons within the event context (Smith, 1984; Smith & Miller, 1983). Event schema tend to be organized episodically around categories of social settings. Event schemas incorporate stimulus configurations likely to be encountered, the categories of people likely to inhabit the setting, and behavior sequences likely to be encountered. Within this automatic process of comprehension could be located a number of operations as well as some schematic content that have causal relevance.

First, one property of this schematic processing is the fitting or matching of incoming data to schematic representations. This has been described in terms of a template-matching process (Hastie, 1981; Tesser, 1978). In either case, congruence of incoming data with schematic event representation results in the data being encoded schematically without further processing and the specific instance being difficult to retrieve. The current observation is but another instance of a previously represented experience. However, the concept of congruence needs elaboration as it bears fundamentally on attribution processes.

Schematic representation of objects, persons, and behaviors has been depicted in terms of category prototypes constructed from a set of experienced exemplars (Ebbesen & Allen, 1979), a set of features often associated with the category (Cantor & Mischel, 1977), or both. Congruence, then, can be seen as a feature detection phenomenon. But, an exhaustive feature-matching process is not sufficiently economic to be proposed as the mechanism underlying schematic encoding. Some features are encountered more frequently than others and, hence, are more diagnostic (Cantor & Mischel, 1979) or representative of categorical inclusion. It has been argued that feature frequency is schematically represented (Hasher & Zacks, in press) in that each association of incoming data with a schematic feature produces a unique memory trace or path. The more paths available, the easier or faster the feature can be referenced. The representativeness of the observed instance of the prototype, then, is reflected in how exhaustive a search is required to discover its schematic representation (Kahneman et al., 1982; Wyer & Srull, 1981). Congruence can be defined in terms of the easy availability of a schema for encoding the features of current instance (Tversky, 1977).

Failure to encode or an exhaustive search for schematic representation of a stimulus, person, or behavior—implying that it is not representative—engages further processing. Schank and Abelson (1977), for example, referred to incongruent information as an obstacle forcing a deviation from the script. The same conclusion is indicated by research demonstrating the advantage of incongruent over congruent information in memory (Bower, Black, & Turner, 1979; Hastie, 1981) given that incongruent data forces a more exhaustive schematic search, building increased numbers of associate links (Srull, 1984). At this point it is important to recall an additional property of event schemas. Schank (1975) and others (Pyszczynski & Greenberg, 1981; Wyer & Carlston, 1979) have argued that event schemas incorporate causal linkages among their elements. As a result, event schemas can serve as plans (Neisser, 1976) directing the search for a schema allowing the processor to understand incongruent information in the context of existing schematic content.

Behavior incongruent with the content of the event schema used to encode the incoming information could result in a number of processing consequences. First, some (incongruent) information may be more deeply processed than other (congruent) information. Second, the processing forced by detection of incongruent information may block or reduce continued comprehension of other aspects of incoming data within the event schema. Alternatively, deeper processing of incongruent information may be parallel to the ongoing comprehension of the event. In either case, increased levels of incongruent data would result in a processing decrement and disadvantage to incongruent information in memory as its level increased (Srull, 1984). Third, because event schemas incorporate causal links between elements, incongruence of one element may lead to increased scrutiny and/or processing of causally associated elements. Incongruent behavior, for example, might result in deeper processing of stimulus attributes if they are scripted as causal factors of behavior. The reverse, of course, also could be anticipated: incongruent stimuli resulting in deeper processing of behavior sequences. An unpleasant facial expression of an ice cream taster may lead to more processing of the flavor being tested. Pistachio flavor ice cream may lead to deeper processing of tasters' facial expressions. In short, the automatic processing of incoming information through event schemas would result in a "texturing" of information. Congruent data are levelled while incongruent information and causally associated elements are highlighted. This texturing of information, in turn, has consequences for (1) subsequent attention-driven conscious processing, and (2) the execution of further schematic processing.

Incongruence increases the probability that the textured information will be taken to conscious processing. In such instances, attention would be drawn to both the behavior and the associated causal element without awareness of the automatic processing having resulted in their salience. The association of the causal element with the behavior comes to conscious processing as an "attributional fact" (O'Leary & Hansen, 1984): Strange behavior, strange person. Undoubtedly in many cases— particularly in the heat of interaction (Enzle, Harvey, & Hansen, 1977; Jones & Nisbett, 1972)—this attributional fact is accepted without further processing beyond that required in lexical memory to state the association. Texturing of information results in ice cream gluttony rendering the child an ice cream lover or the ice cream tasty without apparent conscious thought. These processes constitute minimal causation.

BEYOND MINIMAL CAUSATION

Conscious attention drawn to incongruent information increases the probability of additional processing to discover an explanation (Pyszczynski & Greenberg, 1981; Wong & Weiner, 1981). The texturing of information through automatic processing is likely to direct the execution of this additional processing. Association of person with incongruent behavior would lead to a search of person schemas as a means of encoding and comprehension. The individual processing the child's ice cream in terms of person schemas may encounter "loves ice cream" in his–her "child" schema. Availability of a schematic representation results in the behavior being encoded and understood in terms of the schema. Nonavailability of a schematic representation would result in the behavior not being encoded and forces additional processing. Likewise, association of stimulus with incongruent behavior would lead to a search of stimulus–object schema (or, if the stimulus is a person, person schemas). Encountering a schematic representation leads to the encoding of the behavior in terms of the schema. Failure to discover an available representation forces additional processing. Encoding through person and stimulus schemas can be seen as parallel to the covariation-only inferences depicted in the psychologic model. Two points need to be made about this directed processing. First, because initial (automatic) encoding and comprehension is accomplished within event schemas, it is unlikely that situation—the basis for event schema selection—would enter into subsequent causal processes or be seen as causally relevant to behavior (Moore, Sherrod, Liu, & Underwood, 1979; Wyer, 1981). This is often referred to as a fundamental attribution error (Nisbett & Ross, 1980). Second, because negative instances are not schematically represented, base-rate overestimation of the power of a stimulus to provoke a particular behavior (false consensus) and the proclivity of an individual to engage in a particular behavior is likely (Jones & Nisbett, 1972, Nisbett & Ross, 1980; Taylor & Crocker, 1981).

If an exhaustive search of person schemas reveals no congruent representation (i.e., low distinctiveness with psychologic terminology) or exhaustive search of stimulus schema reveals no congruent representation (i.e., high consensus), additional processing is required in order for the behavior to be understood. Also, it is at this point that the processor may be explicitly oriented toward causal understanding: What caused this to happen? The first resort may be a search of alternative schema: An attempt to encode using stimulus schema following unavailability of congruent representation in person memory and to encode using person schema following unavailability of congruent representation in stimulus memory (Crocker, Hannah, & Weber, 1983). This would parallel the augmentation and discounting inferences of the psychologic model. Failing this would be confusion, causal magic (e.g., ascription to luck) or resort to explicit causal processing.

Causal Schema: Special Theories of Causation

Throughout, I have taken the view that the individual's understanding of causal reality is embedded in event schemas and that attributional processing can be described in terms of the texturing of information resulting in schematic search of person or stimulus schemas toward the comprehension of incongruent information. Kelley (1972b), however, has described a number of causal schemas, including the ANOVA concept, as content-free rubrics for understanding cause in any domain. The existence of such "free-floating"content-free schemas would seem doubtful (Nisbett & Ross, 1980). However, structures for representing and comprehending causal reality outside of event-specific memory seems cognitively economic. I would argue that such schemas would be conceptually organized around causal principles allowing for causal understanding through analogy, providing algorithms for solving causal dilemmas (Nisbett & Ross, 1980) and serving as a last resort for comprehension of incongruent information. For example, a "two heads are better than one" causal schema might embody a theory of causal additivity while a "weak link" causal schema might incorporate a theory of causal nonadditivity. Although such schemata would not be content-free as implied by Kelley (1972b), they could be classed as causal schemata in that access is determined by "causal form" rather than specific content. Each causal schema, then, represents a special theory of causation keyed to the causal features of events.

Causal schemas would incorporate prototypes composed of phenotypic features of effects and the (inter)action of associated causal forces. These schemas allow the processor to access representations of causal reality without the necessity of assembling fragments of causal understanding in event memory. As with other schematic processing, availability of a congruent prototype is indicative of the frequency with which the observed "causal form" has been previously encountered. Also, the ordering of search through prototypes (their accessibility) is presumed to be determined by frequency of prior access. We could expect these prototypes to be organized on the dimensions, among others, of causal complexity (Wimer & Kelley, 1982), effect extremity (Kelley, 1972a) and effect evaluation (Izard, 1982; Weiner, 1982). Each schema would be based on a principle of cause sufficiency so as to suggest the identity of a single cause among an array of many candidates associated with simple or modest effects and the generation of additional causal candidates beyond a single cause associated with complex or extreme effects (Gross, 1983). Each causal schema would allow the individual to comprehend many different categories of events that could be assimilated to its causal form. Causal memory of this sort, allowing access to prototypic representations of cause–effect relationships, would be cognitively economic.

COMMENT

In this chapter I have attempted to produce a model of attribution inferencing compatible with current approaches to social cognition. Why? Attribution theory has just about reached the end of its useful life as a framework for exploring causal thought. In light of more molecular and sophisticated social-cognition models, many of the issues raised by attribution theorists and researchers—for example, differential weighting of distinctiveness and consensus information—seem superficial or more related to formal (causal) problem solving than to the bulk of causal information processing. Likewise, the traditional attribution methodologies—providing preformed causal information ("Most people [verb] X.") and requesting theoretically meaningful attributions ("To what extent was this caused by something about the person?")—seem superficial or even misguided as serious probes of mundane causal information processing. Nevertheless, an obituary would be premature. Attribution theory has been and will continue to be fruitful by way of generating provocative hypotheses about causal understanding and the mediation of social behavior by causal understanding. There is little doubt that the attribution literature will continue to grow if only out of impetus. However its full potential will be realized only if its heuristic value is recognized by those forming the emergent social cognition paradigm. It is what it describes: an algorithm of causal understanding, provoking inquiry. In order to serve this role two things must occur. First, attribution theory must be recognized as describing commonsense understanding that is epiphenomenal to social cognition and constrained to the *what* as opposed to the *how* and *why* of lay epistemology. Second, attribution models must be made compatible with theories of social cognition. This was my intent: not to reincarnate attribution in the guise of a quasi-cognitive theory, but rather to suggest a form more suited to this role before the cognitivists despair of attribution theory.

REFERENCES

Ajzen, I. (1977). Intuitive theories of events and effects of base-rate information on prediction. *Journal of Personality and Social Psychology, 35,* 303–314.

Bargh, J. A. (1984). Automatic and conscious processing of social information. In R. S. Wyer and T. K. Srull (Eds.), *Handbook of social cognition* (Vol. 3). Hillsdale, N.J.: Erlbaum.

Bower, G. H., Black, J. B., & Turner, T. J. (1979). Scripts in memory for text. *Cognitive Psychology, 11*, 177–220.

Cantor, N., & Mischel, W. (1977). Traits as prototypes: Effects on recognition memory. *Journal of Personality and Social Psychology, 35*, 38–48.

Cantor, N., & Mischel, W. (1979). Prototypes in person perception. In L. Berkowitz (Ed.), *Advances in experimental social psychology* (Vol. 12). New York: Academic Press.

Crocker, J., Hannah, D. B., & Weber, R. (1983). Person memory and causal attributions. *Journal of Personality and Social Psychology, 44*, 55–66.

Darley, J. M., & Gross, P. H. (1983). A hypothesis-confirming bias in labeling effect. *Journal of Personality and Social Psychology, 44*, 20–33.

Ebbesen, E. B., & Allen, R. B. (1979). Cognitive processes in implicit personality trait inferences. *Journal of Personality and Social Psychology, 37*, 471–488.

Enzle, M. E., Harvey, M. D., & Hansen, R. D. (1977). Time pressure and causal attributions. *Personality and Social Psychology Bulletin*, 624–627.

Graesser, A. C. (1981). *Prose comprehension beyond the word*. New York: Springer-Verlag.

Hamilton, D. L. (1981). Cognitive representations of persons. In E. T. Higgins, C. P. Herman & M. P. Zanna (Eds.), *Social cognition: the Ontario symposium* (Vol. 1). Hillsdale, N.J.: Erlbaum.

Hansen, R. D. (1980). Commonsense attribution. *Journal of Personality and Social Psychology, 39*, 996–1009.

Hansen, R. D., & Hall, C. A. (1984). *Discounting and augmenting causal forces*. Unpublished manuscript, Yale University and Michigan State University.

Hansen, R. D., & Ronis, D. L. (1984). Search for cause. Unpublished manuscript, Oakland University, Rochester, MI.

Hardy, A., Garland, H., & Stephenson, L. (1975). Information search as affected by attribution type and response category. *Personality and Social Psychology Bulletin, 4*, 612–615.

Hasher, L., & Zacks, R. T. (in press). Automatic processing of fundamental information: the case of frequency of occurrence. *American Psychologist*.

Hastie, R. (1981). Schematic principles in human memory. In E. T. Higgins, C. P. Herman, & M. P. Zanna (Eds.), *Social cognition: the Ontario symposium* (Vol. 1). Hillsdale, N.J.: Erlbaum.

Hastie, R., & Kumar, P. A. (1979). Person perception: personality traits as organizing principles in memory for behaviors. *Journal of Personality and Social Psychology, 37*, 25–38.

Hull, J. G., & West, S. G. (1982). The discounting principle in attribution. *Personality and Social Psychology Bulletin, 8*, 208–213.

Izard, C. E. (1982). Comments on emotion and cognition: Can there be a working relationship. In M. S. Clark & S. T. Fiske (Eds.), *Affect and social cognition*. Hillsdale, N.J.: Erlbaum.

Jennings, D. L., Amabile, T. M., & Ross, L. (1982). Informal covariation assessment: data-based versus theory-based judgments. In D. Kahneman, P. Slovic, A. Tversky (Eds.), *Judgment under uncertainty: heuristics and biases*. New York: Cambridge University Press.

Jones, E. E., & Davis, K. E. (1965). From acts to dispositions: the attribution process in person perception. In L. Berkowitz (Ed.), *Advances in experimental social psychology* (Vol. 2). New York: Academic Press.

Jones, E. E., & McGillis, D. (1976). Correspondent inferences and the attribution cube: a comparative reappraisal. In J. H. Harvey, W. Ickes, & R. F. Kidd (Eds.), *New directions in attribution research* (Vol. 1). Hillsdale, N.J.: Erlbaum.

Jones, E. E., & Nisbett, R. E. (1972). The actor and the observer: divergent perceptions of the causes of behavior. In E. E. Jones, D. E. Kanouse, H. H. Kelley, R. E. Nisbett, S. Valins, & B. Weiner (Eds.), *Attribution: perceiving the causes of behavior.* Morristown, N.J.: General Learning Press.

Kahneman, D., Slovic, P., & Tversky, A. (1982). *Judgment under uncertainty: heuristics and biases.* New York: Cambridge University Press.

Kelley, H. H. (1967). Attribution theory in social psychology. In D. Levine (Ed.), *Nebraska symposium on motivation* (Vol. 15). Lincoln: University of Nebraska Press.

Kelley, H. H. (1972a). Attribution in social interaction. In E. E. Jones and others (Eds.), *Attribution: perceiving the causes of behavior.* Morristown, N.J.: General Learning Press.

Kelley, H. H. (1972b). Causal schemata and the attribution process. In E. E. Jones, D. E. Kanouse, H. H. Kelley, R. E. Nisbett, S. Valins, & B. Weiner (Eds.), *Attribution: perceiving the causes of behavior.* Morristown, N.J.: General Learning Press.

Langer, E. J., Blank, A., & Chanowitz, B. (1978). The mindlessness of ostensibly thoughtful action: the role of "placebic" information in interpersonal interaction. *Journal of Personality and Social Psychology, 36,* 635–642.

Major, B. (1980). Information acquisition and attribution processes. *Journal of Personality and Social Psychology, 39,* 1010–1023.

McArthur, L. A. (1972). The who and what of why: some determinants and consequences of causal attribution. *Journal of Personality and Social Psychology, 22,* 171–193.

McArthur, L. Z. (1976). The lesser influence of consensus than distinctiveness information on causal attributions: a test of the person–thing hypothesis. *Journal of Personality and Social Psychology, 33,* 733–742.

Mitchell, M., Hyde, M., & Friedman, D. (1983). The effect of frequency information on actor-entity attributions. *Personality and Social Psychology Bulletin, 9,* 359–363.

Moore, B. S., Sherrod, D. R., Liu, T. J., & Underwood, B. (1979). The dispositional shift in attribution over time. *Journal of Experimental Social Psychology, 15,* 553–569.

Neisser, V. (1976). *Cognition and reality: principles and implications of cognitive psychology.* San Francisco, CA.: Freeman.

Nisbett, R. E., & Borgida, E. (1975). Attribution and the psychology of prediction. *Journal of Personality and Social Psychology, 32,* 932–943.

Nisbett, R. E., & Ross, L. (1980). *Human inference: strategies and shortcomings of social judgment.* Englewood Cliffs, N.J.: Prentice-Hall.

Nisbett, R. E., & Wilson, T. D. (1977). Telling more than we can know: verbal reports on mental processes. *Psychological Review, 84,* 231–259.

O'Leary, V. E., & Hansen, R. D. (in press). Sex as an attributional fact. *Nebraska Symposium on Motivation.*

Orvis, D., Cunningham, J. D., & Kelley, H. H. (1975). A closer examination of causal inference: the role of consensus, distinctiveness, and consistency information. *Journal of Personality and Social Psychology, 32,* 605–616.

Pyszczynski, T. A., & Greenberg, J. (1981). Role of disconfirmed expectancies in the instigation of attributional processing. *Journal of Personality and Social Psychology, 40,* 31–38.

Ross, L. (1977). The intuitive psychologist and his shortcomings. In L. Berkowitz (Ed.), *Advances in experimental social psychology* (Vol. 10). New York: Academic Press.

Rothbart, M., Evans, M., & Fulero, S. (1979). Confirming events: memory processes and the maintenance of social stereotypes. *Journal of Experimental Social Psychology, 15,* 343–355.

Schank, R. C. (1975). The structure of episodes in memory. In D. G. Bobrow, & A. Collins (Eds.), *Representation and understanding: studies in cognitive science.* New York: Academic Press.

Schank, R., & Abelson, R. (1977). *Scripts, plans, goals and understanding: an inquiry into human knowledge structures.* Hillsdale, N.J.: Erlbaum.

Shaver, K. G. (1981). Back to basics: on the role of theory in the attribution of causality. In J. H. Harvey, W. Ickes, & R. F. Kidd (Eds.), *New directions in attribvtion research* (Vol. 3). Hillsdale, N.J.: Erlbaum.

Smith, E. R. (1984). Attributions and other inferences: processing information about the self versus others. *Journal of Experimental Social Psychology, 20,* 97–115.

Smith, E. R., & Miller, F. D. (1979). Salience and the cognitive mediation of attribution. *Journal of Personality and Social Psychology, 37,* 2240–2252.

Smith, E. R., & Miller, F. D. (1983). Mediation among attributional inferences and comprehension processes: initial findings and a general method. *Journal of Personality and Social Psychology, 44,* 492–505.

Snyder, M. (1981). Seek, and ye shall find: testing hypotheses about other people. In E. T. Higgins, C. P. Herman, & M. P. Zanna (Eds.), *Social cognition: the Ontario symposium* (Vol. 1). Hillsdale, N.J.: Erlbaum.

Snyder, M., & Campbell, B. H. (1980). Testing hypotheses about other people: the role of the hypothesis. *Personality and Social Psychology Bulletin, 6,* 421–426.

Snyder, M., & Cantor, N. (1979). Testing hypotheses about other people: the use of historical knowledge. *Journal of Experimental Social Psychology, 15,* 330–342.

Snyder, M., & Gangestad, S. (1981). Hypothesis-testing processes. In J. H. Harvey, W. Ickes, & R. F. Kidd (Eds.), *New directions in attribution research* (Vol. 3). Hillsdale, N.J.: Erlbaum.

Snyder, M., & Swann, W. B. (1978a). Behavioral confirmation in social interaction: from social perception to social reality. *Journal of Experimental Social Psychology, 14,* 148–162.

Snyder, M., & Swann, W. B. (1978b). Hypothesis-testing processes in social interaction. *Journal of Personality and Social Psychology, 36,* 1202–1212.

Taylor, S. E., & Crocker, J. (1981). Schematic bases of social information processing. In E. T. Higgins, C. P. Herman, & M. P. Zanna (Eds.), *Social cognition: the Ontario symposium* (Vol. 1). Hillsdale, N.J.: Erlbaum.

Taylor, S. E., & Fiske, S. T. (1975). Point of view and perceptions of causality. *Journal of Personality and Social Psychology, 32,* 439–445.

Taylor, S. E., & Fiske, S. T. (1978). Salience, attention, and attribution: top of the head phenomena. In L. Berkowitz (Ed.), *Advances in experimental social psychology* (Vol. 11). New York: Academic Press.

Taylor, S. E., & Fiske, S. T. (1981). Getting inside the head: Methodologies for process analysis and social cognition. In J. H. Harvey, W. Ickes, & R. F. Kidd (Eds.), *New directions in attribution research.* Hillsdale, N.J.: Erlbaum.

Tesser, A. Self-generated attitude change. (1978). In L. Berkowitz (Ed.), *Advances in experimental social psychology* (Vol. 11). New York: Academic Press.

Trabasso, T., Rollins, H., & Shaughnessy, E. (1971). Storage and verification stages in processing concepts. *Cognitive Psychology, 2,* 239–289.

Tversky, A. (1977). Features of similarity. *Psychological Review, 84,* 327–352.

Weiner, B. (1982). The emotional consequences of causal attributions. In M. S. Clark & S. T. Fiske (Eds.), *Affect and cognition.* Hillsdale, N.J.: Erlbaum.

Weiner, B., Russell, D., & Lerman, D. (1978). Affective consequences of causal ascriptions. In J. H. Harvey, W. Ickes, & R. F. Kidd (Eds.), *New directions in attribution research* (Vol. 2). Hillsdale, N.J.: Erlbaum.

Wells, G. L., & Ronis, D. L. (1982). Discounting and augmentation: is there something special about the number of causes. *Personality and Social Psychology Bulletin, 8,* 566–572.

Wimer, S., & Kelley, H. H. (1982). An investigation of the dimensions of causal attribution. *Journal of Personality and Social Psychology, 43,* 1142–1162.

Wong, P. T. P., & Weiner, B. (1981). When people ask why questions and the heuristics of attributional search. *Journal of Personality and Social Psychology, 40,* 650–663.

Wyer, R. S. (1981). An information-processing perspective on social attribution. In. J. H. Harvey, W. Ickes, & R. F. Kidd (Eds.), *New directions in attribution research* (Vol. 3). Hillsdale, N.J.: Erlbaum.

Wyer, R. S., & Carlston, D. E. (1979). *Social inference and attribution.* Hillsdale, N.J.: Erlbaum.

Wyer, R. S., & Srull, T. K. (1980). The processing of social stimulus information: a conceptual integration. In R. Hastie, T. M. Ostrom, E. B. Ebbeson, R. S. Wyer, D. L. Hamilton, & D. E. Carlston (Eds.), *Person memory: cognitive basis for social perception.* Hillsdale, N.J.: Erlbaum.

Wyer, R. S., & Srull, T. K. (1981). Category accessibility: some theoretical and empirical issues concerning the processing of social stimulus information. In E. T. Higgins, C. P. Herman, & M. P. Zanna (Eds.), *Social cognition: the Ontario symposium* (Vol. 1). Hillsdale, N.J.: Erlbaum.

CHAPTER **4**

Implicit Relations between Dispositions and Behaviors: Effects on Dispositional Attribution*

Glenn D. Reeder

INTRODUCTION

Nearly twenty years ago the major statements of attribution theory first appeared (Jones & Davis, 1965; Kelley, 1967). These theories placed Heider's (1958) earlier insights into a systematic framework, allowing research to focus on a set of core concepts. By Kelley and Michela's (1980) count, over 900 published attribution studies appeared in the decade preceding their review. Yet, as noted elsewhere (Eiser, 1983; Shaver, 1981), this research did little to alter the theoretical foundations of the field. This is not to say that theoretical innovation has been lacking (Jones & McGillis, 1976; Kelley, 1973; Kruglanski, 1980; Shaver, 1981), but it has rarely been inspired by empirical research. The rapidly accumulating empirical findings of attribution research have played a minor role in the field's theoretical development (Ross & Fletcher, in press).

The lack of interplay between theory and data is exemplified by work on the discounting principle (Kelley, 1973). This principle is often applied to the case where an observer is given information about both an actor's behavior and the situational demands operating on the actor. In forming an impression of the actor, the observer tends to discount an implied disposition when situational demands appear to have facilitated the actor's behavior. For example, suppose an actor describes him- or herself as very friendly during an interview for a job with the airlines. The interview situation demands just this type of self-description. Accordingly, observers may attribute a moderate or average level of friend-

---

*The author expresses thanks to Garth Fletcher, Tom Shumaker, and Eddy Van Avermaet for helpful comments on an earlier draft of this manuscript.

ATTRIBUTION
Basic Issues and Applications
87

liness to the actor. In this case, the tendency to infer a very friendly disposition is discounted in the direction of a more moderate attribution of friendliness. In contrast, if the employment situation demands less social behavior (as a night watchman's position might), that same very friendly self-description is likely to produce an inference that the actor is, indeed, very friendly (Jones, Davis, & Gergen, 1961).[1]

A large data base indicates that discounting is sometimes strong (Jones et al., 1961), sometimes partial (Jones & Harris, 1967), and sometimes almost completely absent (Messick & Reeder, 1974; Napolitan & Goethals, 1979). The early attribution statements provide little guidance concerning the limits of discounting and, consequently, the research findings are not easily reconciled. An influential study by Jones and Harris (1967) illustrates the issues involved. Observers were shown an essay that either praised or criticized Cuba's Fidel Castro and were asked to infer the writer's "true" attitude. Consistent with the discounting principle, observers gave more extreme ratings of the writer's attitude when the essay topic had been freely chosen rather than assigned to her or him. However, even in the assigned (or no choice) condition the discounting was only partial: A person who wrote in favor of Castro was rated significantly more pro-Castro than one who took the opposite position. This tendency toward partial or insufficient discounting has withstood numerous challenges and apparently is not a simple artifact of the procedure (Jones, 1979).

Researchers disagree on the issue of whether or not such partial discounting represents attributional error (Harvey, Town, & Yarkin, 1981). Regardless of the ultimate status of this controversy, it is clear that the Jones and Harris (1967) results are not easily explained within the frameworks of the original attribution theories (Jones & Davis, 1965; Jones & McGillis, 1976; Kelley, 1973). From the standpoint of these theories, the writer is instructed to argue a given position and, thus, the situational demands provide a sufficient explanation for the behavior. Essays produced under such conditions should carry little information about the writer's private attitude, and observers should attribute a neutral or modal attitude to the writer.

As Jones (1979) concedes, evidence of insufficient discounting requires an explanation outside the bounds of the influential correspondent-inference theory (Jones & McGillis, 1976). This is not to say that

---

[1]The examples discussed in the text describe the discounting of an attitude (or disposition). This process of dispositional discounting is similar to but not isomorphic with the discounting of causes (Kelley, 1973). The relationship between dispositional attribution and causal attribution is addressed in a subsequent section of this chapter.

the theory lacks utility. The provocative data described by Jones and Harris (1967) exemplify its heuristic value. Also, Jones and Davis's (1965) depiction of the naive observer as a logical (amateur) scientist has enabled the theory to serve as a "rational baseline" against which observer error can be detected (Jones, 1978). It is important to note, though, that whatever benefits a normative model may offer in exposing observer error, the error itself requires explanation.

In an effort to further our understanding of the discounting principle, Brewer and I proposed a *schematic model of dispositional attribution* (Reeder & Brewer, 1979). The model outlines various schemata or implicit assumptions that may underlie our understanding of dispositional terms. Specifically, the model examines implicit links between dispositions and the behaviors these dispositions are thought to imply. The model further attempts to specify the role such *implicational relations* play in person perception. As described later, these implicational relations may sometimes be biased or in error. It follows that the attribution process will reflect this influence. Aspects of the attribution process where error is likely to occur are not treated as extratheoretical. Instead, these aspects, whether biased or accurate, form an integral part of the model.

This chapter builds on our earlier analysis (Reeder & Brewer, 1979) in three ways. First, the factors that influence implicational relations between dispositions and behaviors are explored in greater detail. The analysis focuses on several key implicit assumptions that may govern these relations. Second, recent research is reviewed within the framework of the model. Finally, the present approach is discussed within the wider scheme of implicit personality theory.

Two classes of implicit assumptions are believed to influence implicational relations: reinforcement assumptions and schematic assumptions. Each is described in the following sections.

REINFORCEMENT ASSUMPTIONS

Reinforcement assumptions are concerned with the effect of situational demands on behavior. As every psychologist knows, situational variables exert tremendous control over everyday behavior. Observers—who are clearly aware of this tendency—expect that persons will vary their behavior, if possible, in order to best meet environmental contingencies and demands (Ajzen, 1971; Jones & Davis, 1965). For example, suppose an observer is aware that a writer has been instructed to compose an essay supporting forced school busing. Now a writer who privately holds a pro-busing attitude will certainly be expected to write a pro-busing essay. Further, because of the reinforcement assumptions, writers with a moderate attitude might also be expected to write such an essay. Finally, it might seem implausible that a writer with an anti-busing attitude would compose a pro-busing essay. Such a person, however, might write a moderate essay. This ''restrictive'' assumption will be discussed in a later section. The reinforcement assumptions just described are shown in Figure 4.1

Suppose now that the writer does indeed compose a strong pro-busing essay. An observer who is asked to infer the writer's private attitude may experience some uncertainty. Given the expectations (just described) about the link between the writer's attitude and the likely position of the essay, writers with either pro or moderate positions on the issue might have composed the essay. Under these circumstances, observers are likely to estimate that the writer of a strong pro essay holds a private attitude somewhere between a strong pro and a moderate position on the issue (perhaps a moderately pro position).

In the example above, assumptions about implicational relations determine the inferred disposition. These implicational relations, which incorporate the reinforcement assumption, allow the observer to, in effect, infer ''backward'' to a disposition or attitude attribution. This process is offered as an alternative explanation of data usually cited as evidence of discounting (Kelley, 1973). Specifically, a strong pro essay produced under no choice conditions leads to a state of relative uncertainty. The observer who goes on to attribute an attitude may infer that the writer holds a moderately pro private opinion on the issue. In other words, the tendency to infer a strong pro opinion is discounted.

SCHEMATIC ASSUMPTIONS

The second general class of assumptions are called *schematic assumptions*. These assumptions concern the subjective meaning of dispositional terms. In particular, a naive conception of a disposition often

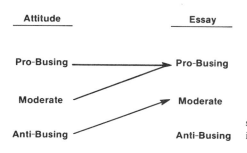

Figure 4.1 Reinforcement assumptions in a case where a pro-busing essay is assigned.

includes expectations about the range of behaviors an actor will perform. For example, a sociable disposition implies mainly sociable behavior, and only rarely very unsociable behavior. These schematic assumptions place limits on the extent to which the reinforcement assumptions are allowed to operate. For example, even if a situation demands very unsociable behavior, a very sociable person might not be expected to meet the demands. A very sociable person might be thought unwilling, or perhaps even unable, to act in a very unfriendly manner.

An earlier article (Reeder & Brewer, 1979) provided a figural description of several representative implicational (or schematic) patterns. These various patterns of implication were then tentatively identified with different traits. The aim was to suggest that a model of attribution must address the *content* of observers' inferences (Carrol, Galegher, & Weiner, 1982; Fiedler, 1982; Schultz & Schleifer, 1983). That is, the attribution process may vary depending on the type of attribution to be made.

Although Reeder and Brewer (1979) described several schematic implicational patterns in figural form, little rationale was included concerning why these relations took a particular form. The present chapter will outline three types of schematic assumptions that may underlie these patterns: assumptions concerned with central tendency, social desirability, and ability. As shown in Figure 4.2, the schematic assumptions combine with reinforcement assumptions to determine implicational relations. These implicational relations, in turn, guide the inference of dispositional characteristics.

IMPLICIT CENTRAL TENDENCY ASSUMPTIONS

In everyday language, dispositional terms are often used to describe an actor's average or most common behavior (Alston, 1975; Fletcher, 1984). We take "Sasha is an extrovert" to mean that Sasha is often out-

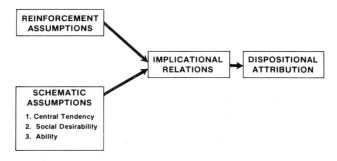

Figure 4.2 The interaction of reinforcement assumptions and schematic assumptions.

going, the life of the party, and so on. Each of Sasha's behaviors may be classified according to the extent it is introverted or extroverted. The information that Sasha is an extrovert lets us know that most of her behavior falls near the extroverted end of the continuum. This *central tendency assumption* is shown graphically in Figure 4.3 (the set of relations is similar to the partially restrictive schema described by Reeder & Brewer, 1979).

Each arrow in the figure connects a dispositional level with a class of behaviors. The arrow indicates that there is a nonzero subjective probability that a person with such a disposition would emit behavior of this sort. Further, thicker arrows suggest stronger implicational links than do thin arrows. It is readily apparent that the strongest implicational links are between correspondent dispositions and behaviors (i.e., an introverted disposition and behavior classified as introverted). Also, persons with an extreme disposition are thought unlikely to behave in a manner that is highly discrepant with that disposition (for example, we don't expect our very introverted friend to regale party guests with a series of jokes).

Several studies have examined perceived disposition–behavior relations directly. These studies suggest that central tendency assumptions are widely applicable to dispositional types, including those dealing with attitudes, preference, morality, and ability. Further, these implicit assumptions are surprisingly strong.

Miller and Rorer (1982) provided what are, perhaps, the first empirical data to support an implicit theory of central tendency. In seeking an explanation of the tendency toward partial discounting in the attitude attribution paradigm, Miller and Rorer (1982) proposed that perceivers "hold implicit theories or expectations concerning the relationship between (a) the writer's attitude and (b) the position or quality of the essay that is produced under assigned-position instructions" (p. 42). Specifically, observers may believe that a writer will produce a strong persuasive essay only if he or she personally endorses that position. In one

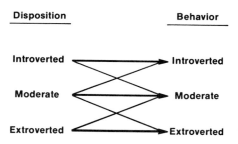

Figure 4.3 Central tendency assumptions for the introverted–extroverted continuum.

portion of their study, observers were told the personal opinions of several writers who were assigned an essay position. Observers were then invited to estimate the probable characteristics of these essays. As the authors had expected, observers believed the writer's personal attitude would be a strong determinant of both essay position and essay quality. For example, when a pro-busing essay was assigned, observers predicted that a writer holding an anti-busing attitude would write a moderate (rather than a pro) essay.

Reeder, Henderson, and Sullivan (1982) extended these findings to include attributions concerned with preference (adventurous–cautious), morality (honest–dishonest), and ability (intelligent–unintelligent). In one part of the study observers were asked questions about the general frequency of behavior: "In general, how often does a very adventurous person act very cautious?" and "In general, how often does a moderate person act very cautious?" The results supported a central tendency assumption. For example, a moderate person was thought far more likely to behave very cautiously than was a very adventurous person. The central tendency assumptions also characterized judgments concerning the behaviors actors might attempt (or intend) and judgments about the potential ability of actors to complete various behaviors.

THE QUESTION OF ACCURACY

Is it possible that observers carry the central tendency assumption too far? In other words, might observers infer too much consistency? A number of social psychologists and philosophers have answered this question with an emphatic "yes." Heider (1958) proposed that Gestalt principles of "form" and "good fit" lead us toward the perception of consistency. Ichheiser carried this idea further by noting a tendency to overestimate the unity of personality:

> Now, if we happen to see a person whom we believe we know very well acting in a manner which is at variance with our expectations, either we are quite shocked and confused or we try to save our own false conception by declaring, "Something is wrong with the person." It does not frequently occur to us that something might be wrong with our own assumptions and interpretations. (1970, p. 52)

Others have relied on terms such as "generalization fallacy" (Locke & Pennington, 1982), "dispositionalist theory" (Nisbett & Ross, 1980), or an "illusion of consistency" (Jones & Nisbett, 1972) to describe similar ideas. Mischel (1968) put forth what is perhaps the strongest statement of this view. After finding little empirical evidence for cross-situational stability in behavior, Mischel was moved to suggest that traits (or consistently stable patterns of behavior) may reside only in the minds of perceivers.

Questions concerning error in attribution are surrounded by controversy (Funder, 1982; Harvey et al., 1981; Reeder, 1982). The difficulties of providing unequivocal evidence of error are formidable. For example, with what criterion should attributions be compared to establish the existence of error (Cline, 1964; Cook, 1979)? Further, the interpretation of deviations from an acceptable criterion can be complex (Cline, 1964; Cronbach, 1955).

Nevertheless, the growing data base on the subject of error cannot be ignored. The present review will focus on studies which provide tentative evidence of an *illusion of consistency:* observers' tendency to overestimate the consistency of behavior. The first such area of research concerns partial or insufficient discounting. The second area involves predicting future behavior and recalling past behavior. These areas of research will be summarized and the issue of error examined briefly. Next, and most important, the question of whether implicational relations offer a reasonable account of these data is addressed.

Partial or Insufficient Discounting

In the introduction of this chapter, evidence of insufficient discounting was outlined (Jones & Harris, 1967). The research indicates that essays produced under "no choice" conditions can prompt observers to attribute essay-consistent attitudes to the writer. Questions concerning the accuracy or normativeness of observers' attributions are clouded by at least two issues. First, much of the research reviewed by Jones (1979) lacks a criterion for assessing error. Perhaps it is actually the case that only persons in favor of a given issue would write an essay taking a strong favorable position. Further, perhaps observers are aware of such a tendency. If so, observers' tendency to attribute essay-consistent attitudes to the writer would not be an error.

Research gives little support to this point of view. For example, the available data suggest that the strength or persuasiveness of essays produced by actual writers (under assigned essay conditions) is, at best, weakly related to the writer's actual attitude (Jones, 1979; Miller, Baer, & Schonberg, 1979). Thus, observers' assumption that a writer's attitude is a strong determinant of essay strength would appear to be in error (Miller & Rorer, 1982). In other words, observers appear to expect too much consistency between a writer's private attitude and the essay such a writer will produce.

Further evidence against the lack of criterion argument comes from studies that employ the writer's own attitude as the criterion of error. Snyder and Jones (1974) instructed half of their subjects to write an essay in favor of Fidel Castro. The remaining subjects were placed in a separate room and instructed to compose an essay defending the virtues of smoking marijuana. Afterwards, the two groups of subjects exchanged essays and each subject estimated the private attitude of a member in the other group. Subjects had earlier recorded their private attitudes on these issues and these actual attitudes were used to assess the existence of error. The results indicate that attributed attitudes were biased in the direction of the assigned essay. For example, writers whose essays defended marijuana were thought to be more pro marijuana than was actually the case.

A recent study by Reeder (1984) extends this line of evidence. Subjects drew straws to determine who would be a writer and who would be an observer. According to condition, the experimenter assigned the writer to compose a pro-busing essay or an essay supporting the drafting of women into the military, respectively. Unlike prior research, observers were present in the same room as the essay topic was assigned and while the writer composed the essay. Afterwards, writers read their essays outloud to the observers. Observers then estimated the private attitude of the writer on an 11-point scale. As in the earlier study (Snyder & Jones, 1974), writers' own attitudes served as the criterion. The results of this study also show that observers systematically over-attribute attitudes in line with the assigned essay (collapsing across the issues, $M = 5.87$ for writer's own attitude versus $M = 7.88$ for attributed attitude). Observers also estimated the attitude of the "typical" student on the target issue. The attitude attributed to the writer was found to be highly discrepant from this measure of typical attitude ($M = 3.75$). In other words, the writer is perceived as holding a uniquely extreme position on the issue. The evidence of insufficient discounting, in summary, remains strong when a reasonable criterion is employed.

A second issue that could potentially cloud the interpretation of insufficient discounting concerns the availability or *salience* of the constraints for the actor (Ajzen & Fishbein, 1983). Research indicates that as the forced nature of the essay assignment is made salient for the observer, the tendency toward insufficient discounting decreases (Miller, Mayerson, Pogue & Whitehouse, 1977). Consequently, it might be argued that attributional error is due to the unrealistically low salience of constraint information in past studies. This argument, however, fails to account for data indicating that error remains when observers have personally experienced these constraints (Snyder & Jones, 1974) or are actually present when the essay assignment is made (Reeder, 1984). Thus, although salience is an important factor, it is apparently not the only determinant of insufficient discounting.

What role might implicational relations play in producing insufficient discounting? It should be clear by now that the present approach (Reeder & Brewer, 1979) views this pattern as a consequence of exaggerated assumptions about central tendency. Observers are apparently unaware that writers holding various attitudinal positions will, when instructed, compose an essay of reasonable quality in the assigned direction (Miller et al., 1979, Miller & Rorer, 1982). Given this lack of awareness, observers tend to view the essay as a "true" reflection of the writer's private attitude. Although there is some discounting of attitude—compared to conditions where writers freely choose the direction of the essay—the discounting is limited by a strong central tendency assumption.

Assumptions about the consistency of behavior may be stronger in some individuals than in others. If these assumptions underlie the insufficient discounting phenomena, individuals who assume stronger consistency should show the least evidence of discounting. Reeder and Spores (1983a) tested this idea. Observers were informed that writers holding various private attitudinal positions on forced busing were instructed to defend one side of the issue. Observers then estimated the quality of essay likely to be produced by these writers. These data allowed observers to be divided into groups holding weak or strong consistency assumptions. Observers with weak consistency assumptions did not view the writer's private attitude as a strong determinant of essay quality. In contrast, those with strong consistency assumptions tended to believe that a high quality essay would be produced only by a writer who personally accepted the assigned essay position.

The remaining part of the Reeder and Spores (1983a) study followed the procedure of an attitude attribution experiment (Jones, 1979). Observers received a description of several writers who composed essays under conditions of constraint ("no choice" conditions). In some cases the assigned essay favored busing, in other cases the essay opposed busing. Observers were then asked to estimate each writer's personal attitude on the issue. In support of prior work (Jones & Harris, 1967), writers identified with a pro- rather than an anti-busing essay were attributed a more pro attitude. Of greater interest, this tendency toward insufficient discounting was magnified among observers who held strong consistency assumptions. That is, observers making strong consistency assumptions attributed attitudes more in line with the essay then did those making weak consistency assumptions. In sum, these data suggest that consistency (or central tendency) assumptions moderate the extent to which the discounting principle is allowed to operate.

PREDICTION AND RECALL

In everyday life it is obvious that a central tendency assumption underlies our predictions about behavior. If we observe a colleague abusing alcohol at a party, we are likely to assume the behavior is not an isolated incident. Not surprisingly, evidence of generalization is common in the attribution literature. Some of the factors that influence this tendency have already been discussed. For example, reinforcement assumptions suggest that observers should generalize less from normative than from counternormative behavior (Cantor & Mischel, 1979, p. 40). Normative (or reward-consistent) behavior may be expected from persons occupying a large range of relevant dispositional levels and, therefore, it has less predictive value. A second factor concerns the extremity of behavior. The observation of extreme behavior leads to greater certainty in predictions than does the observation of less extreme behavior (Lay, Burron & Jackson, 1973). This follows from the central tendency assumption diagramed in Figure 4.3. Relative to more moderate behavior, extreme behavior is implied by only a limited range of dispositional levels.

Reeder and Spores (1983b) found that observers readily predict one immoral behavior from the observation of another. For example, a woman who committed an act of adultery was thought to be much more likely to lie and steal (Ms = 7.21 and 7.09, respectively, on an 11-point scale) than a woman who was not adulterous (Ms = 4.44 and 4.29, respectively). Another group of researchers (Taylor & Crocker, 1981) found that observers' predictions about future behavior were equally extreme regardless of whether a new situation was similar or different from one in which the actor previously had been observed. The authors concluded that observers behave like trait theorists rather than behaviorists.

Central tendency assumptions may also affect our recall of behavior. When recalling the frequency of past behavior, observers seem to equate similarity in meaning with assumptions about frequency (Shweder, 1975; Tversky & Kahneman, 1974). Behaviors that are similar in meaning (such as two extroverted behaviors) are perceived as covarying in the same individual. Also, behaviors which lack similarity of meaning (such as introverted and extroverted behaviors) are assumed *not* to covary in the same person. Shweder (1975) marshaled impressive evidence to support this tendency. Three kinds of data were compared. First, daily check lists of the observed introverted–extroverted behaviors of boys were provided by summer camp counselors. These data might be called the Actual Behavior correlation matrix. Second, the counselors recalled the frequency of these same behaviors at the end of the summer session, providing a Recalled Behavior matrix. Finally, ten of Shweder's students rated the conceptual similarities of these behaviors, generating a Conceptual Similarity matrix. The corresponding values in the three matrices were then compared. This comparison indicated that the correlation between the Recalled Behavior and Conceptual Similarity matrices ($r = .74$) was larger than that between the Actual Behavior and Recalled Behavior matrices ($r = .35$). Thus, when observers attempted to recall the behaviors in question, memory for the actual covariance of behaviors was relatively poor. The recalled covariance appears biased in the direction of an illusion of consistency: Behaviors with consistent meanings were recalled as having covaried within the same individual.

At least under some circumstances, then, observers overestimate the unity of behavior. The data strongly suggest that this tendency plays a role in producing insufficient discounting (Jones, 1979). Further, there is indirect evidence that such a tendency affects judgments involving behavioral prediction and recall. The origins or reasons why observers might overestimate consistency are detailed elsewhere (Nisbett & Ross, 1980; Shweder, 1975). One challenge for future research is to discover the boundary conditions under which an illusion of consistency occurs.

IMPLICIT SOCIAL DESIRABILITY ASSUMPTIONS

A second type of schematic assumption is concerned with social desirability (Ajzen, 1971; Jones & Davis, 1965). For most personality dimensions, one end of the dimension is more socially desirable than the other. For example, on moral dimensions (such as honest–dishonest) it is clear that behavior at the moral end of the continuum is more socially desirable than behavior at the immoral end. Persons occupying various dispositional levels on such a dimension may be assumed likely to direct their efforts toward socially desirable behavior. Thus, observers may assume that most persons will try to behave morally (waiting their turn in line, driving the speed limit, etc.) rather than immorally. This tendency is especially likely when, as is often the case, rewards in the social environment follow socially desirable rather than socially undesirable behavior.

In an effort to explore these assumptions, Reeder et al. (1982) asked observers about the extent to which actors are likely to attempt various behaviors. For example, one pair of questions took the following format: "If a large reward were available for doing so, how likely is it that a person who is very moral (immoral) would try to act very immoral (moral)?" The results clearly support the idea that actors are thought to orient their behavior in the socially desirable direction. Immoral persons are thought highly likely to attempt moral behavior, but moral persons are thought relatively unlikely to attempt immoral behavior. This pattern of assumed implicational relations is shown in Figure 4.4.

Persons with a very immoral disposition are believed likely to attempt behavior spanning the entire continuum from very immoral to very moral (For example, a Mafia chieftain might donate to a charity that publishes a list of its donors). Also, moderate persons are thought to attempt moral behavior more frequently than immoral behavior. Finally, very moral persons are believed to be more or less "restricted" to attempting very moral behavior (see Reeder & Brewer's (1979) description of the hierarchically restrictive schema). In summary, the implicational relations described above show a strong directional tendency toward socially desirable (moral) behavior. The pattern just described is, of course, hardly surprising. However, this assumed pattern gains importance to the extent it influences certain attributional tasks. The following review will focus on asymmetrical discounting and negativity effects when impressions of morality are formed. In each of these areas of research, the role of the social desirability assumption is examined.

ASYMMETRICAL DISCOUNTING IN MORAL ATTRIBUTION

A number of theorists have implied that attributions based on immoral behavior involve different considerations than those following moral behavior (Fincham & Jaspars, 1980; Hamilton, 1980; Kelley, 1971). From the standpoint of implicational relations, it is clear that immoral behavior should appear relatively more informative about the actor's dispositional level. There is a tendency to believe that immoral behavior will be emitted only by persons who actually possess an immoral disposition. Thus, immoral behavior carries a strong message that the actor is immoral. In contrast, moral behavior may often elicit a less certain inference. Both moral *and* immoral persons are thought to act morally

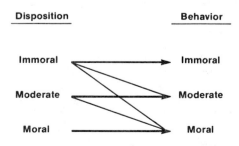

Figure 4.4 Social desirability assumptions showing a directional tendency toward moral behavior.

when it is to their advantage. It follows that attributions based on moral behavior may be less certain and more dependent on situational factors.

The important point is that these implicational relations may set limits on the extent to which discounting is allowed to operate. The implicational relations suggest that, even when there are rewards for immoral behavior, persons with moderate and moral dispositions are thought relatively unlikely to act immorally. Thus, when immoral behavior occurs, observers should be relatively certain the actor is immoral, and little discounting should occur. The research described below lends support to this notion.

In one of the few studies on this topic, Reeder and Spores (1983b) compared attributions based on moral and immoral behavior. In addition to manipulating the actor's behavior, the research also varied situational demands surrounding the behavior. For example, in one scenario a married movie actress is described. She learns that an important movie producer is sexually attracted to her. Prior to meeting with him, she learns that her career will either be helped by sleeping with the producer (immoral demand) or helped by *not* sleeping with him (moral demand). In the latter case, it was clear that the producer preferred to work with serious actresses who did not exploit their sexuality. In the presence of one of these situational demands, the actress committed adultery with the producer (immoral behavior) or did not commit adultery (moral behavior).

Observers judged the actress' level of morality in these various conditions. The implicational relations discussed previously suggest that attributions based on moral behavior will be relatively more subject to discounting than attributions based on immoral behavior. This expectation received support. Attributions based on moral behavior differed significantly as a function of situational demands. In particular, moral behavior in the moral demand condition received a relatively neutral rating. That is, discounting occurred. No such discounting occurred in the immoral behavior condition. Immoral actors were rated relatively immoral regardless of situational demands. Finally, it should be noted that this asymmetrical discounting pattern characterized dispositional attributions but not attributions of causality. Apparently, these two measures are not equivalent in the realm of moral decision making.

NEGATIVITY EFFECTS WHEN IMPRESSIONS ARE FORMED

When forming an impression, observers often integrate several pieces of behavioral information (Anderson, 1974). A striking finding is that negative instances of behavior are given greater weight in the final impression than are positive behaviors (Fiske, 1980; Hamilton & Zanna,

1972; Ostrom & Davis, 1979). For example, an actor who is described by one moral behavior and one immoral behavior is likely to be judged as somewhat immoral. There are many levels of explanation for this robust finding (Kanouse & Hanson, 1972; Peeters, 1971). From the perspective of implicational relations, negative or immoral behavior should be given greater weight because it is considered more diagnostic of the actor's dispositional level (see Figure 4.4). The following sections examine the role of the social desirability assumption in producing a negativity effect.

Impressions of an individual versus a pair of persons. Observers typically assume there is a pattern to an individual's behavior. That is, the behaviors emitted by an individual are not assumed to be a haphazard or random selection from the pool of all possible behaviors. An individual's behavior is expected to form an organized whole (Asch, 1946; Heider, 1958). The social desirability assumption described in Figure 4.4 illustrates one such type of expected organization.

Coovert and Reeder (1985) sought to explore the role of this organization in producing a negativity effect. The research strategy was to compare impressions of an individual with impressions of a social entity which lacked the type of schematic assumptions that apply to an individual. As a means of operationalizing this "control" condition, Reeder and Coovert asked observers to form an impression of a pair of persons. The members of the pair were said to have no relationship with each other. The goal here was to circumvent the "unit formation" (Heider, 1958) or assumed organization that typically underlies impressions of an individual. Specifically, observers may assume that the separate behaviors of unrelated persons do not necessarily obey the social desirability assumption. By definition, this assumption applies only within the context of an individual's behavior. In the absence of this assumed organization, there may be no tendency toward a negativity effect in impressions.

Each stimulus person in the individual condition was described by two behaviors. Each behavior, in turn, was prescaled to represent either high morality (e.g., "rescued a family from a burning house") or low morality (e.g., "used guns on striking workers"). In the pair condition, in contrast, observers judged a pair of stimulus persons. Each stimulus person (in the pair) was described by a single behavior. These behaviors were identical to those employed in the individual condition. The impression rating in the pair condition involved judging the pair as a whole. In summary, the study had a 2 (object of impression: individual vs. pair) × 2 (morality of the first behavior) × 2 (morality of the last behavior) factorial design.

The results reveal a strong negativity effect in the individual condi-

tion: A person described by one moral behavior and one immoral behavior was rated on the immoral side of the scale. In contrast, despite
the fact that judgments were based on identical behaviors, there was no
hint of a negativity effect in the pair condition. The overall impression
of the pair reflected an equal-weight averaging of the stimulus behaviors. This pattern suggests there is something special about impressions
of an individual. From the present perspective this special quality is due
to the assumption that an individual's behavior is organized. The social
desirability assumption describes one aspect of this assumed organization—an aspect that appears to produce a negativity effect in impressions. If observers make assumptions about the organization of behavior
in the pair condition, it is not clear what these assumptions are. It is
reasonable to conclude, however, that the assumed organization for the
pair is not that displayed in Figure 4.4.

Revising an impression of morality. Often times we already possess
an impression of a person. We may have previously labeled them as a
moral or an immoral person. What happens when relevant new information is provided? The present perspective suggests that additional
information that is negative should have more impact than positive information. First, let's consider a person of whom we hold a positive
impression. We expect mainly positive behaviors from such a person. If
we learn that the person has done something immoral—say, poisoned
a neighbor's dog—our image of them is shattered. The impression is
likely to undergo substantial revision.

But consider a person of whom we hold a negative impression. According to the social desirability assumption, we may expect such a person to act in moral was well as immoral ways. Additional information
that the person has acted morally may do little to violate our expectations. Thus little change in our impression is needed. Briscoe, Woodyard, and Shaw (1967) provide evidence of such asymmetrical
impression change. Observers formed an initial impression based on a
paragraph that contained either favorable or unfavorable information
about a person. Then a second evaluatively inconsistent paragraph was
presented. Finally, observers gave a revised impression rating. The results support the argument outlined above. Impressions underwent
greater revision following additional negative (rather than positive) information about the person.

Another study examined response time as observers revised their
impressions (Reeder & Coovert, 1984). According to the reasoning outlined above, the greatest violation of expectations occurs when negative
information is added to a positive impression. Such schema inconsistent

information should greatly increase decision time when a revised impression is formed (Hamilton, Katz, & Leirer, 1980; Markus, 1977). The authors tested this idea by providing observers with an initial set of behaviors that portrayed a stimulus person as either highly moral or highly immoral. Observers then made an initial judgment of the actor's morality.

Response time to form the initial impression did not vary for moral and immoral behavior items. The crucial manipulation involved the presentation in all conditions of a final behavior. This final item (a very moral or very immoral behavior) was always inconsistent with the initial impression. Observers were then requested to provide a second rating of morality. Response time to revise the impression is the main concern. As expected, longer response times occurred when the final item described immoral, as opposed to moral, behavior. It appears, therefore, that when negative information is added to an already existing impression the impression may undergo substantial revision (Briscoe et al., 1967) and the revision itself is relatively time consuming (Reeder & Coovert, 1984).

In summary, there is evidence that a social desirability assumption underlies implicational relations. Persons with undesirable (immoral) dispositions are thought to attempt desirable (moral) behaviors rather frequently. Yet, persons with desirable (moral) dispositions are thought relatively unlikely to attempt undesirable (immoral) behavior. This assumption may set limits on the operation of the discounting principle (Kelley, 1973). Specifically, dispositional attributions of morality based on immoral behavior may be relatively unaffected by situational demands. Finally, these implicational relations may play some role in producing negativity effects in impression formation.

IMPLICIT ABILITY ASSUMPTIONS

Heider (1958) proposed that we are particularly interested in the stable aspects of others' personalities. Perhaps because ability is usually assumed to be stable, it is one of the first judgments we make about others. Heider also theorized that naive observers hold a set of implicit beliefs about how ability operates to shape an actor's behavior. In his discussion of the concept of "can," Heider implied that abilities set limits on a person's behavior. For example, a low level of athletic ability would ordinarily exclude the possibility of an actor's running a 4-minute mile.

Other prominent theorists have similarly discussed the way in which abilities control an actor's range of behavior (Festinger, 1954; Ryle, 1949).

These various accounts share one rather obvious observation: Persons with a high level of ability have a greater range of potential behavior than do persons with a low level of ability. This assumption is also likely to be made by naive observers (Darley & Goethals, 1980).

The implicational relations displayed in Figure 4.5 are based on an ability assumption. Persons with a disposition of high ability are assumed capable of behaviors spanning the entire behavioral continuum (from high ability to low ability). In contrast, persons with moderate and low levels of ability are assumed capable only of behaviors corresponding to their level of ability or behaviors below their level of ability. For example, imagine a movie in which a real life tennis pro plays the part of a rather unathletic musician. If a scene required live action on the tennis court, our tennis pro could probably simulate the musician's low level of tennis skill. But suppose the roles were reversed. The musician is now starring in a picture about a tennis pro. Our assumption now is that any scenes on the tennis court will require a stand-in performer: The musician will be assumed incapable of portraying top quality tennis before the camera.

DISPOSITIONAL ATTRIBUTIONS OF ABILITY

As noted earlier, ability attributions are probably among the first judgments we make about others (Heider, 1958). This importance is reflected in numerous studies of causal attribution in which observers are asked to attribute an actor's achievement behavior to various causes such as ability, effort, task difficulty, and luck (Weiner, 1979). Yet few studies have examined dispositional attributions of ability, or the particular level of ability that is attributed. In everyday life, such judgments are important in our schools, work places, and interpersonal relationships.

We may better understand the reason for this paucity of research if we examine the structure of influential theories of attribution. Heider's (1958) analysis focused on the causal role of ability. These interesting ideas encouraged research on perceived causes (Weiner, 1979), but gave

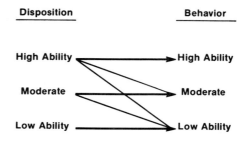

Figure 4.5 Ability assumptions showing a directional tendency toward low-ability behavior.

little direction to research on dispositional attribution. The Jones and Davis (1965) analysis was meant to address dispositional attribution more directly. In their analysis of the attribution process, however, assumptions about the actor's level of ability are a prerequisite to inferences of intentions (and dispositions). That is, the observer decides if the actor possessed a level of ability necessary to have intentionally performed a behavior. This judgment about ability occurs *before* an intention (or disposition) can be deduced. In short, there is a circularity in the model that makes it difficult for the model to handle ability attributions.

The ability assumptions described in Figure 4.5 are a step toward theoretical development in this area. This framework has inspired several studies on the discounting of ability, as described below. Further, these assumptions may play some role in producing primacy effects in ability attribution.

Asymmetrical discounting. Like other schematic assumptions, ability assumptions set limits on discounting. The influence of these assumptions became evident in the course of research by Messick and Reeder. An early experiment (Messick & Reeder, 1972) investigated dispositional attributions of introversion in a job interview scenario. In all conditions observers watched a videotape of a male actor who portrayed himself as introverted. The situational demands surrounding the behavior were manipulated so that the interview situation appeared to demand either introverted or extroverted behavior. When observers judged the actor's level of introversion, there was strong evidence of discounting: lower ratings of introversion occurred when the situation demanded an introverted rather than an extroverted performance.

In a later experiment (Messick & Reeder, 1974), a conceptual replication of the earlier study was undertaken. Only now, the actor portrayed himself as extroverted in the job interview. Little discounting occurred in this study. Regardless of whether the situation demanded introversion or extroversion from the actor, the actor's extroverted behavior led observers to attribute a relatively extroverted disposition. The authors sought to reconcile these findings with their earlier work (Messick & Reeder, 1972) by suggesting that observers might assume extroverted behavior requires more social skill or ability than introverted behavior. Introverts, by this reasoning, might lack the ability to act extroverted. Extroverted behavior could then only have been performed by a "true" extrovert, and accompanying attributions should show little discounting.

Further research (Reeder, Henderson & Sullivan, 1982; Reeder, Messick & Van Avermaet, 1977) tested this ability assumption more directly.

A questionnaire study asked subjects about the role-playing abilities of persons with various dispositions (Reeder et al., 1977). The data from this study clearly indicated that extroverts are believed more capable of introverted behavior than are introverts of extroverted behavior. This kind of asymmetrical role-playing ability was found on other dimensions, including independent–dependent, tolerant–intolerant, optimistic–pessimistic, and intelligent–unintelligent. Assumptions about ability permeate a wide variety of personality dimensions.

Reeder et al. (1977) tested the idea that ability assumptions set limits on discounting. Observers read about a 17-year-old male actor who was attending a high school party. At the party he met an attractive young woman who professed an interest in either intellectual (high-ability) or nonintellectual (low-ability) dating partners. In response to these situational demands, the actor portrayed himself as intellectual in one case and as nonintellectual in another. Observers were asked to rate the actor's intellectuality (or ability). The ability assumptions dictate that only persons with high intelligence are thought capable of highly intelligent behavior and, therefore, attributions based on such behavior should be relatively unaffected by situational demands. In other words, there should be little discounting. Indeed, the data showed that attributions based on low-ability behavior, but not high-ability behavior, were strongly affected by situational demands. The actor in the high-ability (intellectuality) condition was attributed a rather high level of intellectuality regardless of situational demands.

A further study (Reeder, 1979) replicated this finding by showing observers a videotape of an actor playing billiards. Once again attributions of ability (at billiards) based on a skillful performance were relatively unaffected by situational demands. Also, observers showed some evidence of being more certain of their judgments in the high-ability compared to the low-ability conditions.

Would this pattern occur if the actor merely claimed high ability without actually demonstrating his or her talent? Apparently not. Reeder & Fulks (1980) compared attributions based on an overt portrayal of ability with those based on a mere verbal claim of ability. In the overt portrayal condition, observers were shown an actual drawing prepared by a 14-year-old actor. The drawing was well done in one case and a hopeless scribble in another. In the verbal portrayal condition, in contrast, the actor verbally claimed to possess either high ability ("I'm really good at art") or low ability ("I'm not very good at art at all. I'm terrible at it."). Finally, in both the overt and verbal portrayal conditions, situational demands were present for either high- or low-ability behavior. Observers' attributions of artistic ability followed the expected asymmetrical pattern in the overt portrayal condition: attributions based on high-ability behavior were relatively unaffected by situational demands. No sign of asymmetrical discounting was found in the verbal portrayal condition. Instead, attributions in the high- and low-ability cases were both strongly affected by situational demands. It appears that asymmetrical discounting is limited to conditions when the actor provides an actual demonstration of his or her level of ability.

Primacy effects. Jones and his colleagues (Jones, Rock, Shaver, Goethals & Ward, 1968) report a strong primacy effect in the attribution of ability: early information about ability seems to count more than later information. As part of their study, observers learned about an actor who had solved 15 problems out of a series of 30 items. Observers watched the actor work on the problems one at a time. In one condition, it was clear that the 15 solutions had occurred mainly among the early rather than later items in the series (descending condition). In a second condition, the 15 solutions occurred mainly at the end of the series (ascending condition).

Observers were asked to make several judgments about the actor, including a rating of the actor's intelligence. These ratings revealed that the actor in the descending condition—who had solved more problems at the beginning of the series—was perceived more intelligent than one whose solutions occurred at the end. In addition, the descending actor was perceived as solving more problems than the ascending actor. This pattern has been replicated in several more recent studies (Benassi, 1982; Newtson & Rindner, 1979).

An explanation of this finding concerns the point at which observers feel they have sufficient information to make a judgment of ability. Once a subjectively sufficient amount of information is obtained, later information may be ignored. The point at which observers begin to feel confident about the actor's ability may vary for high and low performance. Successful performance may prompt observers to form an early confident attribution about ability. Moreover, given an assumption of high ability, later evidence of unsuccessful performance may be attributed to low motivation. As noted earlier, persons with high ability are assumed capable of low as well as high performance. An early (premature) judgment of high ability could easily lead to error, particularly in a case where performance deteriorates over time.

In contrast, early unsuccessful performance may promote uncertainty (Reeder, 1979). Both high- and low-ability persons are thought capable of an unsuccessful performance. Thus, observers may delay their judgments until later in the series. If so, we might expect more accurate judgments in the ascending condition. The data support this notion. For example, Benassi (1982) reports that descending performers were estimated to have solved 22.18 problems, whereas ascending performers were estimated to have solved 13.18 problems. Given that 15 problems were actually solved, observers in the ascending condition are clearly closer to the mark.

In sum, research on dispositional attributions of ability is concentrated in areas concerned with discounting and primacy effects. In each of these areas an application of the present framework helps to organize experimental findings.

A final point concerns the possibility of identifying particular traits with unique schematic assumptions. Reeder and Brewer (1979) initially proposed that many traits could be identified with a characteristic pattern of implicational relations. For example, traits concerned with ability were said to follow a hierarchically restrictive pattern in which one extreme of the trait continuum is behaviorally restricted and the other is not. Thus, an intelligent person is capable of both intelligent and unintelligent behavior, but an unintelligent person is capable of only unintelligent behavior.

The present analysis is a step toward specifying the schematic assumptions that underlie common implicational patterns. Thus, an ability assumption underlies the hierarchically restrictive pattern of implicational relations for intelligence. Of potentially greater importance, this new approach suggests that more than one schematic assumption may be important for a trait, depending on the type of inference to be made (Reeder et al., 1982). Central tendency assumptions, for example, are probably present when observers estimate the general frequency or variability of ability-related behaviors (intelligent persons are assumed to act at least moderately intelligent most of the time). Under some circumstances, social desirability assumptions might also be relevant to inferences of ability. Observers assume that persons with both high and low ability will ordinarily try to perform at a (socially desirable) high level. In cases where high effort is a sufficient determinant of behavior (for example, when an actor verbally describes him or herself as having high ability), the behavior may not lead to a strong inference of ability (Reeder & Fulks, 1980). In summary, depending on the situation, more than one schematic assumption could apply to a given trait.

THE CONCEPT OF DISPOSITION

The concept of disposition is widely used by psychologists interested in personality and attribution processes. Yet, until recently, it has received only limited theoretical attention in the psychological literature (Buss & Craik, 1983; Fletcher, 1984; Sabini & Silver, 1982). Two major approaches can be distinguished. First, dispositions may be viewed as causal entities that give rise to specific behaviors. In the area of personality psychology, for example, Allport (1966) proposed that "Traits are cortical, . . . having the capacity to gate or guide phasic reactions. . . ." (p. 3). Attribution theorists (Heider, 1958; Jones & Davis, 1965; Kelley, 1967; 1973) have portrayed the social perceiver as searching for the underlying causal relations governing behavior. In their view, observers find trait descriptions useful precisely because traits are perceived to be the causes of stable behavior patterns. This assumption has received wide acceptance in the field. Researchers have routinely asked observers to make a forced choice between attributing an actor's behavior to situational or dispositional causes. Under these circumstances, observers display a tendency to prefer dispositional causes over situational causes as the explanation of behavior (Jones & Nisbett, 1972; Watson, 1982). To date, however, the exact meaning of the assumed causal connection between disposition and behavior is left unclear.

Early attribution models assume that a causal analysis precedes the attribution of specific dispositional qualities. According to these models, observers allocate causality between situational (external) causes and dispositional (internal) causes *before* attributing a specific dispositional level. The evidence does not support this sequence. For example, Smith and Miller (1983) utilized a clever reaction time paradigm to assess the time needed to respond ("yes" or "no") to various questions. Their subjects responded faster when asked about the actor's traits and intentions than when asked about the situational or dispositional causes of behavior. Additional research indicates that causal attributions are affected by different variables than are dispositional attributions (Harvey & Rule, 1978; Reeder & Fulks, 1980). For example, even when behavior is attributed primarily to external causes (and not to internal causes), observers may still attribute a disposition that corresponds to the observed behavior (Reeder & Spores, 1983b). This pattern is unlikely if causal attributions are mediating dispositional attributions. It is probably true that observers often consider situational influences before attributing a disposition to the actor. The observer's use of reinforcement assumptions describes this sequence. But there are neither logical nor empirical reasons to believe that a full causal analysis must precede dispositional attribution (Eiser, 1983).

An alternative view suggests that dispositions summarize observed regularities in behavior. In the field of personality, this approach has been advanced by Buss and Craik (1983). Alston (1975) similarly proposed that certain traits like sociability and persistence are related to behaviors directly on the basis of frequency. Thus, we say a friend is sociable on the basis of frequent observations of our friend's outgoing behavior. In contrast to "frequency traits," other traits have a less direct connection to behavior. Traits involving needs, values, attitudes, and abilities, which Alston calls "purposive-cognitive" traits, are not related to behavior on the basis of mere frequency. For example, a person may have an ability that he rarely exercises. Or "A person may have a strong need for close relationships, but because of a fear of rejection rarely or never seeks to satisfy it," (Alston, 1975, p. 22).

The present approach to attribution likewise conceives of dispositions as summary categories for observed behavior. Observers often employ dispositions to describe a range of behavior that has been observed in the past. Additionally, observers may use dispositions to predict future behavior. The rules governing this range of expected behavior form the major substance of this chapter. Of course, observers also endow dispositions with causal force. However, as Fletcher (1984) implies, this tendency is probably stronger for some types of dispositions (e.g., abilities) than others (e.g., punctuality). The question of whether implicational relations can appropriately be regarded as *causal* relations merits further study.

The present analysis has focused on the disposition–behavior link. Notably missing is the concept of *intention* (Jones & Davis, 1965; Maselli & Altrocchi, 1969). In the Jones & Davis (1965) theory, the process of attribution consists of (1) observing behavior, (2) noting the uniqueness and social desirability of the effects produced by behavior, (3) judging whether the actor had the knowledge or ability to produce these effects, (4) inferring the actor's intention, and (5) inferring a disposition. Only acts which are intentional are presumed to give rise to dispositional inferences. Jones and Davis (1965) are probably correct that unintentional acts are less directly related to corresponding dispositional judgments than are intentional acts. Thus, some harmful acts done unintentionally may not be seen as reflecting a mean or harmful disposition.

Yet observers often rely on unintentional behavior when inferring dispositional qualities (Eiser, 1983). Heider's (1958) analysis of responsibility implies that even in the absence of intentionality, harmful acts which are merely associated with an actor (global association), are committed by the actor (commission), and have foreseeable consequences (foreseeability) may be held against the actor. Thus, a parent's unintentional domination of his or her children may be taken as strong evidence that the parent is "domineering." As a second example, consider the case of dispositional attributions of ability. An athletic competitor who fails miserably in an attempt to break a record may be attributed low ability. Yet it is clear that failure was not the competitor's intention. As these examples suggest, the inference of intention need not be viewed as a precondition for dispositional attribution.

AN ASPECT OF IMPLICIT PERSONALITY THEORY

Research on implicit personality theory has concentrated almost exclusively on the implicative relations between traits (Bruner, Shapiro & Taguiri, 1958) or on the dimensions underlying trait similarity or meaning (Rosenberg & Sedlak, 1972). These efforts have vastly increased our understanding of implicit relations among traits. As Schneider (1973) points out, however, implicit relations between traits (dispositions) and behaviors remain largely unexplored.

Cantor and Mischel's work (1979) represents an exception to this trend. According to their concept of implicit personality theory, social information is organized by a hierarchical system of categories (Rosch & Mervis, 1975). Widely applicable trait types, such as extrovert, represent the most general categories or prototypes, whereas more specific traits and behaviors are organized around the general categories. Unlike most past work on implicit personality theory, which has remained strangely isolated from other areas of social cognition, Cantor and Mischel have applied their perspective to tasks involving the inference of traits (categorization), behavior prediction, and recall of social information.

The present concept of implicational schema (Reeder & Brewer, 1979) focuses exclusively on relations between dispositions and behaviors. In this respect, the domain of the model falls within the more general pattern of relations described by Cantor & Mischel (1979). Another similarity between these approaches is that basic findings are applied directly to other areas of social cognition, particularly dispositional attribution.

CONCLUSION

This chapter explored implicational relations between dispositions and behaviors. The analysis highlighted several key factors that may govern these relations. Two general classes of implicit assumptions—reinforcement assumptions and schematic assumptions—were tentatively proposed. Reinforcement assumptions describe observers' awareness that actors vary their behavior to meet situational demands in the environment. Schematic assumptions, in contrast, are concerned with the range of behaviors a given disposition implies. Schematic assumptions of central tendency, social desirability, and ability may be particularly important.

This approach provides a potentially comprehensive explanation of dispositional discounting (Kelley, 1973). According to the discounting tendency, when situational demands appear to have facilitated an actor's behavior, observers discount an implied disposition (in the direction of making a more moderate dispositional inference). The theoretical account offered here focuses on the role of reinforcement assumptions in producing such discounting. More important, perhaps, are the factors that moderate discounting. Schematic assumptions of central tendency, social desirability, and ability are proposed as setting limits on the extent of discounting. This analysis helps explain limited discounting in such diverse areas as attitude, morality, and ability attribution.

The present perspective is both narrow and broad in its scope. While other attributional models have focused on intentions or causal attributions, the present approach is somewhat narrowly focused on dispositional attributions. Neither the inference of intentions nor causes is viewed as a necessary prerequisite of dispositional attribution. Also, from the standpoint of implicit personality theory, a concern with the disposition–behavior link is similarly narrow. This domain represents only a subset of the prototype-based scheme described by Cantor and Mischel (1979).

On the other hand, the model cuts across a broad array of research topics. In the areas of attribution, both rational and apparently irrational tendencies (i.e., insufficient discounting) are addressed. The model also directs attention to the neglected interconnections that exist between implicit personality theory and attribution. Finally, the model offers insights into areas somewhat peripheral to attribution. For example, the schematic assumptions of social desirability and ability hold the promise of enriching our understanding of the process of impression formation. These assumptions may affect the manner in which information about morality and ability is integrated to form an impression. Future research may find still other applications for these concepts.

REFERENCES

Ajzen, I. (1971). Attribution of dispositions to an actor: Effects of perceived decision freedom and behavior utilities. *Journal of Personality and Social Psychology, 18,* 144–156.

Ajzen, I., & Fishbein, M. (1983). Relevance and availability in the attribution process. In J. Jaspars, F. Fincham, & M. Hewstone (Eds.), *Attribution theory and research: Conceptual, developmental and social dimensions.* London: Academic Press.

Allport, G. W. (1966). Traits revisited. *American Psychologist, 21,* 1–10.

Alston, W. P. (1975). Traits, consistency and conceptual alternatives for personality theory. *Journal for the Theory of Social Behavior, 5,* 17–48.

Anderson, N. H. (1974). Cognitive algebra: Integration theory applied to social attribution. In L. Berkowitz (Ed.), *Advances in experimental social psychology.* (Vol. 7). New York: Academic Press.

Asch, S. E. (1946). Forming impressions of personality. *Journal of Abnormal and Social Psychology, 41,* 258–290.

Benassi, V. (1982). Effects of order of presentation, primacy, and physical attractiveness on attributions of ability. *Journal of Personality and Social Psychology, 43,* 48–58.

Briscoe, M. E., Woodyard, H. D., & Shaw, M. E. (1967). Personality impression change as a function of the favorableness of first impressions. *Journal of Personality, 35,* 343–357.

Bruner, G. S., Shapiro, D., & Tagiuri, R. (1958). The meaning of traits in isolation and in combination. In R. Tagiuri & L. Petrullo (Eds.), *Person perception and interpersonal behavior.* Stanford, CA: Stanford University Press.

Buss, D. M., & Craik, K. H. (1983). The act frequency approach to personality. *Psychological Review, 90,* 105–126.

Cantor, N., & Mischel, W. (1979). Prototypes in person perception. In L. Berkowitz (Ed.), *Advances in experimental social psychology* (Vol. 12). New York: Academic Press.

Carrol, J. S., Galegher, J., & Weiner, R. (1982, August). Dimensional and categorical attributions in expert parole decisions. Paper presented at the meeting of the American Psychological Association, Washington, D.C.

Cline, V. B. (1964). Interpersonal perception. In B. A. Maher (Ed.), *Progress in experimental personality research* (Vol. 1). New York: Academic Press.

Cook, M. (1979). *Perceiving others.* London: Methuen.

Coovert, M. D., & Reeder, G. D. (1985). *Impressions of morality: Differences when the target is an individual vs. a pair of persons.* Manuscript in preparation.

Cronbach, L. J. (1955). Processes affecting scores on "understanding of others" and "assumed similarity." *Psychological Bulletin, 52,* 177–193.

Darley, J. M., & Goethals, G. R. (1980). People's analyses of the causes of ability-linked performances. In L. Berkowitz (Ed.), *Advances in experimental social psychology* (Vol. 13). New York: Academic Press.

Eiser, J. R. (1983). Attribution theory and social cognition. In J. Jaspars, F. Fincham, & M. Hewstone (Eds.), *Attribution theory and research: Conceptual, developmental and social dimensions.* London: Academic Press.

Festinger, L. (1954). A theory of social comparison processes. *Human Relations, 7,* 117–140.

Fiedler, K. (1982). Causal schemata: Review and criticism of research on a popular construct. *Journal of Personality and Social Psychology, 42,* 1001–1013.

Fincham, F. D., & Jaspars, J. M. (1980). Attribution of responsibility: From man the scientist to man as lawyer. In L. Berkowitz (Ed.), *Advances in experimental social psychology* (Vol. 13). New York: Academic Press.

Fiske, S. T. (1980). Attention and weight in person perception: The impact of negative and extreme behavior. *Journal of Personality and Social Psychology, 38,* 889–906.

Fletcher, G. J. O. (1984). Psychology and common sense. *American Psychologist, 39,* 203–213.

Funder, D. C. (1982). On the accuracy of dispositional versus situational attributions. *Social Cognition, 1,* 205–222.

Hamilton, D. L., Katz, L. B., & Leirer, V. O. (1980). Organizational processes in impression formation. In R. Hastie, T. M. Ostrom, E. B. Ebbesen, R. S. Wyer, D. L. Hamilton, & D. E. Carlston (Eds.), *Person memory: The cognitive basis of social perception.* Hillsdale, N.J.: Erlbaum.

Hamilton, D. L., & Zanna, M. P. (1972). Differential weighting of favorable and unfavorable attributes in impressions of personality. *Journal of Experimental Research in Personality, 6,* 204–212.

Hamilton, V. L. (1980). Intuitive psychologist or intuitive lawyer? Alternative models of the attribution process. *Journal of Personality and Social Psychology, 39,* 767–772.

Harvey, J. H., Town, J. P., & Yarkin, K. L. (1981). How fundamental is "The fundamental attribution error"? *Journal of Personality and Social Psychology, 40,* 346–349.

Harvey, M. D., & Rule, B. G. (1978). Moral evaluations and judgments of responsibility. *Personality and Social Psychology Bulletin, 4,* 583–588.

Heider, F. (1958). *The psychology of interpersonal relations.* New York: Wiley.

Ichheiser, G. (1970). *Appearances and realities.* San Francisco: Jossey-Bass.

Jones, E. E. (1978). Update of "From acts to dispositions: The attribution process in person perception." In L. Berkowitz (Ed.), *Cognitive theories in social psychology.* New York: Academic Press.

Jones, E. E. (1979). The rocky road from acts to dispositions. *American Psychologist, 34,* 107–117.

Jones, E. E., & Davis, K. E. (1965). From acts to dispositions: The attribution process in person perception. In L. Berkowitz (Ed.), *Advances in experimental social psychology* (Vol. 2). New York: Academic Press.

Jones, E. E., Davis, K. E., & Gergen, K. J. (1961). Role playing variations and their informational value for person perception. *Journal of Abnormal and Social Psychology, 63,* 302–310.

Jones, E. E., & Harris, V. A. (1967). The attribution of attitudes. *Journal of Experimental Social Psychology, 3,* 1–24.

Jones, E. E., & McGillis, D. (1976). Correspondent inferences and the attribution cube: A comparative reappraisal. In J. Harvey, W. Ickes, & R. Kidd (Eds.), *New directions in attribution research* (Vol. 1). Hillsdale, N.J.: Erlbaum.

Jones, E. E., & Nisbett, R. E. (1972). The actor and the observer: Divergent perceptions of the causes of behavior. In E. E. Jones, D. E. Kanouse, H. H. Kelley, R. E. Nisbett, S. Valins, & B. Weiner (Eds.), *Attribution: Perceiving the causes of behavior.* Morristown, N.J.: General Learning Press.

Jones, E. E., Rock, L., Shaver, K. G., Goethals, G. R., & Ward, L. M. (1968). Pattern of performance and ability attribution: An unexpected primacy effect. *Journal of Personality and Social Psychology, 10,* 317–341.

Kanouse, D. E., & Hanson, L. R. (1972). Negativity in evaluations. In E. E. Jones, D. E. Kanouse, H. H. Kelley, R. E. Nisbett, S. Valins, & B. Weiner (Eds.), *Attribution: Perceiving the causes of behavior.* Morristown, N.J.: General Learning Press.

Kelley, H. H. (1967). Attribution theory in social psychology. In D. Levine (Ed.), *Nebraska Symposium on Motivation.* (Vol. 15). Lincoln: University of Nebraska Press.

Kelley, H. H. (1971). Moral evaluation. *American Psychologist, 26,* 293–300.

Kelley, H. H. (1973). The process of causal attribution. *American Psychologist, 28,* 107–128.

Kelley, H. H., & Michela, J. L. (1980). Attribution theory and research. In M. R. Rosenzweig, & L. W. Porter (Eds.), *Annual Review of Psychology* (Vol. 31). Palo Alto, Calif.: Annual Reviews Inc.

Kruglanski, A. W. (1980). Lay epistemo-logic-process and contents: Another look at attribution theory. *Psychological Review, 87,* 70–87.

Lay, C. H., Burron, B. F., & Jackson, D. N. (1973). Base rates and information value in impression formation. *Journal of Personality and Social Psychology, 28,* 390–395.

Locke, D., & Pennington, D. (1982). Reasons and other causes: Their role in attribution processes. *Journal of Personality and Social Psychology, 42,* 212–223.

Markus, H. (1977). Self-schemata and processing information about the self. *Journal of Personality and Social Psychology, 35,* 63–78.

Maselli, M. D., & Altrocchi, J. (1969). Attribution of intent. *Psychological Bulletin, 71,* 445–454.

Messick, D. M., & Reeder, G. (1972). Perceived motivation, role variations, and the attribution of personal characteristics. *Journal of Experimental Social Psychology, 8,* 482–491.

Messick, D. M., & Reeder, G. D. (1974). Roles, occupations, behaviors, and attributions. *Journal of Experimental Social Psychology, 10,* 126–132.

Miller, A. G., Baer, R., & Schonberg, P. (1979). The bias phenomenon in attitude attribution: Actor and observer perspectives. *Journal of Personality and Social Psychology, 37,* 1421–1431.

Miller, A. G., Mayerson, N., Pogue, M., & Whitehouse, D. (1977). Perceiver's explanations of their attributions of attitude. *Personality and Social Psychology Bulletin, 3,* 111–114.

Miller, A. G., & Rorer, L. G. (1982). On "the rocky road from acts to dispositions": Conceptions of essay diagnosticity in the attitude attribution paradigm. *Journal of Research in Personality, 16,* 41–59.

Mischel, W. (1968). *Personality and assessment.* New York: Wiley.

Napolitan, D. A., & Goethals, G. R. (1979). The attribution of friendliness. *Journal of Experimental Social Psychology, 15,* 105–113.

Newtson, D., & Rindner, R. J. (1979). Variation in behavior perception and ability attribution. *Journal of Personality and Social Psychology, 37,* 1847–1858.

Nisbett, R., & Ross, L. (1980). *Human inference: Strategies and shortcomings of social judgment.* Englewood Cliffs, N.J.: Prentice-Hall, Inc.

Ostrom, T. M., & Davis, D. (1979). Idiosyncratic weighting of trait information in impression formation. *Journal of Personality and Social Psychology, 37,* 2025–2043.

Peeters, G. (1971). The positive–negative asymmetry: On cognitive consistency and positivity bias. *European Journal of Social Psychology, 1,* 455–474.

Reeder, G. D. (1979). Context effects for attributions of ability. *Personality and Social Psychology Bulletin, 5,* 65–68.

Reeder, G. D. (1982). Let's give the "fundamental attribution error" another chance. *Journal of Personality and Social Psychology, 43,* 341–344.

Reeder, G. D. (1984, May). *Searching for a criterion of error in the attitude attribution paradigm.* Paper presented at the meeting of the Midwestern Psychological Association, Chicago, IL.

Reeder, G. D., & Brewer, M. B. (1979). A schematic model of dispositional attribution in interpersonal perception. *Psychological Review, 86,* 61–79.

Reeder, G. D., & Coovert, M. D. (1984, August). *Revising an impression of morality: A reaction time analysis.* Paper presented at the meeting of the American Psychological Association, Toronto.

Reeder, G. D., & Fulks, J. L. (1980). When actions speak louder than words: Implicational schemata and the attribution of ability. *Journal of Experimental Social Psychology, 16,* 33–46.

Reeder, G. D., Henderson, D. J., & Sullivan, J. J. (1982). From dispositions to behaviors: The flip side of attribution. *Journal of Research in Personality, 16,* 355–375.

Reeder, G. D., Messick, D. M., & Van Avermaet, E. (1977). Dimensional asymmetry in attributional inference. *Journal of Experimental Social Psychology, 13,* 46–57.

Reeder, G. D. & Spores, J. M. (1983a, May). *Individual differences in the attitude attribution paradigm.* Paper presented at the meeting of the Midwestern Psychological Association, Chicago, IL.

Reeder, G. D., & Spores, J. M. (1983b). The attribution of morality. *Journal of Personality and Social Psychology, 44,* 736–745.

Rosch, E., & Mervis, C. (1975). Family resemblances: Studies in the internal structure of categories. *Cognitive Psychology, 7,* 573–605.

Rosenberg, S., & Sedlak, A. (1972). Structural representations of implicit personality theory. In L. Berkowitz (Ed.)., *Advances in experimental social psychology* (Vol. 6). New York: Academic Press.

Ross, M., & Fletcher, G. (1985). Attribution and social perception. In G. Lindzey & E. Aronson (Eds.), *The handbook of social psychology* (3rd ed.). San Francisco: Random House.

Ryle, G. (1949). *The concept of mind.* London: Hutchinson's University Library.

Sabini, J., & Silver, M. (1982). *Moralities of everyday life.* Oxford, England: Oxford University Press.

Schneider, D. J. (1973). Implicit personality theory: A review. *Psychological Bulletin, 79,* 294–309.

Shaver, K. G. (1981). Back to basics: On the role of theory in the attribution of causality. In J. Harvey, W. Ickes, & R. Kidd (Eds.), *New directions in attribution research* (Vol. 3). Hillsdale, N.J.: Erlbaum.

Shultz, T. R., & Schleifer, M. (1983). Towards a refinement of attribution concepts. In J. Jaspars, F. Fincham, & M. Hewstone (Eds.), *Attribution theory and research: Conceptual, developmental and social dimensions.* London: Academic Press.

Shweder, R. A. (1975). How relevant is an individual difference theory of personality? *Journal of Personality, 43,* 445–485.

Smith, E. R., & Miller, F. D. (1983). Mediation among attributional inferences and comprehension processes: Initial findings and a general method. *Journal of Personality and Social Psychology, 44,* 492–505.

Snyder, M. L., & Jones, E. E. (1974). Attitude attribution when behavior is constrained. *Journal of Experimental Social Psychology, 10,* 585–600.

Taylor, S. E., & Crocker, J. (1981). *Is the social perceiver a behaviorist or a trait theorist?* Unpublished manuscript.

Tversky, A., & Kahneman, D. (1974). Judgment under uncertainty: Heuristics and biases. *Science, 185,* 1124–1131.

Watson, D. (1982). The actor and the observer: How are their perceptions of causality divergent? *Psychological Bulletin, 92,* 682–700.

Weiner, B. (1979). A theory of motivation for some classroom experiences. *Journal of Educational Psychology, 71,* 3–25.

CHAPTER 5

Motivation and Attribution: The Effects of Control Deprivation on Subsequent Information Processing*

Thane S. Pittman and Paul R. D'Agostino

INTRODUCTION

The title of McArthur's (1972) attribution paper, "The How and What of Why," points to the predominant focus of traditional attribution research, that is, on discovering *what* attributions people make, and *how* they use available information to come to those particular attributions. In the typical attribution study, the experimenter provides information about a behavior and the context in which it occurred, and then asks the subject to answer questions that require making inferences from the information provided. By varying the nature of the behavior and the situation in which it occurs, the investigator is then able to study what inferences will be made given a particular set of information and can discover how the subjects have weighted and combined the available information to come to their attributional conclusions. This strategy has been quite productive, but it leaves aside questions of *when* persons will spontaneously engage in such attributional analyses, since in these studies subjects are explicitly asked to do so. However, it seems intuitively clear that people do not always bother to make attributions about every piece of behavioral information that comes their way, and this fact has been demonstrated in a variety of experimental settings (e.g., Enzle & Schopflocher, 1978; Pittman, Scherrer, & Wright, 1977). A more complete understanding of the way in which attributions play a role in social

*This chapter and the authors' research reported in it were supported by National Science Foundation grants BNS 78-17440 to Thane S. Pittman, and BNS 81-11829 to Thane S. Pittman and Paul R. D'Agostino. We thank Victoria Esses for her comments on an earlier version of this chapter.

117

behavior, then, requires that we focus research on the related questions of when people are likely to initiate attributional activity and why they do so.

RECENT RESEARCH ON THE INSTIGATION OF ATTRIBUTIONAL ACTIVITY

CHARACTERISTICS OF THE STIMULUS INFORMATION

One recent approach taken to investigate under what conditions attributional analyses will be instigated has been to look for features in the stimulus information that might trigger attributions. One finding revealed that unexpected information seems to trigger attributional analyses (Clary & Tesser, 1983; Hastie, 1984; Pyszczynski & Greenberg, 1981; Wong & Weiner, 1981). Another finding disclosed that negative outcomes, both for self and others, seem to stimulate attributional questions (Harvey, Yarkin, Lightner, & Town, 1980; Wong & Weiner, 1981). This general approach appears to be quite useful, but it leads to perhaps a more interesting kind of question: What is it about people that sensitizes them to these features of stimulus information?

INVOLVEMENT WITH THE TARGET PERSON AND WITH THE SITUATION

A second research approach has been to hold the nature of the stimulus information constant and to vary the nature of the perceiver's involvement in the setting. For example, expectations of future interaction with the target person appear to encourage attributional activity (Bersheid, Graziano, Monson & Dermer, 1976; Harvey et al., 1980; Miller, Norman, & Wright, 1978). Likewise, increased involvement with the issue in question through commitment or personal relevance has been shown to trigger attributions (Heller, 1972; Pittman et al., 1977). The Jones and Davis (1965) analyses of personalism and hedonic relevance are also examples of this general approach. These kinds of studies focus more explicitly on the characteristics of perceivers that may lead to the instigation of attributional analyses and raise directly the issue of motivational states of the perceiver that may trigger an interest in drawing inferences from available information.

How might the variety of findings on characteristics of the stimulus information and of the involvement of the perceiver be organized in a more general framework? In the remainder of this chapter we will present an analysis of a general motive that may underly all of these findings, and will review a program of research designed to test and explore a variety of implications of this viewpoint.

CONTROL MOTIVATION AND ATTRIBUTIONAL ACTIVITY

What does motivate us to make attributional analyses? Perhaps Kelley's (1967, 1971) suggestion that we make attributions in order to render the world predictable and controllable is a reasonable place to begin. Kelley suggested that this is the general orientation that disposes us to create causal explanations for the events in our social surroundings. The recent findings on the effects of unexpected information on attributional activity make sense from this point of view. Features in the stimulus information such as unexpected (i.e., not already explained) events, or unusually negative outcomes (which might also be considered to be unexpected), would be precisely the kinds of events that a control-motivated organism should be seeking to explain. However, if the stimulus context is held constant, then additional assumptions about the nature of control motivation need to be made to explain why such information sometimes is and sometimes is not subjected to attributional analysis.

How can we use the concept of control motivation to explain why we sometimes construct causal explanations for particular events, and sometimes do not? The most direct expansion of the control-motivation hypothesis is simply to add the assumption that control motivation is not always the same. When control motivation is strong, we are more likely to be interested in forming attributions than when control motivation is weak. The findings concerning the effects of anticipated future interaction and increased issue involvement on attributional activity can be understood in this light, since control concerns ought to be enhanced by either variable. Neither of these sets of findings, however, can be seen as general tests of our proposed expansion of the control-motivation hypothesis, since the source of increased control motivation and the target of attributional analysis are so closely related. A test of the proposed hypothesis would be relatively straightforward: Create two groups of subjects differing in the strength of control motivation, present information to them in a subsequent, unrelated setting which might be used to form attributions, and compare the tendency to form attributions of the two groups. If the expanded control-motivation hypothesis is correct, then the group with the stronger control motivation should be more likely to engage in attributional analysis.

What might increase or decrease the strength of control motivation? If a person's conceptualizations seem to be working well, that is, if the person is not making erroneous predictions or being confronted with events that imply that he or she does not understand the world in which we live, then control through attributional analysis may not be a particularly strong concern. If, however, one is confronted with an experience that calls his or her conceptualizations into question, that implies that her or his understanding of the world is inadequate, then the motivation to come to a better (and safer) understanding of the environs should increase. In other words, we propose that control motivation can be increased by exposing a person to an experience that, by temporarily depriving the person of control, calls into question his or her ability to predict and control.

This was the approach taken in Pittman and Pittman's (1980) test of the control motivation–attributional activity hypothesis. First, subjects were given an experience with a concept-formation task. The baseline group was shown the task, which consisted of six 10-trial concept-formation problems. They then proceeded to guess on each trial without any feedback, ostensibly to provide a correction for guessing for future use of the test. In other words, while baseline subjects had exposure to the same task used in the experimental conditions, nothing about their experience with the task suggested inadequacy in their conceptualizations. In the experimental conditions, subjects were given random correct–incorrect feedback on two of the problems (low control deprivation) or on all six of the problems (high control deprivation). In both experimental groups, then, subjects were shown a task that appeared to be amenable to analysis and were urged to try to do their best. They then discovered that no matter how hard they tried or what strategy they employed, they could do no better than chance on the problems.

After the concept formation session was completed, subjects were taken to a second experimenter for the second of the two "mini-experiments" for which they had volunteered. The second experimenter, blind to the conditions created by the first experimenter, administered the attribution materials, a mood checklist, and an anagram solution task. The attribution materials used in the second session had been shown to be sensitive to variations in the tendency to utilize available information when forming attributions (Pittman et al., 1977). An informational variation was embedded in a description of a communicator on the first page: Half of the subjects were told that the communicator had written the essay on the following page for payment (external motivational information condition), and the other half were told that the communicator had written the essay in his private journal and had not originally intended that it be published (internal motivational information condition). This information was followed by an essay (on locating nuclear power plants near populated areas), and a set of questions about the communication and the communicator.

The major dependent variable was the amount of external influence attributed by the subjects to the communicator in explaining his motivation for writing the essay. As can be seen in Table 5.1, the attributions of subjects who had been deprived of control were more affected by variations in motivational information than were baseline subjects. A similar pattern of effects was obtained on several other questions about the communicator, including intent to persuade and the extent to which the essay actually represented the author's own opinion. In both the high- and low-deprivation conditions, prior control deprivation did lead to increased utilization of the available attribution-relevant information.

The Pittman and Pittman (1980) data are consistent with the control-deprivation hypothesis prediction, and show that control deprivation led to increased utilization of the available attribution-relevant information. There are, however, a number of possibilities which may explain how this happened. For example, perhaps the control-deprived subjects encoded the motivational information more carefully or with more efficiency, or they may have been more likely to draw inferences at the time information was presented or when the attribution questions were asked, or they tried harder to remember the motivational information at time of recall. The general question here concerns what control-deprived subjects did differently than baseline subjects with the information available to them. To address this question, we designed several studies to explore the information-processing changes produced by prior control deprivation.

Table 5.1

AMOUNT OF EXTERNAL INFLUENCE ATTRIBUTED TO THE WRITER[a]

Control deprivation	Motivational information	
	External	Internal
High	6.29	2.94 •
Low	6.47	1.59
None	5.47	4.06

[a]The higher the score, the greater the external influence on the 7-point scale. Adapted from Pittman & Pittman (1980).

CHANGES IN INFORMATION-PROCESSING STRATEGY FOLLOWING CONTROL DEPRIVATION

Through what process did control-deprived subjects in the Pittman and Pittman (1980) study accomplish their increased utilization of available information in forming attributions? One interesting possibility is that control deprivation may lead subjects to adopt a cautious, conservative information-processing strategy designed to increase the accuracy of their subsequent judgments and decisions. If control deprivation does produce such an information-processing strategy, then control-deprived subjects should be superior to baseline subjects in subsequent cognitive tasks that require careful, accurate processing of input material.

D'Agostino and Pittman (1984) examined the performance of control-deprived and baseline subjects on a sentence recognition task. Following experience with either the baseline or the high-control deprivation procedure from Pittman and Pittman (1980), all subjects studied a list of sentence pairs, some of which consisted of statements which suggested an obvious inference. For example, the sentences (1) John rarely studies for any of his courses and (2) John always gets good grades strongly imply that (3) John is smart. A sentence pair was used as a target pair only if at least 80% of the subjects in a pilot study agreed that a third sentence was implied by the two statements. Filler and buffer pairs consisted of two sentences which did not suggest any obvious implication.

All subjects were then given a recognition test consisting of old sentences, inferences based on old sentences, and new sentences. If control-deprived subjects engaged in more careful and precise processing of the study list, then they should be better able than baseline subjects to recognize old sentences and their associated implications, but they should also be less likely than baseline subjects to confuse these facts with their implications. The recognition test was given under two instruction conditions to assess both of these hypotheses. Under the inference-instruction condition, subjects were told to respond "old" both to sentences that were actually presented as well as inferences based on those sentences. While this condition required knowledge about the study sentences and their implications, it did not require that subjects discriminate between the two types of knowledge. Under the memory-instruction condition, subjects were told to respond "old" only to sentences that had actually been presented. Therefore, this condition required that subjects discriminate between the facts that were studied and their inferences.

The mean percentage of correct responses for target facts and inferences, the major dependent variable, is shown in Table 5.2. The analysis indicated a significant interaction between control deprivation and the inference variable: Under both instruction conditions, control deprivation led to higher recognition performance, but only for inference statements. Consistent with the hypothesis, under the memory instructions control-deprived subjects were better than baseline subjects at recognizing inference items as new sentences. Under the inference instructions, control-deprived subjects were better than baseline subjects at recognizing inference items as implications of the original fact pairs. This enhanced performance of the control-deprived subjects was not attained at the expense of response speed: There were no differences in reaction time between control deprivation and baseline subjects. These data are, then, consistent with the general hypothesis that control deprivation produces a tendency to employ information-processing strategies that are characterized by careful and accurate encoding of facts and their implications.

Why did control-deprived and baseline subjects differ only on inference judgments (and not on facts)? The most likely reason is that only inference judgments were sensitive to the differences in processing that occurred during acquisition. Presumably, inference judgments required that both of the original facts be retrieved in order to validate the inference (Hayes-Roth & Thorndyke, 1979). This nontrivial retrieval requirement would be less difficult if the related facts were organized into higher-order memory units. Careful and deliberate processing of sentence pairs by control-deprived subjects may have increased the likelihood that the relationship between sentences was detected and that these sentences were integrated into a higher-order memory representation. Subsequent judgments that required the retrieval of both sentences would therefore be facilitated. On the other hand, recognition of facts and new sentences required only that a test sentence be compared to individual study sentences. Apparently, this minimal retrieval oper-

Table 5.2

MEAN PERCENTAGE OF CORRECT JUDGMENTS ON INFERENCE AND FACT ITEMS

Group	Inference instructions		Memory instructions	
	Inference	Fact	Inference	Fact
Control deprivation	76	91	84	84
No control deprivation	65	94	70	89

ation required only standard processing of the study list and therefore correct recognition occurred regardless of whether the target sentences had been organized. This is basically an argument for a ceiling effect and leads to the prediction that if the task was made more difficult, control deprivation would facilitate all recognition judgments.

To explore this interpretation, and to test again the hypothesis that control deprivation leads to careful processing of information in subsequent settings, a second experiment was conducted in which subjects studied a short text and were then asked to verify important and unimportant facts and inferences.

The text used in this study was identical to that used by Walker and Meyer (1980). It was roughly 200 words in length and concerned a revolution in the mythical country of Morinthia. The text consisted of two parts, each typed on a separate page, and contained four pairs of critical facts. The facts were categorized into those high in the content structure (important) and those low in the content structure (unimportant).

The verification test consisted of 12 randomly ordered statements. Four of these statements consisted of the logical implication of each pair of critical facts. For example, for the critical pair (1) King Egbert is a dictator and (2) Albert Porfiro hated all dictators, the logical implication was (3) Albert Porfiro hated King Egbert. Two of these inference statements were derived from facts high in the content structure (important true inference) and two from facts low in the content structure (unimportant true inference). In addition, the verification list contained two statements which were explicitly mentioned in the text. One statement was high in the content structure (important true explicit) and one was low in the content structure (unimportant true explicit).

The list also contained six false statements which either contradicted facts stated in the text or were not necessarily true given the information in the text. The identical verification test was administered to both control-deprived and baseline subjects.

Control-deprived and baseline subjects did not differ in the amount of time spent studying the text, in their reaction times during the test phase, or in their judgments concerning false items. Table 5.3 displays the results on the main dependent variable, the proportion of correct responses for the important and unimportant true inference and true explicit items. Although control-deprived and baseline subjects did not differ in their judgments on unimportant items, control-deprived subjects were significantly more accurate on both important inference and important explicit judgments.

The results of this second experiment clearly indicate that control deprivation enhanced subsequent text comprehension. Control-deprived

Table 5.3

MEAN PROPORTION OF CORRECT RESPONSES ON INFERENCE AND FACT JUDGMENTS

	Inference		Fact	
Group	Important	Unimportant	Important	Unimportant
Control deprivation	.73	.54	.96	.71
No control deprivation	.57	.59	.75	.79

subjects were more accurate than baseline subjects on both facts and inferences when this information was important for the understanding of the material they had read. Control-deprived subjects apparently focused their attention on the important aspects of the text. This tendency to prefer central or diagnostic information will be discussed further in a subsequent section.

We have thus far assumed that control deprivation leads to more careful analysis and encoding of subsequent new data; in other words, we have assumed that the effects observed in the studies just reported are derived from storage or encoding phenomena. But this need not necessarily be the case. In fact, the absence of study time differences in the text-processing study described immediately above might imply that the effects are a retrieval phenomenon, although the lack of reaction time differences in both of the preceding studies argues against this interpretation. To determine more clearly whether the enhanced performance of control-deprived subjects is an input phenomenon, we conducted a third study. The text used in this study was again that used by Walker and Meyer (1980).

In the storage condition, subjects first received either the baseline or control-deprivation manipulation, then studied the text, then had a 20-minute delay during which they worked on an interpolated task, and finally were given the verification task. In other words, the storage condition constituted a replication of the previous text study experiment, with the addition of the interpolated delay before the final verification task. In the retrieval condition, subjects first were given the 20-minute delay task (a length of time corresponding to the amount of time taken to complete the control-deprivation task), then studied the text, *then* were given the baseline or control-deprivation manipulation, and finally were given the verification task. Under the storage condition, then, the sequence of events was as follows:

control   ⟶   *text*   ⟶   *20 min*   ⟶   *verification*
manipulation   study   filled delay   task

Under the retrieval condition the sequence was:

$$20 \text{ min} \longrightarrow \text{text} \longrightarrow \text{control} \longrightarrow \text{verification}$$
$$\text{filled delay} \qquad \text{study} \qquad \text{manipulation} \qquad \text{task}$$

This design controlled for the total time spent in the experiment by both storage and retrieval subjects, and controlled the amount of elapsed time between text study and the verification test. The only difference between the storage and retrieval conditions, then, was whether the manipulation of control deprivation came before or after text study. If the effects observed in previous studies are input phenomena, then control-deprived and baseline subjects should differ only in the storage condition; if, on the other hand, those effects are retrieval phenomena, then control-deprived and baseline subjects should differ in both the storage and retrieval conditions.

As can be seen in Table 5.4, the results clearly indicate an input or storage process: Control-deprived subjects were again superior to baseline subjects, but only in the storage condition.

Taken together, these studies are consistent with the hypothesis developed in the beginning of this chapter. Control deprivation causes an increased interest in forming attributions in subsequent settings, and produces a careful information-processing approach that, at least under the kind of circumstances used in these studies, produces superior performance in recognizing both facts and the implications of those facts.

OTHER EFFECTS OF CONTROL DEPRIVATION ON ATTRIBUTIONS

CONTROL DEPRIVATION AND THE PARADOX OF ACCURACY

Although it is clear that the causal attributions of subjects in the Pittman and Pittman (1980) study were differentially influenced by the informational manipulation, it is difficult to say anything about the

Table 5.4

MEAN PROPORTION OF CORRECT RESPONSES

Group	Storage	Retrieval
Control deprivation	.81	.74
No control deprivation	.63	.72

accuracy of those attributions. It seems reasonable for subjects to have made different attributions in the internal and external motivational information conditions, but there were no clear "right" or "correct" answers to the questions about the communicator's motivations. The D'Agostino and Pittman (1984) studies do show superior memory for facts and inferences, and in that sense may be taken as evidence of more accurate processing, but the inferences in those studies were sufficiently straightforward so that they were either made or not made. In other words, the design of those studies was such that errors or biases in inference judgments could not really be studied.

The accuracy question is important, however, and the possibility of an interesting paradox is raised by a consideration of the literature on biases and illusions in social explanation. Studies of biases in the attribution of success and failure to self (e.g., Miller, 1976; Schlenker & Miller, 1977), of overestimation of control over random events (e.g., Langer, 1975; Wortman, 1975), and belief in a controllable or just world (e.g., Lerner, Miller, & Holmes, 1976; Walster, 1966), for example, imply that individuals satisfy a desire for control by developing comforting illusions about the controllable nature of their world. The paradox, of course, is that the more one indulges in such illusions, the worse one's ability to know how to exert real control becomes. Whether or not such illusions are indeed created by control motivation, the question of how experience with lack of control will affect these biases remains. Does deprivation of control enhance the tendency to indulge in illusions and biases, or does it instead lead to attempts to develop accurate understandings in ensuing settings?

Pittman, Quattrone, and Jones (1985) conducted two studies addressed to this question, using the attitude attribution paradigm (Jones, 1979) as the source of biased attributions. In both studies subjects were first given either the baseline or control-deprivation procedure, and then were given attitude attribution materials by a second experimenter. In the attitude attribution paradigm subjects hear or see a speech or an essay, described as having been produced by the target person under no choice conditions, in which either a strong pro or con position is taken on an issue. Even though subjects in these studies know the target person was forced to take the particular position represented in his or her essay, there is still a strong tendency to attribute essay-consistent attitudes to the target person. The difference between attributed attitudes in the pro and con conditions is the index of the size of the attitude attribution error.

Are subjects who have been deprived of control more or less likely to make this error? Using the attribution materials employed in a previous attitude attribution experiment (Jones, Riggs, & Quattrone, 1979), Pittman et al. (1985) found that control-deprived subjects were less influenced by the essay than baseline subjects. This tendency was most pronounced on items calling for generalized trait attributions, a finding consistent with a companion set of studies on the effects of constraint information across levels of inferential generality (Cantor, Pittman, & Jones, 1982). Table 5.5 shows that the significant interaction on attributed liberalism–conservatism was produced by a reduction of speech content effects in the control-deprivation condition. In other words, prior experience with control deprivation caused subjects to be less likely to make the attitude attribution error.

When combined, the D'Agostino and Pittman (1983) and the Pittman et al. (1985) studies imply that control deprivation produces careful and accurate processing of subsequent information, leading to enhanced memory for facts and inferences, and enhanced accuracy in those inferences even under conditions where erroneous inferences are the rule.

Control Deprivation and Changes in Information Seeking

We have seen that control-deprived subjects process new information in a more careful, deliberate, and accurate fashion than baseline subjects. This may represent a preference on the part of control-deprived subjects for forming new conceptualizations directly from the available information, as opposed to trying to interpret new information by relying on prior conceptualizations or preexisting knowledge structures. Given the prior failure of existing conceptualizations, such caution would be sensible. This manner of information processing has been variously described as data-driven, bottom-up, or systematic processing, as opposed to conceptually driven, top-down, or heuristic processing

Table 5.5

MEAN ATTRIBUTED LIBERALISM–CONSERVATISM[a]

Group	Speech content	
	Liberal	Conservative
Control deprivation	11.38	7.69
No control deprivation	14.19	5.31

[a]Attributions were made on a 21-point scale on which 1 denoted conservative and 21 liberal.

(Chaiken, 1980; Lindsay & Norman, 1977; Neisser, 1976; Nisbett & Ross, 1980; Palmer, 1975). Thus, when deprived of control, persons subsequently will adopt a cautious, conservative strategy where ongoing interpretations of the environment are repeatedly checked against a precise and detailed analysis of sensory and perceptual information. That is not to say that control-deprived persons do not engage in conceptually-driven processing at all, but rather that their schema-activated knowledge is more carefully evaluated against available evidence.

If control deprivation does produce such a shift in information-processing strategy, then information preferences might also be expected to change. For example, raw data might be preferred to someone else's potentially erroneous generalizations from those data. Information from a clearly specified source or with a specific referent, might be preferred to information from unspecified sources or with unclear referents. The general point here is that control-deprived persons should prefer to rely on raw data, so that new constructions of those data can be developed with careful attention to accuracy.

Pittman, Cantor, and D'Agostino (1984) tested this prediction by giving control-deprived and baseline subjects choices among sources of information about future interaction partners that were either specific or general. The prediction was that control-deprived subjects would show a preference shift toward specific information.

Following the control-deprivation manipulation, the second experimenter explained to each subject that he or she would be participating in an ongoing personality assessment project that had been underway for some time at a neighboring university. In the current phase of the project, students from the two universities were interacting in the laboratory. Each subject then agreed to come back for an interaction session, working with two different partners on two different tasks, and a time for their appointment was chosen. After explaining the general nature of the tasks that would be used in the next session, the subject was then told that part of the current study involved having one interactant know something about his or her partner before they met. The subject was then told that since their partners had been participating in the project for some time, information had been collected about them from four different categories (cooperativeness–competitiveness, self-esteem, breadth of interest, and organizational style). In each general category, there were test scores from general personality tests and specific personality tests, and behavioral observations from general interaction settings and specific interaction settings. The information, then, represented three independent variables: (1) information category (four levels just named), (2) personality test versus behavioral observation, and

(3) general versus specific information. Each subject was shown a check-list displaying the 16 sources of information for each of their interaction partners and was allowed to choose any five pieces of information for each partner.

When the percentage of choices allocated to each of the four general categories was analyzed, the overall choice patterns of control-deprived and baseline subjects did not differ. However, both groups showed a preference for the cooperativeness–competitiveness category over the other three categories. The cooperativeness–competitiveness choices were sufficiently numerous to allow an analysis of the general–specific and personality–behavior variables.

Within the cooperativeness–competitiveness category, the analysis in-dicated a significant interaction between control deprivation and the general–specific variable. As Table 5.6 indicates, while baseline subjects showed a preference for general information, control-deprived subjects shifted to a preference for specific information, consistent with the hy-pothesis that control deprivation produces a change in information pref-erence toward specific information.

Subjects in the second D'Agostino and Pittman (1984) study described above showed an apparent preference for or focus on important infor-mation. This suggests a second kind of preference shift, namely, a shift to a focus on central or diagnostic information. If control deprivation leads to increased interest in forming accurate causal analyses in sub-sequent settings, then preference for or homing in on central or diag-nostic information would also be expected. Swann, Stephenson, and Pittman (1981) designed an experiment to assess directly whether or not control deprivation produces increased interest in revealing central or diagnostic information. This study was also designed to explore another question. In all of the preceding studies, information was made available to subjects, and the dependent measures focused on some aspect of uti-lization of that information. However, if information was not provided in such convenient form by the experimenter, but instead an opportu-nity was made available for subjects actively to seek out information, would control deprivation produce enhanced curiosity and a willingness to seek out diagnostic information?

Swann et al. (1981) designed their study to explore these questions by creating a setting in which subjects could seek out revealing infor-mation if they so desired. Baseline and control-deprived groups were created as in the previous studies. The second experimenter then ex-plained to each subject that he or she would be asked to conduct an interview with another subject that would be taped for future use in a different study. The experimenter explained that a number of interviews

Table 5.6

PERCENTAGE OF SUBJECT'S CHOICES OF GENERAL
AND SPECIFIC INFORMATION

Group	General	Specific
Control deprivation	48	71
No control deprivation	61	48

were being taped, that the questions being used in the interviews were to vary randomly within a restricted range, and that each interviewer was therefore free to select any 10 questions from a list of 30. These 30 questions had previously been rated by a group of judges from the same subject population who responded to the question: "If you asked this question of a male college freshman, how much do you think you would learn about him?" The 30 questions used in the experiment were divided into 8 diagnostic questions, 14 intermediate questions, and 8 non-diagnostic questions based on the judges' ratings. It was thus possible to assess each subject's interest in learning about the interviewee by measuring the diagnosticity or potential informational value of the 10 questions each subject chose to ask for the interview.

Table 5.7 shows that control-deprived subjects asked significantly more diagnostic questions than did baseline subjects, and this was true whether or not subjects expected to interact with their partners after asking the 10 questions (this latter variable is labeled high and low utility in the table).

When taken together, the focus on important information in the second D'Agostino and Pittman (1984) study, the preference for specific information in the Pittman et al. (1984) study, and the seeking out of diagnostic information in the Swann et al. (1981) study reveal a pref-

Table 5.7

MEAN NUMBER OF DIAGNOSTIC AND NONDIAGNOSTIC QUESTIONS SELECTED[a]

	Question			
	Diagnostic		Nondiagnostic	
Group	Low utility	High utility	Low utility	High utility
Control deprivation	4.35	4.54	1.60	1.00
No control deprivation	3.75	3.85	1.55	.83

[a]Adapted from Swann, Stephenson & Pittman (1981).

erence for causally relevant, revealing information from clearly specifiable sources following an experience with control deprivation.

CONTROL DEPRIVATION AND EFFORT EXPENDITURE

Control deprivation produces careful, accurate processing of subsequent information and a bias toward diagnostic information. Given these kinds of concerns on the part of the control-deprived subjects, we might also expect that they would be willing to expend additional effort in order to acquire information and to process it carefully. However, no direct measure of additional effort expenditure was taken in the studies described thus far. A more direct measure of effort expenditure was taken by D'Agostino and Pittman (1982). Following a manipulation of control deprivation, subjects were given a modified version of a control judgment task described by Alloy and Abramson (1979). Subjects were given two responses (throwing a switch or not throwing a switch). Following the chosen response, a green light either did or did not come on. Subjects were told that they were to determine how much control they had over green light onset by varying their responses and observing the light. Unlike the procedure used by Alloy and Abramson (1979), however, subjects in this study were told that they could take as many trials as they wished before making their judgments. The number of trials taken was the index of the amount of effort expended.

Control-deprived subjects took significantly more trials to make their judgments than did baseline subjects (49.8 vs. 34.4). The actual control judgments of control-deprived and baseline subjects, as well as of a third group of subjects who were not deprived of control but were yoked to the number of trials chosen by control-deprived subjects, did not differ. The results of this study show that control-deprived subjects are willing to expend effort to acquire information.

LIMITATIONS ON THE EFFECTS OF CONTROL DEPRIVATION ON ATTRIBUTIONAL ACTIVITY

PRIOR EXPECTATIONS OF CONTROL AND THE EFFECTS OF CONTROL DEPRIVATION

If one expects to have control but finds that attempts to exert control are ineffective, that experience calls into question one's understanding of the causal underpinnings of the setting. Such an experience should lead one to be cautious and careful in forming causal explanations in new settings. The concept-formation procedure that has been used in all of these experiments to manipulate control deprivation constitutes such an experience: Subjects expect to be able to solve the problems but find that they cannot (Pittman & Pittman, 1979). However, other kinds of experiences in which one has no control may not carry the same kinds of implications. For example, if a person never expects to have control, and the lack of control implies nothing about the adequacy of the person's conceptualizations, then the kinds of subsequent changes that we have seen in the studies reported in this chapter might not follow.

To test this analysis, Pittman (1984) first exposed subjects to uncontrollable, unpredictable 96 dB noise, or to unpredictable but controllable noise, following the procedures used by Glass and Singer (1972) in their studies of the aftereffects of noise. In these procedures, all subjects are told that while they are working on their tasks (simple mathematics and word problems) they will hear random noise bursts. In the uncontrollable conditions, it is clear to subjects from the beginning that they will not be able to control the noise. While this experience may be unpleasant and irritating, it does not carry any negative implications for the adequacy of the subject's conceptualizations.

Following their exposure to the noise, subjects were given either the internal or external motivational information booklets used in the Pittman and Pittman (1980) study, and either the pro or con attitude attribution materials from the Pittman et al. (1983) attitude attribution study. As Table 5.8 shows, uncontrollable noise subjects utilized the motivational information, but controllable noise subjects did not. This finding is consistent with the Pittman and Pittman (1980) findings. However, on the attitude attribution task, uncontrollable noise subjects made greater attitude attribution errors than did controllable noise subjects, a finding opposite that obtained with the concept formation method of control deprivation in the Pittman et al. (1985) study.

Focusing on the discrepant accuracy findings in our studies with the attitude attribution paradigm, we may have the answer to the accuracy versus illusion of control problem. Some motivated errors of attribution may indeed be made in the service of a general control motive, and made in order to make the person feel better even though they are in fact biased or inaccurate. If the person has an experience with deprivation of control such that expected control is lost in a way that challenges the validity of the person's conceptualizations, then accuracy concerns will become paramount, and we should expect to see decreases in motivated errors. If instead the person has an experience with simple lack of control, that is, an experience that may be unpleasant or irritating but one that does not call any of the person's conceptualizations into

Table 5.8

MEAN ATTRIBUTED EXTERNAL INFLUENCE AND ATTITUDE ATTRIBUTION AS A FUNCTION OF CONTROL OVER NOISE[a]

	Attributed externality	
Group	External influence	Internal influence
No control (Control deprivation)	6.19	5.00
Control (No control deprivation	5.00	5.41

	Attitude attribution	
	Liberal speech	Conservative speech
No control (Control deprivation)	15.31	3.63
Control (No control deprivation)	11.33	3.94

[a]On the attributed externality question, 1 denoted internal motivation and 7 external motivation. For the attitude attribution measure, 1 denoted conservative attitude and 21 liberal attitude.

question, then the person's primary concern may focus on feeling better, rather than on accuracy, causing increased indulgence in the emotional balm of biased and illusory feelings of understanding and effectance.

CONDITIONS LEADING TO EFFORT WITHDRAWAL FOLLOWING CONTROL DEPRIVATION

The learned helplessness literature is replete with examples of task performance decrements following control deprivation pretreatments (e.g., Abramson, Seligman & Teasdale, 1978; Seligman, 1975). But in most of our studies, control deprivation led to enhanced performance on cognitive tasks, increased sensitivity to and interest in diagnostic information, and a willingness to expend effort to acquire information. In the Pittman and Pittman (1980) study, both performance decrements (on an anagram solution task) and increased sensitivity to attribution-relevant information were demonstrated in the same subjects following control deprivation. How might we explain the differences in effects obtained on overt task performance (i.e., anagrams) and cognitive performance (e.g., enhanced input processing of information)?

There are several explanations for the performance decrements found in the learned helplessness literature. Learned helplessness theory implicates generalized expectations of the independence of behavior and outcomes as the cause of performance decrements (Seligman, 1975). Attributional egotism theory identifies ego-protective motives as the source of defensive effort withdrawal on tasks where the possibility of another ego-threatening failure exists (Snyder, Stephan & Rosenfield, 1978). A similar analysis is involved in Jones and Berglas's (1978) analysis of self-handicapping strategies designed to blunt the effects of potentially ego-threatening diagnostic failures. The latter two analyses are persuasive and supported by data indicating that when excuses are provided, effort withdrawal is attenuated or reversed (Frankel & Snyder, 1978).

Following the ego-protective effort withdrawal line of reasoning, the tasks on which performance decrements are typical may be seen by subjects as tasks on which diagnostic failure is likely, therefore leading to effort withdrawal as at least an internal excuse. The attributional and information-processing tasks we have used, however, may not have been perceived as particularly difficult (low-failure probability), or in fact may not have been seen as tasks at all, at least in the sense that performance could or would be objectively evaluated. Also, since we have identified the enhanced comprehension effects following control deprivation as input phenomena, the information-processing effects of control deprivation may already have occurred before the phase of the study calling for diagnostic performance was revealed or became an issue.

To test this analysis, D'Agostino and Pittman (1984) designed a fourth study in which a description of the Walker and Meyer (1980) text used in Studies 2 and 3 was added. In this study, following the control deprivation manipulation, the task was described as being moderately difficult, and subjects were told that under similar circumstances most students like themselves had done moderately well, with a few doing very well and a few doing very poorly. These instructions were designed to make it clear that performance on the task would have self-diagnostic or ego-relevant implications. However, half of the subjects were given this description before study time, and half were given this description only after study time. Thus the before and after text conditions differed only in terms of when the moderate-difficulty instructions were given, and in all cases these instructions were given before the final test task.

In this study, unlike any of the others, the results revealed significant differences in text study time. The significant interaction on this measure indicated that control-deprived subjects who were given the moderate difficulty instructions before study time spent less time reading

Table 5.9

MEAN PROPORTION OF CORRECT RESPONSES

Group	Difficulty information	
	Before text study	After text study
Control deprivation	.64	.80
No control deprivation	.75	.69

the text than in any of the other conditions. This is clear evidence for effort withdrawal.

The proportion of correct responses for true inference and true explicit judgments is presented in Table 5.9. The analysis indicated a significant interaction: In the before condition, control-deprived subjects' performance was worse than that of baseline subjects, while in the after condition control-deprived subjects showed enhanced performance, as in the previous studies.

These data support the hypothesis that control-deprived subjects are motivated to protect against further loss of control and self-esteem, and that it is this motivation that guides subsequent information processing. When the threat to self-esteem is minimal, control deprivation may induce an information-processing strategy that emphasizes careful and precise processing of information with less reliance on knowledge structures to select and filter available data. Such a strategy would insure that subsequent judgments and decisions were basd on the accurate processing of all relevant information. This would explain why control-deprived subjects normally perform better than baseline subjects on relatively simple memory and text comprehension tasks. However, if the identical tasks are perceived as a threat to self-esteem as under the before condition in the last study, then rather than risk a further loss of control and self-esteem, control-deprived subjects may simply not study the material very well (that is, may withdraw effort) and attribute subsequent poor performance to a lack of effort.

SOME ISSUES FOR FURTHER RESEARCH

The nature of the control-deprivation experience is one area that deserves further research. We have so far relied primarily on the concept-formation task, using random feedback as the control-deprivation manipulation, and have concentrated our research on the effects produced by this experience. McCaul (1983) split his subjects into depressed and nondepressed groups and then gave them the attribution materials from the Pittman and Pittman (1980) study. The depressed subjects showed the same pattern as control-deprived subjects, that is, increased utilization of the motivational information compared to the nondepressed group. Since control deprivation appears to be a major cause of depression (Seligman, 1975), these data are consistent with the control motivation–attribution analysis we have developed. Similarly, Alloy and Abramson's (1979) finding that depressed subjects are more accurate than nondepressed subjects on some judgment tasks is consistent with our findings. But the different effects caused by the uncontrollable noise manipulation reported in this chapter (Pittman, 1984) point to the necessity of further study on the nature of the control-deprivation experience. Our suggestion that expectation of control accounts for this difference needs further testing.

The Pittman (1984) study raises the issue of possible limitations on the finding that control deprivation leads to more accurate judgments in subsequent settings. There may be some tasks on which improved performance is simply not possible because of limitations on people's ability to change their processing strategies. Some of the errors caused by the use of heuristics reviewed by Nisbett and Ross (1980), for example, may not yield to increased accuracy concerns if perceivers are either unaware of these errors or are unable to change to a more accurate information processing strategy. Griffin (1981) found that the control-deprivation manipulation had no effect on either the "questioner–contestant" effect (Ross, Amabile, & Steinmetz, 1977) or the primacy effect (Jones, Rock, Shaver, Goethals, & Ward, 1968). These studies imply that indeed some errors may be impervious to accuracy concerns, although null effects need to be interpreted with caution.

There may be other tasks where data-driven or bottom-up information-processing strategies are simply not as efficient as conceptually-driven or top-down strategies. If, on these kinds of tasks, control-deprived subjects are still prone to rely more heavily on data-driven processing, then we could expect control deprivation to lead to poorer performance.

The judgment tasks we have employed have not involved strong prior expectations or hypotheses. Instead, subjects were presented with novel data sets from which inferences could be generated. If, however, the judgment task involved strong prior hypotheses, would we find similar effects? The findings to date imply that we would, but the existence of strong hypotheses might tip the scales in the direction of ego-protection. This might be particularly likely in the realm of self-judgments. Our judgment tasks have not involved self-attributions directly. If the task involved judgment of one's own success or failure, for example, it is an open question whether accuracy or ego-protective concerns would prevail.

SUMMARY

We have reviewed a series of studies designed to explore the motivational antecedents of attributional analyses. The first finding was that when control motivation is increased, the likelihood of engaging in attributional analyses of available information in subsequent settings is also increased. This increased likelihood of effortful attributional activity is associated with increased attention to and interest in obtaining central or diagnostic information. Available information is processed in a careful, deliberate fashion that can be characterized as data-driven, bottom-up, or systematic processing. Such processing produced more accurate performance on a variety of tasks.

Perhaps the most distinctive general feature of this research, when considered against the backdrop of current work in social cognition, lies in the emphasis on prior motivational concerns that people may bring to new settings, concerns that shape both the degree of interest in engaging in attributional analyses, and the nature and outcomes of those analyses. People often do enter situations in motivational states caused by prior, unrelated events. Understanding this aspect of motivation is important for the continued development of our knowledge concerning the role of attribution processes in human behavior.

REFERENCES

Abramson, L. Y., Seligman, M. E. P., & Teasdale, J. D. (1978). Learned helplessness in humans: Critique and reformulation. *Journal of Abnormal Psychology, 87,* 49–74.

Alloy, L. B., & Abramson, L. Y. (1979). Judgment of contingency in depressed and nondepressed students: Sadder but wiser? *Journal of Experimental Psychology: General, 108,* 441–485.

Bersheid, E., Graziano, W., Monson, T., & Dermer, M. (1976). Outcome dependency: Attention, attribution, and attraction. *Journal of Personality and Social Psychology, 34,* 978–989.

Cantor, N. E., Pittman, T. S., & Jones, E. E. (1982). Choice and attitude attributions: The influence of constraint information on attributions across levels of generality. *Social Cognition, 1,* 1–20.

Chaiken, S. (1980). Heuristic versus systematic information processing and the use of source versus message cues in persuasion. *Journal of Personality and Social Psychology, 39,* 752–766.

Clary, E. G., & Tesser, A. (1983). Reactions to unexpected events: The naive scientist and interpretive activity. *Personality and Social Psychology Bulletin, 9,* 609–620.

D'Agostino, P. R., & Pittman, T. S. (1982). Effort expenditure following control deprivation. *Bulletin of the Psychonomic Society, 19*, 282–283.

D'Agostino, P. R., & Pittman, T. S. (1984). *The relationship between control deprivation and subsequent information processing strategy.* Unpublished manuscript, Gettysburg College, Gettysburg, PA.

Enzle, M. E., & Schopflocher, D. (1978). Instigation of attribution processes by attribution questions. *Personality and Social Psychology Bulletin, 4*, 595–599.

Frankel, A., & Snyder, M. L. (1978). Poor performance following unsolvable problems: Learned helplessness or egotism? *Journal of Personality and Social Psychology, 36*, 1415–1423.

Glass, D. C., & Singer, J. E. (1972). *Urban stress: Experiments on noise and social stressors.* New York: Academic Press.

Griffin, J. J. (1981). *Control deprivation and subsequent attributional accuracy.* Unpublished honors thesis, Gettysburg College, Gettysburg, PA.

Harvey, J. H., Yarkin, K. L., Lightner, J. M., & Town, J. P. (1980). Unsolicited attribution and recall of interpersonal events. *Journal of Personality and Social Psychology, 38*, 551–568.

Hastie, R. (1984). Causes and effects of causal attribution. *Journal of Personality and Social Psychology, 46*, 44–56.

Hayes-Roth, B., & Thorndyke, P. W. (1979). Integration of knowledge from text. *Journal of Verbal Learning and Verbal Behavior, 18*, 91–108.

Heller, J. F. (1972). *Attribution theory: Self and other attributions as a determinant of attitude change.* Unpublished doctoral dissertation, University of Iowa, Iowa City, IA.

Jones, E. E. (1979). The rocky road from acts to dispositions. *American Psychologist, 34*, 107–117.

Jones, E. E., & Berglas, S. (1978). Control of attributions about the self through self-handicapping strategies: The appeal of alcohol and the role of under-achievement. *Personality and Social Psychology Bulletin, 4*, 200–206.

Jones, E. E., & Davis, K. E. (1965). From acts to disposition: The attribution process in person perception. In L. Berkowitz (Ed.), *Advances in Experimental Social Psychology* (Vol. 2). New York: Academic Press.

Jones, E. E., Riggs, J. M., & Quattrone, G. (1979). Observer bias in the attitude attribution paradigm: Effect of time and information order. *Journal of Personality and Social Psychology, 37*, 1230–1238.

Jones, E. E., Rock, K. G., Shaver, K. G., Goethals, G. R., & Ward, L. M. (1968). Pattern of performance and ability attribution: An unexpected primacy effect. *Journal of Personality and Social Psychology, 10*, 317–340.

Kelley, H. H. (1967). Attribution theory in social psychology. In D. Levine (Ed.), *Nebraska symposium on motivation* (Vol. 15). Lincoln: University of Nebraska Press.

Kelley, H. H. (1971). Attribution theory in social interaction. In E. E. Jones et al. (Eds.), *Attribution: Perceiving the causes of behavior.* New York: General Learning Press.

Langer, E. J. (1975). The illusion of control. *Journal of Personality and Social Psychology, 32*, 311–328.

Lerner, M. J., Miller, D. T., & Holmes, J. (1976). Deserving and the emerging forms of justice. In L. Berkowitz and E. Walster (Eds.), *Advances in Experimental Social Psychology* (Vol. 9). New York: Academic Press.

Lindsay, P. H., & Norman, D. A. (1977). *Human information processing* (2nd ed.). New York: Academic Press.

McArthur, L. Z. (1972). The how and what of why: Some determinants and consequences of causal attribution. *Journal of Personality and Social Psychology, 31*, 171–193.

McCaul, K. D. (1983). Observer attributions of depressed students. *Personality and Social Psychology Bulletin, 9,* 74–82.

Miller, D. T. (1976). Ego involvement and attributions for success and failure. *Journal of Personality and Social Psychology, 34,* 901–906.

Miller, D. T., Norman, S. A., & Wright, E. (1978). Distortion in person perception as a consequence of the need for effective control. *Journal of Personality and Social Psychology, 36,* 598–607.

Neisser, U. (1976). *Cognition and reality: Principles and implications of cognitive psychology.* San Francisco: Freeman.

Nisbett, R., & Ross, L. (1980). *Human inference: Strategies and shortcomings of social judgment.* Englewood Cliffs, N.J.: Prentice-Hall.

Palmer, S. E. (1975). Visual perception and world knowledge: Notes on a model of sensory-cognitive interaction. In D. Norman and D. Rumelhart (Eds.), *Explorations in cognition.* San Francisco: W. H. Freeman & Co.

Pittman, N. L. & Pittman, T. S. (1979). Effects of amount of helplessness training and internal–external locus of control on mood and performance. *Journal of Personality and Social Psychology, 37,* 39–47.

Pittman, T. S. (1984). [Effects of uncontrollable noise on accuracy of the attribution inference process]. Unpublished raw data.

Pittman, T. S., Cantor, N. E., & D'Agostino, P. R. (1984, August). *Changes in information preference following control deprivation.* Paper presented at the meeting of the American Psychological Association, Toronto, Canada.

Pittman, T. S., & Pittman, N. L. (1980). Deprivation of control and the attribution process. *Journal of Personality and Social Psychology, 39,* 377–389.

Pittman, T. S., Quattrone, G., & Jones, E. E. (1985). *Control deprivation and the accuracy of attributional inferences.* Paper presented at the meeting of the Eastern Psychological Association, Boston, MA.

Pittman, T. S., Scherrer, F. W., & Wright, J. B. (1977). The effect of commitment on information utilization in the attribution process. *Personality and Social Psychology Bulletin, 3,* 276–279.

Pyszczynski, T. A., & Greensberg, J. (1981). Role of disconfirmed expectancies in the instigation of attributional processing. *Journal of Personality and Social Psychology, 40,* 31–38.

Ross, L., Amabile, T. M., & Steinmetz, J. L. (1977). Social roles, social control, and biases in social-perception processes. *Journal of Personality and Social Psychology, 35,* 485–494.

Schlenker, B. R., & Miller, R. S. (1977). Egocentrism in groups: Self-serving biases or logical information processing? *Journal of Personality and Social Psychology, 35,* 755–764.

Seligman, M. E. P. (1975). *Helplessness: On depression, development, and death.* San Francisco: Freeman.

Snyder, M. L. Stephan, W. G., & Rosenfield, D. (1978). Attributional egotism. In J. H. Harvey, W. J. Ickes, & R. F. Kidd (Eds.), *New directions in attribution research* (Vol. 2). Hillsdale, N.J.: Erlbaum.

Swann, W. B., Stephenson, B., & Pittman, T. S. (1981). Curiosity and control: On the determinants of the search for social knowledge. *Journal of Personality and Social Psychology, 40,* 635–642.

Walker, C. H ., & Meyer, B. J. F. (1980). Integrating different types of information in text. *Journal of Verbal Learning and Verbal Behavior, 19,* 263–275.

Walster, E. (1966). Assignment of responsibility for an accident. *Journal of Personality and Social Psychology, 3,* 73–79.

Wong, P. T. P., & Weiner, B. (1981). When people ask "why" questions, and the heuristics of attributional search. *Journal of Personality and Social Psychology, 40,* 650–663.

Workman, C. B. (1975). Some determinants of perceived control. *Journal of Personality and Social Psychology, 31,* 282–294.

CHAPTER 6

Social Comparison
of Causal Understandings*

Martha G. Hill, Gifford Weary, Lorraine
Hildebrand-Saints, and Susan D. Elbin

INTRODUCTION

Whether perceivers are conceptualized as logical philosophers (Heider, 1958), information processors (Jones & Davis, 1965), or social scientists (Kelley, 1967), they presumably make attributions in order to understand and predict events in their social environments. Our research has been influenced primarily by Kelley's conceptualization of the "perceiver as social scientist," whose task it is to "locate the source of an event by considering, among other things, the judgments of other persons" (Shaver, 1975, p. 59). The social environment that confronts perceivers is complex and often ambiguous, lacking objective criteria for evaluating the adequacy or quality of one's causal analyses. Consequently, it may be essential for individuals to compare their judgments with judgments of other perceivers to gain a sense of understanding, and hence control, over the social environment: "Veridicality [of social perceptions] must be determined by comparison among a number of perceivers in the sometimes naive hope that their perculiarities will somehow cancel out" (Shaver, 1975, p. 13).

Attribution researchers and theorists have investigated the causes of or basic processes underlying attribution (see Harvey & Weary, 1984). In addition, they have examined the behavioral consequences of an individual's attributions. Less attention has been given to the communicative role of attributions, although it is quite likely that perceivers do communicate their causal analyses to others for a variety of reasons.

*The authors thank Bill Swann for his input regarding our measure of social information seeking. We also thank John H. Harvey for his thoughtful comments on an earlier draft of this chapter.

143

Individuals might communicate their causal analyses as they compare notes with other perceivers, or they might express causal judgments to help establish a particular social identity in order to guide or control others' responses (Weary & Arkin, 1981). Surprisingly little is known about how individuals respond to others' expressed causal attributions. In this chapter we will describe some embryonic work on the interpersonal consequences of expressed or communicated causal judgments. We will begin with a discussion of the communicative role of attributions, followed by a review of some empirical evidence suggesting that what actors say about the causes of their outcomes affects observers' evaluations of them. In addition, we will discuss social comparison processes generally and describe how social comparison of causal judgments provides individuals with self-evaluative feedback. Finally, we will present experimental results from two laboratory studies that evaluated the affective consequences of social comparison of causal judgments.

COMMUNICATIVE ROLE OF ATTRIBUTIONS

Only recently have attribution theorists and researchers begun to examine the influence of self-presentation motivations on the causal inference process. For example, in their investigation of attributional conflict in young couples, Orvis, Kelley, and Butler (1976) concluded that communication of divergent causal explanations is a common and important part of couples' interactions. Orvis et al. also suggested that communicated attributions may serve self-presentational needs. Specifically, within the context of couples' interactions, strategically communicated attributions may be used to defend or justify one's behavior, or to call into question the behavior of one's partner. In a similar vein, Weary (1979) has contended that individuals may ascribe causality for positive and negative outcomes associated with their behaviors in such a way that would avoid embarrassment and/or gain public approval. For example, individuals might not want to accept undue credit for positive outcomes and deny credit for negative outcomes if they are told explicitly that their behavior is the major object of study and if their unrealistically positive self-presentation could be invalidated by their own subsequent behaviors or by others' present or future assessments of their behaviors. The embarrassment resulting from such public invalidation would likely threaten individuals' positive public image. Communicated self-attributions, then, may be important components of individuals' self-presentation strategies, enabling attributors to influence or control their social environment by eliciting or shaping others' evaluations of them (see Weary & Arkin, 1981; Jones & Pittman, 1982).

Despite this emphasis on the possible purposes that strategically communicated attributions may serve, little is actually known about the reactions of observers to individuals' causal judgments for their own or others' behavioral outcomes. This gap in the literature is particularly surprising since the topic of actor–observer differences in attributions has stimulated considerable interest among theorists and researchers (see Jones & Nisbett, 1972; Monson & Snyder, 1977).

OBSERVERS' REACTIONS TO INDIVIDUALS' CAUSAL JUDGMENTS

Several recent studies, however, have examined individuals' reactions to another's strategic causal claims regarding his or her outcomes. An example of such work is a study by Tetlock (1980). That study simulated an experiment by Ross, Bierbrauer, and Polly (1974) in which teachers were led to believe they had been successful or unsuccessful in teaching a lesson to a student. Ross et al. found that teachers tended to take responsibility for failure but attributed success to the student. In this study, Tetlock provided subjects with written descriptions of the Ross et al. procedures and included information indicating that a particular teacher had either succeeded or failed and had made either self-serving attributions (i.e., the teacher had taken credit for success or had denied responsibility for failure) or counterdefensive attributions. Tetlock reasoned that society generally expects teachers to take responsibility for pupil failure but to reward pupil success. Teachers in the Ross et al. study, then, may have strategically selected attributions that were in accord with normative requirements of the teacher role in an attempt to create a positive public image. In accord with this reasoning, Tetlock found that his subjects evaluated the teacher who made counterdefensive attributions more positively than the teacher who made self-serving attributions.

Another example of work in this area is a study reported by Forsyth, Berger, and Mitchell (1981). In that study, groups of subjects received success or failure feedback following a "survival exercise" group discussion. Each subject had served as group leader for part of the exercise and, therefore, had contributed to the group outcome. Following the feedback, subjects completed self-rating forms that included a measure of personal responsibility and subsequently were given bogus forms presumably completed by other group members. Subjects then completed co-member evaluations based upon the bogus self-rating forms. Forsyth et al. found that group members who presumably had taken credit for the group's success or had blamed others for the group's failure were evaluated least favorably by fellow group members.

These studies (Forsyth et al., 1981; Tetlock, 1980) provide evidence that what actors say about the causes of their own outcomes affects observers' evaluations of them. However, the studies only begin to examine the processes underlying individuals' reactions to others' expressions of their causal judgments generally. It is important to note that in each of the studies described, situational cues were available regarding the social desirability of attributions. Individuals whose attributions were consistent with those cues were evaluated more positively by observers. The results of these studies suggest that individuals may select strategically attributions that are in accord with situational or normative requirements in order to create a positive public image. In addition, the results suggest that observers' reactions may be influenced in part by the extent to which actors' causal claims are in accord with or in violation of situational constraints or social norms.

In order to understand more fully the processes underlying individuals' reactions to others' communicated causal explanations, it may be important to examine observers' evaluative reactions under conditions where there are few if any situational cues regarding the social value or desirability of particular causal explanations. It is surely the case that there are many everyday situations where individuals' expressions of their causal judgments for events have little or no presentational value. Since such expressed causal judgments may evoke important reactions from others, it is important to understand the nature and basis of those reactions. In addition, it is likely that observers implicitly make attributions for actors' outcomes and that observers' reactions involve a comparison of their own and actors' causal attributions. That is, the degree of similarity between observers' and actors' causal attributions may influence in important ways the observers' reactions. The studies we will present later in this chapter focused upon observers' reactions to others' expressed causal judgments under conditions where both had made causal attributions for an event and their judgments were compared. Before turning to a description of the studies, let us discuss how observers might respond to another's similar or dissimilar causal explanation for an event when there are few if any cues as to the socially desirable attribution.

SOCIAL COMPARISON

Causal analysis often involves subjective judgments in complex, ambiguous social situations that are likely to evoke in the perceiver feelings of uncertainty regarding the quality or accuracy of his or her judgments. Those feelings of uncertainty may be important antecedents of social comparison processes. More specifically, social comparison theory (Festinger, 1954) suggests that individuals have a need to evaluate their opinions and abilities. In the absence of objective criteria regarding the accuracy or favorability of opinions, abilities, or judgments, the need to evaluate can be satisfied by comparison with other people. Presumably, when individuals engage in social comparison, they experience both a need for accuracy and a desire for favorable self-evaluations (Gruder, 1977; Thornton & Arrowood, 1966). They may select different comparison others, depending upon the predominance of self-evaluative or self-enhancement needs.

SELF-EVALUATION, SOCIAL COMPARISON, AND CONSENSUAL VALIDATION

It is important here to make a distinction between social comparison and consensual validation and to discuss the relationship between these processes and individuals' needs for self-evaluation. Mettee and Smith (1977) argued that social comparison, in a broad sense, subsumes consensual validation since consensus information is derived from others. They reasoned that "Consensual validation pertains to the confirmation of *already existing* reality conceptions, whereas social comparison pertains to the *discovery and construction* of reality" (p. 70). An individual who is concerned with determining "reality" and uncertain about his or her ability to do so, is faced with a different sort of problem than the individual who already has decided upon what is "real" and is concerned with confirming that "reality."

The distinction between self-evaluation/social comparison and consensual validation becomes particularly important when we consider similar and dissimilar others as sources of informational feedback. In the case of consensual validation, the positive or negative value of socially derived information is determined by the degree to which it confirms or agrees with established conceptions of reality. That is, when an individual is seeking agreement, he or she is likely to find others' similarity inherently positive and dissimilarity inherently negative. In the case of self-evaluation/social comparison, similarity and dissimilarity are not intrinsically positive or negative, respectively. The positivity of socially derived informational feedback depends upon its *usefulness* to the perceiver. Indeed, there may be conditions under which dissimilar comparison others might be preferred. For example, an individual's desire to establish his or her uniqueness is likely to engender a preference for dissimilar others (see Fromkin, 1972).

SOCIAL COMPARISON OF CAUSAL JUDGMENTS

As we have suggested previously, causal judgments often are made in complex, ambiguous social situations. Consequently, an individual who has evaluated and made causal attributions for an event may experience a heightened sense of uncertainty regarding the quality or accuracy of his or her judgments. That is, the perceiver may ask "Have I attended to the important aspects of this situation?" or "Is my analysis reasonable?". The perceiver's uncertainty may motivate the search for social comparison information (e.g., others' causal judgments). When perceivers ask, "How do others interpret this situation?", another's expressed causal explanation for an event provides relevant self-evaluative feedback. It provides the perceiver with some evidence of the quality of his or her causal analysis. The socially derived informational feedback, then, may serve to reduce the perceiver's uncertainty regarding the correctness of the newly constructed conception of reality. The self-evaluative information provided by comparison of causal judgments may be critically important to the attributor who presumably seeks to understand and gain control over the social environment (Harvey & Weary, 1981).

Little attention has been paid to the affective consequences of self-evaluative feedback provided by the social comparison of newly constructed interpretations of reality (e.g., causal judgments). Information that is more accurate and more effective in reducing the perceiver's uncertainty should produce more positive sentiment for the source of that information. Similar others generally are seen as providing more accurate and greater uncertainty-reducing information (Festinger, 1954). The expression by another of similar causal explanations for an event should provide an individual with validation for his or her understanding of the event. Such validation should reduce the individual's uncertainty about the adequacy of his or her causal explanation and should lead to the feeling of positive sentiment toward the other. The expression of dissimilar causal explanations for the event, however, should provide invalidation, increase uncertainty, and lead to the feeling of negative sentiment toward the other.

The studies to be presented in the following section were designed to test the previously discussed reasoning regarding the effects of perceived concordance of causal understandings on interpersonal evaluations. Our conceptualization is extrapolated from Byrne's work on attitude similarity; however, it is important to note that the vast majority of similarity–attraction studies have been concerned with the effects of validation or invalidation of an already existing attitude or belief. The research herein represents an extension as it focuses explicitly on similarity of *attributional* judgments and the effects of validation or invalidation of a newly constructed interpretation of an event (see Mettee & Smith, 1977).

LABORATORY STUDIES OF THE AFFECTIVE CONSEQUENCES OF THE SOCIAL COMPARISON OF CAUSAL ATTRIBUTIONS

The studies presented here have examined the reactions of observers to a second observer's causal attributions for an event. Those reactions were evaluated within a context where there was a necessary and explicit comparison of observers' newly constructed causal judgments. In each of the studies, subjects made causal attributions for a hypothetical actor's behavioral outcome and subsequently compared their attributions with those of another participant.

STUDY 1

In a study presumably concerned with the processes involved in jury decision making, an observer-subject and an observer-participant read, from the perspective of jurors, a case summary that described an accident. Observer-subjects made causal attributions for the accident and subsequently learned that their causal judgments were similar or dissimilar to the participant-observer's. To rule out the possibility that similarity might be confounded with the perceived accuracy or social desirability of causal judgments, subjects also learned that their judgments were consistent (socially correct) or inconsistent (socially incorrect) with the causal judgments made by the majority of previous participants in the study. While the social correctness or incorrectness might be expected to provide subjects with some degree of validation or invalidation, respectively, for their causal understanding of the accident, it seemed likely that this effect would be modest compared to the validation or invalidation provided by a salient, specific other. Con-

sequently, the principal prediction was that there would be a main effect
of similarity of causal judgment on subjects' evaluations of the second
observer-participant.

In addition to investigating the effects of similarity and social correctness of causal judgments on interpersonal evaluations, we also were
interested in examining the effects of importance of causal understanding. It is undoubtedly true that causal understandings vary in importance for attributors. For example, it probably is more important to
understand what caused the break-up of one's marriage than to understand the causes of a very minor argument with one's spouse. Moreover, when one's causal understanding of an event is more important,
it seems reasonable to expect that validation or invalidation of this understanding would be more important. In the present experiment, subjects were led to believe that the case summary they read described a
real case that had involved litigation (high-importance condition) or a
hypothetical case that was just developed for use in the experiment (low-
importance condition). We anticipated that the effects of similarity of
causal judgments on subjects' evaluations of the second observer would
be more pronounced in the high-importance conditions.

METHOD

Subjects. Subjects were undergraduates (52 males, 28 females) at
Ohio State University who participated in order to fulfill an introductory
course requirement. Subjects were randomly assigned to the eight experimental conditions.

Procedure. Subjects were told that the purpose of the study was to
examine jury decision-making processes and that they would be asked
to read a description of and to make various judgments about an accident. The experimenter further explained that while the subject and another participant (a female confederate) would be reading the same case
summary and following the same procedures, they had been placed in
separate rooms because the presence of others could subtly influence
judgments.

In the high-importance conditions, the study was described as one of
a series of studies commissioned by the Select Committee on Judicial
Reform designed to evaluate the effectiveness of 18–23-year-olds as jurors. Subjects were told that the case they would read was a real case
that actually had involved litigation against a party for property damage
and personal injury.

In the low-importance conditions, the study was presented as part of an undergraduate research project. Subjects were told that the case study they would read described a hypothetical accident similar to cases decided daily in the court system. The experimenter emphasized that although the accident could have happened, it did not.

Next, each subject was given a booklet including a case summary and two questionnaires. The case summary described a situation in which multiple factors contributed to a car accident.[1] The damages for the accident, including property and personal injuries received by a bystander, were estimated at $3,500. The first questionnaire assessed the extent to which subjects believed the driver was responsible for the accident and the extent to which the accident was due to factors beyond the driver's control. The second questionnaire was designed to check the perceived importance of causal understanding. Subjects were asked to rate how important it was to them to understand the facts of the case and the causes of the accident. In addition, a question was included to assess whether subjects recalled that the case was real or hypothetical.

The experimenter instructed the subjects to read the case summary and to answer the questions that followed it. She then joined the confederate in the adjacent room, presumably to explain the experiment to her.

When the experimenter was sure that subjects had completed reading the case summary and answering the questionnaires, she rejoined them. In order to justify taking the booklet and to complete the experimental manipulations, the experimenter next explained to subjects that in an actual jury situation they would have had an opportunity to discuss their viewpoints with other jurors before reaching a consensus on the cause of the accident. She suggested that since that had not been possible, they might like to see the other ''juror's'' (confederate's) evaluation of the case. Subjects' booklets were then taken to the adjacent room presumably to show the attributions to the other participants. In actuality, the experimenter made ratings for the confederate on each attribution measure that were either similar (a 1-point difference) or dissimilar (a 7-point difference) to the subjects' actual ratings. The confederate's bogus attributions then were shown to subjects, and the similar or dissimilar nature of their judgments was noted.

After providing the similarity information, the experimenter left the room to return the confederates' booklets and to get the final question-

---

[1]Data from 60 pilot subjects indicated that the actor ($M = 1.62$, $SD = 3.7$) and situational factors ($M = 1.77$, $SD = 3.68$) were viewed as equally responsible for the accident. In addition, the variances of subjects' ratings on the two attributional scales suggested that there was no clear consensus as to the correct judgment.

naire. When the experimenter returned, she informed subjects how their causal judgments compared to those made by previous participants in the study. Subjects in the socially correct condition were told that the majority of others, about 80%, had found the actor "about as responsible" as the subject had. Subjects in the socially incorrect condition were told that the majority (80%) of others had found the actor either significantly more or less (depending on subjects' ratings) responsible for the accident.

In the final phase of the experiment, all subjects were asked to complete a final questionnaire giving their impressions of the experiment. This questionnaire included measures designed to check on the manipulation of similarity and social correctness of causal understandings and four 9-point scales on which subjects were asked to rate the other participant on each of four characteristics (reasonable, pleasant, open-minded, and friendly). After subjects finished this questionnaire, they were thoroughly debriefed and dismissed.

RESULTS

Manipulation checks. To check on the manipulation of the independent variable of importance of causal understanding, subjects completed two measures. First, subjects were asked to indicate whether the case summary they read described a real accident or a hypothetical event. All subjects correctly recalled that the case they had read was real or hypothetical. Subjects also were asked to rate on a 15-point scale (-7, not at all; $+7$, very important) how important they felt it was to understand the facts of the case and the causes of the accident. Subjects' ratings were analyzed using a $2 \times 2 \times 2$ (Similarity × Importance × Social Correctness) analysis of variance: no significant effects were found ($Ms = 6.5$ and 6.2 for high- and low-importance conditions, respectively). This latter analysis raises concerns about the effectiveness of the importance manipulation.

To check on the manipulations of perceived similarity and social correctness of causal understanding, subjects were asked to rate on two 15-point scales the degree to which they believed (1) their own and the other participant's understanding of the case was similar and (2) their causal judgments were similar to those of previous participants in the study. Separate $2 \times 2 \times 2$ (Similarity × Importance × Social Correctness) analyses of variance performed on subjects' ratings yielded only the predicted main effect on the similarity ($F[1, 72] = 559.31$, $p < .001$) and social correctness ($F[1, 72] = 617.51$, $p < .001$) check measures. These independent variables, then, were successfully manipulated.

Evaluation index. Subjects were asked to rate on four 9-point scales the extent to which the other participant seemed reasonable, pleasant, open-minded, and friendly. Subjects' ratings on these four scales were highly intercorrelated ($ps < .001$) and, consequently, were summed and divided by 4 to yield a single evaluation index. A 2 × 2 × 2 (Similarity × Importance × Social Correctness) analysis of variance of the evaluation index yielded a highly significant main effect for similarity ($F[1, 72] = 106.76, p < .0001$). Subjects in the similar judgment condition ($M = 7.28$) evaluated the other participant more positively than did subjects in the dissimilar judgment condition ($M = 5.21$). The analysis also yielded a significant Similarity × Importance × Social Correctness interaction ($F[1, 72] = 6.27, p < .02$). Tests of simple interaction effects for Similarity × Importance of Causal Understanding were significant only for socially correct judgments ($F[1, 72] = 6.59, p < .025$). Examination of the means presented in Table 6.1 reveals that similarity resulted in more positive evaluations of the other participants than did dissimilarity with this effect being particularly pronounced when subjects' causal judgments were relatively important and socially correct. The results of tests of simple main effects within level of correctness of causal judgment are illustrated in Table 6.1.

Discussion

It has been suggested in this paper that when individuals are uncertain about the accuracy or quality of their judgments, they may find that others' expressed causal judgments provide relevant self-evaluative

Table 6.1

Means for the Evaluation Index: Study 1[a]

Importance of causal understanding	Socially correct		Socially incorrect	
	Similar judgment	Dissimilar judgment	Similar judgment	Dissimilar judgment
High	8.05$_a$	5.05$_b$	7.0$_d$	5.43$_e$
	(10)	(10)	(10)	(10)
Low	6.98$_c$	5.43$_b$	7.08$_d$	4.95$_e$
	(10)	(10)	(10)	(10)

[a]The higher the mean, the more positive the evaluation. The numbers in parentheses indicate the numbers of subjects in each experimental condition. Within level of correctness of causal judgment, means with common subscripts are not significantly different.

information and consequently, may influence individuals' affective responses to comparison others. More specifically, we predicted that the expression by another of similar causal explanations for an event would lead to the feeling of positive sentiment toward the other. Such positive sentiment presumably is a consequence of validation of the causal understanding which, in turn, engenders feelings of confidence in one's own judgment and, hence, one's sense of control. The results indicated that a second observer was evaluated more positively by observer-subjects in the similar than in the dissimilar judgment conditions. Moreover, this effect was obtained regardless of the social correctness of causal understanding. At least in the present experiment, it would seem that individuals want to find support for their causal view of an event, even when that view may be incorrect.

Little support was found for the predicted interaction between similarity and importance of causal judgments. It was predicted that positive and negative evaluations of another associated with similar and dissimilar causal judgments, respectively, would be more pronounced in the high- than in the low-importance conditions. However, importance of causal understanding resulted in more pronounced evaluations only under similar-socially correct judgment conditions. Examination of the check evidence suggests that our manipulation of importance of causal understanding was not successful. Specifically, it seems that we were not successful in creating conditions of low-importance. The experimental instructions likely contributed to this lack of success. That is, when introducing the experimental task, the experimenter pointed out to all subjects that the focus of the study was jury decision-making processes. Within this context, it seems reasonable to argue that subjects may have been highly motivated to evaluate carefully the case before making their judgments. Also, the fact that these apparently important judgments would be known by the experimenter may have enhanced even more the importance of their causal explanations.

It is important to note that we have taken null effects associated with the independent variable of social correctness as support for our prediction that similarity of causal judgments would exert a more potent effect on subjects' evaluations of the observer-participant than would the social correctness of those judgments. While in some cases this position might be questionable, the results of the manipulation check measure indicated that subjects recalled correctly the social consensus information provided by the experimenter. However, it still could be argued that subjects in the present study did not make maximum use of this experimenter-generated consensus information or that this information was not effective in altering subjects' assessments of the social desirability of their causal judgments. This seems unlikely for at least three reasons. First, the consensus manipulation employed was a relatively strong one (80 vs. 20%). Second, care was taken to assure that the accident was viewed as equally attributable to the driver and situational factors and that there was no clear consensus as to the correct attribution (see footnote 1); in this way, we attempted to minimize subjects' tendencies to infer high consensus from their own judgments. Third, social correctness information was presented after information about the importance and similarity of causal judgments. All three of these factors have been shown to increase the impact of explicit consensus information (Kassin, 1979).

The above reasoning is not meant to imply that the social correctness of causal judgments would not exert an influence on interpersonal evaluations under other conditions. Indeed, in a situation where self-presentational motivations are maximally aroused, the perceived social correctness of another's causal explanations would likely influence evaluations of the comparison other. We will return in the second study to a discussion of this possibility.

STUDY 2

The second investigation was conducted primarily for two reasons. First, in addition to examining the effects of attributional social comparison feedback on interpersonal attraction, we also wanted to assess the impact of such feedback on subsequent social information gathering activities vis-à-vis the comparison other. A major goal of social comparison processes is the reduction of uncertainty regarding one's construction of social reality. However, it should be evident that not all forms of comparison feedback may satisfy this goal. For example, we have argued in this chapter that the expression by another of dissimilar causal judgments for an event may engender greater uncertainty about the adequacy of that judgment. It seems likely that in response to such feedback, various uncertainty-reduction strategies might be tried. One strategy, particularly when the comparison cannot be avoided, might involve the gathering of additional information about the comparison other in order to ascertain the reason for the discrepancy in causal understandings.

The second major purpose of the study was to examine how the arousal of self-presentational concerns may affect observers' reactions to comparison feedback. Several researchers (Wheeler, Shaver, Jones, Goethals, Cooper, Robinson, Gruder, & Butzine, 1969; Wilson & Benner, 1971) have suggested that under private conditions, the usefulness or uncertainty reduction potential of the comparison information determines individuals' reactions to comparison others; under public, evaluative conditions, the favorability of the information takes on added importance. We would like to argue that the presentational implications of individuals' reactions to comparison others also become important in determining the effects of social comparison information under such conditions. For example, in the face of negative comparison feedback, very positive evaluations of or the avoidance of additional information about a comparison person might be seen as strategic attempts to repair a public image that has been hurt by the feedback. Conversely, very negative evaluations or the gathering of much information might be seen as defensive reactions. Since such presentational strategies would likely create an even less positive public image, a more effective strategy for individuals who publicly receive negative feedback might be to respond to comparison others in a moderate, ambiguous fashion. Individuals who experience a positive comparison, however, do not need to worry about repairing or protecting a damaged public image and may adopt more self-enhancing presentational strategies.

In the present study, the effects of similarity and social correctness of causal understandings for an event on evaluations of and the amount of social information seeking about the comparison other were examined under conditions designed to exaggerate (immediate evaluation) or minimize (delayed evaluation) observers' self-presentational concerns. In a study presumably concerned with jury decision making, an observer-subject and a second observer-confederate read a description of a situation that led to an accident. Observer-subjects made causal attributions for the accident and learned that these judgments would be evaluated at the end of the experimental session by an expert committee. Subjects then learned that their causal judgments were either similar or dissimilar to the other participant's and consistent (socially correct) or inconsistent (socially incorrect) with the judgments made by the majority of previous participants in the study. Half of the subjects learned at this time that the expert evaluation had to be postponed for an unspecified time.

Based on the above reasoning, we expected that subjects' primary motivation under delayed evaluation conditions would be the reduction of uncertainty regarding their causal judgments. Since this need should be best served by a salient and specific other's expression of concordant judgments, we expected that similarity would result in *more* favorable evaluations and *less* need for additional information than dissimilarity of causal understandings. As in Study 1, we expected the effects of social correctness compared to similarity of causal judgments to be modest. However, manipulation of this variable might provide subjects with some degree of validation or invalidation for their causal understandings. When subjects are less concerned about the correctness of their judgments, we might anticipate *more* favorable evaluations of and *less* information gathering about the comparison other.

Under immediate evaluation conditions, where self-presentational concerns presumably would be aroused, we expected that subjects would have some anxiety about the public, expert evaluation of their performance on the experimental task. Consequently, we anticipated that the favorability of the comparison would be determined primarily by information about the social correctness of causal understandings. Specifically, if subjects believe their judgments are incorrect, the comparison experience should be negative, even though the comparison other also may be incorrect. Since very favorable or very unfavorable reactions to the comparison person might be recognized by the expert committee as tactics designed to minimize the unfavorable repercussions of incorrect judgment feedback, under similar- and dissimilar-incorrect judgment conditions, moderation of subjects' evaluations and information gathering activities was expected. Under positive comparison conditions, however, subjects should be able to enhance their public esteem by highlighting via their reactions to the comparison person the desirability of the correct judgment feedback. Consequently, we expected that when subjects' judgments were socially correct, similarly correct others would be evaluated *more* favorably than dissimilar (and incorrect) judgment others. However, we also predicted that *less* information would be gathered under similar than dissimilar judgment conditions. This latter prediction was based on the notion that when a comparison is positive, subjects will try to solicit information that by implication may enhance the desirability of or their responsibility for the favorable feedback; information about an incorrect other is more likely than information about a similarly correct other, to enhance subjects' already positive, public identities.

METHOD

Subjects. Subjects were undergraduates (40 males, 40 females) at Ohio State University who participated in order to fulfill an introductory course requirement. They were assigned randomly and equally to the eight experimental conditions.

Procedure. The study was described as one of a series of studies commissioned by the Select Committee on Judicial Reform designed to evaluate the effectiveness of 18–23-year-olds as jurors. Subjects were told that the case they (and the second [female] participant in the adjacent room) would read was a real case that actually had involved litigation against a party for property damage and personal injury. Subjects also were told that as soon as the session was completed, they would meet with three members of the judicial reform committee who would evaluate their reactions to the case and to the study.

Next, subjects were given a booklet that included the same case summary and attribution measures used in Study 1. The experimenter instructed subjects to read the case summary and to answer the questions that followed it. She then joined the other participant (confederate) in the adjacent room—presumably to explain the experiment.

When the experimenter was sure that subjects had completed reading the case summary and answering the questions, she rejoined them. Using the same procedure employed in Study 1, she then manipulated the similarity and social correctness of subjects' causal understandings. The experimenter next told subjects in the immediate evaluation conditions that she just had received a note indicating that the three members of the Committee on Judicial Reform had arrived. Subjects were reminded that they would meet with the members shortly at which time their judgments and decision making strategies would be evaluated. In the delayed evaluation conditions, subjects were told that the note indicated a couple members of the committee were unable to make the evaluation session today. It was explained that the evaluation would be postponed to a later date, and because of the inconvenience, subjects would not be required to attend. The evaluation would instead be based on subjects' written responses to the experimental questionnaires.

All subjects then received a list of 21 potential questions a juror deliberating this case might ask another juror.[2] The experimenter explained that in normal jury decision-making situations, jurors exchange

[2]Questions for the measure of information seeking were selected from pilot data. Prior to the experiment, 60 questions concerning the jury case, how jurors might make decisions about the case, and jurors' personal characteristics were generated by the experimenters. Sixty-seven psychology students read a summary of the case used in Study 1 and made decisions about the actor's responsibility for the accident. Subjects then were given the list of 60 questions that "they might ask of another juror in an actual jury case." Subjects read each of the questions and responded to two items: "How much personal information do you feel could be gained from this question?" and "How much information relevant to the jurors' decisional process could be gained from this question?" Responses could range from 1 (very little) to 7 (a great deal of information). Twenty-one questions with the lowest standard deviations on both dimensions (personal, decisional information) were selected. Based on pilot subjects' mean ratings, the 21 questions were categorized according to whether they were likely to elicit a high, moderate, or low amount of personal and decision-relevant information. Those questions with a mean rating between 1.0 and 3.0, 3.75 and 4.2, and 5.0 and 7.0 were categorized as low, moderate, and high, respectively, on each of the informational dimensions (see Table 6.3).

information and ideas. In order to make this study more like an actual jury case, subjects were asked to select any number of questions they would like to ask the other "juror" in the study (it was emphasized that in selecting the questions, there was no right or wrong strategy).

Following this task, the experimenter placed the list of questions in a folder on the desk and asked all subjects to complete the final questionnaire. This questionnaire included measures designed to check on the manipulation of similarity and social correctness of causal understandings and six 9-point scales in which the subjects were asked to rate the other participant on each of six characteristics (reasonable, pleasant, open-minded, sincere, friendly, and honest). Finally, subjects were debriefed and dismissed.

RESULTS

Manipulation checks. At the outset of the debriefing session, subjects were asked a question designed to check on the manipulation of immediate or delayed evaluation. Debriefers asked the subject if and when their judgments would be evaluated. All subjects correctly answered that their judgments would be evaluated by a judicial reform committee. Subjects in the immediate evaluation condition acknowledged that the evaluation would take place immediately following the session. All subjects in the delayed evaluation condition told the debriefer about the cancellation of the evaluation session and that they were not required to attend it. The manipulation of the evaluation variable, then, was successful.

To check on the manipulations of perceived similarity and social correctness of causal understanding, subjects were asked to rate on two 15-point scales the degree to which they believed (1) their own and the other participants' understanding of the case was similar and (2) their causal judgments were similar to those of previous participants in the study. Separate $2 \times 2 \times 2$ (Similarity $\times$ Social Correctness $\times$ Evaluation) analysis of variance performed on subjects' ratings yielded the predicted main effect on the similarity ($F[1, 72] = 1371.83$, $p < .0001$) and social correctness ($F[1, 72] = 617.51$, $p < .001$) check measures. These independent variables, then, were successfully manipulated.

Evaluation index. Subjects were asked to rate on 9-point scales the extent to which the other participant seemed reasonable, pleasant, open-minded, sincere, friendly, and honest. Subjects' ratings on these scales were highly intercorrelated ($ps < .01$) and, consequently, were summed and divided by 6 to yield a single attraction index.

For ease of presentation and to provide more specific tests of the predictions, separate analyses of variance were conducted within the immediate and the delayed evaluation conditions. Within the delayed evaluation conditions, analysis of variance revealed the predicted main effect for similarity ($F[1, 36] = 17.46$, $p < .0002$). Subjects in the similar judgment condition ($M = 6.52$) evaluated the other participant more positively than did subjects in the dissimilar judgment condition ($M = 5.27$). The analysis also yielded, as predicted, a significant but weaker main effect for social correctness of causal judgments ($F[1, 36] = 6.51$, $p = .02$). Subjects whose judgments were socially correct ($M = 6.28$) evaluated the other participant more favorably than did subjects whose judgments were socially incorrect ($M = 5.52$).

Within the immediate evaluation conditions, a 2×2 (Similarity $\times$ Social Correctness) analysis of variance yielded a significant main effect for similarity ($F[1, 36] = 12.88$, $p < .001$) such that similarity resulted in more favorable evaluations of the comparison other than did dissimilarity of causal understandings. This effect, however, was qualified by a significant Similarity $\times$ Social Correctness interaction ($F[1, 36] = 6.31$, $p < .02$). Examination of the means presented in Table 6.2 reveals that similarity resulted in more positive evaluations of the other participant only when subjects' judgments were socially correct. The results of a priori pairwise comparisons (Dunn, 1961) conducted within level of immediate or delayed evaluation are illustrated in Table 6.2.

Social information seeking measure. Subjects were asked to select from the list of 21 questions those items they would like to ask the other participant in the study (see Table 6.3). Overall, subjects asked an average of 5.33 questions. Separate 2×2 (Similarity $\times$ Social Correctness) analyses of variance conducted within the immediate and delayed eval-

Table 6.2

MEANS FOR THE EVALUATION INDEX: STUDY 2[a]

	Immediate evaluation		Delayed evaluation	
	Socially correct	Socially incorrect	Socially correct	Socially incorrect
Similar judgment	7.65$_a$	6.61$_b$	6.92$_c$	6.12$_c$
	(10)	(10)	(10)	(10)
Dissimilar judgment	5.95$_b$	6.31$_b$	5.63$_d$	4.91$_d$
	(10)	(10)	(10)	(10)

[a]The higher the mean, the more positive the evaluation. The numbers in parentheses indicate the number of subjects in each experimental condition. Within level of evaluation, means with common subscripts are not significantly different.

Table 6.3

MEASURE OF INFORMATION SEEKING[a]

	Categorization of questions	
Question	Personal	Decision-relevant
1. How similar to the actual jury decision-making process was this task?	L	L
2. In your opinion, how safe was the neighbor's shed?	L	H
3. What is your favorite passion?	H	L
4. Do you think all this could have been avoided if Mr. J had hired a professional to do the job?	L	M
5. What is your grade point average?	H	L
6. Do you think this case would be clear to anyone who read it?	L	H
7. Have you ever served on a jury before?	L	M
8. Did you feel there was enough information to arrrive at a decision?	M	H
9. How common are such accidents?	L	M
10. Do you think financial damages should have been awarded in this case?	L	H
11. Are you the oldest, youngest, or in the middle of your brothers and sisters?	H	L
12. How carefully did you read the case study?	M	H
13. What other preventive measures might Mr. J have taken?	L	H
14. Does "intention" make a difference in responsibility?	M	H
15. What is your religion?	H	L
16. What is your age?	H	L
17. Did you feel sorry for Mr. J?	H.	H
18. Are you interested in law?	M	L
19. Do you feel your views on most matters agree with other's views?	H	M
20. How many criminal justice or law courses have you had?	M	L
21. How easy did you think it was to arrive at a decision?	H	M

[a]H denotes a high, M a moderate, and L a low rating on that dimension.

uation conditions on the total number of questions chosen revealed no significant main or interaction effects. Post hoc analyses of the questions according to their informational characteristics (i.e., elicitation of high, moderate, or low personal and decision-relevant information) revealed significant effects only for those items designed to elicit highly personal information. Specifically, a two-way analysis of variance conducted within delayed evaluation conditions revealed that subjects chose significantly fewer questions of a highly personal nature to ask the similar ($M = .65$) as compared to the dissimilar ($M = 1.25$) judgment other ($F(1, 36) = 3.96$, $p = .05$). Within the immediate evaluation conditions, however, subjects whose judgments were socially correct ($M = 1.25$) sought more highly personal information from the other participant than did subjects whose causal judgments were socially incorrect ($M = .53$; $F[1, 36] = 3.85$, $p = .057$).

DISCUSSION

The results for the evaluation index provide strong support for the a priori hypotheses. Under delayed evaluation conditions, subjects' primary motivation was expected to be the reduction of uncertainty about the adequacy of their judgments. Consequently, we anticipated that subjects' expression of positive sentiment toward the other participant would result from validation via the comparison feedback of their causal understandings of the event. The results indicated that, as predicted, the other participant was evaluated more favorably by subjects in the similar than in the dissimilar judgment conditions. More favorable evaluations of the other also were found for socially correct than for incorrect judgment conditions. It appears that in the present investigation the explicit, albeit delayed, evaluation of causal judgments made the validation provided by the correctness feedback more important than it was in Study 1. It is important to note, however, that the effects of social correctness still were relatively modest compared to those of similarity of causal judgments.

Under immediate evaluation conditions, we expected the presentational implications of subjects' reactions to the other participant to be an important determinant of the effects of similarity and social correctness of causal understandings. Specifically, we expected that subjects who had received comparison feedback indicating that their causal judgments were correct would try to enhance their public esteem by highlighting the desirability of the feedback. One way to accomplish this would be to evaluate very favorably a similarly correct other. However, subjects in the immediate evaluation conditions who received information indicating that their causal judgments were incorrect were expected to have concerns about the presentational effectiveness of making very favorable or unfavorable evaluations of the other. To avoid further damage to their public esteem, these subjects were expected to moderate their evaluations of the similar and dissimilar judgment other. Analyses of the evaluation measure supported these predictions. Under immediate evaluation conditions, the similar judgment other was evaluated more favorably than the dissimilar judgment other only when subjects' judgments were socially correct.

The results for the measure of information seeking were considerably weaker. None of the predicted effects was obtained when the total number of questions chosen was examined; however, post hoc analyses of questions likely to elicit highly personal information did reveal several effects consistent with the predictions. Specifically, under delayed evaluation conditions, more information of a highly personal nature was sought from dissimilar than similar judgment others. Such information seeking presumably resulted from the greater uncertainty reduction needs engendered by the other's expression of discordant causal judgments. In addition, under immediate evaluation conditions, more highly personal information was sought from the comparison other only when the information might by implication reflect favorably on subjects, that is, only when their judgments were socially correct. It is interesting to note in this regard that the highly personal questions asked most often by socially correct judgment subjects included, "Did you feel sorry for the defendant?" and "How easy did you think it was to arrive at a decision?". It is difficult to imagine how the other participant's responses to such questions could not have positive presentational implications for subjects whose causal judgments were correct.

Why were the results for the measure of information seeking so weak? There are at least two possible reasons. First, information gathering activities may not be major consequences of social comparison processes. Second, our measure of information seeking may not have been sensitive enough to detect differences in social information seeking in response to comparison feedback about causal judgments. While future research will decide which, if either, of these two explanations is correct, our hunch is that the second possibility is the more likely one. The measure of information seeking was developed specifically for this study and, consequently, had not previously been employed. Moreover, only about 5 of the 21 questions were chosen by subjects. It may well be that our measure simply did not sample broadly enough those questions that would have allowed subjects to enhance or protect their public images or reduce uncertainty about the adequacy of their causal judgments.

CONCLUDING REMARKS

Several authors have speculated that causal attributions play an important role in interpersonal evaluative activities (Orvis et al., 1976). However, most of the research examining the relationship between attributional and evaluative processes has focused on the reactions of observers to the causal attributions made by an *actor* for his or her performance outcome (Carlston & Shovar, 1983; Forsyth et al., 1981; Tetlock, 1980). More specifically, it has focused on the question of whether actors' self-serving attributions are effective in gaining the approval of others. In the current chapter, we have presented the results of two studies that examined the reactions of observers to a *second observer's* causal attributions for an *actor's* outcome. For reasons outlined earlier, we have placed our research within the context of social comparison theory. It is important to note, however, that there may be several limitations to the generalizability of our findings. First, it is not clear what role social comparison processes may play in observers' reactions to actors' self-attributions. Second, in both Studies 1 and 2, observer-subjects were asked explicitly to make attributions for an event and then were forced into a direct comparison with another. Mettee and Smith (1977) argued that such a comparison is likely to be competitive. Future research will need to determine the effects of attributional comparison feedback when the situation is not competitive.

REFERENCES

Carlston, D. E., & Shovar, N. (1983). Effects of performance attributions on others' perceptions of the attributor. *Journal of Personality and Social Psychology, 44*(3), 515–525.
Dunn, O. J. (1961). Multiple comparisons among means. *Journal of the American Statistical Association, 56,* 52–64.
Festinger, L. (1954). A theory of social comparison processes. *Human Relations, 7,* 117–140.
Forsyth, D. R., Berger, R. E., & Mitchell, T. (1981). The effects of self-serving vs. other-serving claims of responsibility on attraction and attribution in groups. *Social Psychology Quarterly, 44*(1), 59–64.
Fromkin, H. L. (1972). Feelings of interpersonal undistinctiveness: An unpleasant affective state. *Journal of Experimental Research in Personality, 6,* 178–185.
Gruder, C. L. (1977). Choice of comparison persons in evaluating oneself. In J. M. Suls & R. L. Miller (Eds.), *Social comparison processes: Theoretical and empirical perspectives.* Washington, D.C.: Hemisphere Publishing.
Harvey, J. H., & Weary, G. (1981). *Perspectives on attributional processes.* Dubuque, Iowa: William C. Brown.
Harvey, J. H., & Weary, G. (1984). Current issues in attribution theory and research. *Annual Review of Psychology, 35,* 427–459.
Heider, F. (1958). *The psychology of interpersonal relations.* New York: Wiley.
Jones, E. E., & Davis, K. E. (1965). From acts to dispositions: The attribution process in person perception. In L. Berkowitz (Ed.), *Advances in experimental social psychology* (Vol. 2). New York: Academic Press.
Jones, E. E., & Nisbett, R. E. (1972). The actor and the observer: Divergent perceptions of the causes of behavior. In E. E. Jones, D. Kanouse, H. H. Kelley, R. E. Nisbett, S. Valins, & B. Weiner (Eds.), *Attribution: Perceiving the causes of behavior.* New York: General Learning Press.

Jones, E. E., & Pittman, T. S. (1982). Toward a general theory of strategic self-presentation. In J. Suls (Ed.), *Psychological perspectives on the self.* Hillsdale, NJ: Erlbaum.

Kassin, S. M. (1979). Consensus information, prediction, and causal attribution: A review of the literature and issues. *Journal of Personality and Social Psychology, 37,* 1966–1981.

Kelley, H. H. (1967). Attribution in social psychology. In D. Levine (Ed.), *Nebraska Symposium on Motivation.* Lincoln: University of Nebraska Press.

Mettee, D. R., & Smith G. (1977). Social comparison and interpersonal attraction. In J. M. Suls & R. L. Miller (Eds.), *Social comparison processes: Theoretical and empirical perspectives.* Washington, D.C.: Hemisphere Publishing.

Monson, T. C., & Snyder, M. (1977). Actors, observers, and the attribution process: Toward a reconceptualization. *Journal of Experimental Social Psychology, 13,* 89–111.

Orvis, B. R., Kelley, H. H., & Butler, D. (1976). Attributional conflict in young couples. In J. H. Harvey, W. J. Ickes, & R. F. Kidd (Eds.), *New directions in attribution research* (Vol. 1). Hillsdale, NJ: Erlbaum.

Ross, L., Bierbrauer, G., & Polly, S. (1974). Attribution of educational outcomes by professional and nonprofessional instructors. *Journal of Personality and Social Psychology, 29,* 609–619.

Shaver, K. G. (1975). *An introduction to attribution processes.* Cambridge, Mass.: Winthrop Publishers.

Tetlock, R. E. (1980). Explaining teacher explanations of pupil performance: A self-presentation interpretation. *Social Psychology Quarterly, 43,* 283–290.

Thornton, D. A., & Arrowood, A. J. (1966). Self evaluation, self-enhancement, and the locus of social comparison. *Journal of Experimental Social Psychology,* Suppl. 1, 40–48.

Weary, G. (1979). Self-serving attributional biases: Perceptual or response distortions? *Journal of Personality and Social Psychology, 37,* 1418–1420.

Weary, G., & Arkin, R. M. (1981). Attributional self-presentation. In J. H. Harvey, W. J. Ickes, & R. F. Kidd (Eds.), *New directions in attribution research.* Hillsdale, NJ: Erlbaum.

Wheeler, L., Shaver, K. G., Jones, R. A., Goethals, G. R., Cooper J., Robinson, J. E., Gruder, C. L., & Butzine, K. W. (1969). Factors determining choice of a comparison other. *Journal of Experimental Social Psychology, 5,* 219–232.

Wilson, S. R., & Benner, L. A. (1971). The effects of self-esteem and situation upon comparison choices during ability evaluation. *Sociometry, 34*(3), 381–397.

PART II

APPLICATION OF ATTRIBUTION THEORY AND RESEARCH

This part contains three chapters concerned with applications of attributional ideas and findings to various problems in living. In Chapter 7, Arkin and Baumgardner provide a discussion of self-handicapping and how people appear to use this strategy of self-presentation in a variety of societal contexts. The concept of self-handicapping, first introduced by Berglas and Jones (1978) has been shown to help clarify why a person might consume a debilitating drug, consume alcohol, reduce effort on achievement tasks, and engage in other types of behavior that on the surface may appear to be deleterious to the individual. But as Arkin and Baumgardner cogently argue, such behavior appears to serve the function of maintaining one's sense of personal control in a complex, fast-paced, and frequently challenging social environment. At the same time, Arkin and Baumgardner also note that the evidence suggests that objectively the self-presentational utility of self-handicapping may be much less than most handicappers imagine.

Fincham (Chapter 8) discusses attributional processes in close relationships. He reviews and critically evaluates much of the research that has become prominent in the last few years. He also extends current theoretical analysis to include attention to the natural interdependence of attribution, affect, and behavior. Fincham's statement represents not only a thoughtful critique of the limitations of some attribution approaches to understanding and treating relationship dilemmas, but also a scholarly presentation of the potential of the attributional perspective in addressing relationship questions and problems. He reasonably asks that more attention be given to research on basic attributional principles as they operate in relationship contexts.

The final chapter in this part by Anderson and Arnoult (Chapter 9) focuses on attributional models of depression, loneliness, and shyness. These "problems in living," so much a part of our time, appear to be particularly amenable to attributional analysis concerned with how people understand the bases of their troubling feelings and thoughts. Anderson and Arnoult present a compelling case for the importance of the controllability and the locus of attributional style dimensions in every-day problems in living. For example, people who tend to feel that they can control the factors leading to negative events are less depressed than are those who do not typically feel capable of controlling them. This chapter is filled with leads about useful directions for research on attribution as a social and personality dynamic and as a central concept in the understanding and treatment of clinically manifest thoughts and emotions.

CHAPTER 7

Self-Handicapping*

Robert M. Arkin and Ann H. Baumgardner

INTRODUCTION

In Western society, an excellent candidate in the race for most important attribute is ability, or competence (see Anderson, 1968; Festinger, 1954; White, 1959). We live in a world where a great deal of what we do is evaluated, both by ourselves and by others, with an eye toward assessing the level of ability underlying performance (Darley & Goethals, 1980). Performance on the tennis court, in the classroom, in the concert hall, and across a table for two is scrutinized closely to determine athletic, intellectual, artistic, or social competence.

Commonly, attribution theory has been considered the study of the process by which people form causal interpretations of events around them. However, the attribution approach also encompasses this more general process of how people go about attributing personal characteristics, feelings, and traits to objects in their social context. To create a meaningful view of their social world, people "must answer questions not only about the 'whyness' of things, but about their 'whatness' as well" (Kanouse & Hansen, 1971, p. 47). The same trait term used to describe why an event transpired (e.g., failure due to an individual's lack of effort) is easily translated to a trait ascription (he is lazy; see Jones & Davis, 1965). It is partly for this reason that the topics of attribution and self-concept have been married in a great deal of contemporary research and have contributed so substantially to the growing body of work that has come to be called social cognition (Fiske & Taylor, 1984).

The *self-serving bias in causal attribution* refers to a rather pervasive tendency of individuals to attribute successful outcomes to themselves and

*Part of this chapter was written while the first author was on leave at the University of Oxford; thanks are due the social psychology group at Oxford for their hospitality and support. Thanks are also due John Harvey, Richard Petty, Catherine Riordan, and Gifford Weary for their insightful comments on an earlier version of this paper.

unsuccessful outcomes to other factors (e.g., Weary & Arkin, 1981). In the case of the self-serving bias, the intimate link between questions of "whyness" and "whatness" is clear. By denying personal responsibility for unsuccessful outcomes, the negative quality of the bad news is vastly reduced; although the failure has occurred and cannot be reversed, the implications of the failing outcome in determining one's level of ability is minimized. Put simply, by attributing an unsuccessful outcome to some extraneous external cause, one can sever the usual link between performance and evaluation. In contrast, by assuming personal responsibility for successful outcomes, the positive quality of the good news can be increased; the implication of the success in determining one's level of ability is maximized by asserting the link between performance and evaluation.

The self-serving bias in causal attribution is a fairly clear use of attributional principles aimed at protecting or sustaining one's image. A more subtle use of attributional principles would consist of performing only certain behaviors or manipulating the context proactively, so that only desired inferences about personal qualities could be drawn. This more subtle maneuver relegates the use of attributional principles to a rather high plane, in that the attributional rules must be applied proactively, before a given behavioral sequence is undertaken, rather than retroactively, after some outcome has occurred. It is also rather more refined because it argues that people must have a fairly sophisticated knowledge of how various behaviors tend to be interpreted by the average perceiver (Schneider, 1981).

The purpose of this chapter is to review the literature and discuss the theoretical, methodological, and a few of the applied aspects of this subtle use of attributional principles to manage one's image. The introduction of the term *self-handicapping* (Jones & Berglas, 1978) sets the stage for this integration of attribution theory and impression management; the term refers to an individual's attempt to reduce a threat to esteem by actively seeking or creating inhibitory factors that interfere with performance and thus provide a persuasive causal explanation for potential failure. The introduction of extraneous interfering causal factors obscures the link between performance and evaluation, at least in the case of that potential failure, and mitigates the impact of the failure feedback; as with the self-serving bias phenomenon, the failure is not viewed as a reflection of low ability or competence. Yet the probability of failure is increased by the introduction of the "handicap," rendering success less likely. To quote the authors directly: "The self-handicapper, we are suggesting, reaches out for impediments, exaggerates handicaps, and embraces any factor reducing personal responsibility for mediocrity and enhancing personal responsibility for success'' (Jones & Berglas, 1978, p. 202).

This gives every appearance of being a sophisticated use of Kelley's (1971) discounting and augmentation principles. In the case of mediocre or failing performance, the role of the individual's ability must be discounted as a causal factor, since another plausible cause (i.e., the handicap) is present. In the case of successful performance (which may be unlikely after the introduction of the impediment) the role of the individual's ability as a cause is augmented because the success occurred in spite of the adverse circumstances.

We begin the chapter with a brief overview of the relevant literature and then attempt to fashion a taxonomy or organizational scheme to spell out some dimensions of self-handicapping that we hope will prove heuristic. Next, we discuss in detail the motivational basis of self-handicapping, attempt to integrate our taxonomic scheme with the discussion of motives, and close with some speculative analyses of the likely effectiveness of self-handicapping.

SELF-HANDICAPPING STRATEGIES

A BRIEF OVERVIEW

As discussed previously, the goal of the self-handicapper is to discount ability as a determinant of poor performance and to augment ability as a determinant of good performance. Ideally, the impediment chosen should be one that places the actor in the least negative light possible. Minimally, the handicap must not reflect an attribute that seems related to low ability. Maximally, the ideal handicap would give every appearance of interfering with performance, but in reality would serve as a minimal impediment to achievement.

However, research on self-handicapping has not addressed individuals' preferences for one or another self-handicapping alternative. Instead, the studies have presented subjects with an option to self-handicap along only a single route. Nevertheless, several self-handicapping strategies have been investigated and the evidence seems persuasive that people do use attributional principles, via self-handicapping, to regulate their image.

In an initial demonstration of drug use as a self-handicap, Berglas and Jones (1978) gave subjects who had previously succeeded at a task, but did not expect that success to recur on a repetition of the task, the opportunity to choose to protect themselves by ingesting a debilitating drug. By taking the drug, the subjects were able to manipulate the situation such that their first successful performance might be seen as based on their "true" abilities, because the impending failure, if it occurred, would be seen as attributable to the debilitating drug.

The inhibiting drug choice paradigm has been used in a few replications of the original self-handicapping finding (e.g., Gibbons & Gaeddert, 1984; Kolditz & Arkin, 1982; Tucker, Vuchinich, & Sobell, 1981). These studies have been carried out with different purposes in mind (e.g., see Kolditz & Arkin, 1982), yet the basic phenomenon seems reliable. For instance, Tucker et al. (1981) replicated the Berglas and Jones methodology using alcohol consumption as the dependent measure. They found that subjects who expected to fail drank greater quantities of alcohol, presumably as a means to undermine the competence implications of their "impending" failure.

The finding that ingesting a debilitating drug functions as a self-handicap suggests that chronic drug or alcohol use might, at least in part, be attributable to chronic self-handicapping (see Jones & Berglas, 1978).

Along conceptually similar lines, but with different theoretical underpinnings, M. L. Snyder and his colleagues (Frankel & M. L. Snyder, 1978; M. L. Snyder, Smoller, Strenta, & Frankel, 1981) reasoned that lack of effort could also serve as a useful impediment to performance and thus obscure ability inferences based upon failing outcomes. Drawing from the Heiderian (1958) idea that ability and effort are inversely related, they argued that the individual who expects to fail will reduce effort and thus minimize the likelihood of an attribution of low ability. Using a learned helplessness sort of paradigm, they found that subjects who had previously succeeded but expected to fail did withdraw effort. Strategic reductions in effort have been found in other studies as well (Baumeister, Hamilton, & Tice, 1984; Pyszczynski & Greenberg, 1983). For instance, Pyszcynski and Greenberg (1983) found that subjects who expected to fail reduced intended effort, but only when confronted with an ego-involving task. This finding suggests that the importance of one's performance influences the decision to self-handicap.

Taken together, these studies all show self-handicapping strategies that may be classified as acquisitions of impediments of an internal but ability-irrelevant nature. Taking a debilitating drug, consuming alcohol, and reducing effort all obscure the inference that poor performance is due to incompetence, but each reflects an internal "disposition" that itself is not particularly flattering. Another class of handicap might include setting the stage so that a poor performance would be attributable to an *external* impediment. For example, such a ploy could be used by the weekend athlete who socially compares solely with those obviously out of his league, such as marathon runners. Under such circumstances, losing a race could not be viewed as diagnostic of poor ability; the runner has simply chosen an inordinately difficult goal and the negativity of the imminent failure is mitigated.

Rhodewalt and Davison (1984) have demonstrated choice of a situational impediment as a self-handicapping strategy under conditions similar to those employed in the Berglas and Jones (1978) paradigm. Subjects who had previously performed well, but did not expect their success to recur in an upcoming performance, self-handicapped by choosing to listen to performance-debilitating music rather than facilitative or neutral music. In a similar way, Greenberg (1983) found that subjects led to expect failure chose goals that were very difficult (i.e., chose a task which would require a particularly high score to warrant "success"). Inherent in the choice of very difficult goals or impossible circumstances is the avoidance of any information that is diagnostic of poor performance. Interestingly, the elimination of the diagnostic implications of performance may reduce the anxiety associated with performance evaluation and thus contribute to an actual improvement in performance (Brodt & Zimbardo, 1981; Weiner & Sierad, 1975). For example, Leary (1983a) found that socially anxious individuals, exposed to a distracting noise that would supposedly interfere with an ability to interact successfully with others, were less anxious and actually performed better during a social interaction than their counterparts not exposed to the handicap.

One theme that runs throughout the studies discussed thus far is that self-handicaps involve the active acquisition of internal (e.g., drug ingestion or reduced effort) or situational (e.g., choice of difficult goals or distracting noise) impediments to performance. However, a more liberal interpretation of self-handicapping could include other strategies comprised of verbal self-reports or claims of handicaps. C. R. Snyder and his colleagues (Smith, C. R. Snyder, & Handelsman, 1982; Smith, C. R. Snyder, & Perkins, 1983; C. R. Snyder & Smith, 1982) have conducted several studies demonstrating the use of strategic claims (i.e., the avowal of a handicap that is already present or may not be present at all) in evaluative settings. They suggest that symptoms such as social or test anxiety can be strategically used to protect esteem in the same way as a self-handicap that is acquired.

Smith, C. R. Snyder, and Handelsman (1982) examined the self-report of test anxiety as a self-handicapping strategy. Prior to a test, high and low test-anxiety subjects were either informed that test anxiety inhibits performance on the test, does not inhibit performance on the test, or were given no instructions. They found that anxious subjects reported more anxiety than usual, except when anxiety was portrayed as not inhibiting at all. Snyder et al. argued that test-anxious individuals may utilize their symptoms as a means to circumvent uncertainty regarding future outcomes. This finding has been replicated by Greenberg, Pyszczynski and Paisley (1984); however these authors found that this effect only occurred when extrinsic incentives for good performance were relatively low. The use of symptoms as accounts for future negative evaluation has been extended beyond test anxiety; other studies have indicated that shyness, depression, and hypochondriacal complaints may be used in the same fashion (Baumgardner, Lake & Arkin, 1984; Smith et al., 1983; C. R. Snyder, Smith, Augelli, & Ingram, 1983).

Interestingly, Smith et al. found that their subjects' strategic ploy was not designed to protect prior performance. In the self-handicapping studies carried out previously, a prior success, one which was not clearly based upon ability, was necessary to promote self-handicapping. This discrepancy regarding the necessary and sufficient antecedents of self-handicapping raises the question of whether handicapping is designed to protect oneself from the implications of a likely failure, to protect the ability implications of a prior success, or perhaps both.

One resolution of the discrepancy could rest with the nature of the self-handicapping strategy available to subjects. In the Smith et al. study, a verbal claim, rather than the active acquisition of a handicap, was investigated. It may have been easier for subjects to "pull-off" such a claim (i.e., require less strategic effort) and thus the precipitating conditions for such a strategy need not be so strong. In the Jones and Berglas paradigm, where subjects who self-handicapped had to ingest a pill, participants were perhaps willing to do so only when the stakes were relatively high. More specifically, the *acquisition* of a handicap (rather than the mere verbal claim of a handicap) may require direct threats to prior ability ascriptions *and* likely future failure. Of course, further research may show that expectation of failure is indeed sufficient to elicit all forms of handicapping.

In a related controversy, the question has been raised as to whether people are ever inclined to self-handicap subsequent to failing a task. Both Rhodewalt and Davison (1984) and Weidner (1980) found that only persons who are especially resistant to viewing themselves as out of control. (e.g., Type A individuals) handicapped in the face of prior failure. Baumgardner et al. (1984) uncovered another important qualification. They argued that the individual who has failed publicly should be less likely to claim a handicap, since handicapping only the future performance could not ameliorate the negative evaluation based on the earlier performance. (Moreover, if the handicap itself has negative self-relevant implications, the "handicapper" may do even more serious damage to his or her image rather than repair a spoiled image.) They found that subjects reported a greater degree of depressive symptoms (which had been characterized by the experimenter as an impediment) only when they believed that the experimenter was unaware of their prior poor performance. Together, these studies suggest that self-handicapping can occur subsequent to failure, but only when the candidate for handicapping still has something clear to protect (e.g., an unspoiled public identity; an exaggerated sense of personal efficacy).

What is perhaps most intriguing about the preponderance of the research discussed thus far is the nature of the attributional strategy. Subjects who self-handicap by ingesting a drug, consuming alcohol, or expressing depressive symptoms are discounting an ability attribution for poor performance but are not necessarily discounting an internal attribution for that performance. For instance, the individual who performs poorly due to being intoxicated avoids being labelled stupid or incompetent, but she is still drunk. Likewise, the individual who claims test anxiety may avoid an ability attribution for failure, but still must contend with the negative implications of the label "test anxious." Self-handicapping therefore appears to reflect a powerful motivation to avoid ability inferences. However, before turning to a discussion of the motivational bases of self-handicapping, it may be useful and instructive to attempt organizing the self-handicapping strategies into some sensible scheme.

ORGANIZATIONAL SCHEME

As the preceding discussion suggests, self-handicapping can be viewed along several dimensions. Research examining symptom self-reports consists of *claims* of internal (but nonability) handicaps (such as claiming test anxiety). This can be contrasted with self-handicapping which entails the *acquisition* of an impediment to accurate appraisal (such as ingesting a debilitating drug or alcohol, or reducing effort). These examples of symptom self-report and acquired handicaps are similar in that both accentuate ability-irrelevant *internal* attributions. This class of *internal* factors can be contrasted with *external* factors such as the choice of difficult goals, or nondiagnostic contexts. Considering these dimensions together, a taxonomy emerges whereby self-handicaps can be classified in one of four quadrants: *internal-acquired, internal-claimed, external-acquired,* and *external-claimed* (see Figure 7.1).

There are no data bearing on what type of handicapping strategy an individual is likely to adopt, should he have a choice. Nevertheless, it is interesting to speculate what might transpire if a potential handi-

Action

		Acquired	Claimed
Locus	Internal	Drug ingestion Alcohol consumption Reduced effort	Test anxiety Social anxiety Physical complaint Depression
	External	Choosing poor performance conditions Difficult goal choice	Asserting the difficulty of a task

Figure 7.1 Taxonomy of self-handicaps.

capper had a choice among options. With regard to the internality–externality of handicaps, it seems that an internal handicap (i.e., drug ingestion or reduced effort), whether acquired or claimed, should carry more negative repercussions for the self-handicapping individual. For example, to fail because one is drunk should be viewed more negatively than failure attributable to an impossible task. This supposition is derivable from Weiner's (Weiner, Russell, & Lerman, 1978) account of the attributional determinants of affect; the internal–external attributional dimension is said to determine affect (primarily) and only internal attributions for success and failure produce affects such as pride and shame, respectively. Therefore, given a choice, an individual might opt for an external handicap if one is available. However, a disadvantage of external handicaps is that they may be less persuasive than the more costly, internal sort of handicap; specifically, they may be more subject to public scrutiny and consequently more easily "discovered" by a skeptical audience.

In predicting whether an individual will opt for an internal versus an external handicap, another factor is likely to prove crucial. The importance of appearing able, or at least not incompetent, in a given setting may well determine whether an individual will choose an internal or an external handicap. Because internal handicapping is more costly, this choice probably occurs more readily in situations where it is very important to the individual to be convincing with his handicap. Moreover, if it is particularly important to portray oneself as able (or not unable), then perhaps one is more willing to incur such costs.

The acquired–claimed dimension refers to the distinction between an actual behavioral manuever (acquisition) and a verbal claim designed to portray a handicap. Rather than dichotomous, it may be helpful to view this dimension more as a continuum from overt or active behavior (e.g., ingesting a drug, choosing a difficult goal) at one extreme to mere self-serving attributions (e.g., "my poor performance was due to bad luck") at the other. Somewhere between these poles lies the verbal claim (such as test anxiety). The individual who claims a handicap is not drawing a causal inference directly, and is not dealing merely with past behavior; rather she is attempting to set up an inference process such that the intended attribution is logically derivable from that claim. In claiming that her test anxious state will account for any poor performance *in the future*, the individual fosters but does not directly provide a nonability attribution for impending failure.

Notably, an acquired handicap appears to carry the greatest potential costs. The acquired handicap may actually make failure more likely, but a mere claim of a handicap does not affect the likelihood of failure. Moreover, it may be worth noting that an acquired handicap carries a special risk of its own. Not only is the inference process described in the paragraph above necessary, but it is also necessary that the behavior (e.g., a lack of effort) is perceived and construed as a handicap. In short, the sophistication of the inferences necessary for acquired handicaps is much greater than for mere claims of handicaps.

In addition to the two conceptual dimensions described above, self-handicapping can be characterized along two rather more motivational dimensions (see Figure 7.2). First, while there is considerable evidence that self-handicapping occurs, it is not yet clear whether these behaviors serve primarily public (i.e., impression management) or private (i.e., self-esteem) goals. Most of the studies previously reviewed did not vary the impression management motives of subjects, although those that have done so (e.g., Baumgardner, et al., 1984; Kolditz & Arkin, 1982) have found increases in self-handicapping under conditions engendering impression management motives. This raises the question of whether acquiring or claiming an impediment will occur for purely private reasons at all. We shall leave a discussion of this issue until the next section, on motivational underpinnings of self-handicapping.

For reasons of exposition, we have focused on handicaps as strategies to "discount" the competence implications of failure. However, the original theoretical statement expressly included the "augmenting" of success as well. The individual who succeeds in spite of an impediment,

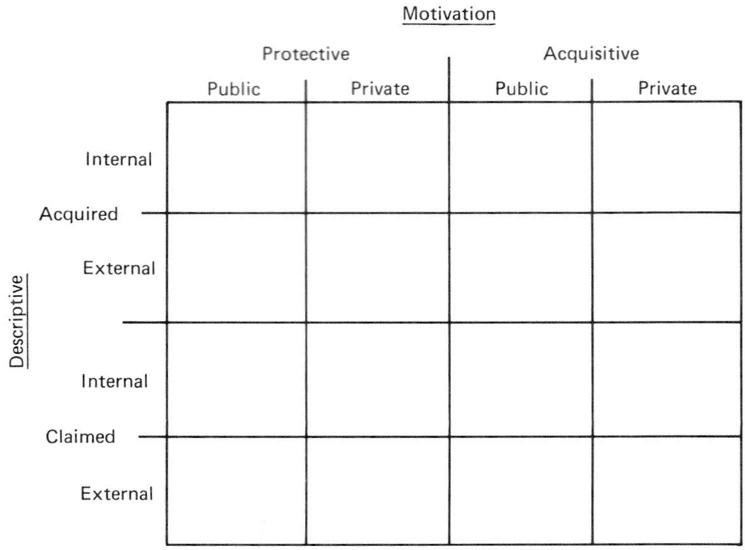

Figure 7.2 Taxonomy of descriptive and motivational dimensions underlying self-handicapping.

has achieved a truly impressive performance, and would warrant more extreme ability attribution than the person who succeeds without the impediment (see especially Heider, 1958, and Kelley, 1971). The original demonstration and all subsequent investigations of self-handicapping have retained the confounding of these two potentially separable processes. The theoretical and empirical separation of these two processes seems very desirable to the present authors.

For instance, Arkin (1981) proposed two primary approaches an actor might take in accomplishing self-presentation: the *acquisitive* style and the *protective* style. The individual who behaves in an acquisitive manner seeks out situations where a positive presentation of self is possible and attempts to garner social approval when appropriate. The individual who engages in a protective self-presentation style avoids situations where losses in approval are likely, and engages in a variety of protective presentations when complete avoidance is not possible. It seems possible to draw the analogy that the self-handicapper who expects failure and wishes to discount the impending failure is engaging in protective self-presentation, whereas the self-handicapper who expects to succeed and wishes to augment the success is engaging in acquisitive self-presentation. If, as Arkin (1981) argued, there are powerful individual differences and powerful contextual factors determining who adopts these two styles and when, it seems important to unconfound these two motive systems in the self-handicapping arena as well. More specifically, if the weight of the evidence shows that self-handicapping occurs solely among persons who tend to expect failure and in contexts where failure seems likely, then it may turn out that self-handicapping is primarily a *protective* strategy.

We might add briefly that the acquisitive brand of self-handicapping seems unlikely because of some unique costs associated with it. The person who self-handicaps when he or she expects to succeed would be presented with a dilemma; if the handicap is adopted, then the individual may lose a chance to prove he or she is able (i.e., failure becomes more probable) and be forced to fall back on failure attributable to the handicap. All else being equal, a demonstration of high ability would seem preferable to ambiguous failure. Nevertheless, because people may occasionally be motivated to demonstrate true excellence, acquisitive forms of handicapping may indeed occur. Moreover, because handicaps could serve to lower expectancies or criteria for success, the "unique costs" may often be minimized. However, "claimed" handicaps of an acquisitive type should be much more common because they automatically carry fewer costs. Colloquially, these might be referred to as "hedging one's bet."

THE MOTIVATIONAL BASES AND ETIOLOGY OF SELF-HANDICAPPING

SELF-ESTEEM AND SOCIAL ESTEEM

The motivational basis of self-handicapping would seem to be obvious. Self-handicapping is a "response to an anticipated loss in self-esteem" (C. R. Snyder & Smith, 1982, p. 107). When Jones and Berglas (1978) first introduced the term self-handicapping, they placed the basis of the phenomenon squarely under the time-honored umbrella of the motive to protect or sustain self-esteem. They argued that the self-handicapping individual must have a precarious and fragile, but not entirely negative, self-concept. The "perpetual loser" who has little or no self-esteem after a long and scarring history of inadequacy is not a prime candidate for self-handicapping; the very basis of the self-handicapping strategy must be "that the strategist has something to protect" (Jones & Berglas, 1978, p. 205).

In proposing self-esteem protection as the basis of self-handicapping, Berglas and Jones (1978) discussed self-presentational motives and acknowledged that the ambiguity created by the handicap could help the individual maintain a positive (if tenuous) public image. Individuals could embrace or espouse a handicap for that reason, rather than for the purpose of avoiding sustained damage to their self-esteem. Nevertheless, they asserted that handicapping would occur "even in the absence of others" (Jones & Berglas, 1978, p. 202) and "under conditions of total privacy" (Berglas & Jones, 1978, p. 407). In their oft-cited demonstration of self-handicapping, they included a variable that was designed to lay the self-presentational interpretation to rest. In one set of experimental conditions the experimenter was explicitly unaware of the subject's performance. Self-handicapping occurred without regard to the privacy or publicity of the subject's performance.

However, Kolditz and Arkin (1982) harbored doubts about the Berglas and Jones (1978) attempt to rule out self-presentation. For instance, although the experimenter was blind to the subject's performance in the "privacy" conditions, an experimental assistant was not. Subjects, especially male subjects for whom the self-handicapping effect emerged most clearly, may have felt they had to maintain a positive image in the eyes of the experimental assistant—who happened to be a young woman. Moreover, drug choice, Berglas and Jones's dependent variable, was an overt, public behavior in all conditions and if subjects had any doubt about the privacy of their performance, prudence may have led them to self-handicap just in case their performance would become public knowledge.

Based upon an impression management framework, Kolditz and Arkin (1982) varied the publicity of the drug choice itself and the relative publicity of subjects' performance. When subjects made their drug choice in total privacy, where their choice of a performance-inhibiting drug could not serve as a self-presentation strategy, self-handicapping was almost eliminated. The publicity of subjects' performance had a similar, albeit weaker, impact on subjects' self-handicapping tendencies. In sum, this comparatively strong test of the impact of publicity pointed clearly to a self-presentation interpretation of the phenomenon.

It seems possible to reconcile this finding with the Jones and Berglas original *theoretical* position in two ways. First, characteristics of the task in the Berglas and Jones experimental paradigm may explain the restriction of self-handicapping to public circumstances. If the task was not very relevant or compelling to subjects (i.e., did not engage self-esteem concerns), but at the same time was taken by the experimenter to be very important, then it would seem sensible for subjects not to bother with the rather effortful and perhaps disagreeable acquisition of the handicap (taking the drug) in total privacy; nevertheless, the self-presentational value of handicapping in the public conditions would remain quite clear.

This resolution seems unlikely at first. Because the Berglas and Jones task was a test of "intellectual performance," the test should have been very compelling to the undergraduate participants. However, subjects were told the test contained a set of items designed expressly to "discriminate the uppermost levels of intellectual potential"; they were told to expect scores no higher than about the 60th or 70th percentiles. This characterization may have placed it out of the league of most of the participants, and they may have decided the test held no real diagnostic value for them personally. This would sap the need to protect one's self-esteem in the private conditions, yet would leave intact the self-presentational value of handicapping in the public conditions. A genuine test of the self-esteem proposition would require a task where a failing performance was a definite threat to subjects' self-esteem.

A second reconciliation focuses on the nature of the subject populations that participated in both of these studies. Jones and Berglas (1978) emphasized that the basis of self-handicapping is "control of the actor's *self*-attributions of competence and control" (p. 407). Their case for this proposition was based substantially on their analysis of the etiology of the tendency to self-handicap. Their analysis, which we shall take up shortly, places the origin of the tendency to self-handicap in an individual's early history. The result of the individual's unique experience is an exaggerated importance of competence; the self-handicapper is said to have "an abnormal investment in the question of self-worth" (Jones & Berglas, 1978, p. 205).

Thus, the individual who should be expected to self-handicap under private as well as public conditions may not be the average, normal, well-adjusted person: "people who know they have the talent and resources to master life's challenges are not likely to hide behind the attributional shield of self-handicapping" (Berglas & Jones, 1978, p. 406). Instead, the individual who is likely to self-handicap under most circumstances, including under conditions of total privacy, is the individual who has the unique complement of experiences that places self-esteem at risk. The subjects in the Berglas and Jones and the Kolditz and Arkin studies were surely, for the most part, average, normal and well-adjusted undergraduate students. While the average, normal and well-adjusted undergraduate is certain to be concerned with effective impression management, this sort of person is probably not the best candidate for studying the sort of self-handicapping that derives from deep-seated uncertainty about one's competence.

The impression management brand of self-handicapping should occur for most individuals under most (public) circumstances. It is essentially an individual's response to a self-presentational predicament, the prime components being a prior success (creating a future obligation or future expectation of further success) and the individual's subjective expectation that the success may not be repeatable. The individual self-handicaps because the self-presentational costs of a clear and unambiguous failure are greater than the potential rewards of success (which is, of course, unlikely anyway). Any factor that makes salient the likelihood of failure or makes salient the costs of failure (i.e., disapproval) would serve to increase the probability of self-handicapping. For instance, Berglas and Jones's (1978) "noncontingent success" would serve to undermine one's subjective probability of a repeatable success. Alternatively, fostering attention to potential losses as opposed to potential gains (Canavan–Gumpert, 1977) should elicit a situationally specific form of conservatism (see Arkin, 1981) and thus promote self-handicapping.

The predisposition to prefer self-handicapping (to rigorous tests of one's competence) has not received much attention. However, Jones and Rhodewalt (1982) have developed a scale to assess people's general tendencies to handicap, and Rhodewalt, Saltzman, and Wittmer (in press) and Baumeister and Kahn (1982) have used the instrument in initial tests of its utility. Rhodewalt et al. (in press) found that high and low self-handicapping members of the Princeton University men's swim team practiced about the same amount prior to a relatively unimportant meet, but that high self-handicapping persons practiced much less than their low self-handicapping counterparts prior to a very important meet. This sort of effect was replicated in a second study using professional golfers. Baumeister and Kahn (1982) found that obese persons who scored high on the Self-Handicapping Scale tended to blame their problems on obesity whereas their non-handicapping counterparts did not.

The Self-Handicapping Scale "probes the respondent's tendency to use such self-handicapping behaviors as lack of effort ('I would do a lot better if I tried harder'), illness ('I suppose I feel under the weather more often than most people'), or procrastination ('I tend to put things off to the last minute')" (Rhodewalt, et al., in press, p. 5). While these items focus on the report of various handicapping strategies, they also seem to reflect a general sort of negative, self-critical ideation. Numerous personality inventories seem to measure cognitions reflecting self-doubts, or shaky self-confidence. Negative thoughts are a component of scales of social anxiety, shyness, depression, social desirability, individuation, test-anxiety and many others (cf. Arkin, 1981). However, Weinstein (1968) and others have suggested that the classic case may be general measures of self-esteem. Not surprisingly, then, the Self-Handicapping Scale is highly correlated with self-esteem ($r \simeq -.50$) (F. Rhodewalt, personal communication, February, 29, 1984). Nevertheless, the magnitude of this correlation leaves much variance unique to the Self-Handicapping Scale; further research using the scale may well demonstrate its theoretical and practical utility.

We are aware of only one study that includes a measure of self-esteem and uncovers what could be construed as self-handicapping (however, see also Bernstein, Stephenson, Snyder & Wicklund, 1983). Shrauger and Osberg (1980) recognized that "spending less time at an activity would seemingly result in attributions that facilitated a more favorable self-concept" (p. 362), but they focused upon the attributional inferences and not the effort itself. They found that low self-esteem subjects took the least time of any group of subjects in preparing for a task; this placed them in position to assign the attributions for failure to lack of effort and for success to ability, which they did. However, this was only true of low self-esteem subjects who had moderately high performance expectancies, who seem most analogous to individuals who have had prior successes, but still harbor doubts about their competence. Ironically, the low self-esteem subjects who said they expected to fail spent the most time of any group preparing for the task, almost as though they were overzealously attempting to overachieve. Consequently, the net effect was that their zealous expenditure of effort led them to minimize the role of ability when they succeeded, a type of behavioral–attributional pattern that would surely tend to sustain their low performance expectancies and augment their self-doubts.

Before leaving the topic of self-esteem and social esteem it seems important to be clear by what we mean by self-handicapping in private, and what we mean to imply when we suggest that phenomenon is associated with individual differences in self-doubts, or shaky self-confidence.

Several authors in the impression management area have argued for a process that might be called, loosely, self-presentation to the self (e.g., Schlenker, 1980, p. 92). By this they mean that individuals manage their impressions, especially in private contexts, in order to impress themselves with their matching or meeting of certain personally held standards of behavior. This sort of behavior does not strike us as self-presentational at all, but rather seems more appropriately characterized as the sort of matching-to-standard type of behavior studied by those interested in self-regulation (cf. Carver & Scheier, 1981); the point of the attempts at matching-to-standard is to enhance one's sense of "fit" with the environment, and thus to enhance one's general sense of control over events as they transpire. In short, an individual will attempt a task (in private) to see if it can be done, or adopt a stance or assume a role (in private) similarly to see if it "works." This is not done to achieve self-praise, but instead for purposes of testing one's limits and enhancing one's viability when genuine challenges are posed. Likewise, the individual who self-handicaps in private, should that ever be demonstrated persuasively, would not do so solely for purposes of managing his or her impression of self, but instead to avoid information that would serve to increase one's sense of vulnerability when genuine challenges are posed. This discussion raises the general question of the role of control in self-handicapping, and self-presentation generally, and it is to this issue that we turn next.

SEEKING AND MAINTAINING CONTROL/EFFECTANCE

Speaking pragmatically, one's goal in life must be to function effectively, behaving in ways that will maximize pleasure and minimize pain. To accomplish this, a person must have some measure of personal control over his or her own actions and the environment. Perhaps more importantly, an individual must *believe* in his or her own efficacy; if one does not, the likelihood of initiating potentially rewarding actions and continuing such actions to their completion may be diminished (e.g., Bandura, 1977; Deci, 1975). In the extreme, this may even lead to the sort of inaction associated with learned helplessness (e.g., Seligman, 1975). There is extensive and growing evidence that people strongly value and are reluctant to relinquish the perception of control (e.g., Berscheid, Graziano, Monson & Dermer, 1976; Langer, 1975, 1984). Indeed, the entire topic of self-evaluation, under the guise of attribution theory and social comparison theory, has been laid at the doorstep of control motivation: the individual seeks understanding "as a means of encouraging and maintaining his effective exercise of control in that world . . . his latent goal in gaining knowledge is that of effective management of himself and his environment" (Kelley, 1971, p. 22).

The way an individual construes self-relevant events can contribute to (or detract from) an individual's sense of effective control. For example, in the "self-serving bias" people attribute their successes to personal factors (ability and effort) but attribute their failures to environmental factors (bad luck or task difficulty); it has been suggested that by doing so, people can gain feelings of control over their present and future outcomes (cf. Weary & Arkin, 1981). A sense of personal causation (for positive outcomes) is an important factor contributing to a sense of personal efficacy.

In contrast, a feeling of personal causation for negative outcomes has been characterized as the most debilitating pattern of self-relevant ideation, but only if the causal responsibility is assigned to a stable element of the self (such as one's ability or competence); this attributional pattern has been viewed as the core event in the development of personal learned helplessness (e.g., Abramson, Seligman & Teasdale, 1978), test-anxiety (Arkin, Kolditz & Kolditz, 1983), social anxiety (Leary, 1983b) and other phenomena. If the causal responsibility is assigned to an unstable and controllable element of the self (i.e., one's effort), however, the individual's resistance to the debilitating after-effects of failure is increased; the individual's sense of efficacy is retained, and the person is likely to try and try again following a failure. In short, the stylistic preference for making lack of effort attributions for failure (among low test-anxious, high self-esteem, or low socially anxious persons) contributes to a sense of personal efficacy. There is no evidence that such individuals actually expend insufficient effort when they report their lack of effort as the cause of their unsuccessful performance, only that they prefer to believe that their effort is the culprit.

If the preference to view effort as responsible for failure can be seen as a strategy for maintaining one's sense of personal efficacy, then it seems reasonable to view the withholding of effort (and any other handicap) as a *behavioral* (rather than merely cognitive) attempt to implicate non-ability causes of failure, and thus, in a similar way, sustain one's sense of personal efficacy. While the actual withholding of effort (or acquisition of some other handicap) does not imply that there will be a remarshalling of genuine effort in the future, it would serve to protect the individual's fragile sense of personal competence for the moment; this would serve to forestall the debilitating effects of failure that result from a clear and indisputable attribution to lack of ability, and prevent the individual from the paralytic and painful results of having to give up hope.

Ironically, then, self-handicapping can be viewed as a strategy for maintaining one's sense of personal control. It is not the sort of personal control that is ordinarily discussed in the literature of social psychology; instead, self-handicapping would be viewed as a sort of "enabling tactic," a strategy that would permit the individual to maintain public esteem and the "illusion of control," but would not contribute directly to any genuine sense of control. The self-handicapper would be able to maintain face in social relations, because self-doubts are prevented from becoming certain disabilities. But the individual does not enjoy any increase in genuine control. A similar distinction has been drawn by Rothbaum, Weisz and Snyder (1982). They proposed that people are not only interested in "primary control," where they can bring the environment into line with their wishes, but also are motivated to achieve "secondary control" (if primary control is impossible), where they can bring themselves into line with environmental forces. Self-handicapping may be a form of control that rests somewhere between these two.

If it is, then the determinants of an individual's choice of a primary form of control versus self-handicapping may be analogous to Wortman and Brehm's (1975) analysis of responses to uncontrollable outcomes. They argued that small exposure to helplessness training produces "reactance" (additional efforts at primary control), but that continuing helplessness training produces learned helplessness (giving up). Perhaps an expectation of control promotes primary control efforts, but a growing fear of failure makes self-handicapping progressively more attractive (see Figure 7.3). Persons high and low in self-esteem (or high and low on the Self-Handicapping Scale) may well vary in the point of inflection in the curve predicting switches from primary control to self-handicapping. One doubt about this analogy is whether persons who are dubious they will succeed will sometimes exert prodigious amounts

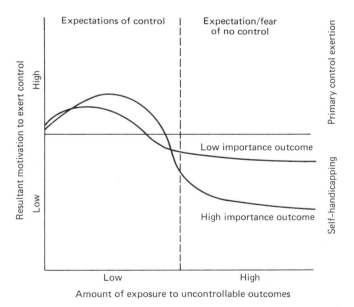

Figure 7.3 Self-handicapping as a function of expectations of control: primary control versus secondary control (after Wortman & Brehm, 1975).

of effort, as though they were overzealous overachievers (cf. Shrauger & Osberg, 1980).

AVOIDING DIAGNOSTICITY

One implication of the foregoing analysis of personal control motivation is that individuals who suffer from anxious uncertainty and self-doubts can only sustain their sense of personal efficacy by avoiding a clear test of their competence. This seems to fly in the face of a great deal of social psychological theorizing, which has assumed that individuals seek accurate information about their environment and their place in it (e.g., Festinger, 1954; Heider, 1958). It would seem that, on occasion the benefits of self-handicapping simply outweigh the benefits of a clear and precise self-evaluation.

However, recent evidence suggests that the individuals who are likely to self-handicap actually prefer to avoid diagnostic information. For instance, Sachs (1982) gave subjects contingent or noncontingent feedback on a test and then, following Trope (1975), had subjects select additional problems from item groups that varied in diagnosticity. He found that the contingent success subjects preferred the diagnostic items, while the noncontingent success subjects preferred the nondiagnostic items. In another demonstration of active avoidance of diagnosticity, Meyer and Starke (1982) found that persons high in self-concept (of ability) chose to score an intelligence test rather than a nonachievement test after they had completed both, whereas the low self-concept subjects preferred to learn about their performance on the nonachievement test (see Willerman, Lewit, & Tellegen, 1960, for a similar finding). In a very intriguing extension, Strube and Roemmele (1984) recently found that only low self-esteem individuals who scored high on the Self-Handicapping Scale avoided diagnosticity, and that was true only when the diagnosis was likely to be unflattering. These studies support the notion of evaluation avoidance, and suggest that self-handicapping is done to avoid a clear and unbiased test of one's ability.

Trope (1975) originally found that individuals who were low in achievement motivation tended to avoid diagnostic information, while persons high in achievement motivation clearly sought it out. Arkin and Haugtvedt (1984) recently replicated this finding using a measure of test anxiety. They also created a new set of conditions in which subjects were told that an electronic apparatus had been designed to filter out the interfering cognitions ordinarily associated with test-anxiety, and that test-anxious subjects would therefore be able to enjoy a rare opportunity to diagnose their abilities (with the effects of interfering thoughts held constant across participants). Test anxious subjects avoided the diagnostic items even more when the electronic gear (that would provide the more precise, and tailor-made diagnostic test of their competence) was present. This suggests that avoiding self-examination is precisely what some people may wish to accomplish.

The net result of avoiding diagnostic opportunities so judiciously is that the individual will suffer anxious uncertainty (that social psychologists have been reasonably certain people wanted to reduce whenever possible, e.g., see Festinger, 1954, especially). Yet it appears that anxious uncertainty is preferable to a clear and unambiguous test of one's competence among persons inclined to self-handicap. Thus we seem to have a self-perpetuating cycle in which anxious uncertainty produces behavior that can only sustain a high level of anxious uncertainty.

ATTRIBUTE AMBIGUITY

Uncertainty is not always undesirable, however. Snyder and Wicklund (1981) argued that the classic attribution paradigm has a "built-in bias." The attributor moves naturally in the direction of specificity, singling out certain causes as primary and discarding others. However, Snyder and Wicklund argued that "rather than narrowing the range of causes to arrive at a single, dominant explanation, we should at times expect the attributor to attempt to break open the range of causality— to locate multiple causes, and to render the end result of the 'search' for causality ambiguous" (Snyder & Wicklund, 1981, p. 198). This sounds remarkably like what occurs with self-handicapping.

However, the motivational basis for seeking "attribute ambiguity" was described very differently than the motivational basis of self-handicapping, which we have outlined here. Snyder and Wicklund proposed attribute ambiguity as a defense against being viewed in a stereotyped way, as predictable, or as inflexible. They proposed that people like to think that "they possess abilities and personalities that allow a full range of behaviors" because the possession of some disposition can have "control-reducing implications" (p. 199).

Though Snyder and Wicklund do not discuss it in just this way, the attribution of high ability can certainly be limiting. As Jones and Berglas (1978) point out, success often carries a future obligation to perform at a high level and often at increasingly high levels. Marecek and Mettee (1972) found that subjects low in self-esteem rejected responsibility for a sudden increase in performance, even intentionally performing less well on subsequent trials—presumably to dispel any high expectations fostered by the strong performance. Mettee (1971) found that this only occurred when subjects thought they were to be evaluated further.

In sum, self-handicapping appears to be one very specific brand of attribute ambiguity-seeking, in that the motivational basis of the two sorts of behavioral arenas is the same in some respects (i.e., both are designed to enhance one's sense of, or "illusion of," control). Yet they differ in that one (attribute ambiguity) is driven by feelings of reactance (cf. Brehm, 1966) and an acquisitive desire to regain a broad spectrum of control, while the other (self-handicapping) is driven by fears of failure and a protective desire to settle for ambiguity regarding whether control is present when one fears real control may be unattainable.

ETIOLOGY

The etiology of the tendency to self-handicap is perhaps the most fascinating aspect of the entire topic. In an insightful discussion, to which we cannot do justice in our limited space here, Jones and Berglas (1978) write a prescription for producing anxious uncertainty in an individual and, thus, an overriding concern with the question of self-worth. In one scenario, the child cannot determine whether rewards that are contingently based upon performance (i.e., praise for good work) would continue to be present in the absence of the good performance (i.e., whether or not unconditional love is present). Such a child may be driven to overachievement, where the crucial test of the presence of love without good performance is avoided through a zealous expenditure of effort. However, the alternative path, of the underachiever, can also result from this dilemma. The child who tries and fails dares a direct test of parental love; but by withholding effort, the child can try to maintain "a precarious hold on the illusion of love and admiration" (Jones & Berglas, 1978, p. 204).

Another scenario involves insufficiently contingent reinforcement. The individual who has suffered a reinforcement history that is chaotic or capricious may have difficulty discerning what rewards have been for, and may therefore view "ill-gotten gains" as precarious and likely to be unattainable in the future. Because the rewards have not been contingent upon performance, even if abundant (as in Seligman's theory of success depression, 1975), the rewards are uninformative concerning one's competence. This set of circumstances would also place one's self-esteem at risk. Self-handicapping would merely preserve the ambiguity of the deservingness of past reward and the prospect of future reward.

INTEGRATING MODEL AND MOTIVES

In previous sections of this chapter we have addressed motivational issues as well as behavioral manifestations of self-handicapping. Figure 7.4 reiterates the organizational scheme (see Figure 7.2) that emerged from these discussions. With regard to motivation, the individual who chooses to self-handicap was characterized as concerned over either social or self-esteem, and self-handicapping was viewed as based on either acquisitive or protective motives. Self-handicapping in public was linked with how the individual appears to others. On the other hand, self-handicapping in private was linked with self-evaluation, and was viewed as most likely to occur among populations of persons who have an abnormal investment in their sense of self-worth. Although it is conceivable that self-handicapping may occasionally be designed to augment a positive presentation of self, this was certainly not our focus here; indeed, we know of no direct evidence that this occurs. By contrast, the data are quite convincing that self-handicapping occurs where individuals expect a negative evaluation; this suggests a "protective" motivational basis for most self-handicapping (though direct tests are needed), and implicates the discounting principle rather than the augmentation principle in most instances of handicapping.[1]

In addition to these motivational variables, Figure 7.4 includes dimensions of behavioral strategies people might employ in attempts to self-handicap. A major distinction we have drawn is between acquired and claimed handicaps. The individual who "acquires" a handicap actually takes on an impediment to performance; the probability of failure is therefore increased in his or her attempt to attribute poor performance to the handicap. The "claimed" handicap merely involves stating that such a handicap is present. We argued that the acquisition of a self-handicap involves greater strategic planning and probably greater motivation than merely claiming a handicap. Finally, acquired or claimed handicaps may be either internal or external; that is, the individual may intend a performance to be attributed to some aspect of the self (e.g., low effort, a debilitating drug or alcohol, test-anxiety, etc.) or some aspect of the environment (e.g., inordinately difficult goals, a poor test, etc.). A self-handicap that is internal may be more effective in that it is less amenable to public scrutiny, and perhaps more clearly debilitating;

[1]This conclusion is consistent with recent evidence that discounting effects far exceed augmentation effects in social judgment (Hansen & Hall, 1984). Further, Reeder and Brewer's (1979) analysis of implicational schemata point precisely to the self-handicapping context as the prototypical circumstance where discounting would have greatest utility: one success in a string of less auspicious outcomes (see especially page 77).

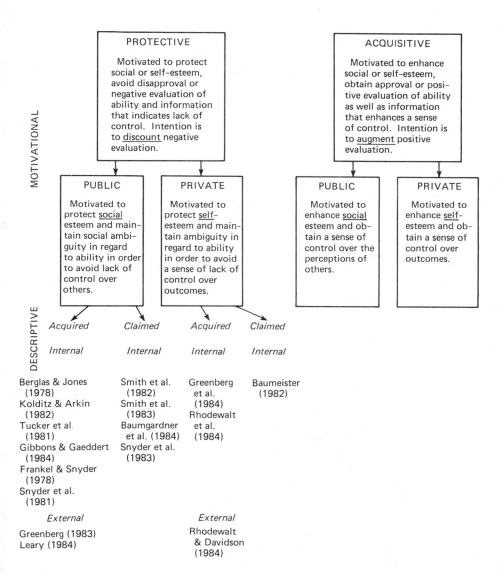

Figure 7.4 An integration of model and motives: motivational and behavioral manifestations. (Although the Greenberg et al., 1984, and Rhodewalt and Davison, 1984, studies are placed in the private category, there is not unequivocal support that self-handicapping occurred in truly private conditions. However, in both studies, the authors claim that self-handicapping was private.)

yet such a handicap may also carry more negative implications for the actor in that internal handicaps ordinarily produce negative personal and social evaluations.

As can readily be seen from Figure 7.2, there are many combinations in the panorama of self-handicapping types for which there is no evidence. This is not meant to imply, for instance, that acquisitive forms of handicapping simply do not exist; instead, the organizational scheme is offered to show retrospectively where research efforts have been directed and to indicate prospectively where future research endeavors would be especially useful. In particular, the absence of studies showing self-handicapping under clearly private circumstances is a notable problem in discerning the precise motivational basis of handicapping, and outlining the parameters of its occurrence. Similarly, a clear exposition of the conditions promoting acquisitive and protective forms of handicapping would be useful from a theoretical as well as a practical (i.e., therapeutic) perspective; it seems likely that only protective forms of self-handicapping become problematic for the individual in negotiating everyday life. Finally, only further research can clarify whether or not the current weight of the evidence, which shows the acquisition or claiming of internal handicaps predominantly, reflects the predilection of human beasts in the social wild or solely the theoretical predilection of social and personality psychologists.

EFFECTIVENESS OF SELF-HANDICAPPING

One of the weakest links in the impression management literature is an analysis of the impact of self-presentation, both on the audience or target of self-presentation and on the self. There are a number of reasons for the relative lack of clarity, theoretically or empirically, about this link in the self-presentation process. One is certainly the comparative recency of attempts to integrate the impression management approach with attribution processes (cf. Crittenden, 1983; Harvey & Weary, 1984; Orvis, Kelley & Butler, 1976; Weary & Arkin, 1981).

However, it is perhaps this aspect of the impression management viewpoint that holds the most promise to contribute to the panorama of topics in social psychology that often come under the umbrella heading "the self in social interaction," and to provide an integrated and comprehensive theory of interpersonal relations. Questions concerning the direct impact of self-presentational behavior on self-concept, the actual reactions of others to various self-presentational behaviors, the presenter's perception of others' reactions to presentational attempts, and so forth, all bear on the course and outcome of everyday interaction. Because of the unique nature of the self-handicapping strategy, answers to these sorts of questions in that behavioral arena seem particularly important.

Unfortunately, there is as yet no evidence bearing upon the impact, or effectiveness, of self-handicapping. However, some educated guesses can be made, and some intriguing hypotheses generated, by exploring some related literatures.

AUDIENCE REACTION TO SELF-PRESENTATION

Research on audience response to self-presentation overtures is scant, yet what is available at present paints a very straightforward and predictable picture. For instance, accurate presentations of self are the most favorably received (Schlenker & Leary, 1982). This is hardly surprising, given the relative importance of traits like honesty and sincerity in impression formation (Anderson, 1968). Therefore, a very positive, self-enhancing presentation of self will be effective in generating favorable evaluations from an audience if the presenter "has the goods" to back up the claim. However, very positive, self-enhancing claims are just as effective when the audience is merely unaware of any contradictory evidence (Schlenker & Leary, 1982). This may help account for the tendency of individuals to describe themselves in terms consistent with negative information about themselves that is already known, but compensate for this by enhancing their claims on dimensions about which the audience has no prior knowledge (Baumeister & Jones, 1978). Similarly, individuals confronted with further tests of their competence modestly attribute their successes to good fortune and their failures to themselves, reversing the usual self-serving bias in causal attribution (e.g., Wortman, Costanzo & Witt, 1973); this makes sense when the premium on accurate presentations of self is considered. Indeed, it appears conditions that tend to promote "counterdefensive," or modest presentations of self (Weary, 1978) are precisely those circumstances in which modest evaluations are perceived as most honest and sincere (Shovar & Carlston, 1979; Tetlock, 1980) and most indicative of competence (Tetlock, 1980).

To offer attributions that are at variance with objective facts, or which violate the general "norm for internality" (which dictates that people should be responsible for their own outcomes; Jellison & Green, 1981), is a risky business. For example, when people deny personal responsibility for an unsuccessful outcome, as occurs in instances of the rather pervasive self-serving bias, it is necessary to violate the "norm for internality'' to dissociate oneself from the negative outcome. This is a presentational tactic that people high in social anxiety (i.e., low in self-esteem) are commonly unwilling to attempt (Arkin, Appelman & Burger, 1980); it may require greater social skills, or a greater sense of self-confidence, to try such a tricky tactic. In a similar way, Ungar (1980) found that persons who were relatively certain of their likely performance presented themselves in a way consistent with their expectations, but that persons who were uncertain of their likely performance presented themselves positively; he argued that ''self-enhancement motives are of sufficient strength to occasion *risk-taking* in self-presentations when subjects believe they have a chance of succeeding'' (p. 165; italics original). One predictable exception to the principles of accuracy and internality, taken together, is that an actor who modestly underestimates a clearly superior performance is perceived more favorably than an accurate, but seemingly boastful, actor who acknowledges having done very well (Schlenker & Leary, 1982).

Another, rather surprising exception to the principles of accuracy and internality—one which bears directly on the likely effectiveness of self-handicapping—is that an actor who is self-deprecating by predicting an inferior performance is disliked, even if the prediction is borne out in reality through a poor performance (Schlenker & Leary, 1982). If one can safely generalize from this finding, it argues that poor performance cannot be redeemed by an honest expression of personal responsibility for the negative event. Coupled with the risk associated with denial of responsibility for negative outcomes, this places the individual who anticipates failing in a very difficult predicament. The predicament is all the more problematic for the individual low in self-esteem, who is disinclined to risk attributional self-presentation anyway (Arkin et al., 1980). As a consequence, self-handicapping may be a particularly attractive strategic maneuver; it not only averts the objective failure, but also alleviates the necessity of risking further damage to one's image by having to provide some account for the failure.

Another related literature also bears on the utility of self-handicapping. Precious little is known about how self-appraisal is affected by strategic self-presentation, but what is known is quite consistent in its implications. Jones, Rhodewalt, Berglas, and Skelton (1981) suggested that ''self-presentational actions are likely to make one of the competing alternative views of the self salient'' (p. 408). Therefore, measures of self-evaluation should show carry-over effects of flattering and unflattering presentations of self; this view is entirely consistent with what has been argued of late about the malleability of self-concept (e.g., Ross, Lepper & Hubbard, 1975). Jones et al. (1981) found that subjects led to behave in a self-enhancing way subsequently showed elevated self-esteem, and that subjects instructed to be self-deprecating showed lowered self-esteem. Beyond the reactions of others, then, people must monitor their likely presentation of self and make appropriate adjustments to avoid unflattering portrayals of self because of self-perception processes (Bem, 1972).

Self-concept is also affected by self-presentation through the mediational role of audience reaction. There is abundant evidence that self-evaluations are influenced by feedback received from others (Shrauger & Schoenemann, 1979). For instance, Gergen (1965) found that observers' agreement with a positive self-presentation raised the presenter's self-esteem; this change in self-concept was lasting, at least through the post-experimental interview. Because it is usually normative to do so (Blumberg, 1972), others are likely to accept the individual's presentation of self at face value, setting in motion changes in self-concept.

Yet, the individual who harbors self-doubts and is plagued by concerns over disapproval will be inclined to engage in a protective sort of self-presentation (cf. Arkin, 1981), including modesty, conformity, neutrality in opinions, and self-deprecation. Although such strategies enable the presenter to avoid threatening signs from others that his (positive) self-presentation is being challenged, the individual will still be evaluated negatively and sustain real losses in future commerce with others. Because direct protective self-presentation can result in fairly unfavorable evaluations, it may be more effective to avoid risks in interpersonal relations by engaging in self-handicapping. While both protective self-presentation and self-handicapping share the property of being risk avoidance–safety seeking interpersonal strategies, self-handicapping may be preferred if the threat to one's self-concept is truly compelling and complete avoidance of the task is impossible.

Finally, then, this raises the question of just how self-handicapping may be perceived when it occurs. Unfortunately, there is nothing published on this question. Nevertheless, some hints about how it might be perceived can be derived from an analysis of the relationship between ability and effort attributions in the achievement motivation literature. Even though effort withdrawal is only one variety of self-handicapping, the implications of this type may map well onto the process as a whole.

THE ABILITY–EFFORT TRADEOFF IN SOCIAL PERCEPTION

According to Heider (1958), perceived ability and motivation have an inverse relationship. Consequently, the harder a person is believed to have worked for a given level of success, the less ability will be attributed to him; conversely, greater attribution to ability would occur when effort is lower. The reverse side of this theoretical coin is that failure could be due to lack of ability only, lack of effort only, or to a combination of both. Yet, if lack of effort is clearly present, according to the discounting principle (cf. Kelley, 1971), inferences about lack of ability are less clear. By the same token, if lack of ability is clearly present inferences about lack of effort are less certain. It is a very small theoretical step to posit that self-handicapping, in the form of effort withdrawal, rests on the Heiderian notion that ability and effort are inversely related. Individuals can obscure the impact of ability upon poor performance by withdrawing effort only if the Heiderian model is accurate.

Although Heider's (1958) model seems so intuitively likely, there is at least some evidence that observers do not follow the predicted pattern. Two experiments have found that attributions of ability and motivation are positively related (when performance was controlled) rather than inversely related (Felson & Bohrnstedt, 1980; Kepka & Brickman, 1971). Felson and Bohrnstedt (1980) attributed this finding to "a halo effect in which teachers perceive bright students as highly motivated . . . or perceive highly motivated students as bright, or it may be that students who are well-liked are attributed more ability and motivation" (p. 804). But, there was no indication this positive correlation was stronger at the upper end of the scale than at the lower end of the scale; in short, teachers also perceived unmotivated students as unable, and this finding casts considerable doubt upon the long range utility of a self-handicapping strategy for purposes of impression management. However, Surber (1984) recently demonstrated considerable individual differences in observers' inferences about the relationship of ability and effort in producing success and failure (see also Nicholls, 1984).

Regardless, we have argued that people do engage in self-handicapping, and that it is probably predominantly a strategy adopted by persons with powerful self-doubts, or low self-evaluations. Touhey and Villemez (1980) uncovered a very intriguing effect that suggests actors, in particular actors who are prone to engage in self-handicapping, follow the Heiderian formula.

They found that persons high in need-for-achievement increased their judgments of their ability in response to an effortful success; by contrast, individuals low in need-for-achievement increased their judgments of their ability following less effortful successes. Thus, only low need-achieving actors, who are high in test-anxiety (and thus are high in self-doubts), follow the Heiderian model. For unknown reasons, then, it may be that persons with considerable self-doubt view ability and effort as inversely related and base their use of the self-handicapping strategy on that perception; consistent with this view, Riggs (1982) found that the self-handicapping tactic of effort withdrawal emerged only among underachievers who believed that effort had an impact on their performance. Yet, paradoxically, observers of their behavior, more often average to high in self-confidence than not, would tend to apply a completely different metric in assessing the actor's competence. If actors do not recognize their difference from observers, it could reflect a gap in their "applied person perception" skills (cf. Schneider, 1981).

In sum, self-handicapping may be a very useful strategy for obscuring the impact of poor performance on ability inferences, but only for a rather select group of individuals and mostly concerning their own self-perceptions; as far as the self-presentational utility of self-handicapping, it may be smaller than most self-handicappers imagine.

SUMMARY

We have discussed self-handicapping as a subtle use of attributional principles designed to manage one's image. The individual who self-handicaps performs only certain behaviors, or manipulates the environment, such that only desired inferences can be made; specifically, our reading of the literature suggests that self-handicapping is driven by an individual's desire to discount low ability as a cause of an imminent failure.

A typology was proposed to organize the various self-handicaps that have been investigated thus far. A wide variety of handicaps are available to the individual who wishes to avoid a clear diagnosis of incompetence, including internal-acquired (e.g., drug ingestion, effort reduction), external-acquired (e.g., difficult goal or testing conditions), internal-claimed (e.g., self-reported anxiety or depression), and external-claimed (self-reported environmental impediments).

In addition, the motivational bases and effectiveness of these strategies were analyzed. It was argued that the decision to self-handicap is often based on one's motivation to protect social esteem. However, the likelihood that people self-handicap to protect self-esteem seems high, and the motivation for such a self-deceptive maneuver was, ironically, laid at the doorstep of the rather pervasive human desire for control. A discussion of individual differences led us to propose that the latter motivational basis for handicapping may most readily be aroused in persons who harbor self-doubts and are plagued by concerns over disapproval, whereas the former motivational basis is pervasive, making self-handicapping an intrinsic part of everyday social relations.

At first glance, self-handicapping appears to be an effective image management strategy. However, a review of research brought together with a widely-cast net suggests that self-handicappers, as actors, may well use rules of inference that are not shared by observers of their behavior. Therefore, the self-presentational utility of self-handicapping may be much smaller than most handicappers imagine. By contrast, the inferential tendencies of persons who harbor self doubts and suffer from anxious uncertainty may contribute to the lure of self-handicapping for these persons. The consequence may be a vicious cycle of anxious uncertainty fueled by behaviors that serve only to reinforce self doubts.

REFERENCES

Abramson, L. Y., Seligman, M. E. P., & Teasdale, J. D. (1978). Learned helplessness in humans: Critique and reformulation. *Journal of Abnormal Psychology, 87,* 49–74.

Anderson, N. H. (1968). Likeableness ratings of 555 personality-trait words. *Journal of Personality and Social Psychology, 9,* 272–279.

Arkin, R. (1981). Self-presentation styles. In J. T. Tedeschi (Ed.), *Impression management theory and social psychological research.* New York: Academic Press.

Arkin, R. M., Appelman, A. J., & Burger, J. M. (1980). Social anxiety, self-presentation, and the self-serving bias in causal attribution. *Journal of Personality and Social Psychology, 38,* 23–35.

Arkin, R. M., & Haugtvedt, C. (1984). Test-anxiety, task difficulty and diagnosticity: The roles of cognitive interference and fear of failure as determinants of choice of task. In H. van der Ploeg, R. Schwarzer, & C. D. Spielberger (Eds.), *Advances in test anxiety research* (Vol. 3). Hillsdale, N.J.: Erlbaum.

Arkin, R. M., Kolditz, T. & Kolditz, K. (1983). Attributional style of the test-anxious student. *Personality and Social Psychology Bulletin, 9,* 271–280.

Bandura, A. (1977). Self-efficacy: Toward a unifying theory of behavioral change. *Psychological Review, 84,* 191–215.

Baumeister, R. F., Hamilton, J. C., & Tice, D. M. (1984). *Public versus private expectancy of success: Confidence booster or performance pressure.* Unpublished manuscript, Case Western Reserve University, Cleveland.

Baumeister, R. F., & Jones, E. E. (1978). When self-presentation is constrained by the target's knowledge: Consistency and compensation. *Journal of Personality and Social Psychology, 36,* 608–618.

Baumeister, R. F., & Kahn, J. (1982). *Obesity as a self-handicapping strategy: Don't blame me, blame my fat.* Unpublished manuscript, Case Western Reserve University, Cleveland.

Baumgardner, A. H., Lake, E. A., & Arkin, R. M. (1984). *Claiming depression as a self-handicap.* Unpublished manuscript, University of Missouri, Columbia.

Bem, D. J. (1972). Self-perception theory. In L. Berkowitz (Ed.), *Advances in experimental social psychology* (Vol. 6). New York: Academic Press.

Berglas, S., & Jones, E. E. (1978). Drug choice as a self-handicapping strategy in response to noncontingent success. *Journal of Personality and Social Psychology, 36,* 405–517.

Bernstein, W. M., Stephenson, B. O., Snyder, M. L., & Wicklund, R. A. (1983). Causal ambiguity and heterosexual affiliation. *Journal of Experimental Social Psychology, 19,* 78–92.

Berscheid, E., Graziano, W., Monson, T. & Dermer, M. (1976). Outcome dependency: Attention, attribution, and attraction. *Journal of Personality and Social Psychology, 34,* 978–989.

Blumberg, H. H. (1972). Communication of interpersonal evaluations. *Journal of Personality and Social Psychology, 23,* 157–162.

Brehm, J. W. (1966). *A theory of psychological reactance.* New York: Academic Press.

Brodt, S. E., & Zimbardo, P. G. (1981). Modifying shyness-related behavior through symptom missattribution. *Journal of Personality and Social Psychology, 41,* 437–449.

Canavan-Gumpert, D. (1977). Generating reward and cost orientations through praise and criticism. *Journal of Personality and Social Psychology, 35,* 501–513.

Carver, C. S. & Scheier, M. F. (1981). *Attention and self-regulation: A Control Theory approach to human behavior.* New York: Springer-Verlag.

Crittenden, K. S. (1983). Sociological aspects of attribution. *Annual Review of Sociology, 9,* 425–446.

Darley, J. M. & Goethals, G. R. (1980). People's analysis of the causes of ability-linked performances. In L. Berkowitz (Ed.), *Advances in experimental social psychology,* (Vol. 13). New York: Academic Press.

Deci, E. L. (1975). *The psychology of self-determination.* Lexington, MA: D. C. Heath.

Felson, R. B. & Bohrnstedt, G. W. (1980). Attribtions of ability and motivation in a natural setting. *Journal of Personality and Social Psychology, 39,* 799–805.

Festinger, L. (1954). A theory of social comparison processes. *Human Relations, 7,* 117–140.

Fiske, S. T., & Taylor, S. E. (1984). *Social cognition.* Reading, MA: Addison-Wesley.

Frankel, A., & Snyder, M. L. (1978). Poor performance following unsolvable problems: Learned helplessness or egotism. *Journal of Social Psychology, 36,* 1415–1423.

Gergen, K. J. (1965). The effects of interaction goals and personalistic feedback on the presentation of self. *Journal of Personality and Social Psychology, 1,* 413–424.

Gibbons, F. X. & Gaeddert, W. P. (1984). Focus of attention and placebo utility. *Journal of Experimental Social Psychology, 20,* 159–176.

Greenberg, J. (1983). *Difficult goal choice as a self-handicapping strategy.* Unpublished manuscript, Ohio State University, Columbus, OH.

Greenberg, J., Pyszczynski, T., & Paisley, C. (1984). *The effect of extrinsic incentives on the use of test anxiety as an anticipatory attributional defense: Playing it cool when the stakes are high.* Unpublished manuscript, University of Arizona, Tucson.

Hansen, R. D., & Hall, C. A. (1984). Discounting and augmenting causal forces. Unpublished manuscript, Oakland University, Rochester, MI.

Harvey, J. H., & Weary, G. (1984). Current issues in attribution theory and research. *Annual review of psychology, 35,* 427–459.

Heider, F. (1958). *The psychology of interpersonal relations.* New York: Wiley.

Jellison, J. M., & Green, J. (1981). A self-presentation approach to the fundamental attribution error. *Journal of Personality and Social Psychology, 40,* 643–649.

Jones, E. E., & Berglas, S. (1978). Control of attributions about the self through self-handicapping strategies: The appeal of alcohol and the role of underachievement. *Personality and Social Psychology Bulletin, 4,* 200–206.

Jones, E. E., & Davis, R. E. (1965). From acts to dispositions: The attribution process in person perception. In L. Berkowitz (Ed.), *Advances in experimental social psychology* (Vol. 2). New York: Academic Press.

Jones, E. E., & Rhodewalt, F. (1982). Self-handicapping scale. Departments of Psychology, Princeton University and University of Utah.

Jones, E. E., Rhodewalt, F., Berglas, S., & Skelton, J. A. (1981). Effects of strategic self-presentation on subsequent self-esteem. *Journal of Personality and Social Psychology, 41,* 407–421.

Kanouse, D. E., & Hansen, L. R. (1971). Negativity in evaluations. In E. E. Jones, D. E. Kanouse, H. H. Kelley, R. E. Nisbett, S. Valins, & B. Weiner (Eds.), *Attribution: Perceiving the causes of behavior.* New York: General Learning Press.

Kelley, H. H. (1971). Attribution in social interaction. In E. E. Jones, D. E. Kanouse, H. H. Kelley, R. E. Nisbett, S. Valins, & B. Weiner (Eds.), *Attribution: Perceiving the causes of behavior.* New York: General Learning Press.

Kepka, E. J., & Brickman, P. (1971). Consistency versus discrepancy as clues in the attribution of intelligence and motivation. *Journal of Personality and Social Psychology, 20,* 223–229.

Kolditz, T. A., & Arkin, R. M. (1982). An impression management interpretation of the self-handicapping strategy. *Journal of Personality and Social Psychology, 43,* 492–502.

Langer, E. J. (1975). The illusion of control. *Journal of Personality and Social Psychology, 32,* 311–328.

Langer, E. J. (1984). *The psychology of control.* Beverly Hills, CA: Sage Press.

Leary, M. R. (1983a). *Understanding social anxiety: Social, personality, and clinical perspectives.* Beverly Hills, CA: Sage Publications.

Leary, M. R. (1983b). *Social anxiety and interpersonal concern: Testing a self-presentational explanation.* Unpublished manuscript, University of Texas, Austin, TX.

Maracek, J., & Mettee, D. (1972). Avoidance of continued success as a function of self-esteem, level of esteem certainty, and responsibility for success. *Journal of Personality and Social Psychology, 22,* 98–107.

Mettee, D. R. (1971). Rejection of unexpected success as a function of the negative consequences of accepting success. *Journal of Personality and Social Psychology, 17,* 332–341.

Meyer, W. U., & Starke, E. (1982). Own ability in relation to self-concept of ability: A field study of information-seeking. *Personality and Social Psychology Bulletin, 8,* 501–507.

Nicholls, J. G. (1984). Achievement motivation: Conceptions of ability, subjective experience, task choice, and performance. *Psychological Review, 91,* 328–346.

Orvis, B. R., Kelley, H. H., & Butler, D. (1976). Attributional conflict in young couples. In J. H. Harvey, W. J. Ickes, & R. F. Kidd (Eds.), *New directions in attribution research* (Vol. 1). Hillsdale. NJ: Erlbaum.

Pyszczynski, T., & Greenberg, J. (1983). Determinants of reduction in intended effort as a strategy for coping with anticipated failure. *Journal of Research in Personality, 17,* 412–422.

Reeder, G. D., & Brewer, M. B. (1979). A schematic model of dispositional attribution in interpersonal perception. *Psychological Review, 86,* 61–79.

Rhodewalt, F., & Davison, J. (1984). *Self-handicapping and subsequent performance: The role of outcome valence and attributional certainty.* Unpublished manuscript, University of Utah, Salt Lake City.

Rhodewalt, F., Saltzman, A. T., & Wittmer, J. (in press). Self-handicapping among competitive athletes: The role of practice in self-esteem protection. *Basic and Applied Social Psychology.*

Riggs, J. M. (1982). *The effect of performance attributions on choice of achievement strategy.* Unpublished doctoral dissertation, Princeton University, Princeton, NJ.

Ross, L., Lepper, M. R., & Hubbard, M. (1975). Perseverance in self-perception and social perception: Biased attributional processes in the debriefing paradigm. *Journal of Personality and Social Psychology, 32,* 880–892.

Rothbaum, F., Weisz, J. R., & Snyder, S. S. (1982). Changing the world and changing the self: A two-process model of perceived control. *Journal of Personality and Social Psychology, 42,* 5–37.

Sachs, P. R. (1982). Avoidance of diagnostic information in self-evaluation of ability. *Personality and Social Psychology Bulletin, 8,* 242–246.

Schlenker, B. R. (1980). *Impression management: The self-concept, social identity, and interpersonal relations.* Monterey, CA: Brooks-Cole.

Schlenker, B. R., & Leary, M. R. (1982). Audiences' reactions to self-enhancing, self-denigrating, and accurate self-presentations. *Journal of Experimental Social Psychology, 18,* 89–104.

Schneider, D. J. (1981). Tactical self presentation: Toward a broader conception. In J. T. Tedeschi (Ed.), *Impression management theory and social psychological research.* New York: Academic Press.

Seligman, M. E. P. (1975). *Helplessness: On depression, development, and death.* San Francisco: Freeman.

Shovar, N. & Carlston, D. (1979). *Reactions to attributional self-presentation.* Paper presented at the annual meetings of the Midwestern Psychological Association, Chicago.

Shrauger, J. S., & Osberg, T. M. (1980). The relationship of time investment and task outcome to causal attributions and self-esteem. *Journal of Personality, 48,* 360–378.

Shrauger, J. S., & Shoenemann, T. J. (1979). Symbolic interactionist view of self-concept: Through the looking glass darkly. *Psychological Bulletin, 86,* 549–572.

Smith, T. W., Snyder, C. R., & Handelsman, M. M. (1982). On the self-serving function of an academic wooden leg: Test anxiety as a self-handicapping strategy. *Journal of Personality and Social Psychology, 42,* 314–321.

Smith, T. W., Snyder, C. R., & Perkins, S. C. (1983). The self-serving function of hypochohdriacal complaints: Physical symptoms as self-handicapping strategies. *Journal of Personality and Social Psychology, 44,* 787–797.

Snyder, C. R., & Smith, T. W. (1982). Symptoms as self-handicapping strategies: The virtues of old wine in a new bottle. In G. Weary & H. Mirels (Eds.), *Integrations of clinical and social psychology.* New York: Oxford University Press.

Snyder, C. R., Smith, T. W., Augelli, R. W., & Ingram, R. E. (1983). On the self-serving function of social anxiety: Shyness as a self-handicapping strategy. Paper presented at the 1983 annual meeting of the American Psychological Association, Anaheim, CA.

Snyder, M. L., Smoller, B., Strenta, A., & Frankel (1981). A comparison of egotism, negativity, and learned helplessness as explanations for poor performance after unsolvable problems. *Journal of Personality and Social Psychology, 40,* 24–30.

Snyder, M. L., & Wicklund, R. (1981). Attribute ambiguity. In J. H. Harvey, W. J. Ickes, & R. F. Kidd (Eds.), *New directions in attribution research* (Vol. 3). Hillsdale, N.J.: Erlbaum.

Strube, M. J. & Roemmele, A. (1984). *Self-enhancement, self-assessment and self-evaluative task choice.* Unpublished manuscript.

Surber, C. F. (1984). Inferences of ability and effort: Evidence of two different processes. *Journal of Personality and Social Psychology, 46,* 249–268.

Tetlock, P. E. (1980). Explaining teacher explanations of pupil performance: A self-presentational interpretation. *Social Psychology Quarterly, 43,* 283–290.

Touhey, J. C., & Villemez, W. J. (1980). Ability attribution as a result of variable effort and achievement motivation. *Journal of Personality and Social Psychology, 38,* 211–216.

Trope, Y. (1975). Seeking information about one's own ability as a determinant of choice among tasks. *Journal of Personality and Social Psychology, 32,* 1004–1013.

Tucker, J. A., Vuchinich, R. E., Sobell, M. B. (1981). Alcohol consumption as a self-handicapping strategy. *Journal of Abnormal Psychology, 90,* (3) 220–230.

Ungar, S. (1980). The effects of certainty of self-perceptions on self-presentation behaviors:

A test of the strength of self-enhancement motives. *Social Psychology Quarterly, 43,* 165–172.

Weary, G. (1978). Self-serving biases in the attribution process: A re-examination of the fact or fiction question. *Journal of Personality and Social Psychology, 36,* 56–71.

Weary, G., & Arkin, R. (1981). Attributional self-presentation. In J. H. Harvey, W. Ickes, & R. F. Kidd (Eds.), *New directions in attributional research* (Vol. 3). New York: Erlbaum.

Weidner, G. (1980). Self-handicapping following learned helplessness treatment and the Type A coronary-prone behavior pattern. *Journal of Psychosomatic Research, 24*(6), 319–325.

Weiner, B., Russell, D., & Lerman, D. (1978). Affective consequences of causal ascription. In J. H. Harvey, W. Ickes, and R. F. Kidd (Eds.), *New directions in attribution research* (Vol. 2). Hillsdale, NJ: Erlbaum.

Weiner, B., & Sierad, J. (1975). Misattribution of failure and enhancement of achievement strivings. *Journal of Personality and Social Psychology, 31,* 415–421.

Weinstein, E. (1968). The development of interpersonal competence. In D. Goslin (Ed.), *Handbook of socialization theory and research.* Chicago: Rand McNally.

White, R. W. (1959). Motivation reconsidered: The concept of competence. *Psychological Review, 66,* 297–333.

Willerman, B., Lewit, D., & Tellegen, A. (1960). Seeking and avoiding self-evaluation by working individually or in groups. In D. Willner (Ed.), *Decisions, values, and groups.* New York: Pergamon Press.

Wortman, C. B., & Brehm, J. W. (1975). Responses to uncontrollable outcomes: An integration of reactance theory and the learned helplessness model. In L. Berkowitz (Ed.), *Advances in experimental social psychology* (Vol. 8). New York: Academic Press.

Wortman, C. B., Costanzo, P. R., & Witt, T. R. (1973). Effect of anticipated performance on the attributions of causality to self and others. *Journal of Personality and Social Psychology, 27,* 372–381.

CHAPTER 8

Attributions in Close Relationships*

Frank D. Fincham

INTRODUCTION

Psychologists from a variety of subdisciplines are paying an increasing amount of attention to the study of close relationships (see Argyle & Henderson, in press; Kelley, Berscheid, Christensen, Harvey, Huston, Levinger, McClintock, Peplau, & Petersen, 1983; Levinger, 1980). The present chapter considers this trend within the subdisciplines of social and clinical psychology. As social psychology assumes its role in the emerging interdisciplinary science of close relationships, it seems natural to consider how its dominant theoretical framework, attribution theory, might facilitate our understanding of such relationships. Consideration of this issue is equally propitious from the perspective of clinical psychology, as recent attempts to develop cognitive therapies for relationship problems have been dominated by an attribution perspective (e.g., Baucom, 1981; Berley & Jacobson, 1984; Epstein, 1982). This chapter therefore explores the utility of theory and research on attribution in the study of close relationships and in the treatment of relationship problems.

The first section examines the concepts of attribution and close relationships; a critical evaluation of existing research on attributions in close relationships is presented next. In the third section, an attempt is made to pose some important questions for such research and to outline their clinical implications. Finally, the benefits of investigating attribution processes in close relationship are discussed.

*I thank Garth Fletcher, Lisa Gaelick, Jolene Galegher, Audrey Hokoda, Fred Kanfer, Susan Kemp-Fincham, and David White for their critical comments on an earlier draft of this chapter.

ON THE UBIQUITY OF THE TERMS
ATTRIBUTION AND *CLOSE RELATIONSHIP*

A recent treatise on close relationships (Kelley et al., 1983) makes repeated reference to attributions, yet classic papers on this topic (e.g., Jones & Davis, 1965) are not cited. Some initial insight on why this might be the case can be gained by exploring the possible referents of "attribution" and "close relationships." This task involves more than a linguistic exercise, as the conclusions drawn regarding the central task of this chapter depend, in part, on the level at which these two terms are construed.

Considerable debate has occurred in recent years regarding the nature of an *attribution*. As originally conceived by Heider (1944), attribution concerned "unit formation" between effects and their origins or causes. This usage, which is limited specifically to *causal* attribution, may be considered the narrow sense of the term. It is also sometimes unwittingly used to indicate evaluative judgments, a practice which presumably derives from the intuitive notion that such judgments are based on causal attributions. *Attribution* has also been depicted as dealing with answers to "why" questions (Kelley, 1972) or seeking "sufficient reasons" for behavior (Jones & Davis, 1965, p. 220). In this usage, attribution becomes synonymous with commonsense explanations for events which may or may not involve causal attribution. This view of attribution denotes the broad sense of the term, and it is the one used in the current chapter, unless otherwise specified.

Like attribution, *close relationship* has a broad set of referents. Attempts to communicate clearly what is meant by this term "carry clouds of ambiguity" (Berscheid & Peplau, 1983, p. 12). Not surprisingly, there has been little agreement as to when people are in a "relationship" with each other, or as to what criteria should be used in classifying a relationship as "close." Kurt Lewin (1948), in one of the first social psychological analyses of an intimate relationship (marriage), seems to capture what stands at the core of attempts to characterize close relationships in various disciplines. He concludes that each of the characteristics of such relationships "makes for a high degree of interdependence" (p. 89). Contemporary researchers (Kelley et al., 1983), building on this core feature, have argued that closeness in relationships is a function of the degree of mutual impact or interdependence assessed along the dimensions of (1) frequency of impact; (2) degree of impact per occurrence; (3) the extent to which the impact involves a diverse series of activities; and (4) the existence of interconnected activity over time. High scores on all four of these dimensions define a close relationship.

The preceding description of close relationships may be considered incomplete by some scholars. For example, it begs the question of what constitutes sufficiently influential impact to characterize a relationship as close, while its quantitative emphasis seems to underplay qualitative aspects of a relationship, such as Lewin's (1948) condition that partners affect each other in their "central regions." Nonetheless, this atheoretical description is adopted here to facilitate comparability across writers. The modifier "close" will be omitted when referring to such relationships in the remainder of the chapter. Although the observations made might be useful for understanding relationships in general, the focus of attention is limited largely to the marital dyad because it is commonly accepted as an obvious example of a close relationship.

Before examining relevant research, it should be noted that the foregoing attempt to clarify attribution and close relationship captures neither the range nor complexity of the issues involved in research on these topics. However, it is necessitated by the ubiquity of these terms, which in the author's view constitutes the single most significant barrier to progress in both areas of research. The present discussion of such basic notions may be overly simple or erroneous, but it is offered in the belief that science is advanced more by error than by confusion.

CURRENT ATTRIBUTION RESEARCH AND CLOSE RELATIONSHIPS

The investigation of attributions for interpersonal behavior constitutes a major portion of attribution research. In the vast majority of cases, however, judgments are made about a stranger or hypothetical other on the basis of highly restricted information and for the purpose of complying with experimenter instructions. Each of these characteristics casts doubt on the relevance of such research for understanding attributions in relationships. For example, Knight and Vallacher (1981) show that attributors who believed themselves to be interacting with another person manifested a diametrically opposed pattern of attributions for that person's positive (situationally attributed) versus negative (dispositionally attributed) behavior compared to attributors who only expected to interact with the person at a later time. Detached observers did not make differential attributions for these two forms of behavior. In a similar vein, persons tend to make stronger internal attributions for positive behavior performed by a friend or a spouse than for an acquaintance (Taylor & Koivumaki, 1976). Such data suggest that the findings of basic attribution research should not be extrapolated without question to the study of close relationships.

RESEARCH IN SOCIAL PSYCHOLOGY

A striking difference between attribution in relationships and traditional attribution research in the laboratory is poignantly illustrated by
an early study of attributional conflict in young couples. Orvis, Kelley,
and Butler (1976) had subjects recount instances where each partner had
different attributions for a behavior by listing the behavior, their explanation for it, and their partner's explanation. Several interesting findings emerged, not the least of which is that subjects apparently had little
difficulty generating examples of attributional conflict which constituted
a "nearly complete summary of 'ways to aggravate, frustrate, threaten,
anger or embarrass your partner' " (Orvis et al., 1976, p. 370). In view
of the negative behaviors generated, it is perhaps not surprising that a
major finding concerns differences between actor (the person emitting
the offensive behavior) and partner (the offended spouse) explanations.
Partners tended to give explanations in terms of the actor's personal
characteristics (e.g., inability, habits) or attitudes toward the partner
(e.g., lack of concern, negative feelings). In contrast to the relative stability implied by the above explanations, actors tended to see their behavior as a single incident which they attempted to excuse (e.g., gave
explanations involving circumstances, other people or objects, or their
own psychological or physical state) or to justify (e.g., by appeal to
norms, the behavior's true intent, or appreciation of its desirability).

The above actor–partner differences were confirmed by Passer, Kelley,
and Michela's (1978) examination of the meaning given to various explanations. Undergraduate students judged the similarity between the
13 categories of explanations obtained in Orvis et al.'s (1976) study either
from the perspective of the actor or the partner. In both conditions, the
valence of the attitude toward the partner constituted one dimension in
the multidimensional scaling analyses. In the actor condition, the second dimension, intentional–unintentional, reflected the difference between excusing and justifying explanations. The remaining dimension
in the partner condition contrasted the actors' traits with their states or
circumstances.

In sum, these two studies suggest that actors' preferred explanations
for their negative behavior reflect a positive attitude toward the partner;
whereas, partners' preferred explanations are defined by the actor's
negative attitude and/or negative traits. These findings thus introduce
into the literature a new dimension which shows that attributions are
not value-neutral. The robustness of this dimension is demonstrated in
a more recent study which also found an evaluative dimension (as well
as intentionality and stability dimensions) for attributions regarding self-

and partner behavior deemed to be emotionally significant by the attributor (White, 1983). The existence of such a dimension suggests that the satisfaction experienced by partners may covary with attributions.[1]

Before considering research pertaining to relationship satisfaction, it is worth noting factors which limit the generalization of these findings. First, the explanations pertained only to instances of attributional conflict. Non-conflict contexts or those in which attributions are not communicated may yield different attribution patterns.[2] Second, where multiple explanations were given, only the most prominent one as defined by the experimenters, was coded. Third, where a sequence of events was given only the most immediate one was coded. The above issues may be particularly important in relationships (see the section, "Research in Clinical Psychology"). Finally, a subsequent, complementary study (Harvey, Wells, & Alvarez, 1978) suggests that couples are unaware of their actual attributional divergence. This stands in contrast to the ease with which Orvis et al. (1976) were able to examine attributional conflict. The contradiction may, however, be more apparent than real. Harvey et al. (1978) examined ratings of attributions for sensitive relationship conflicts (Orvis et al. 1976 specifically avoided these) in what turned out to be highly satisfactory relationships (couples expected their relationships to continue indefinitely and scored 9.6 on an 11-point scale of relationship satisfaction). Thus ignorance of attributional divergence for sensitive relationship issues may be associated with greater relationship satisfaction. This possibility remains an hypothesis, however, as attributional divergence was not examined in relation to satisfaction.

Indirect evidence suggests that attribution processes are indeed associated with relationship satisfaction. Thompson and Kelley (1981) found that relationship satisfaction correlated with partner responsibility for positive relationship events ($r = -.14$, Experiment 1), while estimated success of the relationship related to partner responsibility for conflict resolution, for carrying the conversation when the couple is alone, and accepting responsibility for inconveniencing the other ($r = -.24$, $-.27$ and $+.36$, respectively, Experiment 3).[3] The mere existence of such correlations is noteworthy as subjects again included partners who perceived their relationships to be highly successful (mean

[1]White (1983) found only a weak relationship between the evaluative dimension and satisfaction, a result which may reflect the limited variability obtained on the latter variable.
[2]Kelley (1979, p. 106) cites further research by Orvis which suggests that Orvis et al.'s (1976) findings obtain only when attributions are communicated.
[3]The negative correlations indicate that lower satisfaction is associated with greater responsibility assigned to the partner.

of 8.1 on a 10-point scale). In a similar vein, Sillars's (1981) research on roommate conflict shows that attributing the cause of the conflict to the roommate, as well as the tendency to see the conflict as stable, was greatest when relationship satisfaction was low.

RESEARCH IN CLINICAL PSYCHOLOGY

More direct evidence is provided by recent studies which investigate attributions in distressed relationships. The differences between distressed and nondistressed couples in both negative and positive spouse behaviors (e.g., Gottman, 1979; Jacobson, Folette, & McDonald, 1982; Jacobson, Waldron, & Moore, 1980; Wills, Weiss, & Patterson, 1974) have led researchers to examine attributions for behaviors that differ in valence separately. The issues investigated are usually some variant of the hypotheses (1) distressed couples are more likely to make causal attributions which undermine or neutralize positive spouse behavior but which accentuate the impact of negative behaviors (attribution hypothesis); (2) these inferences are related to subsequent responses to such behavior (attributional hypothesis; see Kelley & Michela, 1980).

Jacobson, McDonald, Follette, and Berley (in press), for example, investigated the first of these hypotheses by examining the extent to which distressed spouses (one partner scored below 100 on the Dyadic Adjustment Scale) attribute positive partner behaviors to "external" factors while attributing negative behavior to "internal" factors. Unknown to one spouse, the other was instructed to "act positive" or "act negative" on a conflict resolution task following which the uninformed spouse rated a set of causal attributions for their partner's behavior. Overall, there was a tendency to favor internal attributions, which is consistent with previous research showing that partner behavior is explained in dispositional terms (cf. Kelley, 1979), but differences nonetheless emerged between the two groups. Distressed couples rated negative spouse behavior more internally, whereas, nondistressed couples did so for positive spouse behavior.

Unfortunately, the interpretation of these results is somewhat ambiguous. It is not clear that the attributions rated reflect the internal–external dimension, a dimension which is tricky to operationalize and has created some confusion among attribution researchers (cf. Ross, 1977). Consider the attributions "She was trying to please me" and "He wanted to put on a good performance for the camera." The first is considered internal, the second external. Yet the structure of each is identical as the motivation occurs in the actor and is directed to an external source. What is at issue is the external target (spouse vs. camera); the first attribution is an example of an interpersonal attribution (what is the partner like in relation to *me*?; cf. Newman, 1981a, 1981b and the section, "Conclusion"), whereas the second is not. Moreover, the attributions also differ on causal dimensions other than the internal-external one. In addition, it is unlikely that this dimension of attribution alone mediates behavior exchanges, and its centrality to relationship attributions cannot be established by fiat in this manner (cf. Ross & Fletcher, in press). As a consequence, our own research has utilized several causal dimensions.

The starting point for this research was the clinical observation that spouses presenting themselves for therapy often feel helpless relative to the marriage and believe that there is little they can do to change their partner's behavior or improve the relationship. Consequently, the attribution dimensions which theoretically mediate learned helplessness were therefore investigated (Abramson, Seligman, & Teasdale, 1978). More specifically, it was expected that spouses seeking marital therapy would make more spouse (external), global, stable, and uncontrollable causal attributions for negative spouse behaviors than their nondistressed counterparts, while the inverse pattern would obtain for positive spouse behavior (attribution hypothesis).[4] The role of these attribution dimensions in mediating intended responses to spouse behavior was also evaluated (attributional hypothesis).

In the first study (Fincham & O'Leary, 1983), couples presenting for therapy and happily married couples completed an attribution questionnaire comprising 12 spouse behaviors (6 positive and 6 negative). These behaviors described commonly occurring acts (e.g., your spouse pays careful attention to what you are saying) which reflected the various categories of marital behavior included in the daily checklists used in behavioral marital therapy (Weiss & Perry, 1979). Respondents named the major cause of each behavior and then rated it on the four causal dimensions. In addition, they indicated the affective impact of the behavior and their most likely response to it. The results indicated that distressed spouses rated causes of negative behavior as more global; whereas nondistressed spouses considered causes of positive behaviors more global. The control dimension yielded a reliable difference only for positive acts (nondistressed more controllable than distressed), although the groups also tended to differ in the predicted direction regarding negative acts (p < .10). Attribution ratings predicted a significant portion of the variance in behavioral intentions only for positive spouse behaviors. However, path analyses suggested that the effect of

[4]The control dimension was included on the basis of our clinical observations and its centrality in previous attribution research (Weiner, 1979).

attributions on behavioral intentions was mediated by their impact on affect.

The relative lack of group differences in ratings of causal attributions was surprising but can be understood by reexamining previous writings on the topic. This exercise is also instructive because it illustrates the barrier to research progress posed by the ubiquitous nature of the term attribution. Clinicians point out that couples "typically view therapy as a way to demonstrate . . . that they are blameless and that the other is at fault" (Jacobson & Margolin, 1979, p. 108; see also Wright & Fichten, 1976). However it is unclear from previous research whether attributions for partner behavior were investigated in terms of perceived cause, responsibility, credit, or blame as the terms are used interchangeably in these reports (e.g., Sillars, 1981; Thompson & Kelley, 1981). In laboratory research people respond differently to such questions when judging hypothetical vignettes (Fincham &Jaspars, 1980; Fincham & Shultz, 1981; Shultz & Schleifer, 1983), and it is thus possible that in the context of our study spouses made similar distinctions. This possibility might also account for the low relationship found between causal attributions and intended behavior, as there is evidence to suggest that punishment is not determined directly by causal attributions but is, instead, mediated by attributed blame (Fincham & Roberts, in press; Jaspars, Hewstone, & Fincham, 1983). If this analysis is correct, attributions regarding blame, or the proposed bases for this attribution (e.g., intentional nature of actor's behavior, actor's motivation), may not only be more important in distinguishing distressed from nondistressed groups, but also in predicting behavioral responses. Such a position is consistent with theoretical statements which view attributions of intent as pivotal to the occurrence of family violence (Doherty, 1981a; Gelles & Strauss, 1979; Hotaling, 1980).

The preceding study was therefore replicated with some refinements to the attribution questionnaire and respondents were also asked to infer the extent to which the behavior reflected the spouse's positive or negative intentions, was selfishly motivated, and was blameworthy or praiseworthy, (Fincham, Beach, & Nelson, 1984). Again clear group differences in the predicted direction were obtained on the global causal dimension for both positive and negative events. A further difference was that nondistressed spouses rated the causes of positive events as more stable than did distressed spouses. These slightly stronger findings on the causal dimensions are partly attributable to the use of a more depressed clinic sample. With depression as a covariate, differences on the stability dimension disappeared. As expected, strong differences were found for perceived blame, inferred intent, and motivation for both positive and negative behaviors (distressed spouses inferred more negative intentions, selfish motivations, and judged behavior as more blameworthy in both cases). Moreover, behavioral intentions were more strongly correlated with these latter attributions (r_{pos} , .55 to .77; r_{neg} , .61 to .76) than the causal attribution dimensions (r_{pos} , $-.15$ to .30; r_{neg} , $-.08$ to $-.37$).

These data are consistent with two previous studies. Sillars's (1981) study on roommate conflict, for example, similarly suggests that blaming one's roommate for the conflict is associated with conflict escalation, while the low correlations between causal attributions and behavioral intentions concur with results from a study which examined actual spouse behavior. Doherty (1982) found that the tendency of newlywed wives to infer negative intentions or traits was positively associated with observed negative criticism of spouse ($r = .32$) and self-reported angry responses to coercive statements by the spouse ($r = .29$). No relationships were found for husbands. It should be noted, however, that attributions were assessed indirectly via responses to vignettes portraying hypothetical persons. Thus, this study exhibits limitations similar to the research described above.

In order to investigate the validity of data obtained by the use of stimuli comprising hypothetical partner behavior a third study was conducted (Fincham, 1984). Spouses in this investigation wrote down the two most important difficulties they experienced in their marriage and answered attribution questions pertaining to these difficulties. Again distressed spouses saw the causes of the difficulties as more global and were more likely to manifest negatively valenced attributions for the difficulties. Thus despite the criticism of research using hypothetical stimuli, the pattern of results using the two methodologies is quite similar. This observation is consistent with results from a study by Madden and Janoff-Bulman (1981) which showed no differences between wives' attributions of blame for hypothetical vignettes of conflict situations and the actual conflicts experienced with husbands. In both cases greater husband blame was also associated with lower marital satisfaction.

In a further study (Fincham, Beach, & Baucom, 1984), we obtained data on actor–partner differences in attributions made by distressed and nondistressed spouses. An Actor–Partner × Group interaction was obtained for both positive and negative events which showed that distressed spouses manifest large partner–actor differences in attributions relative to nondistressed spouses. Distressed spouses saw their own behavior as more positively motivated, reflective of something about themselves, and more deserving of praise than positive partner behavior; whereas, for negative actions causes of own behavior were seen as more external, less stable, and less global. These findings suggest that a precept for happy marriage is to "attribute thy partner's behavior as thou would thine own."

In sum, our research emphasizes the importance of attending to relationship satisfaction when examining attributions in relationships, the necessity of investigating numerous causal dimensions, and suggests that attributions of fault or liability are pivotal in relationships. These conclusions, however, should be considered tentative given the limitations of this research. Chief among these is the cross-sectional nature of the research which precludes analysis of the causal relationship between attributions and relationship satisfaction and the fact that it, like most attribution research, fails to capture the richness and complexity of naturally occurring attributions.[5] The latter is, however, evident in research on relationship termination.

Research on relationship termination has focused on explanations given for marital separation or divorce (Fletcher, 1983; Harvey, et al., 1978; Kitson & Sussman, 1982; Newman, 1981c). Perhaps the most striking feature of these data are their richness and complexity which contrasts with attribution theory's picture of people as cognitive misers. For example, Fletcher (1983) found that the explanations of a "large number of respondents" (p. 256) did not terminate with dispositional attributions but mentioned background factors, such as upbringing, which might account for them. However, as Harvey et al. (1978) argue, researchers need to rule out artifactual explanations, such as the need of separating spouses, to develop rationales which will facilitate the legal-psychological dissolution for their relationship. Whether the need to develop elaborate accounts is artifactual rather than intrinsic to the phenomenon is perhaps arguable, but their point is well taken. Post relationship explanations regarding the relationship are quite likely different to those given in the context of an ongoing relationship. Changes in such explanations (Newman & Langer, in press) for instance, are likely to reflect intrapersonal processes rather than relationship processes. Consequently, the details of these studies are not apposite in the present context.

Conclusion

In concluding this brief review, it is worth noting that attribution researchers might profit from paying more explicit attention to characteristics which differentiate relationships. The recurrent emergence of

[5]Both issues are currently under investigation in our laboratory.

intimate–distant, positive–negative, and equal–unequal dimensions in perceptions of relationships has led to the suggestion that they may represent a framework which structures knowledge about relationships (Wish, Deutsch, & Kaplan, 1976). It would be surprising if attributions were not affected by these differences in relationships. Already the importance of the intimate–distant dimensions has begun to emerge. However, it is apparent that little attempt has been made thus far to differentiate between types of relationships along this dimension. Thus subject samples sometimes comprise a mixture of dating and married couples, even though there may be important differences between these two kinds of relationships which influence the attribution process. For instance, Lederer and Jackson (1968) believe that marriage produces profound changes in a relationship as it becomes compulsory, rather than voluntary, and clinicians are familiar with the spouse who is unclear as to whether a given behavior is due to their own or partner's volition, or to the exigencies of conforming to the state of marriage (Haley, 1963, p. 120). From an attributional perspective, marriage thus confers an additional potential cause for partner behavior allowing use of the discounting principle (Kelley, 1972).

There is some evidence that the positive–negative dimension may also be important both as an attribution dimension and in terms of understanding the attributions made by couples who vary on this dimension. Thus wittingly or not, attribution research has mirrored two of the dimensions underlying the perceived structure of relationships. The third, equal–unequal, is less evident. Its most obvious instantiation is that of the parent–child relationship, and in this form some research interest is evident. Both developmental and clinical psychologists have begun to evaluate parent perceptions of child behavior (Larrance & Twentyman, 1983; Rosenberg & Repucci, 1983). With few exceptions, however (e.g., Compas, Friedland-Bandes, Bastien, & Adelman, 1981; Dix & Grusec, in press), the research is not conducted within an attribution framework and hence this application currently remains a potential yet to be fully realized.

TOWARD A MORE SYSTEMATIC EXAMINATION OF ATTRIBUTIONS IN CLOSE RELATIONSHIPS

It is apparent that research on attributions in relationships is in its infancy and comprises largely isolated sets of studies unrelated to a more comprehensive research framework. Consequently, there is the temptation to propose a model regarding attributions in relationships in the hope of providing such a framework. This temptation is resisted as relationship researchers have for too long erected "large and complex theories . . . without having the data base on which such theories should depend" (Duck, 1980, p. 117). Several theoretical papers on attributions in relationships have emerged recently despite the evidently meager data base in this field (e.g., Arias, in press; Berley & Jacobson, 1984; Doherty, 1981a, b; Epstein, 1982; Fincham, 1983; Hotaling, 1980; Kelley, 1979; Newman, 1981a, b; Newman & Langer, in press; Weiss, 1981). None appear to have provided an integrative research framework, and the contribution of yet another is not clear.

Given the above observation, it is appropriate to consider how research on attributions in relationships is best facilitated. To this end, the perspective of a neophyte is adopted and some simple questions regarding attributions in relationships are articulated. These are discussed in terms of equally obvious distinctions which may provide a rough framework for future research. As clinical application cannot always await the resolution of basic research questions, the clinical implications of each question are also outlined. In this regard, several caveats are apposite. First, only selected clinical issues highlighted by an attribution perspective are considered (see Christensen, 1983, for a more comprehensive treatment of intervention in close relationships). Second, specific events comprise the unit of analysis rather than general descriptions of relationship problems, as this level of analysis is deemed necessary for successful therapy (Christensen, 1983; Jacobson & Margolin, 1979). Third, most of the observations made pertain to behavioral marital therapy.

THE OCCURRENCE OF ATTRIBUTIONS IN RELATIONSHIPS

The most fundamental query the neophyte might make is as simple as it is obvious: "Do attributions occur in relationships?" It is easy to dismiss this iconoclastic question as it seems difficult to conceive of a relationship devoid of attributions. However, before doing so it is instructive to consider the nature of interchanges between partners that form the basis of their interdependence and hence their existence in a "close relationship." A useful distinction in this regard is that between exchange interactions, where benefits of equivalent value are exchanged, and communal interactions, in which benefits are given in accordance with the perceived need of another (Clark & Mills, 1979). In the present context, it is noteworthy that the attributions made by the recipient of the benefit differ in the two interactions—exchange behaviors are seen to be motivated by the receipt of a future reciprocated benefit and hence are means to an end; whereas communal acts are intrinsically rewarding, serving as an end in themselves.

According to the definition outlined earlier, relationships may entail either form of interaction. However, they are ideally characterized by communal interactions, a property which from a lay perspective, at least, might be considered one of their defining features. Given this viewpoint, it makes sense to consider seriously our initial question: Do partners try to create a stable environment by making causal attributions for each other's behavior? Perhaps not. Merely attending to possible extrinsic causes for relationship behavior has been associated with lower scores on Rubin's love scale while consideration of intrinsic causes shows a similar tendency (Seligman, Fazio, & Zanna, 1980). Seeking causes for relationship behavior may therefore detract from the perception of the relationship as intrinsically rewarding. As Snyder and Wicklund (1981) eloquently state, "an intimate relationship is practically defined in terms of its ambiguity of cause, and this is the magic that appeals to its participants" (p. 218).

Why then is it difficult to conceive of a relationship devoid of attributions? Several answers are possible, only some of which will be mentioned. First, there are many sources other than causal analyses (e.g., use of scripts) which can be used to establish a predictable reality. To the extent that these sources "explain" perceived behaviors and are hence subsumed under the term *attribution*, relationships cannot be regarded as attribution free. Second, causal attributions may comprise part of the perception of relationship behavior (see the next section). Third, the plausibility of the preceding argument rests on several unarticulated assumptions. In explicitly discussing the assumptions made regarding two underlying dimensions, the phase of a relationship and relationship expectations, it will be clear that there is no simple answer to our initial question.

RELATIONSHIP PHASES

It is quite likely that attribution processes are integrally related to the phase of a relationship. At the very least researchers need to distinguish between the formation, maintenance, and dissolution of relationships following the tradition of family sociology, where these phases comprise distinct research literatures. With one exception (Newman & Langer, in press), this dimension has been neglected in theoretical formulations relating to attributions in close relationships.

The importance of this dimension is, however, readily apparent. During the formation of a close relationship, deliberate attribution making is likely to be highly functional in reducing ambiguity and facilitating information processing of relationship behavior. Attributions of all sorts are no doubt salient as partners begin to construct and refine conceptions of what the partner and the relationship is like. As these conceptions become well specified, the relationship enters the maintenance phase.

During the maintenance phase, the existence of stable conceptions of the relationship allows greater predictability and reduces the need to make attributions regarding relationship behavior. When attributions are made, they may reflect more about the person's beliefs about the relationship than the behavior judged. The relative comfort of this phase contrasts with the dissatisfaction and pain surrounding the relationship dissolution phase. Here attributions are again likely to be critical in assisting spouses to understand what is happening in the relationship. However, as termination takes place each person is likely to evidence greater concern regarding the provision of attributions that are socially acceptable in their environment.

This thumbnail sketch suggests that the very occurrence of mindful attributions may be a barometer of relationship development. Although interesting, this hypothesis is perhaps overly simple as it is related to a second important dimension, namely, relationship expectations.

RELATIONSHIP EXPECTATIONS

Individuals entering a relationship do so with expectations regarding both the content and causes of appropriate relationship behavior which shape and are ultimately shaped by relationship experience. Expectations most likely facilitate processing of partner behavior by directing attention to particular information. In the early stages of the relationship, for example, this may take the form of selective attention to positive aspects of the partner's behavior, which no doubt facilitates the formation of a close relationship. Ultimately such processes result in causal schemata regarding relationship behavior.

The view that attributions and expectations are inseparable contrasts with traditional attribution research where covariation and configuration models of attribution (Kelley, 1967, 1972) have spawned largely separate literatures. At present, little is known about the interaction between existing expectations and the processing of available, causally relevant information (Ajzen, 1977; Metalsky & Abramson, 1980), although there is evidence that the violation of expectations instigates the attribution process (Pittman & D'Agostino, Chapter 5, this volume; Pyszczynski & Greenberg, 1981; Wong & Weiner, 1981). Much more attention needs to be focused on this issue if attribution research is to be useful in understanding relationships. At the very least, data is needed on the conditions under which the perception of partner behavior is assimilated to existing expectations and vice versa.

The explicit consideration of expectations illuminates other aspects of attribution research on relationships. For example, it may explain why causal attributions are often equated with perceived blame. Given a set of expectations for reasonable relationship behavior, a causal inquiry regarding the partner's behavior can amount to a charge which requires rebuttal. The issue of responsibility seems most relevant here, and, as responsibilities exist in relation to duties, causal perception as traditionally conceived in the attribution literature need not even be at issue. The quintessence of responsibility is answerability or accountability, and hence the provision of attributions in the form of justifications or excuses (Orvis et al., 1976) may prevent relationship conflict by ''verbally bridging the gap between action and expectation'' (Lyman & Scott, 1970, p. 112). To the extent that such accounts are indicative of the actor's positive attitude towards the partner they confirm the value of the relationship for both partners and suggest that attributions may serve as repair mechanisms in a relationship. More importantly, when an attribution functions in this manner, it is likely to preserve the set of expectations that gave rise to the initial enquiry. Determination of the conditions that give rise to successful accounts may provide some understanding regarding the relationship between existing expectations and new input information. Moreover, it is important to clarify whether attributions in relationships always follow the rules of responsibility attribution rather than causal attribution.

Returning to our original question regarding the occurrence of attributions in relationships, it can be seen that by implicitly assuming a relationship in the maintenance phase and the occurrence of expectation-congruent behavior only, it is possible to argue that attributions have no place in a relationship. Explicit examination of these assumptions shows, therefore, that the more appropriate question to ask is *when* mindful attributions occur in relationships and not *whether* they occur.

CLINICAL IMPLICATIONS

The observations made in relation to relationship phases, when considered in conjunction with data on behavior exchange in marriage, yield an interesting hypothesis. Distressed spouses tend to be more affected by immediate, negative spouse behavior (Jacobson et al. 1980; Jacobson et al., 1982) and are more likely to reciprocate it (Gottman,

1979; Margolin & Wampold, 1981) than nondistressed spouses who tend to exchange high rates of positive behaviors noncontingently (Gottman, Notarius, Markman, Bank, Yoppi, & Rubin, 1976). It is quite possible that causal attributions mediate the contingent exchanges which occur in distressed couples while the noncontingent exchanges of happy couples are consistent with the proposal that the maintenance phase of a relationship is characterized by a relative lack of attribution making. This leads to the hypothesis that high rates of causal attributions in marriage may indicate spouse dissatisfaction. If correct, helping a spouse make more benign attributions for his or her partner's behavior may be insufficient in marital therapy (Baucom, 1981; Epstein, 1982; Berley, & Jacobson, 1984). Failure to extinguish deliberate causal analysis of partner behavior may allow the quid pro quo exchanges, which characterize distressed marriages, to be maintained.

In this regard, possibly the best that can be done is to ensure that positive behavior change is seen to occur in the absence of environmental constraints. This would maximize the reinforcing value of such behavior and may ultimately remove the necessity of making attributions for it. To this end, strategies which increase the perceived choice of the behavior-changing spouse are likely to be most appropriate. This implies some alterations in the implementation of behavior change in marital therapy. Hence, for example, rather than have spouses request behavior changes from one another (Jacobson & Margolin, 1979), each should her- or himself generate possible changes that might increase his or her spouse's satisfaction. Similarly, implementation of such changes should not be based on reciprocal behavior change contracts (O'Leary & Turkewitz, 1978) but should be unilateral. Finally, therapist directives relating to behavior change should not be too specific lest change be attributed to the therapist.

The second dimension considered above, the expectation–attribution relationship, gives rise to the notion that in relationships questions of responsibility rather than perceived causality are at issue. Explicit consideration of attributions as responsibility judgments might prove useful to therapists as a conceptual framework for integrating several seemingly disparate cognitive therapy techniques and as a tool in working with couples. For instance, it alerts spouses to the fact that what they might consider innocent attribution inquiries are really accusations of blame. This could render the accused partner's defensive reaction and the couple's possible escalation of conflict more comprehensible. It opens the way for evolving more appropriate means of handling such inquiries and may naturally lead to communication training, a commonly used procedure in marital therapy (Segraves, 1982). More importantly, consideration of the duties which give rise to responsibilities entails explicit examination of relationship expectations. The importance of this exercise is emphasized by the fact that the consideration of expectations comprises "much of what occurs in good marital therapy" (O'Leary & Turkewitz, 1978, p. 247). Where unrealistic expectations are at issue, the irrational beliefs underlying them serve as the appropriate target of internvention (Ellis & Harper, 1977; Epstein & Eidelson, 1981). Such beliefs (e.g., disagreement between spouses is destructive; partner's approval is necessary) are often not obvious, but considering relationship problems within the present framework directs attention to their possible existence. This is an important asset, as the identification and challenging of unrealistic expectations or myths is one of the most widely advocated procedures in cognitive approaches to marital therapy (Baucom, 1981; Berley & Jacobson, 1984; Epstein, 1982).

Capacity responsibility, or the preconditions which must be met before a person can be held responsible for his or her actions, encapsulates a second common cognitive restructuring procedure used with couples, namely relabelling (Jacobson & Margolin, 1979). Often this takes the form of reframing a distressing spouse behavior attributed to a negative trait (e.g., lack of communication resulting from distrustfulness) as a skill deficit (e.g., lack of communication skills). Teaching couples to consider explicitly the capacities necessary for holding someone responsible may help prevent the need for relabelling.

Finally, utilization of the criteria for responsibility attribution may also be useful in therapy. For example, consideration of Heider's (1958) levels of responsibility attribution would lead distressed spouses to ask questions such as: Is the upsetting event caused by my spouse? Is my spouse's behavior in this regard intentional? If not, is the event foreseeable from my spouse's perspective? If so, is there a justification for my spouse's behavior? In regard to the last question, it would be important to have spouses realize that the actor alone knows the reasons for his or her behavior (Locke & Pennington, 1982). Even though the attributor may wish to provide a negative causal explanation of the reasons themselves, or dispute the beliefs on which the reasons for their spouse's conduct rest, consideration of the behavior in terms of the actor's reasons is likely to render it more understandable and, most likely, less malevolent.

The adoption of the above framework in the context of facilitating behavior change would, by virtue of its novelty for couples, also direct attention to each spouse's processing of such change. Explicit processing of change is necessary to promote the emergence of more adaptive conceptions of the relationship. Lack of attention to the processing of positive behavior changes might otherwise result in their being assimilated to existing malfunctional expectations (e.g., "She or he is only doing this because it was a homework assignment").

Introducing "responsibility attribution" explicitly into therapy also has obvious dangers. It may potentially reinforce the adverserial system which characterizes distressed relationships. However, its apparent relevance to distressed couples makes it an attractive possibility in the initial stages of therapy. This does not mean that it should be used literally to help determine blame. Rather, like any approach adopted in marital therapy, it needs to be introduced in the context of mutual cooperation and collaboration. Despite possible dangers, such an approach seems more appropriate than a previously implemented attribution intervention which teaches couples to make attributions in accordance with the covariation principle (Baucom, 1981), a procedure requiring a "mere statistician" (Ross, 1977).

In sum, it is suggested that attributions may be an index of distress and of underlying expectations that need to be changed as well as being the subject of change themselves. The next issue to be addressed concerns not only attributions per se but also the subject matter to which they pertain.

THE SUBJECT OF ATTRIBUTIONS IN RELATIONSHIPS

Our neophyte might next inquire about the subject matter of attributions. What are attributions made about in relationships? This is a poignant question, as the duration of relationships over time requires that events for which attributions are made be extracted from the ongoing flow of interaction. Moreover, once extracted the event is likely to be understood in the context of its location within a temporal sequence of cause–effect relationships. Unfortunately, little is known about this process but its importance in relationship research is emphasized by the reciprocal determinism which characterizes dyadic interaction. As a given act by one spouse is simultaneously a stimulus (insofar as it is followed by a partner behavior) and a response (insofar as it follows a partner behavior), any attempt to impose a linear cause–effect structure is quite arbitrary. This does not imply that such structures are alien to partner's perceptions of their relationships, as it is generally believed that our information-processing capacities force us to segment perceptual inputs into units (Dickman, 1963; McClintock, 1983). Unfortunately, basic attribution research is again of little assistance in understanding segmentation of the behavior stream (cf. Newtson, 1976).

Communication theorists have, however, long recognized that people "punctuate" the flow of interaction by pairing events in a way that introduces the impression of cause–effect relations (Watzlawick, Beavin, & Jackson, 1967). Once a starting point is established, the causal ordering of events becomes obvious to the perceiver. *Faulty punctuation*, where each partner sees his or her behavior as a response to the other's prior action (e.g., wife nags . . . husband withdraws . . . wife nags . . . husband withdraws), is particularly apparent in conflict situations and is seen as the root of relationship problems (Watzlawick, et al., 1967).

While such a characterization is valuable, it does not capture fully the richness of attribution in relationships. For example, partner behavior may be attributed to multiple causes, which may or may not occur in the immediately preceding interaction, or to an immediate cause, which is itself seen as the endpoint of a sequence of events extending far into the past. Both kinds of causes have been found in relationships (Fletcher, 1983; Orvis et al., 1976), but, as in traditional attribution research, the issues of multiple causation and causal chains have been neglected (Fincham & Shultz, 1981; Fincham & Roberts, 1984). Yet variability in attributions on such dimensions might be important in understanding relationships. A person who attributes his or her partner's negative behavior to a disposition but then proceeds to view that disposition as a result of the partner's upbringing is likely to be more tolerant and patient, at least initially, than one who stopped his or her analysis after inferring a disposition.

In fact the extraction of meaningful behavior units and their causal analysis in relationships is likely to be quite complex. It presumably involves monitoring and coordinating information derived from behavior chains of both partners, as well as cognizance of potential causes which lie outside the immediate interaction sequence. Differences in the perceived salience of each of these elements may result in complex interactions between them. For instance, if the perceiver's own behavioral chain is very salient, the unit extracted from interaction may comprise a fine-grained segment of their own behavior that is explained in terms of prior sections within their own behavioral chain. Similarly, equal attention to both persons' chains, as well as extrinsic causes, may result in a sequence of own and other behavior as the perceptual unit and an attribution pertaining to the relationship itself. Several other possibilities exist, but it is sufficient to note that the nature of an attribution in a relationship cannot easily be divorced from the very behavior that it explains. The fact that different classes of behavior evoke different explanations has only recently gained the attention of attribution researchers (Lalljee & Abelson, 1983).

Once we recognize that people segment ongoing behavior into meaningful units and impose causal structures on these units, a number of questions related to attribution processes become apparent. Perhaps the most basic include (1) identifying and characterizing behavioral segments and causal structures; (2) determining whether these two processes are distinguishable or, as has been suggested, whether the reasons for behavior enter into the very perception of meaningful behavioral units (Newman, 1981a, b; Orvis et al., 1976), (3) finding out if sequences of events are organized primarily in causal rather than other terms, and so forth (cf. Kelley, 1983). Even the simplest of these questions is not readily amenable to empirical analysis, which may account for the paucity of research in this area (McClintock, 1983). However, the potential utility of an attribution approach in understanding relationships will only be fully realized once these questions are addressed. The necessity for this research approach is emphasized by the fact that the absence of studies requiring subjects to abstract information from behavior has led to distorted conceptualizations of relationships (Duck, 1980).

CLINICAL IMPLICATIONS

The previously stated observations again suggest interesting possible differences between distressed and nondistressed spouses. The notion of faulty punctuation noted by clinicians can be translated into the hypothesis that distressed spouses more likely give proximal causes for relationship behavior, while nondistressed spouses might trace causality through intervening events to more distal causes. In a similar vein, one might hypothesize that distressed spouses are more likely subject to the prejudice, noted by Mill, that a phenomenon can have no more than one cause. They might seek *the* cause of distressing spouse behavior rather than entertain the notion of multiple causation. Needless to say, research will help us decide the validity of such hypotheses.

As regards therapy, it appears that attributions may once again be indicative of issues that might have to be addressed in treatment. Of all the available explanations for the distressing event, why has the spouse chosen this particular one? Has she or he simply overlooked other possible causes, or have these been considered and rejected? Answers to such questions are likely to provide useful diagnostic information. Perhaps the most important therapeutic implication involves altering the perceived causal structures of distressed spouses. For example, spouses entering therapy often make attributions which suggest no possibility of change (e.g., "He or she did it because he or she is just naturally mean"). Changing such attributions to increase a sense of mastery over the problem (e.g., "We seem to snap at each other when we are tired") is often seen as a precondition to therapeutic change. This is implicit in the "reframing" of problems by systems oriented therapists (e.g., Minuchin, 1974) and the induction of a "collaborative set" in behavioral therapy (Jacobson & Margolin, 1979).

Awareness of the fact that spouses segment interaction and select the cause of the event from a range of conditions and complex causal connections suggests several possibilities for changing attributions in therapy. Redirecting attention to aspects of the event that have been overlooked may lead to the event's being seen as part of a larger sequence of events. Similarly, further segmentation of an event might naturally lead to a different attribution. Judicious use of "why" questions can be used to trace causation to prior events and so on. Thus the popular notion of reattribution (see Wilson, Chapter 1, this volume; Fincham, 1983) need not be achieved by explicitly focussing on causes per se. It is also apparent that new attributions are no more "correct" than those they replace, which suggests that the notion of attribution "error" in relationships (Berley & Jacobson, in press; Newman, 1981a, b) is untenable. It would be more appropriate and less emotive, though perhaps not as clinically satisfying, to describe attributions as more or less functional for a given purpose. The process of reattribution in therapy, therefore, should not be considered independently of therapeutic goals. Research on reattribution would also be improved by recognition of the functional nature of attributions.

The Nature of Attributions in Relationships

A third question which may legitimately be asked is "What kinds of attributions occur in relationships?" This question is considered in terms of the level at which attributions are made as well as the content of such attributions.[6]

Levels of Attribution

A distinction frequently made in attribution research is that between the implicit attribution of causes, a relatively unreflective and less conscious process likely to be part of the interpretation of an event as discussed earlier, and explicit attribution processing of the sort that occurs when subjects provide a thoughtful analysis of an event subsequent

[6]Traditional dimensions along which attributions can be classified are not considered as they were discussed in the section, "Current Attribution Research and Close Relationships" and their implications for relationships are also elaborated by Doherty (1981a).

to its occurrence (Langer, 1978; Lloyd-Bostock, 1983). Clearly it is the latter sort of attribution which has been investigated in relationships. It would be useful, however, to distinguish between explicit attributions which remain private to the individual and those that are communicated to the partner. These two levels of attribution are obviously not totally different, independent phenomena, since both are influenced by the social context in which they are made, but it is only the latter that achieves the status of a social act.

When attributions are viewed as social acts that comprise part of the relationship dialogue, it becomes apparent that they can be studied in the same manner as any other behavior. For instance, a functional analysis in which the stimuli preceding the verbalization of an attribution and its consequences are systematically monitored would elucidate the conditions under which causal attributions are articulated in a relationship and would show how they are shaped by its development (see Kidd & Amabile, 1981). Intuitively, it would make some difference if an attribution were spontaneously articulated or was a response to an inquiry from the partner. In regard to the former, the goals of the attributor in the relationship and the perceived consequences of the attribution for the relationship need to be considered. To fully understand an attribution in the latter case, the enquiring partner's knowledge and the purpose of his or her inquiry need to be considered. In sum, the context surrounding the articulation of an attribution in a relationship is critical to understanding it.

Once attributions are investigated as part of the relationship dialogue, it is apparent that they can be made at a further level. Attributions themselves may be subject to causal analysis. Such meta-attributions are likely to be most obvious when a spouse does not find his or her partner's causal attributions acceptable, although they may also occur on the basis of inferred partner attributions. The investigation of attributions as independent, rather than dependent variables, suggests a fertile area for future research (see Hill, Weary, Hildebrand-Saints, & Elbin, Chapter 6, this volume).

THE CONTENT OF ATTRIBUTIONS

Orthogonal to the level at which an attribution is made is the content of an attribution. Despite the laudable attempt to solicit attributions from subjects, it is apparent that researchers have viewed these data in a limited way, focussing on such traditional categories as internal (dispositional) and external (situational) attributions. Exactly what constitutes an internal or external attribution in a relationship is, however, moot. Do "internal" attributions apply only to individual partners or also to properties of the relationship? Is a spouse's influence on his or her partner coded as an "external" attribution or do situational influences reside only outside of the dyad?

Attempts to categorize attributions in relationships elucidate the limitations of the caterogies utilized to date. Newman (1981a, b; Newman & Langer, in press) notes, for example, that attributions such as "my partner has a poor attitude about me" are not clearly internal attributions even though they are treated as such (Orvis et al., 1976). Nor are they clearly situational. Similarly, it is difficult to understand why a (dispositional) category "partner insensitivity" might contain attributions such as "lack of mutual affection" or "absence of emotional support" (Harvey, et al., 1978). Consequently, Newman (1981a) has proposed an interpersonal attribution category which focusses on "one's perception of 'self in regard to other' and 'other in regard to self' " (p. 63).

The recognition of attributions which focus on interaction is an important addition to the literature. However, Newman's (1981a, b) analysis appears to be incomplete. It is possible to distinguish between an interactive attribution which maintains a focus on the partner (e.g., "She does not trust me"; "Partner has a poor attitude about me") and one which is truly relational (e.g., "There is a lack of trust between us", "lack of mutual affection"). It might, however, be argued that such a distinction is one of form, not content. It is noteworthy that similar differences in "form" on the internal–external attribution dimension have been found to have "psychological meaning" (Fletcher, 1983).

In sum, it seems helpful to make conceptual distinctions between internal and external attributions (causes which are intrapersonal or reflective of something about the spouse and causes outside of the spouse or which would influence anyone—both exclude causes residing in the dyad), interpersonal attributions (causes which related to the spouse vis-à-vis his or her partner), and relationship attributions (causes which reflect properties of the dyad itself).

CLINICAL IMPLICATIONS

Distressed and nondistressed spouses are likely to differ on both of the dimensions discussed above. To the extent that distress reflects a breakdown in the acceptance of accounts, distressed spouses may make more meta-attributions than their nondistressed counterparts. In terms of the content of attributions, intriguing possibilities arise. The interdependence manifest in relationships leads to the suggestion that intrapersonal causes of behavior may tend to be attributed interpersonally by the partner (Newman & Langer, in press). This relationship analogue of the fundamental attribution error may, however, require some modification when considered in terms of relationship satisfaction. It seems reasonable to hypothesize that distressed spouses make more negative interpersonal attributions than their happily married counterparts. However, do nondistressed spouses make positive interpersonal attributions for partner behavior resulting from intrapersonal causes? As distressed spouses are encouraged to make relationship attributions in therapy, does this imply that nondistressed spouses are more likely to make such attributions?

Several implications for therapy concerning the nature of attributions in relationships have already been mentioned. What remains is to consider the broader context in which attributions occur. Hence, it is not only the attribution itself which may be the focus of attention in therapy, but also the conditions which instigated it, the goals of each partner, secondary gains associated with it, and so on.

ATTRIBUTION, AFFECT, AND BEHAVIOR IN RELATIONSHIPS

Having explored the nature of attributions in relationships, our neophyte might finally ask whether such attributions matter: Do they influence spouses' affect and behavior toward one another? Any answer to such a question is based largely on assumption—attribution researchers have been preoccupied with the antecedents of attributions (attribution theories) rather than their consequences (attributional theories). This situation precludes a demonstration of how attributions influence affect and behavior (Kelley & Michela, 1980), a lacuna seen to limit severely the application of attribution research (Eiser, 1983). In this regard the attribution literature reflects the malaise of its parent discipline, psychology, where the relationships among cognition, affect, and behavior are poorly understood. As a consequence, only a few, limited observations are made regarding the appropriateness of the above question.

As psychology "went cognitive" in the seventies (Dember, 1974), it seemed natural that attribution theory assumed center stage and that affect, behavior, expectations, and so on became "postcognitive." However, as we mature into the "affective eighties" (Fincham & O'Leary, in press; Zajonc, 1980), there is the danger of unproductive debate regarding the primacy of attributions. Recalling the resolution of the nature-nurture controversy is instructive—it suggests that we direct our attention to the interaction of attributions and other variables specifying the conditions under which attributions tend to influence affect–behavior and vice versa (for a different perspective on this issue, see Coyne, 1982). Only then, will we know when it is appropriate to apply attribution theory.

In the context of relationships, the proposed interdependence between attribution, affect, and behavior is particularly important. The duration of the relationship over time has two important implications. First, attributions made for a past event may be influenced as much by the event's perceived consequences as its perceived antecedents. Second, attributions can be confirmed or disconfirmed by the spouse's subsequent behavior. Such observations suggest that attribution theorists are guilty of faulty punctuation and that an absolute distinction between attribution and attributional theories is untenable (cf. Eiser, 1983). In short, it is as imprudent to deny that attributions influence behavior–affect as it is to assert that they are its primary determinants in relationships.

CLINICAL IMPLICATIONS

It would be presumptuous to draw any specific implications from the above global comments. However, they do point to the potential shortsightedness of dogmatically adhering to a framework that points to one response channel as primary. Hence, for example, the inadequacy of assuming that affect and cognition naturally follow behavior change is a shortcoming of behavioral marital therapy that is now recognized by its proponents (e.g., Baucom, 1981; Jacobson, 1984; Margolin, 1983). Similarly, we need to remind ourselves that attributions comprise only one component in the acquisition, maintenance, and remediation of clinical problems.

This does not imply that time devoted to attributions in marital therapy is ill spent. On the contrary, clients' beliefs that attributions are connected to affect and behavior necessitate attention to them, regardless of the relationship revealed by science. Moreover, attributions can become functionally autonomous and themselves be the source of relationship discontent. While it would be foolish not to focus directly on attributions in such cases, this need not preclude attention to behavioral or affective factors. For instance, recent research illustrating the impact of mood on cognitive processes (e.g., Wright & Mischel, 1982; Schwartz & Clore, 1983) suggests that altering resistant negative attributions to positive ones might be facilitated by prior induction of a positive mood. Nor is it being suggested that attribution change is not sometimes a prerequisite for other kinds of changes (cf. Kihlstrom & Nasby, 1981). It is rather a matter, to paraphrase Paul's (1969) well-known question of: "What response channel or combination thereof is the most effective focus for this couple, at this time, with what aspect of their problem, under which set of circumstances and how will it work?" (p. 62).

What might our neophyte finally conclude from the above inquiries? Most obviously they generate more questions than answers. Hence she or he may suspect, correctly, that the issues discussed are representative rather than exhaustive of those relating to attributions in relationships. In addition, they concern only the perspective of the individual. A whole new set of questions would emerge if attributions of the dyad were treated as the unit of analysis. Our neophyte would also conclude that many of the distinctions and issues elaborated are familiar ones. Their familiarity has not, however, ensured their inclusion in recent relationship research on attributions nor indeed have they necessarily received the attention they deserve in basic attribution research. In sum, it might be concluded that our understanding of attributions in relationships is currently inversely proportional to the magnitude of the challenge this task poses and that our charting of this domain has only just begun. Hopefully, the preceding discussion provides a rough cartography of this terrain for future research.

CONCLUSION

A fuller understanding of our initial observation regarding the neglect of classic attribution theories in statements about relationships is now possible. The lack of research testing basic attribution processes (e.g., correspondent inferences, augmentation, covariation) in the context of ongoing behavioral sequences makes it difficult to judge their significance for interpersonal interactions (Ross & Fletcher, in press). The limitations of these statements is also apparent in the present context. For example, it is quite likely that spouses infer dispositions from unintentional behaviors (e.g., carelessness) as well as intentional ones (Jones & Davis, 1965) and that they clearly use more than covariation information in making attributions (Kelley, 1972). Indeed, the simpleminded questions posed regarding attributions in relationships reveals a paucity of basic attribution research relevant to them.

The study of attributions in relationships thus promises to enrich attribution theory, and it is in such applications that the future of attribution research may lie (Harvey & Harris, 1983). Conversely, an attribution perspective is potentially fruitful for the study of close relationships. Both social and clinical psychologists are becoming increasingly enthusiastic about such a possibility. This combination is likely to be potent and it has already resulted in the exciting methodological innovation of coding attributions from conversation transcripts (Peterson, Luborsky, & Seligman, 1983; Larrance & Twentyman, 1983).

The broad scope of attribution theory is likely to ensure its exploration in relationship research. Herein, however, lies a potential danger. It is already apparent that citation of "attribution theory" in this area is not always informed by an appreciation of basic attribution research. At worst, this makes the link between the application of attribution theory and its parent field tenuous and, at best, results in the rediscovery of existing findings and distinctions. In any event, the confusing usage of this term is exacerbated in the emerging relationship literature on this topic where it often serves as a synonym for cognition. The continued vitality of attribution research requires greater differentiation between types of attributions, the content to which they pertain, and how these interact with the attribution process. Such a development implies the promulgation of content-related "minitheories" of attribution relevant to relationships. In the interest of promoting the collaboration of social and clinical psychologists in achieving this goal, it is appropriate to remind clinicians of Lewin's (1951) famous observation "that there is nothing as practical as a good theory" and for social psychologists to remember his admonition *not* to "look toward applied problems with highbrow aversion" (p. 51). Only by following Lewin's original mandate is a true understanding of attributions in close relationships likely to emerge.

REFERENCES

Abramson, L. Y., Seligman, M. E. P., & Teasdale, J. D. (1978). Learned helplessness in humans: Critique and reformulation. *Journal of Abnormal Psychology, 87*, 49–74.

Ajzen, I. (1977). Intuitive theories of events and the effects of base-rate information on prediction. *Journal of Personality and Social Psychology, 35*, 303–314.

Argyle, M., & Henderson, M. (in press). *Rules of relationships.* London: Heinemann.

Arias, I. (in press). Assessment of cognition. In K. D. O'Leary (Ed.), *Assessment of marital discord.* Hillsdale, NJ: Lawrence Erlbaum.

Baucom, D. H. (1981, November). Cognitive behavioral strategies in the treatment of marital discord. Paper presented at the 15th Annual Convention of the Association for the advancement of Behavior Therapy, Toronto.

Berley, R. A., & Jacobson, N. S. (1984). Causal attributions in intimate relationships: Toward a model of cognitive-behavioral marital therapy. In P. Kendall (Ed.), *Advances in cognitive–behavioral research and therapy* (Vol. 3). New York: Academic Press.

Berscheid, E., & Peplau, L. A. (1983). The emerging science of relationships. In H. H. Kelley, E. Berscheid, A. Christensen, J. H. Harvey, T. L. Huston, G. Levinger, E. McClintock, L. A. Peplau, & D. R. Peterson (Eds.), *Close relationships.* New York: Freeman.

Christensen, A. (1983). Intervention. In H. H. Kelley, E. Berscheid, A. Christensen, J. H. Harvey, T. L. Huston, G. Levinger, E. McClintock, L. A. Peplau, & D. R. Peterson (Eds.), *Close relationships.* New York: Freeman.

Clark, M. S., & Mills, (1979). Interpersonal attraction in exchange and communal relationships. *Journal of Personality and Social Psychology, 37*, 12–24.

Compas, B. E., Frieland-Bandes, R., Bastien, R., & Adelman, H. S. (1981). Parent and child causal attributions related to the child's clinical problem. *Journal of Abnormal Child Psychology, 9*, 389–397.

Coyne, J. C. (1982). A critique of cognitions as causal entities with particular reference to depression. *Cognitive Therapy and Research, 6*, 3–13.

Dember, W. (1974). Motivation and the cognitive revolution. *American Psychologist, 29*, 161–168.

Dickman, H. R. (1963). The perception of behavioral units. In R. G. Barker (Ed.), *The stream of behavior*. New York: Appleton-Century-Crofts.

Dix, T. H., & Grusec, J. E. (in press). Parent attribution processes in child socialization. In I. Sigel (Ed.), *Parental belief systems: Their psychological consequences for children*. Hillsdale, NJ: Lawrence Erlbaum.

Doherty, W. J. (1981a). Cognitive processes in intimate conflict: I. Extending attribution theory. *The American Journal of Family Therapy, 9*, 1–13.

Doherty, W. J. (1981b). Cognitive processes in intimate conflict: II. Efficacy and learned helplessness. *The American Journal of Family Therapy, 9*, 35–44.

Doherty, W. J. (1982). Attribution style and negative problem solving in marriage. *Family Relations, 31*, 23–27.

Duck, S. W. (1980). Personal relationship research in the 1980s: Towards an understanding of complex human sociality. *Western Journal of Speech Communication, 44*, 97–103.

Eiser, R. J. (1983). From attributions to behavior. In M. Hewstone (Ed.), *Attribution theory: Social and functional extensions*. Oxford: Blackwells.

Ellis, A., & Harper, R. (1977). *A guide to successful marriage*. Los Angeles: Wilshire. (Original work published 1961)

Epstein, N. (1982). Cognitive therapy with couples. *The American Journal of Family Therapy, 10*, 5–16.

Epstein, N., & Eidelson, R. J. (1981). Unrealistic beliefs of clinical couples: Their relationship to expectations, goals and satisfaction. *The American Journal of Family Therapy, 9*, 13–22.

Fincham, F. D. (1983). Clinical applications of attribution theory: Problems and prospects. In M. Hewstone (Ed.), *Attribution theory: Social and functional extensions*. Oxford: Blackwells.

Fincham, F. D. (in press). Attribution processes in distressed and nondistressed couples: II. Responsibility for marital problems. *Journal of Abnormal Psychology*.

Fincham, F. D., Beach, S., & Baucom, D. (1984). *Attribution processes in distressed and nondistressed couples: IV. Self versus partner attributions for spouse behavior*. Manuscript submitted for publication.

Fincham, F. D., Beach, S., & Nelson, G. (1984). *Attribution processes in distressed and nondistressed couples: III. Causal and responsibility attributions for spouse behavior*. Manuscript submitted for publication.

Fincham, F. D., & Jaspars, J. M. F. (1980). Attribution of responsibility: From man the scientist to man as lawyer. In L. Berkowitz (Ed.), *Advances in experimental social psychology* (Vol. 13). N. Y.: Academic Press.

Fincham, F. D., & O'Leary, K. D. (1983). Causal inferences for spouse behavior in maritally distressed and nondistressed couples. *Journal of Social and Clinical Psychology, 1*, 42–57.

Fincham, F. D., & O'Leary, K. D. (in press). Assessment of affect. In K. D. O'Leary (Ed.), *Assessment of marital discord*. Hillsdale, NJ: Lawrence Erlbaum.

Fincham, F. D., & Roberts, C. (in press). Intervening causation and the mitigation of responsibility for harm doing: II. The role of limited mental capacities. *Journal of Experimental Social Psychology.*

Fincham, F. D., & Shultz, T. R. (1981). Intervening causation and the mitigation of responsibility for harm doing. *British Journal of Social Psychology, 20,* 113–120.

Fletcher, G. J. (1983). The analysis of verbal explanations for marital separation: Implications for attribution theory. *Journal of Applied Social Psychology, 13,* 245–258.

Gelles, R. J., & Straus, M. A. (1979). Determinants of violence in the family: Toward a
theoretical integration. In W. R. Burt, R. Hill, F. Nye, & I. Reiss (Eds.), *Contemporary
theories about the family* (Vol. 1). New York: The Free Press.

Gottman, J. M. (1979). *Marital interaction: Experimental investigations.* New York: Academic
Press.

Gottman, J., Notarius, C., Markman, H., Bank, S., Yoppi, B., & Rubin, M. E. (1976).
Behavior exchange theory and marital decision making. *Journal of Personality and Social Psychology, 34,* 14–23.

Haley, J. (1963). *Strategies of psychotherapy.* New York: Grune & Stratton.

Harvey, J. H., & Harris, B. (1983). On the continued vitality of the attributional approach.
In M. Hewstone (Ed.), *Attribution theory: Social and functional extensions.* Oxford:
Blackwells.

Harvey, J. H., Wells, G. L., & Alvarez, M. D. (1978). Attribution in the context of conflict
and separation in close relationships. In J. H. Harvey, W. Ickes, & R. F. Kidd (Eds.),
New directions in attribution research (Vol. 2). New York: Brunner/Mazel.

Heider, F. (1944). Social perception and phenomenal causality. *Psychological Review, 51,*
358–384.

Heider, F. (1958). *The psychology of interpersonal relations.* New York: Wiley.

Hotaling, G. T. (1980). Attribution processes in husband–wife violence. In M. A. Straus
& G. T. Hotaling (Eds.), *The social causes of husband–wife violence.* Minnesota: University of Minnesota Press.

Jacobson, N. S. (1984). The modification of cognitive processes in behavioral marital therapy: Integrating cognitive and behavioral intervention strategies. In K. Halweg & N.
S. Jacobson (Eds.), *Marital interaction: Analysis and modification.* New York: Guilford.

Jacobson, N. S., Follette, W. C., & McDonald, D. W. (1982). Reactivity to positive and
negative behavior in distressed and nondistressed married couples. *Journal of Consulting and Clinical Psychology,* 706–714.

Jacobson, N. S., & Margolin, G. (1979). *Marital therapy.* New York: Brunner /Mazel.

Jacobson, N. S., McDonald, D. W., Follette, W. C., & Berley, R. A. (in press). Attribution
processes in distressed and nondistressed married couples. *Cognitive Therapy and
Research.*

Jacobson, N. S., Waldron, H., & Moore, D. (1980). Toward a behavioral profile of marital
distress. *Journal of Consulting and Clinical Psychology. 48,* 696–703.

Jaspars, J., Hewstone, M., & Fincham, F. (1983). Attribution theory and research: The
state of the art. In J. Jaspars, F. Fincham, M. Hewstone (Eds.), *Attribution theory and
research.* New York: Academic Press.

Jones, E. E., & Davis, K. E. (1965). From acts to dispositions: The attribution process in
person perception. In L. Berkowitz (Ed.), *Advances in experimental social psychology*
(Vol. 2). New York: Academic Press.

Kelley, H. H. (1967). Attribution in social psychology. *Nebraska Symposium on Motivation,
15,* 192–238.

Kelley, H. H. (1972). *Causal schemata and the attribution process.* Morristown, NJ: General
Learning Press.

Kelley, H. H. (1979). *Personal relationships: Their structure and processes.* Hillsdale, NJ: Erlbaum.

Kelley, H. H. (1983). Perceived causal structures. In J. Jaspars, F. Fincham, & M. Hewstone (Eds.), *Attribution theory and research.* New York: Academic Press.

Kelley, H. H., Berscheid, E., Christensen, A., Harvey, J. H., Huston, T. L., Levinger, G., McClintock, E., Peplau, L. A., & Petersen, D. R. (1983). *Close relationships.* New York: Freeman.

Kelley, H. H., & Michela, J. L. (1980). Attribution theory and research. In M. Rosenzweig & L. Porter (Eds.), *Annual Review of Psychology* (Vol. 13). Palo Alto, CA: Annual Review Inc.

Kidd, R. F., & Amabile, T. M. (1981). Causal explanations in social interaction: Some dialogues on dialogue. In J. H. Harvey, W. Ickes, & R. F. Kidd (Eds.), *New directions in attribution research* (Vol. 3). Hillsdale, NJ: Erlbaum.

Kihlstrom, J., & Nasby, W. (1981). Cognitive tasks in clinical assessment: An exercise in applied psychology. In D. Kendall & S. Hollon (Eds.), *Assessment strategies for cognitive behavioral interventions.* New York: Academic Press.

Kitson, G., & Sussman, M. B. (1982). Marital complaints, demographic characteristics, and symptoms of mental distress in divorce. *Journal of Marriage and the Family, 44,* 87–101.

Knight, J. A., & Vallacher, R. R. (1981). Interpersonal engagement in social perception: The consequences of getting into the action. *Journal of Personality and Social Psychology, 40,* 990–999.

Lalljee, M., & Abelson, R. P. (1983). The organization of explanations. In M. Hewstone (Ed.), *Attribution theory: Social and functional extensions.* Oxford: Blackwells.

Langer, E. J. (1978). Rethinking the role of thought in social interaction. In J. H. Harvey, W. J. Ickes, & R. F. Kidd (Eds.), *New directions in attribution research* (Vol. 2). Hillsdale, NJ: Erlbaum.

Larrance, D. T., & Twentyman, C. T. (1983). Maternal attributions and child abuse. *Journal of Abnormal Psychology, 92,* 449–457.

Lederer, W. J., & Jackson, D. D. (1968). *The mirages of marriage.* New York: Plenum.

Levinger, G. (1980). Toward the analysis of close relationships. *Journal of Experimental Social Psychology, 16,* 510–544.

Lewin, K. (1948). The background of conflict in marriage. *Resolving social conflicts: Selected papers on group dynamics.* New York: Harper & Row.

Lewin, K. (1951). Problems of research in social psychology. In D. Cartwright (Ed.), *Field theory in social science: Selected theoretical papers by Kurt Lewin.* New York: Harper & Row.

Lloyd-Bostock, S. (1983). Attributions of cause and responsibility as social phenomena. In J. Jaspars, F. Fincham, & M. Hewstone (Eds.), *Attribution theory and research.* New York: Academic Press.

Locke, D., & Pennington, D. (1982). Reasons and other causes: Their role in attribution processes. *Journal of Personality and Social Psychology, 42,* 212–223.

Lyman, S. M., & Scott, M. B. (1970). *A sociology of the absurd.* New York: Appleton-Century-Crofts.

Madden, M. E., & Janoff-Bulman, R. (1983). Blame, control, and marital satisfaction: Wives' attributions for conflict in marriage. *Journal of Marriage and the Family, 44,* 663–674.

Margolin, G. (1981). Behavioral marital therapy: Is there a place for passion, play, and other non-negotiable dimensions? *The Behavior Therapist, 6,* 65–68.

Margolin, G., & Wampold, B. E. (1981). Sequential analysis of conflict and accord in distressed and nondistressed partners. *Journal of Consulting and Clinical Psychology, 49,* 554–567.

McClintock, E. (1983). Interaction. In H. H. Kelley, E. Berscheid, A. Christensen, J. H. Harvey, J. L. Huston, G. Levinger, E. McClintock, L. A. Peplau, & D. R. Petersen (Eds.), *Close relationships*. New York: Freeman.

Metalsky, G. I., & Abramson, L. Y. (1980). Attributional styles: Toward a framework for conceptualization and assessment. In P. C. Kendall & S. D. Hollon (Eds.), *Cognitive-behavioral interventions: Assessment methods*. New York: Academic Press.

Minuchin, S. (1974). *Families and family therapy*. Cambridge, MA: Harvard University Press.

Newman, H. (1981a). Communication within ongoing intimate relationships: An attributional perspective. *Personality and Social Psychology Bulletin, 7*, 59-70.

Newman, H. (1981b). Interpretation and explanation: Influences on communicative exchanges within intimate relationships. *Communication Quarterly*, 123-132.

Newman, H. (1981c). Post divorce attribution as a function of the attribution of responsibility. *Sex Roles, 7*, 223-232.

Newman, H., & Langer, E. J. (in press). Investigating the development and courses of intimate relationships: A cognitive model. In L. Y. Abramson (Ed.), *Social-personal inference in clinical psychology*. New York: Guilford Press.

Newtson, D. (1976). Foundations of attribution: The perception of ongoing behavior. In J. H. Harvey, W. J. Ickes, & R. F. Kidd (Eds.), *New directions in attribution research* (Vol. 1). Hillsdale, N J: Erlbaum.

O'Leary, K. D., & Turkewitz, H. (1978). Marital therapy from a behavioral perspective: In T. J. Paolino & B. S. McCrady (Eds.), *Marriage and marital therapy*. N.Y.: Brunner-Mazel.

Orvis, B. R., Kelley, H. H., & Butler, D. (1976). Attributional conflict in young couples. In J. H. Harvey, W. Ickes, & R. Kidd (Eds.), *New directions in attribution research* (Vol. 1). Hillsdale, NJ: Erlbaum.

Passer, M. W., Kelley, H. H., & Michela, J. L. (1978). Multidimensional scaling of the causes for negative interpersonal behavior. *Journal of Personality and Social Psychology, 36*, 951-962.

Paul, G. L. (1969). Behavior modification research: Design and tactics. In C. M. Franks (Ed.), *Behavior therapy: Appraisal and status*. New York: McGraw-Hill.

Peterson, C., Luborsky, L., & Seligman, M. E. P. (1983). Attributions and depressive mood shifts: A case study using the symptom-context method. *Journal of Abnormal Psychology, 92*, 96-103.

Pyszczynski, T. A., & Greenberg, J. (1981). Role of disconfirmed expectancies in the instigation of attributional processing. *Journal of Personality and Social Psychology, 40*, 31-38.

Rosenberg, M. S., & Repucci, N. D. (1983). Abusive mothers: Perceptions of their own and their child's behavior. *Journal of Consulting and Clinical Psychology, 51*, 674-682.

Ross, L. (1977). The intuitive psychologist and his shortcomings. Distortions in the attribution process. In L. Berkowitz (Ed.), *Advances in experimental social psychology* (Vol. 10). New York: Academic Press.

Ross, M., & Fletcher, G. (in press). Attribution and social perception. In G. Lindzey & E. Aronson (Eds.), *Handbook of social psychology* (3rd ed.). London: Addison-Wesley.

Schwarz, N., & Clore, G. L. (1983). Mood, misattribution, and judgments of well-being: Informative and directive functions of affective states. *Journal of Personality and Social Psychology, 45*, 513-523.

Segraves, R. T. (1982). *Marital therapy: A combined psychodynamic-behavioral approach*. New York: Plenum Press.

Seligman, C., Fazio, R. H., & Zanna, M. P. (1980). Effects of salience of extrinsic rewards on liking and loving. *Journal of Personality and Social Psychology, 38*, 453-460.

Shultz, T. R., & Schleifer, M. (1983). Towards a refinement of attribution concepts. In J.

Jaspars, F. Fincham, & M. Hewstone (Eds.), *Attribution theory and research*. New York: Academic Press.

Sillars, A. L. (1981). Attributions and interpersonal conflict resolution. In J. H. Harvey, W. Ickes, & R. F. Kidd (Eds.), *New directions in attribution research* (Vol. 3). Hillsdale, NJ: Erlbaum Associates.

Snyder, M. L., & Wicklund, R. A. (1981). Attribute ambiguity. In J. H. Harvey, W. J. Ickes, & R. F. Kidd (Eds.), *New directions in attribution research* (Vol. 3). Hillsdale, NJ: Lawrence Erlbaum Associates.

Taylor, S. E., & Koivumaki, J. H. (1976). The perception of self and others: Acquaintanceship, affect and actor–observer differences. *Journal of Personality and Social Psychology, 33*, 403–408.

Thompson, S. C., & Kelley, H. H. (1981). Judgments of responsibility for activities in close relationships. *Journal of Personality and Social Psychology, 41*, 469–477.

Watzlawick, P., Beavin, J., & Jackson, D. (1967). *Pragmatics of human communication: A study of interactional patterns, pathologies, and paradoxes*. New York: W. W. Norton.

Weiner, B. (1979). A theory of motivation for some classroom experiences. *Journal of Educational Psychology, 71*, 3–25.

Weiss, R. L. (1981). The new kid on the block: Behavioral systems approach. In E. E. Filsinger, R. A. Lewis, & P. McAvoy (Eds.), *Assessing marriage*. Beverly Hills, CA: Sage.

Weiss, R. L., & Perry, B. A. (1979). Assessment and treatment of marital dysfunction. Eugene: Oregon Marital Studies Program. (Available from R. L. Weiss, Department of Psychology, University of Oregon, Eugene, Oregon 97403.)

White, D. M. (1983). Affect and causal attribution in marital conflicts: An exploratory study. Unpublished Master's thesis, University of Illinois.

Wills, T. A., Weiss, R. L., & Patterson, G. R. (1974). A behavioral analysis of the determinants of marital satisfaction. *Journal of Consulting and Clinical Psychology, 42*, 802–811.

Wish, M., Deutsch, M., & Kaplan, S. J. (1976). Perceived dimensions of interpersonal relations. *Journal of Personality and Social Psychology, 33*, 409–420.

Wong, P. T., & Weiner, B. (1981). When people ask "why" questions, and the heuristics of attributional search. *Journal of Personality and Social Psychology, 40*, 650–663.

Wright, J., & Fichten, C. (1982). Denial of responsibility, videotape feedback and attribution theory: Relevance for behavioral marital therapy. *Canadian Psychology Review, 17*, 219–230.

Wright, J., Mischel, W. (1982). Cognitive social learning person variables. *Journal of Personality and Social Psychology, 43*, 901–914.

Zajonc, R. (1980). Feeling and thinking. *American Psychologist, 35*, 151–175.

CHAPTER 9

Attributional Models of Depression, Loneliness, and Shyness

Craig A. Anderson and Lynn H. Arnoult

INTRODUCTION

In recent years, the mental health community has become increasingly aware of the problems of nonclinical populations. An amazingly large proportion of the U.S. population suffers from one or more of these "everyday problems in living" (Anderson & Arnoult, in press), such as depression, loneliness, and shyness. According to Secunda (1973), 15% show significant depressive symptoms at any given time. Bradburn (1969) reported that 26% are lonely. Zimbardo, Pilkonis, and Norwood (1974) showed that about 40% of high school and college students believe themselves to be dispositionally shy.

The costs of such problems, in terms of personal anguish and disrupted familial and other interpersonal relationships, are both high and obvious. Less obvious are the costs of these problems to our society as a whole. Such costs include those associated with divorce, mental health costs, and on-the-job losses due to absenteeism, low productivity, failed interpersonal communications, and other organizational problems that arise from ineffective interpersonal interactions.

Advances in several areas of psychological theory and a gradual eroding of once solid boundaries between these areas have led to exciting, promising approaches to the study of these everyday problems in living. In this chapter we will examine briefly several of these developments, noting proposed causal factors. We will then concentrate on recent attributional models and will present data that support and refine the attributional style models. Finally, we will examine in some detail the issue of direction of causality in attributional models and present data sup-

ATTRIBUTION
Basic Issues and Applications

235

porting the view that attributional style is a causal factor in depression, loneliness, and shyness.[1]

DEFINING THE PROBLEMS

Depression, loneliness, and shyness are difficult to define precisely. What does a person mean who says "I am depressed"? What features lead one to define oneself as lonely or shy? How does one measure these problems? How are the problems interrelated? To understand the meaning of these problems, we adopted the prototype perspective of Horowitz and his colleagues (e.g., Horowitz, French, & Anderson, 1982). In this view each problem is seen as consisting of a "fuzzy set" of features. No single feature is necessarily present when the problem is present, but sufficiently large combinations allow placement in the category. Measurement of the problems is also difficult and will be discussed shortly. First, consider the meaning of the problems.

THE PROTOTYPE APPROACH

Horowitz and colleagues have borrowed the prototype approach from the cognitive literature on categorization (e.g., Rosch, Mervis, Gray, Johnson, & Boyes-Braem, 1976). Briefly, a prototype of a concept or category is the set of the most common features or members of that category. A given instance is classified as a member of a given category quickly and easily if it possesses many of the most important prototypic features. Thus, a sparrow is a good example of the category "bird" (it has many prototypic features), whereas a penguin is a poor example (it has few prototypic features).

Horowitz et al. (1982) used this approach to study the meaning of depression and loneliness. Subjects were asked to think of someone they knew who was lonely or who was depressed. Next, they wrote down the person's most usual feelings, thoughts, and behaviors. Several judges independently tabulated these features. Features that had been listed by at least 20% of the subjects in their descriptions of lonely or of depressed people were defined as prototypic of that category.

For loneliness, 18 prototypic features resulted. An examination of these features, presented in Table 9.1, reveals that lonely people are seen

---

[1]When discussing depression we are referring primarily to moderate levels of unipolar or reactive depression, although some studies under consideration have used more severely depressed populations. We expect the basic findings presented in this chapter to apply to severe unipolar or reactive depression also.

Table 9.1

PROTOTYPIC FEATURES OF LONELINESS[a]

Feels separate from others, different	Feels inferior, worthless, inadequate
Feels isolated	Thinks "Something is wrong with me; I
Feels excluded from activities, not part of	am inferior"
a group	Feels paranoid
Thinks "I am different from everybody	Feels angry
else"	Feels depressed
Thinks "I don't fit in; I am alienated	Feels sad, unhappy
from others"	Avoids social contacts; isolates self from
Feels unloved, not cared for	others
Thinks "Other people don't like me"	Works (or studies) hard and for long
Thinks "I want a friend"	hours
Thinks "I don't know how to make	Is quiet, reserved, introspective
friends"	

[a]From Horowitz, L. M., French, R., & Anderson, C. A. (1982). The prototype of a lonely person. In L. Peplau & D. Perlman (Eds.), *Loneliness: A sourcebook of current theory, research, and therapy,* (pp. 183–205). New York: John Wiley & Sons. Copyright 1982 by John Wiley & Sons. Adapted by permission.

(by lonely and nonlonely subjects; see Horowitz et al., 1982) as having thoughts, feelings, and behaviors reflecting separation from other people. Overall, loneliness seems to be a fairly clear and internally consistent problem.

Depression, on the other hand, was seen as a much more heterogeneous problem. Forty features were included in the prototype. Table 9.2 presents these features of depression. Interestingly, almost all of the features of loneliness appeared in the depression prototype. Thus, if we know that a person is lonely, we also know that he or she has at least some significant features of depression. Note also that whereas most of the loneliness features reflect interpersonal problems, many of the depression features do not. In other words, a lonely person has primarily interpersonal problems, whereas a depressed person may or may not have interpersonal problems.

To date, similar prototype analyses have not been conducted on shyness. We expect that such analyses would reveal a prototype that overlaps considerably with both loneliness and depression. First, some of the interpersonal features of loneliness and depression will also probably appear for shyness. Second, some of the noninterpersonal features of depression will probably fit shyness. For example, shy people are often seen as feeling "nervous, anxious, and afraid." Research on the prototype of shyness would help clarify the relationships between these problems in living.

Table 9.2

PROTOTYPIC FEATURES OF DEPRESSION[a]

Feels helpless, ineffective	Lacks energy, has trouble getting any-
Thinks "I am inferior"	thing productive done
Feels inferior, worthless, inadequate	Sleeps a lot
Thinks "I am inferior; I lack worth and	Drinks alcohol as an escape
ability"	Eats too much
Feels self-pity	Feels lonely
Thinks "I'm unattractive (ugly, fat, un-	Feels alone, different from everyone
appealing, sloppy)"	else
Feels hopeless, pessimistic	Feels isolated
Has a pessimistic attitude, expects the	Thinks "No one understands me"
worst	Feels unloved, not cared for
Thinks of committing suicide	Thinks "No one really loves me"
Thinks "Life is meaningless, not worth	Avoids social contacts, isolates self from
living"	others
Feels angry	Is quiet, doesn't speak much
Is quick-tempered, easily angered	Is "out of it," seems to be in another
Feels paranoid, doesn't trust others	world
Thinks "Everyone is against me"	Is self-involved, preoccupied
Feels nervous, anxious, afraid	Doesn't laugh, smile, have fun
Overreacts to insignificant things	Feels like crying
Feels frustrated	Cries easily
Feels overwhelmed, can't cope	Feels sad, unhappy
Feels sleepy, tired, unenergetic	Thinks "I am unhappy"
Feels unmotivated, lacks initiative	Looks sad

[a]From Horowitz, L. M., French, R., & Anderson, C. A. (1982). The prototype of a lonely person. In L. Peplau & D. Perlman (Eds.), *Loneliness: A sourcebook of current theory, research, and therapy*, (pp. 183–205). New York: John Wiley & Sons. Copyright 1982 by John Wiley & Sons. Adapted by permission.

MEASURING DEPRESSION, LONELINESS, AND SHYNESS

The prototype approach to defining these problems in living suggests a means of developing measures of the problems. One could simply combine the features of each problem into rating scales on which subjects rate the relevance of each feature to themselves. The more relevant the features are to a given person, the more that person "belongs" to that problem category. Indeed, Horowitz et al. (1982) have shown that when relatively many prototypic features of loneliness are contained in a description of a target person, that person is likely to be described by others as lonely.

There are numerous scales designed to measure these various problems in living. Interestingly, the techniques used to generate items for these scales closely parallel the prototype approach. Typically, the researchers generate a pool of items that describe the symptoms or features of the problem in question. Subjects are then asked to indicate which items are self-descriptive, or to rate the self-descriptiveness, relevance, or frequency of occurrence of the items. For example, the UCLA Loneliness Scale consists of 20 self-referent statements generated by people working with the problem of loneliness (Russell, Peplau, & Ferguson, 1978; Sisenwein, 1965). Subjects simply indicate how often they feel as described in each statement.

The most commonly used measures of depression, loneliness, and shyness share this prototype-like approach to construction. In addition, the items contained in depression and loneliness scales correspond closely to the prototypes presented earlier. The UCLA Loneliness Scale, for example, contains the items "I lack companionship" and "My interests and ideas are not shared by those around me" (Russell, Peplau, & Cutrona, 1980; Russell et al., 1978). These correspond to the loneliness prototype features "Feels separate from others" and "Thinks 'I am different from everybody else.'"

The prototype approach suggests that measures of loneliness and depression will correlate highly; the prototypes overlap. Because we also expect the shyness prototype to overlap, we expect measures of shyness to correlate highly with depression and loneliness. Research supports this prediction (e.g., Anderson & Harvey, 1984). This presents a problem for research into potential differences between these problems in living. One cannot be sure that a measure of depression, for instance, is not inordinately contaminated by loneliness. Anderson and Harvey (1984) have recently addressed this issue in an empirical investigation using confirmatory and exploratory factor analyses on self-report measures of these problems in living. They used the short form of the Beck Depression Inventory, the revised UCLA Loneliness Scale, the Shyness Scale (Cheek & Buss, 1981), and the Social Anxiety Scale (Fenigstein, Scheier, & Buss, 1975). As expected, depression, loneliness, and shyness (including social anxiety) were interrelated. Also, it was discovered that several of the items loaded too highly on an unpredicted factor. For example, two loneliness items loaded higher on depression than on loneliness. Thus, it was suggested that these scales be modified slightly to insure factorially pure (but not orthogonal) measures of these constructs.

These various considerations, then, provide us with a good grasp of the meaning of these problems and acceptable scales with which to measure them. We now turn to a consideration of the causes of these problems.

CAUSES OF THE PROBLEMS

Before considering specific causal factors, it is worthwhile to note that three types of causes are generally distinguished—predisposing, precipitating, and maintaining. A predisposing cause is a factor that is present prior to the onset of the problem and that makes one susceptible to the problem or "at risk." A precipitating cause is a factor or event that triggers the onset of the problem. A maintaining cause is one that keeps the problem going once it has started. A given causal factor may be important in more than one sense. For instance, poor social skills may be a predisposing factor for loneliness; the person may have few sources of social support. It may also be a maintaining factor; once a person becomes lonely after losing a close friend (a precipitating factor), he or she may be unable to patch up the friendship or to find new friends.

Another means of discriminating causal factors is classifying them as stress factors, skill factors, or cognitive factors. Obviously these categories overlap, and there are many possible interactions between factors from different categories. Each set of factors, however, reflects a different perspective for viewing the problems in living.

STRESS FACTORS

One set of causal factors in depression, loneliness, and shyness consists of the everyday stresses that people experience. The causal role of stressors in these problems in living is acknowledged in several types of psychological models, ranging from reinforcement theories (e.g., Ferster, 1973, 1974; Lewinsohn, 1974; Lewinsohn, Youngren, & Grosscup, 1979) to psychodynamic theories (e.g., Freud, 1925). The underlying theme is that some people experience stresses that are sufficiently disruptive to interfere with the maintenance of a normal, optimistic, approach to life. The onset of feelings of depression, loneliness, or shyness may be triggered by a sudden loss or failure, such as the death of one's spouse or loss of a job. The problem may be maintained by a low rate of positive reinforcement, which can lead to low motivation, poor performance, and continued low positive reinforcement. A. A. Lazarus (1968) claims that even when there is no apparent loss, a maladaptive reaction may be triggered by anticipation of loss or expectation of nonreinforcement. Considerable empirical evidence supports the notion that environmental stressors are associated with problems in living and will not be reviewed here (e.g., Cutrona, 1982; O'Hara, Rehm, & Campbell, 1982; Paykel et al., 1969).

A number of researchers, however, have noted that stressful experiences do not always produce maladaptive reactions. Events that precipitate depression in some people, for instance, apparently are successfully negotiated by others. Paykel (1974) proposed that such differences are due to individual vulnerability or predisposition. Some personality types may be more vulnerable to certain kinds of stresses than other types. (See R. S. Lazarus, 1966, and Brown, 1974, for similar analyses.) In addition, the effects of a given stressor appear to depend upon the coping resources available, including intrapersonal factors (e.g., health, energy, self-esteem, problem-solving skills) and situational and environmental factors (e.g., time, money, information, social status, social support). Furthermore, the individual's appraisal of available coping resources may be influenced by the presence of cumulative stress from other recent experiences and by previous successful or unsuccessful coping with a similar source of stress. (See Dohrenwend & Dohrenwend, 1974; Folkman, Schaefer, & Lazarus, 1979; Paykel, 1974, for discussions of these factors.) In sum, stress factors are very important in problems in living, but the effects of such stressors depend to a great extent on other mediating variables.

SKILL FACTORS

A second set of factors consists of deficits in a person's skills. These factors are seen, typically, as interacting with stress factors. A person may receive few positive reinforcements because he or she lacks the skills necessary for producing successes in various domains.

A number of studies have, in fact, shown that people suffering from one or more everyday problems in living (i.e., depression, loneliness, shyness) often perform less well at various tasks than their nondebilitated counterparts. Horowitz et al. (1982) had lonely and nonlonely subjects generate solutions to hypothetical problem situations. Most of the situations were of an interpersonal nature, such as making new friends in a new neighborhood. One situation was noninterpersonal; it involved a person attempting to find a lost watch. On the noninterpersonal situation, lonely and nonlonely subjects did not differ in the number or the rated quality of proposed solutions. On the interpersonal situations, however, lonely subjects generated significantly fewer solutions and their solutions were rated as being of poorer overall quality than those of nonlonely subjects.

W. Jones and colleagues (Jones, 1982; Jones, Hobbs, & Hockenbury,

1982) also report evidence that loneliness is a social-skills problem. In dyadic interactions between new acquaintances, Jones (1982) found that lonely people made more self-statements, asked fewer questions, responded more slowly to their partner's statements, and changed the topic of conversation more often than did nonlonely people. Possible consequences of these behavioral patterns were suggested by the finding that lonely people were perceived as less attractive than nonlonely people.

Pilkonis (1977) has shown performance differences between shy and nonshy people in opposite-sex interactions. Subjects reporting for an experiment were seated next to an opposite-sex confederate for a 5-minute waiting period. During that time, shy subjects took longer for their first utterance, spoke less frequently, allowed more long silences to develop, and were less willing to break silences than the nonshy subjects. Lewinsohn (1974) provides a cogent discussion of the skill deficit–low reinforcement position on depression. Several studies have demonstrated such skills deficits in depressed people. Fisher-Beckfield and McFall (1982) found incompetence (as measured by their Problem Inventory for College Students) to be a concomitant of depression. Gotlib and Asarnow (1979) found a negative relationship between interpersonal problem-solving ability and depression in mildly and clinically depressed college students. Lewinsohn, Mischel, Chaplin, and Barton (1980) had depressed and nondepressed subjects participate in a social interaction task. Observer ratings of the social interactions yielded effects suggestive of social skills deficits in the depressed. Coyne (1976) measured the responses of subjects who interacted with either depressed or nondepressed target subjects. Subjects reported feeling more depressed, anxious, and hostile and were more rejecting of the target when the target was a depressed person. These results all suggest that the behavior of depressed people might lead to less positively reinforcing behavior from others.

However, one major problem with the skills approach is that it is often difficult to know whether a person has failed because of a lack of ability, a lack of motivation, or interfering anxiety. Such different interpretations of the poor performances of depressed, lonely, and shy people yield quite different implications for therapy. We will return to this point later. In sum, though, it appears that at least part of the problems of depressed, lonely, and shy people may be caused by their ineffective behaviors. For some of these people, this may reflect real skill or ability deficits.

COGNITIVE FACTORS

Several lines of investigation suggest that cognitive factors underlie problems in everyday living. By cognitive factors we do not mean lack of knowledge (such as social skills). Rather, cognitive factors here refer to beliefs, perceptual styles, or ways of viewing the world. For example, Beck and his colleagues postulate that depressed people have negative beliefs or expectations about themselves, their current situation, and their future (Beck, Rush, Shaw, & Emery, 1979). These negative views can lead one to interpret events in a pessimistically biased fashion and to behave in less than optimal ways. Such a negative world view can also lead, eventually, to poor performances, failures and losses, and ultimately can become a self-fulfilling prophecy.

There are several other cognitive positions that make similar claims. Ellis' rational–emotive approach (1962), for instance, points to irrational belief systems as causes of depressed people's problems. Bandura's social learning theory (1977b), with its emphasis on the causal significance of efficacy and outcome expectancies as determinants of motivation and performance, can also be seen as a cognitive approach.

Although research on these cognitive factors has yielded somewhat mixed results (see Coyne & Gotlib, 1983), most researchers agree that depressed and nondepressed people see their worlds quite differently. For instance, Kuiper and his colleagues have shown that depressed people have a distinctly negative self-schema (see Kuiper, Olinger, & MacDonald, in press, for a review of much of this literature).

A final cognitive factor concerns how people interpret or explain their performance outcomes to themselves. There may be consistent differences in the ways people make attributions for such outcomes, and these individual differences in attributional styles may be important predisposing and maintaining causes of everyday problems in living (e.g., Abramson, Seligman, & Teasdale, 1978; Anderson, 1983b; Anderson & Arnoult, in press; Anderson, Horowitz, & French, 1983; Weiner, 1979).

Before moving on to the attributional style literature, a few concluding comments on causal factors are in order. First, we hasten to point out that the above sketches of stress, skills, and cognitive factors are both brief and selective. The sketches were included merely to draw the reader's attention to a number of the more successful approaches. Second, it should be pointed out that most people working on problems in living acknowledge that all these types of factors (stresses, skills, cognitions) are important. Clearly, one's outcomes in the world (including stresses) are important in determining one's mood state, motivation, self-beliefs, and so on. Similarly, one's skills influence one's outcomes. Finally, how one interprets an outcome influences whether the outcome is seen as a success or a failure, as well as one's affective reactions and self-beliefs. In short, we claim that cognitive positions also incorporate (often implicitly) the skill and stress positions.

ATTRIBUTIONAL STYLE MODELS AND DATA

AN OVERVIEW OF ATTRIBUTION THEORY

Attribution theory has been of interest to social psychologists for some time (e.g., Bem, 1972; Heider, 1958; E. E. Jones & Davis, 1965; Kelley, 1967, 1973). This work has focussed on a set of attribution-related questions. How do people explain events that they observe happening to themselves or to others? What factors determine whether or not an attribution will be made? How is a particular attribution chosen? What effects do different attributions have on subsequent behaviors, emotions, or beliefs? Although an extensive review of attribution theory is beyond the scope of this chapter, a limited discussion of some of the high points and of our own perspective will facilitate later discussions of the attributional style research.

People do not generate causal explanations or attributions for every observed event. Several recent studies suggest that people are most likely to engage in attributional processes in response to events that are concrete, important, unusual, or surprising (Anderson, 1983a; Pyszczynski & Greenberg, 1981; Wong & Weiner, 1981). The particular attribution that will be made depends upon a host of factors. For instance, Taylor and her colleagues have demonstrated that a variety of perceptual features, such as visual prominence or solo status within a group, influence responsibility attributions (see Taylor & Fiske, 1978). Other well documented attributional determinants include the pattern of prior event outcomes in the same situation (e.g., E. E. Jones & Goethals, 1971), information about event distinctiveness and consistency (e.g., Kelly, 1973), perspective of the attributor, as actor or observer (e.g., E. E. Jones & Nisbett, 1971; Monson & Snyder, 1977), and prior beliefs or expectations concerning the to-be-explained event (e.g., Wetzel, 1982).

The processes through which these factors operate are not well understood. One promising possibility has recently been suggested by Kruglanski (1980) and Anderson (1983c, in press). We may view the attribution process as a two stage process. In the first stage, problem formulation, plausible causal candidates for an observed event are generated. In the second stage, problem resolution, the generated causal candidates are examined and evaluated until the ''best'' attribution (or combination) is chosen. Various perceptual (salience) effects on attributions may have their impact on both stages. For example, when an observer must attribute responsibility for a group outcome, a visually prominent person in the group will more likely be included on the plausible-causal-candidate list because he or she easily comes to mind. That person's actual contributions to the group may also be better recalled in the problem resolution stage because of the increased attention elicited by the visual prominence. Other factors may have their impact primarily on one stage only.

There are few directly relevant tests of this model, but two sets of predictions derived from this view have been confirmed. First, this model suggests that different types of situations will lead to generation of different types of plausible causal candidates; that is, each type of situation has its own *causal structure.* Anderson (1983c) has convincingly demonstrated this by finding significant differences in the types of causal candidates generated for the four situation types created by crossing interpersonal versus noninterpersonal with success versus failure situation variables. Second, and as predicted by the model, Anderson (in press) has shown that final attributions of actor and observer subjects are strongly influenced by the causal structure of the target situations.

One final set of questions addressed by attribution researchers concerns the effects of self-attributions on subsequent motivation, performance, and affect. Many relevant data sets come from the achievement domain. Of particular interest here are studies examining the effects of different kinds of attributions for failure on subsequent success expectancies, motivation, and performance. For example, it has been shown that attributing failure to lack of ability often leads to lower success expectancies and motivation than does attributing the same failure to lack of effort (see Weiner, 1972, 1974, 1979, for reviews of much of this literature).

This type of attribution research suggests a possible tie to the problems of depression, loneliness, and shyness. One puzzling feature of these problems is that people suffering from one or more of them frequently fail to attempt to resolve their problem. Depressed people often avoid potentially rewarding activities and give up easily in the face of failure. Lonely people tend to avoid the one-on-one situations that are necessary to the development of close personal relationships. Shy people also avoid social situations and seldom attempt to learn or to enact appropriate social behaviors. In sum, these everyday problems in living often appear to be motivational, rather than skill or stress problems. Attribution theory suggests a plausible motivational model for these problems. Different attributional models of the problems differ in their specifics, but overlap considerably in their general form.

Basically, these various models postulate that the debilitated groups (i.e., depressed, lonely, or shy) tend to make maladaptive self-attributions. This maladaptive attributional style presumably contributes to the observed motivational and performance deficits through the process sketched out in Figure 9.1. This attributional model is, of course, oversimplified but it does make clear the assumptions behind the major attributional models of motivation. Attributions for performance outcomes influence a person's success expectancies. These expectancies in turn influence the person's motivation level. Included in the motivation construct may be variables such as persistence, commitment, and attitude or approach to the task. Motivation level, then, influences task performance and outcome. The outcome, of course, can then influence further attributions, completing the cycle.

How does this model explain the motivational and performance deficits of our debilitated groups? Assume for a moment that a hypothetical person A attributes interpersonal failures to unchangeable personal characteristics, such as ability or personality deficits. Further assume that A agrees to work as a volunteer for the Red Cross, with the task of convincing other people to donate blood. This task will result in a high failure rate. When A attributes such failures to ability deficits, his or her success expectancies will decrease. Failure becomes expected; there is no perceived possibility of improvement. These low success expectancies will lead to low motivation, indicated perhaps by low persistence, unenthusiastic persuasion attempts, and lack of effort to learn how to do better. Such a behavior pattern will lead to an even higher failure rate, which would seem to confirm the initial ability attribution.

Consider now person B, who attributes failure to strategic behavioral errors. When faced with the Red Cross failures, B will assume he or she did something wrong in the persuasion attempts and will try to learn how to do better. Success expectancies will remain fairly high, as will

Figure 9.1 The generalized attribution model of motivation and performance.

motivation, indicated by high persistence, enthusiastic persuasion attempts, and efforts to improve. This behavior pattern will lead to more successes, both in absolute and relative terms.

Note that in Figure 9.1 and in the previous scenarios there is no mention of affective reactions. Most researchers in this area agree that the affective component is a major part of the problems in living, and that it is strongly influenced by some component in this model. There is disagreement on where affect should be placed in the model. Some see affect as resulting primarily from the performance outcome—success leads to positive mood, failure to negative mood. Others suggest that the attribution in combination with the performance outcome determines the affective response. Finally, recent data suggest that some affects are outcome bound (e.g., happiness—success; frustration—failure), whereas some are tied to more specific attributions for an outcome (e.g., pride—success due to ability; incompetence—failure due to lack of ability) (Weiner, Russell & Lerman, 1979). It is also not clear whether affective reactions have any direct, causal impact on other components in this model, or whether they are best viewed as by-products of the other components. Although answers to these affect questions are important, they are not essential for our present purpose of examining attributional models of those problems. We now turn to those models and relevant data.

WEINER'S ATTRIBUTION MODEL

For a more complete statement of Weiner's attribution model, the reader is referred to several of his summary statements (Weiner, 1972, 1974, 1979).

Most of the early research in this area used various achievement tasks. Early researchers examining achievement motivation and responses to success and failure focussed on the locus of the perceived causes. Weiner challenged this focus, noting that much research confounded the locus dimension (internal versus external) with the stability dimension (stable versus unstable). Weiner suggested that these dimensions be factorially crossed, producing four attributions that were prototypes for the resulting four-cell table. Ability was seen as stable and internal; effort as unstable and internal; task difficulty as stable and external; luck as unstable and external. More recently a third attributional dimension, control, has been proposed. This produces an eight-cell, three dimension model (Locus × Stability × Control). It is important to note that Weiner's control dimension is not restricted to the actor's control over the cause. This shift in focus for the control dimension resulted from the difficulty in conceptualizing an external but controllable cause. This problem is supposedly resolved by noting that an external cause (e.g., a teacher's bias) may be controlled by the external agent (e.g., the teacher), even though the actor-attributor (the student) can not control it (see Weiner, 1979). Weiner is not convinced of the value of the control dimension, however, because it is clearly not orthogonal to stability and locus (Weiner & Litman-Adizes, 1980). In addition to classifying attributions, this model also posits that attributions varying along these three dimensions produce consistent effects on several kinds of variables. Specifically, the stability dimension is linked to expectancy changes, the locus dimension is linked to esteem-related emotions, and control is linked to certain interpersonal judgments.

Finally, although this model was originally developed in achievement settings, Weiner and others have explicitly applied it to the problems of loneliness and depression (Peplau, Russell, & Heim, 1979; Weiner, 1979; Weiner & Litman-Adizes, 1980). Both the locus and the stability dimensions are linked to these problems through their impact on motivation. The stability of attributions influences motivation through success expectancies. The locus of attributions influences motivation by influencing the value of the consequences (affective reactions) of various outcomes. Weiner bases such predictions on an expectancy–value model of motivation (Atkinson, 1964; Weiner, 1972, 1974) in which the intensity of motivation is jointly determined by the success expectancies and the value of the goal object. (Note that the generalized attribution model in Figure 9.1 implicitly adopts a similar expectancy-value model, but does not necessarily assume that affective reactions directly influence the value of a goal object.) The control dimension is not explicitly linked to problems in living by Weiner, primarily because it appears to be related to locus and stability. Overall, then, the Weiner model predicts that attributional style differences on the locus and stability dimensions (and by inference the control dimension) will correlate with levels of everyday problems in living.

LEARNED HELPLESSNESS

Learned helplessness originally referred to a laboratory phenomenon in which animals exposed to uncontrollable (inescapable) aversive stimuli in one setting displayed "helpless" behavior in another setting. That is, even when the animal could escape aversive stimulation in the second setting, it typically would fail to do so. Noting the similarities to the behavior pattern of depressed people, Seligman proposed that some types of depression may essentially be a human learned helplessness behavior pattern resulting from uncontrollable experiences (Seligman, 1975). This model of depression underwent a radical change in 1978, primarily because the learned helplessness–depression data from humans did not fit the (original) animal model very well. Excellent presentations of these problems and of the reformulated learned helplessness model may be found in Abramson et al., (1978) and in Abramson, Garber, and Seligman (1980).

The reformulated model is an attributional one and draws heavily on Weiner's work. The model posits that exposure to uncontrollable events elicits attributions that vary on three critical dimensions. Two of the dimensions, locus (internal–external) and stability (stable–unstable) are essentially the same as in Weiner's model. (Note that the locus dimension was relabeled "internality" by Abramson et al. (1978). We will use "locus.") The third dimension, globality (global–specific), refers to the range of situations to which the attribution is seen as applicable. Global causes are important in a wide range of situations, whereas specific ones are tied to a few situations (or one).

Perceiving and expecting response-outcome noncontingency (uncontrollability) leads to four types of depression-related components—depressed affect, lowered motivation, cognitive deficits (e.g., inability to learn response contingencies), and lowered self-esteem. The generality of the depression is influenced by the globality of the attributions. The chronicity (or duration) is influenced by the stability of the attributions. The self-esteem component is influenced by the locus of the attributions. Presumably, the motivational and cognitive deficits are influenced by the attributions through the person's expectations concerning likely future success or failure.

The experimental orientation of the learned helplessness tradition implies a situationist position on depression. That is, depression is largely a result of situational factors that influence outcomes (positive or negative), perceptions of uncontrollability, and attributions for those outcomes. In addition, the model explicitly predicts the existence of a maladaptive attributional style that is associated with depression. Specifically, depressed people are predicted to make more internal, global, and stable attributions for negative outcomes and more external, specific, and unstable attributions for postive outcomes, relative to nondepressed people. Similar predictions would seem to apply to the problems of loneliness and shyness.

Although this model clearly states that attributional style is a causal factor in depression, it does not state what type of causal factor it is. The model certainly implies that it is a maintaining cause. The maladaptive attributional style would tend to lead to continued failure or negative outcomes in many situations, as suggested earlier in Figure 9.1. If such a maladaptive style is acquired in the absence of depression, it may also serve as a predisposing cause. Data relevant to these two questions will be considered later.

CONTROLLABILITY AS AN ATTRIBUTIONAL DIMENSION

Weiner's model and the reformulated learned helplessness model are extremely similar in form and content. Weiner is not sure that a third attributional dimension (in addition to locus and stability) is needed, but postulates that controllability is important. The learned helplessness model postulates a third dimension of globality and excludes controllability as an attributional dimension. It appears that the learned helplessness theorists prefer to think of controllability (and uncontrollability) as a characteristic of events, rather than of attributions. The notion is that the dimensions of locus, stability, and globality capture any controllability differences in attributions, making it superfluous as an attributional dimension.

Other researchers have questioned this dismissal of controllability as an attributional dimension. Indeed, several have suggested that the perceived controllability of a cause may be the most important factor in determining future motivational, cognitive, and performance effects of negative outcomes (e.g., Anderson & Arnoult, in press; Anderson et al., 1983; Wortman & Dintzer, 1978). We suggest that changes in success expectancies as a result of an outcome depend primarily on the extent to which the perceived cause of the outcome is seen as modifiable, changeable, or controllable by the person.[2] If a negative outcome is seen as being caused by a controllable factor, subsequent success expectancies (hence, motivation and performance) should not be adversely affected. If controllability explains the various attributional style–problems in living data as well as the locus and stability and globality dimensions, then there is no reason to adopt the more complex models. That is, the controllability of attributions may determine success expectancy changes, motivation, performance, and affect (including self-esteem). On the other hand, the controllability dimension may not be sufficient. Locus may be particularly important in determining affective reactions.

---

[2]We prefer the term changeability (Anderson et al., 1983) because it implies some control in the future, whereas controllability may be either future or past directed. Because of the popularity of the control concept, and because data shows that subjects see the two as having the same meaning (when the control questions are future oriented, Anderson, 1983c), we have decided to use controllability with this future-oriented focus.

In any case, an examination of the empirical relationships between these attributional style dimensions and depression, loneliness, and shyness is warranted.

SUCCESS OF VARIOUS CAUSAL DIMENSIONS IN PAST RESEARCH

The overriding attributional style model of problems in living, as presented in Figure 9.1, explicitly predicts that measures of problems in living will correlate significantly with measures of attributional style. Four dimensions have emerged as the major contenders; these are locus, stability, globality, and controllability. For negative outcomes, the models predict that the debilitated people (the depressed, lonely, or shy) will make relatively more internal, stable, global, and uncontrollable attributions than the nondebilitated. For positive outcomes, the predictions have been less clear. Positive outcomes do not typically yield depressed affect, regardless of the attribution. One might thus expect little relationship between attributional style for positive outcomes and problems like depression. Consider, though, a lonely person who views herself as socially inept. She may attribute an enjoyable experience on a blind date to the extraordinary social skills of the dating partner. By attributing the positive outcome to such a personally uncontrollable cause, she will still have low expectations for future dates (with other people) and may display the low motivation and the consequent poor social performance that frequently lead to her social failures. Thus, the attributional models may be seen as predicting debilitated people to make relatively more external, unstable, specific, and uncontrollable attributions for positive outcomes than the nondebilitated.

The prototype approach to these everday problems in living suggests which types of situations will most likely lead to the predicted attributional style–problems in living correlations. The depression prototype contains both interpersonal and noninterpersonal features; thus, we expect depression to correlate with attributional style for both interpersonal and noninterpersonal situations. However, most problems presented in therapy are interpersonal (Horowitz, 1979), and the depression prototype is more interpersonal than not. The attributional style–depression relationship may thus be stronger for interpersonal situations than for noninterpersonal ones. The loneliness prototype was almost exclusively interpersonal. This suggests that the attributional style–loneliness relationship will be considerably stronger for interpersonal situations than for noninterpersonal ones. As pointed out earlier, shyness seems to overlap with both loneliness and depression, though no prototype data exist to test this notion. The interpersonalness of shyness seems to suggest, however, that its relationship to attributional style will be strongest in interpersonal situations.

Before examining the data on the attributional style relationships, consider how attributions and attributional styles are measured. Early researchers simply presented subjects with two or more causes that were to be rated, checked, or compared. One popular approach had subjects rate the importance of ability and luck as determinants of their outcome. A better, but still inadequate, approach used the four attributional factors from Weiner's early Locus × Stability model. These approaches suffered from several major problems. First, subjects were restricted to causes that may not have been relevant to them or to their task. Second, many of the researchers made claims about the effects of different causal dimensions, but dimensionality was never directly assessed. Third, by presenting a list of causal factors the researchers may have made salient one or more causes that the subject would not ordinarily consider. If we adopt the two-stage attribution process presented earlier it becomes clear that these methods permit the researcher to influence the attributions at the problem-formulation stage. Other problems with these and similar measurement approaches are cogently discussed by Elig and Frieze (1979), and Deaux and Farris (1980).

One solution to several of these problems is to gather only open-ended attributions. That is, one simply asks the subject to write out the cause or causes of the event in question. These open-ended causes may then be classified or rated by other judges. This technique is usually considered too time consuming and is sometimes plagued with interrater reliability problems. A related solution is to use a forced-choice type format, but to derive the experimenter-provided list of causes from an open-ended pretest study. This technique also has drawbacks. The researcher cannot make unambiguous statements about the dimensionality of the attributions. Also, the problem of making all the listed attributions equally salient exists. This technique does allow the researcher to get fairly naturalistic attributions with an objective measurement technique, which may be sufficient for many research questions (see Anderson et al., 1983).

For research primarily directed at causal dimension questions, the best solution appears to be to have subjects generate open-ended attributions, which they then rate on the causal dimensions of interest. In the typical attributional style study, subjects imagine themselves in hypothetical situations, write out the major cause of each situation outcome, and then rate each cause on the relevant causal dimensions (see Anderson & Arnoult, in press; Seligman, Abramson, Semmel, & von Baeyer,

1979). The one major problem with this technique is that the experimenter selects the causal dimensions. The dimensions selected may not be the most relevant to the particular question or phenomenon under study. If, for instance, controllability is the best underlying dimension for understanding depression, the learned helplessness researchers will fool themselves and mislead others by measuring only locus, stability, and globality. The bulk of the attributional style research has been guided by the learned helplessness model of depression.

Several studies have examined controllability (or similar notions) for depression. Most such studies, however, have adopted a *past-oriented* perspective to the attributional dimension of controllability. We suspect this orientation (e.g., "Could you have controlled . . ." or "How much control did you have . . .") derives from viewing controllability as a feature of situations. The attributional model, though, implies a future-oriented view of controllability. That is, people's success expectancy changes, and subsequent motivation and performance, should be linked to their perceptions of how much they believe they can change, modify, or control, *in the future*, the causal factors that led to past successes or failures. Past-oriented assessments of controllability may reflect self-blame or self-credit tendencies, rather than expectancy-relevant attributional features. For example, two adolescent males may both attribute an interpersonal failure (e.g., getting turned down for a date) to a cause they had been unable to control (e.g., not being able to ask for the date in a self-assured manner). But this past-orientation does not predict their expectancy changes, motivation, or performance in the future. One may believe that he can change his self-presentation by practice; from the future perspective, this cause is seen as controllable, and future successes may be expected. The other may believe that he cannot improve with practice; this cause is uncontrollable from both the past and the future perspectives, and only more failure is expected. In our view, then, controllability as an attributional style dimension must be assessed from a future-oriented perspective. This can be done with several types of questions, such as "How controllable is this cause?", "To what extent can you change this factor?", or "Do you expect to be able to modify this cause in similar situations in the future?".

We reviewed all the available studies of attributional style and depression. The results are summarized in Table 9.3.[3] Several rather strict criteria were used in selecting these results from the myriad studies

---

[3]In any such tabulation, there are always arbitrary decisions concerning inclusion versus exclusion of borderline studies. Since the results are generally the same regardless of inclusion criteria, we are confident that our summary is accurate.

Table 9.3

STUDIES OF DEPRESSIVE ATTRIBUTIONAL STYLE

CORRELATIONAL ANALYSES: CORRELATIONS OF ATTRIBUTIONAL STYLE MEASURES WITH DEPRESSION

Study	Subjects[a]	n	Outcome[b]	Locus	Globality	Stability
Blaney et al., 1980	Students, sample 2	322–379	P	−.19**	.02	−.14**
			N	.07	.23**	.14**
Feather, 1983[c]	Students and other adults	248	P	−.16*	−.11	−.18**
Golin et al., 1981[d]	Students	180	N	.11	.17**	.15*
First session			P	−.17*	.02	−.05
			N	.10	.11	.20**
Second session			P	−.22**	−.13	−.16*
			N	.18*	.16*	.23**
Hammen & deMayo, 1982	Teachers	75	N	.10	—	.16
Johnson et al., 1983[c]	Students	144	P	.00	−.07	−.14
			N	.17*	.16	−.05
Manly et al., 1982	Pregnant women	55	P	.04	.14	−.09
			N	.10	.10	−.03
Metalsky et al., 1982	Students	277	N	.08	.19**	.24**
Seligman et al., 1979	Students	143	P	−.22**	−.04	−.28**
			N	.41**	.35**	.34**

GROUP DIFFERENCES ANALYSES: MEAN ATTRIBUTIONAL
STYLE SCORES FOR DEPRESSED AND NONDEPRESSED GROUPS

	n	Valence[b]			
Harvey, 1981[e]					
Female students					
D	45	P	.46	—	.46
ND	46	P	.59	—	.45
F			8.63**	—	.00
D	45	N	.51	—	.44
ND	46	N	.40	—	.43
F			6.71**	—	.13
Raps et al., 1982					
Male inpatients					
D	30	P	4.93	5.10	4.90
NDS	15	P	5.67	5.27	5.57
NDM	61	P	5.49	5.31	5.53
F			3.60*	.30	4.08*
D	30	N	4.90	4.84	4.89
NDS	15	N	3.51	4.10	4.01
NDM	61	N	4.30	3.65	4.06
F			7.34**	8.25**	7.67**
Sweeney et al., 1982[f]					
Students					
D	20	P	5.18	5.33	5.47
ND	20	P	5.92	5.42	5.88
F			5.84*	.15	4.16*
D	20	N	4.85	4.34	4.80
ND	20	N	4.38	3.48	3.87
F			1.98	5.71*	8.43**

[a] D, depressed; ND, nondepressed; NDS, nondepressed schizophrenic; NDM, nondepressed medical; F, F-test.
[b] P, positive outcome; N, negative outcome.
[c] One-tailed tests were converted to two-tailed tests for consistency with results of the other studies.
[d] Some ps reported by Golin et al. were apparently incorrect. Therefore, we are reporting here the results of our tests of these correlations ($df = 178$).
[e] Harvey reported mean proportions of internal and stable causes given for an event.
[f] These results were not presented in the article, but were obtained in a personal communnciation with Paul Sweeney, March 30, 1984. We thank him for his assistance.
*$p < .05$.   **$p < .01$.

addressed to attributional style issues. These criteria were (1) individual dimensions were reported, (2) dimensional locations of causes were empirically determined, not interpreted (e.g., ability and effort versus luck and task difficulty as the internal-external locus constitutes an interpretation), (3) positive (success) and negative (failure) situations were distinguished, (4) depression and attributional style were measured concurrently, and (5) a given administration of a measure was used only once (e.g., attributional style correlations with two different depression measures were not both included in the table; when both the Beck Depression Inventory (Beck et al., 1961) and the Multiple Affect Adjective Checklist (Zuckerman, Lubin, Vogel, & Valerius, 1964) were used, only the BDI results were included), (6) when both correlational and extreme groups analyses were reported, only the correlational results were included, (7) only published studies were included, (8) controllability results assessed in a past-oriented focus were excluded, (9) studies with unselected samples smaller than 50 or with selected samples smaller than 15 were excluded. These criteria eliminated studies examining controllability in all cases except one, which we consider shortly.

Table 9.3 is divided into two sections. The top reports the zero-order correlations between attributional style measures and depression. The bottom presents means for depressed versus nondepressed groups on attributional style measures.

Overall, the results suggest that there is at least a weak relationship between attributional style and depression. For positive outcomes, increasing levels of depression are associated with more external and unstable attributions. For negative outcomes, increasing levels of depression are associated with more internal, global, and stable attributions. Globality of attributional style for positive outcomes does not appear to be related to depression. In addition, the attributional style–depression relationships displayed in Table 9.3 are quite weak, and there are reversals for each of the dimensions.

Hammen and deMayo (1982) had subjects rate the controllability of their attributions for negative outcomes with a future-oriented focus. In addition, subjects rated the locus and the stability of their attributions. Whereas neither locus nor stability correlated significantly with depression (as in Table 9.3 above), controllability was highly correlated ($r = .42$, $p < .01$). As our model predicts, those who felt they could control the factors leading to the negative events were less depressed than those who felt they had less (or no) control.

There have been few studies of the relationship between attributional style and loneliness or shyness. Anderson et al. (1983) showed that lonely people attribute interpersonal failures more to character deficits and less to behavioral mistakes than do nonlonely people. Teglasi and

Hoffman (1982) found evidence of locus and stability differences in at-tributional style between shy and nonshy subjects. These two studies suggest that our attributional model is relevant to loneliness and shy-ness, but more data are needed.

Confounding of Dimensions of Causality

Although the research on the relationships between attributional style and problems in living supports the generalized attributional model, it does not provide confirmation of the specific models. One major prob-lem in choosing between the various dimensions is their apparent in-terrelatedness. Indeed, if these four dimensions were truly independent of each other, we would have no selection problem—all four would be kept on the basis of the reviewed results. The practice of creating fac-torial models of these dimensions and then filling in each of the result-ing cells with one or more intuitive examples has misled some people into viewing the dimensions as orthogonal. The difficulty in creating causes that are external, stable, and controllable has led some research-ers (e.g., Weiner, 1979) to point out the probable nonorthogonality of dimensions of causality. A common distinction frequently made now is between logical and empirical orthogonality. Two (or more) dimensions are said to be *logically* orthogonal if there exists at least one cause in each cell of the relevant factorial model. Two (or more) dimensions are *em-pirically* orthogonal if the population of causes is uniformly (or equally) distributed among the cells (or if they do not correlate significantly).

Although the logical orthogonality concept may at first appear both arbitrary and vacuous, it serves one important function. By manipulat-ing causal attributions (experimentally or statistically) in a dimensionally orthogonal way, researchers may be able to examine the effects of dif-ferent attributional dimensions on different outcome measures. For ex-ample, one might want to test the prediction that the stability of attributions determines the change in expectancies resulting from suc-cess or failure. Both the Weiner and the learned helplessness models suggest that one such test would entail manipulating ability versus ef-fort attributions. This manipulation presumably controls for locus, since both ability and effort are internal. However, ability and effort clearly differ on controllability. Should results be assigned to stability or to con-trollability effects? In addition, past researchers using this approach have failed to assess the dimensional locations of the specific attributions being manipulated. Many assume, for instance, that both ability and effort are internal. But are they equally internal? Because we do not know, dimensional statements regarding the outcome are speculations at best.

We do not mean to imply that this approach is hopeless. With proper methodological refinements, such as assessing the dimensional locations of various attributions, attempts to control for the effects of various causal dimensions will likely lead to considerable advances in attributional models. This may be accomplished either by choosing empirically determined orthogonal manipulations or by statistically controlling for different dimensions. Our current concern, however, is with the extent of empirical relatedness in these causal dimensions. Two rather different techniques have been used to address this question. One methodological feature required for examination of this question is that the causes examined for dimensional interrelatedness must be generated by subjects in an unbiased format. The approach taken by the three studies to be examined here was to have subjects consider a set of hypothetical situations and to write down the major cause of the outcome for each situation. The dimensional locations of these causes were assessed and correlated.

In the first study to address this issue explicitly, Anderson (1983c) asked a group of subjects to examine the 20 hypothetical situations from the Attributional Style Assessment Test-I (ASAT-I, Anderson et al., 1983) and to list possible reasons for the outcome of each. The ASAT-I situations encompass a broad range of situations divided into four types—interpersonal failure, noninterpersonal failure, interpersonal success, and noninterpersonal success. Abstract versions of the causes were created and identical causes combined, resulting in a total of 63 different causes. Another group of subjects rated these 63 different causes on each of six causal dimensions, including locus, stability, globality, and controllability. The average dimensional ratings of the causes thus defined the dimensional locations of each cause. The cause "worked hard" could thus be located on each of six causal dimensions. The dimensional locations of the 63 causes were then correlated and yielded strong patterns of intercorrelations. These results for the four dimensions of present interest are listed in Table 9.4. Briefly, the only correlation that was not statistically significant was between stability and globality.

The other two studies relevant to the orthogonality question used quite different techniques (Anderson, in press; Anderson & Arnoult, in press). Anderson (in press) had subjects, both as actors and as observers, generate open-ended attributions for each of the 20 ASAT-I situations. Judges then classified each attribution as being one of the 63 causes identified by Anderson (1983c), and dimension scores were assigned accordingly. For each of the 40 items (20 actor attributions, 20 observer), the dimensional correlations were calculated across subjects. The average interdimensional correlations were all highly significant. As can be

Table 9.4

INTERCORRELATIONS OF CAUSES ON THE DIMENSIONS OF LOCUS, STABILITY, GLOBALITY, AND CONTROLLABILITY[a]

	Locus			Stability			Globality		
	r (61)[b]	r (76)[c]	r (205)[d]	r (61)[b]	r (76)[c]	r (205)[d]	r (61)[b]	r (76)[c]	r (205)[d]
Controllability	.68***	.75***	.48***	.45***	.46***	.17*	.42***	.55***	.20**
Globality	.40**	.49***	.25***	.19	.25*	.33****			
Stability	.66***	.70***	.22**						

[a]In all studies, larger dimension scores indicate a cause to be more internal, stable, global, and controllable. Numbers in parentheses indicate degrees of freedom.

[b]From Anderson, C. A. (1983c). The causal structure of situations: The generation of plausible causal attributions as a function of type of event situation. *Journal of Experimental Social Psychology, 19,* 185–203. Copyright 1983 by Academic Press. Adapted by permission.

[c]From Anderson, C. A. (in press). Actor and observer attributions for different types of situations: Causal structure effects, individual differences, and the dimensionality of causes. *Social Cognition.*

[d]From Anderson, C. A., & Arnoult, L. H. (in press). Attributional style and everday problems in living: Depression, loneliness, and shyness. *Social Cognition.*

*$p < .05$.   **$p < .01$.   ***$p < .001$.

seen in Table 9.4, the pattern was very similar to that found in Anderson (1983c).

In the final study, Anderson & Arnoult (in press) had subjects generate open-ended self attributions for each of the 20 ASAT-I situations. Subjects then rated their own causes on five dimensions—locus, stability, globality, controllability, and intent. In this study, then, the dimensional locations of subject-generated attributions were determined entirely by the subjects who generated the causes. Again, for each situation, the interdimensional correlations were calculated across subjects and averaged across situations. The correlations were all significant and as shown in Table 9.4, were similar to results of the previous studies. Overall, then, the results conclusively demonstrated that the four dimensions of primary interest are not empirically orthogonal. Internal causes are also relatively more stable, controllable, and global than are external causes, for example.

What does this tell us about attributional models of problems in living? The main point is that any simple zero-order correlation between a dimension of attributional style and some problem in living is subject to serious confounding. Is a correlation between globality and depression, for instance, due to globality of attributional style or to the controllability component of the globality measure? Two implications follow from this confounding. First, the presence of a significant zero-order correlation between a problem in living and a dimensional measure of attributional style does not unequivocally support that causal dimension as a factor in the problem. Any such zero-order correlation may be entirely spurious. Second, the models proposed by Weiner and the learned helplessness theorists may be too complex. There may be a single underlying causal dimension that relates to the motivational, cognitive, and affective features of various problems in living. Of course, two or more dimensions may be needed. We propose that controllability is the primary dimension affecting success expectancies, motivation, and performance (hence, outcomes and affect). It also seems reasonable to postulate an additional need for the locus dimension, related primarily to affect. In the next section we present an empirical test of these predictions.

AN EMPIRICAL TEST OF UNCONFOUNDED ATTRIBUTIONAL STYLE DIMENSIONS

To address the dimensionality question we recently conducted a large scale questionnaire study (Anderson & Arnoult, in press). College students completed the modified depression scale (MDS), the modified loneliness scale (MLS), and the modified shyness scale (MSS) proposed by Anderson and Harvey (1984). These scales are modifications of the Beck Depression Inventory (short form; Beck & Beck, 1972), the UCLA Loneliness Scale, and the Shyness and Social Anxiety scales, as mentioned earlier in this chapter.

In addition, subjects completed an open-ended version of the ASAT-I (Anderson et al., 1983). In this version, subjects examined each of 20 hypothetical situations, wrote down a self-attribution for each situation, and rated their attributions on the five causal dimensions of locus, stability, globality, controllability, and intentionality. Intentionality attributional style did not reliably predict the problems in living; it will therefore not be considered in the remainder of this chapter.

As previously mentioned, there are four types of situations sampled by the ASAT-I. These are interpersonal failure (e.g., "While working as a volunteer caller for the American Red Cross, you failed to persuade very many people to donate blood"); noninterpersonal failure (e.g., "You have just failed the midterm test in a class"); interpersonal success (e.g., "You have just attended a party for new students and made some new friends"); and noninterpersonal success (e.g., "You have just won a competitive match in a sporting event"). By examining the relationships between attributional style and problems in living separately for each situation type and each problem, we were able to test the prototype-derived notions of loneliness as primarily interpersonal and depression as both interpersonal and noninterpersonal. We also tested for attributional style effects in both success and failure situations. The most important feature of this study, though, was that we were able to test the suitability of various causal dimensions for inclusion in attributional models of depression, loneliness, and shyness. We assessed attributional style for all four major causal dimensions and used the intercorrelations of these dimensional attributional styles to examine the predictive value of each dimension while statistically controlling for the others.

Regression analyses were conducted to see whether each causal dimension of attributional style could, by itself, predict each of the three problems in living. To test this, the four attributional style measures of each dimension (e.g., interpersonal failure locus, noninterpersonal failure locus, etc.) were entered as predictors of each problem in living in separate multiple regressions. As expected, each dimension yielded a significant multiple correlation for each of the problems, all $ps < .05$. The largest R (.35) was between stability attributional style and shyness. The smallest (.22) was between globality attributional style and loneliness.

These significant Rs indicate that each dimension *could* belong in the attributional model of problems in living. They do not demonstrate which ones *do* belong. What is needed is an examination of the *unique* predictiveness of each causal dimension independent of the other dimensions. We conducted a series of regression analyses to determine the unique (or independent) contribution of each dimension as predictors of the problems in living. That is, we calculated the predictive increment in R^2 of each dimension, controlling for the other three dimensions. This was done separately for each situation type and for each problem in living. There were, thus, 12 separate tests (4 situation types × 3 problems in living) of significance of the unique or unconfounded explained variance for each dimension.

The results of these analyses were quite clear. Controllability was the most important dimension, yielding significant increments in 7 of the 12 possible cases (3 for depression, 2 each for loneliness and shyness). Globality and stability added little predictive power. Globality yielded no significant increments to the prediction of any of the problems; stability yielded only 1 barely significant increment out of 12 tests, and this was for shyness. Locus appeared to be of marginal utility, adding significant increments in 3 of 12 tests (2 for depression, 1 for shyness). A fourth increment, interpersonal failure locus predicting loneliness, was marginally significant ($p < .07$).

Perhaps the most convincing finding was the result of analyses pitting the controllability dimension against the other three combined (which, of course, constitutes the learned helplessness model). This procedure gives a great advantage to the learned helplessness model, because it allows confounded variance to count for the learned helplessness dimensions, whereas only unconfounded variance counts for controllability. That is, the learned helplessness increment includes the confounded locus–stability, locus–globality, and stability–globality variance as well as unconfounded variance from locus, stability, and globality. The controllability increment includes only the unconfounded variance of controllability. Despite this advantage, the learned helplessness dimensions did not fare well against controllability. As shown in Table 9.5, controllability contributed significant predictive increments in 7 of 12 tests (as mentioned earlier), but the combined learned helplessness dimensions yielded only two significant increments.

Subsequent analyses revealed that dropping the globality and stability dimensions from the attributional model yielded no significant decrements in predictive power (in 12 such tests). Interestingly, locus did add significant predictive power to controllability but only for failure situations. For depression, locus attributional style added significant increments when assessed for both interpersonal and noninterpersonal situations. For loneliness and shyness, however, locus attributional style added significantly only when assessed for interpersonal failures.

Table 9.5

Increments in R^2 for the Learned Helplessness Dimensions (Including Confounded Variance) Versus Controllability (Unconfounded Variance Only)

Problem	Interpersonal failure	Noninterpersonal failure	Interpersonal success	Noninterpersonal success
Depression				
Locus, stability, and globality[a]	.058**	.026	.020	.008
Controllability[b]	.056***	.040**	.012	.045**
Loneliness				
Locus, stability, and globality	.029	.005	.021	.008
Controllability	.043**	.002	.022*	.017
Shyness				
Locus, stability, and globality	.058**	.022	.015	.024
Controllability	.033**	.013	.028*	.010

[a]Significance tested by $F(3,202)$.
[b]Significance tested by $F(1,202)$.
$*p < .05$. $**p < .01$. $***p < .001$.

In sum, these results support the general attributional style model presented in Figure 9.1. In addition, the causal dimensions of attributional style best suited for models of problems in living are controllability and locus. Table 9.6 contains the beta weights and the multiple correlations obtained by entering both locus and controllability attributional styles as predictors of the three problems in living. The directions of the attributional style relationships with depression, loneliness, and shyness were as expected. The signs of beta weights indicated that people with high levels of these problems tended to attribute failures to more uncontrollable, internal causes than did people not suffering from the problems. Also, the debilitated tended to attribute successes to more uncontrollable, external causes relative to the nondebilitated people. A simpler approach to combining these attributional style dimensions is to compute a unit-weighted composite, based on the predicted relationship for each dimension. For success situations both controllability and locus were expected to correlate negatively with problems in living (and they did), so the success composites were formed by summing the dimensions. For failure situations, controllability was again expected to correlate negatively with the problems, but locus was expected to correlate positively (i.e., more internal attributions for failure by the debilitated). Thus, the failure composites were formed by subtracting the locus scores from the controllability scores. The composite attributional style correlations with problems in living were therefore expected to be negative. Table 9.6 also contains these correlations.

Examination of these composite correlations reveals several interesting points. All the correlations were negative (as predicted), and most were highly significant. The magnitude of the correlations within each problem is also informative. For depression, there were no significant differences between the correlations as a function of situation type. For both loneliness and shyness, however, attributional style for interpersonal situations produced larger correlations than did the corresponding attributional style for noninterpersonal situations. These patterns support our earlier speculations, from the prototype approach, that interpersonal attributional styles would be relatively more important for loneliness and shyness. However, this distinction produced a significant difference in correlations only between the loneliness–failure correlations ($p < .02$).

THE CAUSALITY ISSUE

The attributional style model of problems in living, depicted in Figure 9.1, suggests examination of three kinds of evidence. First, if attributional style is a cause (maintaining, predisposing, or both), then there

Table 9.6

RESULTS FROM THE TWO-DIMENSION CONTROLLABILITY–LOCUS MODEL OF ATTRIBUTIONAL STYLE

Problem	Interpersonal failure			Noninterpersonal failure			Interpersonal success			Noninterpersonal success		
	Beta[a]	R[b]	r[c]	Beta[a]	R[b]	r[c]	Beta[a]	R[b]	r[c]	Beta[a]	R[b]	r[c]
Depression												
Controllability	-.16***	.26***	-.25***	-.14**	.20*	-.20**	-.08	.22**	-.22**	-.16***	.26***	-.22**
Locus	.13**			.10*			-.08			.02		
Loneliness												
Controllability	-.30**	.21**	-.20**	-.07	.06	-.02	-.23*	.28***	-.27***	-.22*	.20*	-.20**
Locus	.21*			-.02			-.20			.07		
Shyness												
Controllability	-.38**	.22**	-.22**	-.24	.12	-.12	-.35**	.26***	-.26***	-.26	.23**	-.22**
Locus	.35**			.20			-.19			-.20		

[a]Beta weights when both predictors are in the regression equation.

[b]Multiple correlation; problem predicted by locus and controllability attributional style.

[c]Unit-weight attributional style correlation with problem.

*$p < .05.$ **$p < .01.$ ***$p < .001.$

should be significant, meaningful correlations between attributional style and concurrent problems in living. The data we've reviewed provide strong support for this prediction. Second, the model implies that appropriate attributional interventions should lead to predictable changes in problem-related features, (i.e., success expectancies, motivation, performance, and by implication, affect). This prediction holds, of course, only if attributional style is a maintaining cause. Third, problems in living at one point in time should be predictable by an attributional style that has developed (and been measured) at an earlier point in time. This prediction holds only if attributional style is a predisposing cause. We will consider this predispositional prediction first.

CORRELATIONAL DATA FOR A CAUSAL MODEL

Concurrent correlational data, such as those presented in the previous section, cannot reveal the direction of causality. It may be that problems in living cause people to develop the maladaptive attributional styles rather than vice versa. A number of statistical techniques have been developed that purportedly allow causal inferences from correlational data, for example, path analysis, cross-lagged correlation analysis, and various hierarchical regression analyses on longitudinal data. In our view, the assumptions required for these models to be valid are virtually never met in this domain. On the other hand, we agree with many researchers that these and similar techniques may be useful in the examination of complex domains, as long as it is clear that causality cannot be unequivocally established by the techniques.

A number of researchers have turned to these approaches in this area with mixed results. Several studies purportedly show attributional style to be a predisposing cause of problems in living (e.g., Firth & Brewin, 1982; Metalsky et al., 1982; O'Hara et al., 1982), while others claim to have demonstrated that attributional style is not a predisposing cause (e.g., Lewinsohn, Steinmetz, Larson, & Franklin, 1981; Manly, McMahon, Bradley, & Davidson, 1982; Peterson, Schwartz, & Seligman, 1981). Interestingly, one of the studies that failed to support the predisposition causal prediction did provide some support for the maintaining cause position (Lewinsohn et al., 1981).

Our examination of these and related studies yielded no clear answer to the predisposition question. We feel there is some indication that attributional style is a predisposing cause of problems in living, but the evidence is not strong enough to provide a conclusive answer.

EXPERIMENTAL ANALOGUES

The ideal methodology for addressing the causality questions is experimental. A simple three-group experiment could answer many of our questions. We might randomly assign subjects to a maladaptive attributional style, a no-manipulation, or an adaptive attributional style condition. We could then gather follow-up measures of problems in living at periodic intervals and see if significant differences emerge.

Obviously, such an experiment is impossible for ethical reasons. A number of analogues to this have been conducted over the years. In some studies, attributions for performance at a particular task have been manipulated and subsequent success expectancies, motivation, or performance assessed. Much of the work summarized earlier is of this type. (See Weiner, 1979, for a recent review.) Admittedly, many of these studies involve rather trivial experimental tasks such as solving anagrams. But the results from experiments using more complex tasks are pretty similar and generally support the idea that attributions are important determinants of motivation (including success expectancies), performance, and affective reactions.

In one such study, Anderson and Jennings (1980) induced subjects to attribute initial failures at interpersonal persuasion either to lack of ability or to use of an ineffective strategy. The persuasion task was getting college students to donate blood to a local blood bank. The results were that after initial failures, strategy condition subjects had higher success expectancies and expected considerably more improvement with practice than did ability condition subjects.

In a follow-up study, Jennings (1980) used a similar manipulation and task but also assessed actual performance (observer ratings). He replicated the expectancy difference between ability and strategy attribution subjects. Jennings also found that subjects led to attribute initial failures to ineffective strategies later changed their strategies more often and improved their persuasive appeals significantly more than did subjects led to attribute initial failures to lack of ability.

We may also view a number of therapy-type studies as analogues to our ethically impossible ideal experiment. In the achievement domain, several researchers have successfully modfied ''helpless'' behaviors by use of an attribution retraining program (e.g., Andrews, & Debus, 1978; Chapin & Dyck, 1976; Dweck, 1975). For example, Fowler and Peterson (1981) preselected grade school children on the basis of reading difficulties and maladative attributional styles. During the training period these children attempted to read easy and difficult sentences arranged in two different partial reinforcement schedules. Some subjects also received either direct or indirect attribution instructions emphasizing effort for successes and lack of effort for failures. The results, measured by persistence at a reading task, indicated that the attribution manipulations produced significant increases in motivation.

In the clinical domain, several therapy studies on depression suggest that attributional style change is important to alleviation of depression (e.g., see Layden, 1982; Rehm, 1977; Rehm, 1982; Rehm & O'Hara, 1979). In addition, a number of the more successful cognitive and cognitive-behavior therapies seem to have built-in attributional manipulations. For example, both in Beck's cognitive therapy and in Bandura's self-efficacy therapy clients are led through success experiences designed to demonstrate that they have the capacity to succeed. These approaches also emphasize a problem-solving, effortful approach that looks very much like an attempt to provide clients with perceptions of controllability. (See Bandura, 1977a, for an overview of self-efficacy theory; see Beck et al., 1979, for a look at cognitive therapy for depression. See also Mahoney, 1974, and Meichenbaum, 1977, for similar cognitive behavioral approaches.) Rehm's self-management therapy for depression explicitly incorporates attributional components (Rehm, 1977).

To date, however, the specific effects of the attributional components in these therapies have not been clearly tested. In addition, there are logical problems in this approach. The attribution model predicts that giving subjects the adaptive attributional style should yield especially large increases in success expectancies, motivation, and performance of initially debilitated subjects. Since nondebilitated subjects presumably make such attributions already, the manipulation designed to give them adaptive ones should have little impact. The therapy studies, both in achievement and clinical contexts, have not examined this is detail. It may be that "effort" exhortations, for instance, will yield equally impressive improvement in debilitated and nondebilitated subjects, indicating a lack of specificity of effect predicted by the model. Obviously, the simple experimental analogue studies with nondebilitated subjects (e.g., Anderson & Jennings, 1980) do not address this specificity of effects notion either.

The Correlational Experiment

To establish that attributional style is a maintaining cause of problems in living, one needs to show three effects. First, one must show a relationship between attributional style and the problems in living (or primary characteristics of the problems, such as the motivational or performance deficits). Second, changes in attributional style brought about by some intervention must yield corresponding changes in the problems (or in the related characteristics). Third, these attribution induced changes must be larger for those subjects given attributions that differ from their typical style than for subjects given attributions that are similar to their typical style.

The minimal design for testing these notions is what we call the *correlational experiment*. In this design, subjects are preselected on the basis of the hypothesized causal factor. Both high- and low-scoring subjects are selected. In the present context, the preselection factor would be controllability attributional style. Subjects in each of these *correlationally* selected groups are then assigned to one of three experimental treatments. One treatment is a no-manipulation control. A second treatment manipulates the hypothesized causal factor to be high. The third treatment manipulates that factor to be low. In our present case, the second and third treatments would be attribution manipulations providing either controllable (adaptive) or uncontrollable (maladaptive) attributions for some task or set of outcomes. All subjects perform the relevant tasks under these conditions, and the hypothesized affected variables are assessed. In this case, these dependent variables might be global problems in living or more specific related variables such as success expectancies, motivation, and performance. By use of appropriate statistical contrasts, one can then assess the fit between the obtained results and those predicted by the causal model.

This type of correlational experiment could not be conducted in a clinical setting, for it would require a manipulation designed to make some people more depressed, lonely, or shy. It can be conducted in more limited laboratory settings where the manipulations are likely to be less powerful, less enduring, and more easily eradicated.

Anderson (1983b) has examined the attribution model in Figure 9.1 with such a correlational experiment. College student subjects were preselected on the basis of the controllability (or changeability) of their attributional styles for interpersonal failures (Anderson et al., 1983). Half of the subjects made relatively frequent attributions to uncontrollable, characterological causes (ability and personality traits) and relatively infrequent attributions to controllable, behavioral causes (strategy and effort). The other half of the subjects had the reverse attributional style. Subjects participated in an interpersonal persuasion task under one of three randomly assigned attribution manipulations. The manipulations consisted of suggesting that performance (success or failure) on the upcoming task depended upon a person's persuasive abilities and relevant personality traits (i.e., the character style), persuasive strategies and effort (i.e., the behavior style), or no attributions were mentioned.

The specific task was to contact other university students by telephone and to try to convince them to donate blood to a local blood bank. The subjects were given one week to work on this task after which they returned to the lab and completed several questionnaires. This task was chosen for several reasons. First, it is a complex, interpersonal task of the type that is especially difficult for people with the problems in living (Horowitz et al., 1982). Second, the task guarantees fairly high-failure rates, which is important since people with problems in living often show heightened deficits after initial failures. Third, the task allowed the collection of fairly straightforward success expectancy, motivation, and performance measures. Success expectancies were assessed by asking subjects to predict their success rate in an upcoming blood drive. A task persistence measure (number of calls made during the experimental week) and a commitment measure (willingness to participate as a caller in an upcoming blood drive) were combined as a measure of motivation. Actual success rate during the experiment consitituted the performance measure.

The results, presented in Figure 9.2, strongly supported our attributional model. (Note that Figure 9.2 presents the results of a composite index of the success expectancy, motivation, and performance measures; the results for each of these measures were individually significant as predicted, as well.) When attributions were not manipulated, behavior style subjects had higher success expectancies, demonstrated greater motivation, and produced better success rates than did character style subjects. When attributions were experimentally manipulated, corresponding behavior and character style subjects were not significantly different from each other. Instead, success expectancies, motivation, and success rates were all determined by the attribution manipulation. Finally, note that effects of the attribution manipulation were specific to the groups for which the manipulations were different from the customary attributional style. That is, the strategy–effort manipulation had a large impact on character style subjects but little impact on behavior style subjects. Similarly, the ability–trait manipulation had a large impact on behavior style subjects but no impact on character style subjects. Overall, the observed pattern of means conformed quite closely to the pattern predicted by the attributional style model, as was shown by the highly significant predicted contrast effect ($p < .001$) and the nonsignificant residual variance ($p > .50$).

These results demonstrated attributional style to be a maintaining cause of the motivational and performance deficits of people with these

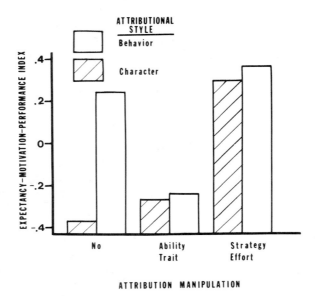

Figure 9.2 Composite index of success expectancies, motivation, and performance as a function of attributional style and attribution manipulation. (From Anderson, C. A. [1983b]. Motivational and performance deficits in interpersonal settings: the effect of attributional style. *Journal of Personality and Social Psychology, 45,* 1136–1147. Copyright 1983 by American Psychological Association.)

problems in living. It is important to note that the attributional styles examined by Anderson (1983b) had previously been found to correlate with depression and loneliness (Anderson et al., 1983). Furthermore, premeasures of depression and loneliness indicated that the character style groups were more depressed and lonely than the behavior style groups (Anderson, 1983b). Although shyness was not assessed in either of those studies, the results of Anderson and Arnoult (in press) in conjunction with the results shown in Figure 9.2 clearly suggest that attributional style is a maintaining cause of all three types of problems in living.

The success rate results of Anderson (1983b) have additional implications about the causes of these problems in living. If depressed, lonely, and shy people experience frequent interpersonal failure because of true skill deficits, then a strategy–effort attribution manipulation should not improve their success rate but only their motivation. However, the character style subjects in the strategy–effort manipulation group had significantly higher success rates than their ability–trait and no-manipulation counterparts; indeed, their success rates were not reliably different from the best performing group of behavior style subjects. This suggests that a significant portion of people suffering from these various problems in living obtain their high failure rates because of motivational rather than skill deficits.

SUMMARY AND CONCLUSIONS

We have covered a great deal of material in this chapter, ranging from the definitions of problems in living, through assessement techniques and attribution theory, to attributional models and empirical tests of those models. In any chapter of this sort, differences between the theories of different research groups tend to be over-emphasized. Although we feel that our emphasis on controllability as an attributional dimension represents a definite improvement over earlier attribution models, we would like to point out that the major tenets of those models remain unchanged. The common model is a motivational one that adapts many ideas from expectancy–value theory. Attributions affect expectancies (and possibly goal values), subsequent motivation, and performance. In short, our approach differs little from and owes an intellectual debt to the Weiner group and the learned helplessness group.

We have additionally emphasized the attributional aspects of problems in living at the expense of the stress and skills aspects. Once again, this is a function of chapter writing and not a negative assessment of the value of these different aspects. Clearly, depression, loneliness, and shyness result from a host of intra- and interpersonal factors. Which factors are most important for a specific client in therapy or for a broader population of people must be determined before appropriate therapy or social intervention can be created.

In reviewing the relevant theoretical and empirical literatures for this chapter, we were struck by the relative lack of high quality research and the difficulty of conducting such research. We include our own studies among those that could, retrospectively, have been better conceived or conducted. But on the whole, the set of studies reviewed here, each with its own particular strengths and weaknesses, has produced a fairly convincing picture of problems in living. There are a number of gaps in the research, however, that offer exciting research possibilities. We will mention only a few.

The prototype approach to the study of depression and loneliness has proved useful in helping define these problems. A similar analysis of shyness would improve our understanding of this problem and would suggest therapeutic strategies for it. (See Horowitz, Weckler & Doren,

1983, for a discussion of therapeutic implications deriving from the prototype approach.)

Although our data suggest that controllability and locus attributional styles are of primary importance in everyday problems in living, much work remains to be done on this model. We have not, for instance, identified specific effects of attributional dimensions on specific dependent variables. Is locus primarily related to self-esteem and other affective variables? Does controllability primarily influence changes in success expectancies? Related questions concerning affect remained unanswered. Where does affect fit in the model? Is affect a direct cause as well as an effect? If so, how does it influence motivation, performance, or attributional style?

The development of different attributional styles is also an area that requires further investigation. What kind of child-rearing practices, family environments, and life experiences lead to particularly adaptive or maladaptive attributional styles? At the present time, it is not even clear that attributional styles are predisposing causes of problems in living. It may be that the maladaptive style develops concurrently with the problems, serving only as a maintaining cause. Or, the style may be dormant in depression-prone individuals until negative life events begin to overwhelm them.

More and better longitudinal studies may help answer some of these developmental and causal questions. More experiments with clinical populations are also needed. To conduct these studies properly, though, we need to have a better idea of the dimensional locations of different types of causes. Otherwise, manipulations of different attributions in the clinic or the lab may confound several dimensions, severely limiting theoretical gains. In addition, the specific effects of the attributional components of various therapies need more investigation.

Finally, the notion of "adaptive" versus "maladaptive" attributional styles needs to be examined carefully. Throughout much of this chapter we have implied that there exists such a simple dichotomy. However, what is adaptive for one person in one situation may be maladaptive for another. For example, a first-semester freshman may attribute his feelings of depression and loneliness to a lack of effort in making new friends. He may then make more of an effort by attending various social functions, organizing small pizza parties, and trying hard to behave in a friendly fashion. If the person has the requisite social skills, the effort attribution is probably more adaptive than an ability attribution for the initial problem. Another person in the same situation but without necessary social skills may be better off making an ability attribution for the situation. An effort attribution may induce the same type of high motivation, but the lack of skills may cause these efforts to result in more frequent and more devastating failures. Also, the effort attributions may lead the person to ignore academic demands as "just one more party" may be desired to attempt to make new friendships. An ability attribution may be more adaptive here by preventing more social embarrassments or by leading the person to seek social skills assistance.

The adaptive–maladaptive question may simply be an issue of attributional accuracy. We suspect that accurate attributions are usually more adaptive than inaccurate ones (assuming one can identify what is accurate). But in some cases, an inaccurate attribution may be more beneficial in the long run. For instance, attributions to controllable causes (e.g., strategy) may maintain high motivation longer than attributions to uncontrollable ones (chance). In some truly uncontrollable situations, persistence for whatever reason, including an inaccurate attribution, may ultimately yield success.

A better understanding of these various questions will, we feel, lead to improvements in therapy, in the socal structuring of our institutions (e.g., universities), and in the quality of life in general.

REFERENCES

Abramson, L. Y., Garber, J., & Seligman, M. E. P. (1980). Learned helplessness in humans: An attributional analysis. In J. Garber & M. E. P. Seligman (Eds.), *Human helplessness: Theory and applications.* New York: Academic Press.

Abramson, L. Y., Seligman, M. E. P., & Teasdale, J. D. (1978). Learned helplessness in humans: Critique and reformulation. *Journal of Abnormal Psychology, 87,* 49–74.

Anderson, C. A. (1983a). Abstract and concrete data in the perseverance of social theories: When weak data lead to unshakeable beliefs. *Journal of Experimental Social Psychology, 19,* 93–108.

Anderson, C. A. (1983b). Motivational and performance deficits in interpersonal settings: The effect of attributional style. *Journal of Personality and Social Psychology, 45,* 1136–1147.

Anderson, C. A. (1983c). The causal structure of situations: The generation of plausible causal attributions as a function of type of event situation. *Journal of Experimental Social Psychology, 19,* 185–203.

Anderson, C. A. (in press). Actor and observer attributions for different types of situations: Causal structure effects, individual differences, and dimensionality of causes. *Social Cognition.*

Anderson, C. A., & Arnoult, L. H. (in press). Attributional style and everyday problems in living: Depression, loneliness and shyness. *Social Cognition.*

Anderson, C. A., & Harvey, R. J. (1984). *Discriminating between problems in living: An examination of measures of depression, loneliness, shyness, and social anxiety.* Manuscript submitted for publication.

Anderson, C. A., Horowitz, L. M., & French, R. (1983). Attributional style of lonely and depressed people. *Journal of Personality and Social Psychology, 45,* 127–136.

Anderson, C. A., & Jennings, D. L. (1980). When experiences of failure promote expectations of success: The impact of attributing failure to ineffective strategies, *Journal of Personality, 48*, 393–407.

Andrews, G. R., & Debus, R. L. (1978). Persistence and causal perception of failure: Modifying cognitive attributions. *Journal of Educational Psychology, 70*, 154–166.

Atkinson, J. W. (1964). *An introduction to motivation.* Princeton, NJ: Van Nostrand.

Bandura, A. (1977a). Self-efficacy: Toward a unifying theory of behavioral change. *Psychological Review, 84*, 191–215.

Bandura, A. (1977b). *Social learning theory.* Englewood Cliffs, NJ: Prentice-Hall.

Beck, A. T., & Beck, R. W. (1972). Screening depressed patients in family practice: A rapid technic. *Postgraduate Medicine, 52*, 81–85.

Beck, A. T., Rush, A. J., Shaw, B. F., & Emery, G. (1979). *Cognitive therapy of depression.* New York: Guilford Press.

Beck, A. T., Ward, C. H., Mendelson, M., Mock, J., & Erbaugh, J. (1961). An inventory for measuring depression. *Archives of General Psychiatry, 4*, 561–571.

Bem, D. J. (1972). Self-perception theory. In L. Berkowitz (Ed.), *Advances in experimental social psychology* (Vol. 6). New York: Academic Press.

Blaney, P. H., Behar, V., & Head, R. (1980). Two measures of depressive cognitions: Their association with depression and with each other. *Journal of Abnormal Psychology, 89*, 678–682.

Bradburn, N. (1969). *The structure of psychological well-being.* Chicago: Aldine.

Brown, G. W. (1974). Meaning, measurement, and stress of life events. In B. S. Dohrenwend & B. P. Dohrenwend (Eds.), *Stressful life events: Their nature and effects.* New York: John Wiley & Sons.

Chapin, M., & Dyck, D. G. (1976). Persistence in children's reading behavior as a function of N length and attribution retraining. *Journal of Abnormal Psychology, 85*, 511–515.

Cheek, J. M., & Buss, A. H. (1981). Shyness and sociability. *Journal of Personality and Social Psychology, 41*, 330–339.

Coyne, J. C. (1976). Depression and the response of others. *Journal of Abnormal Psychology, 85*, 186–193.

Coyne, J. C., & Gotlib, I. H. (1983). The role of cognition in depression: A critical appraisal. *Psychological Bulletin, 94*, 472–505.

Cutrona, C. E. (1982). Transition to college: Loneliness and the process of social adjustment. In L. A. Peplau & D. Perlman (Eds.), *Loneliness: A sourcebook of current theory, research, and therapy.* New York: John Wiley & Sons.

Deaux, K., & Farris, E. (1980). *Causal attributions for performance: Approaching substance via method.* Unpublished manuscript, Purdue University, Department of Psychology, West Lafayette, IN.

Dohrenwend, B. S., & Dohrenwend, B. P. (1974). Overview and prospects for research on stressful life events. In B. S. Dohrenwend & B. P. Dohrenwend (Eds.), *Stressful life events: Their nature and effects.* New York: John Wiley & Sons.

Dweck, C. S. (1975). The role of expectations and attributions in the alleviation of learned helplessness. *Journal of Personality and Social Psychology, 31*, 674–685.

Elig, T. W., & Frieze, I. H. (1979). Measuring causal attributions for success and failure. *Journal of Personality and Social Psychology, 37*, 621–634.

Ellis, A. (1962). *Reason and emotion in psychotherapy.* New York: Lyle Stuart.

Feather, N. T. (1983). Some correlates of attributional style: Depressive symptoms, self-esteem, and Protestant ethic values. *Personality and Social Psychology Bulletin, 9*, 125–135.

Fenigstein, A., Scheier, M. F., & Buss, A. H. (1975). Public and private self-consciousness: Assessment and theory. *Journal of Consulting and Clinical Psychology, 43*, 522–527.

Ferster, C. B. (1973). A functional analysis of depression. *American Psychologist, 28,* 857–870.

Ferster, C. B. (1974). Behavioral approaches to depression. In R. J. Friedman & M. M. Katz (Eds.), *The psychology of depression: Contemporary theory and research.* Washington, D. C.: Winston.

Firth, J., & Brewin, C. (1982). Attributions and recovery from depression: A preliminary study using cross-lagged correlation analysis. *British Journal of Clinical Psychology, 21,* 229–230.

Fisher-Beckfield, D., & McFall, R. M. (1982). Development of a competence inventory for college men and evaluation of relationships between competence and depression. *Journal of Consulting and Clinical Psychology, 50,* 697–705.

Folkman, S., Schaefer, C., & Lazarus, R. S. (1979). Cognitive processes as mediators of stress and coping. In V. Hamilton & D. M. Warburton (Eds.), *Human stress and cognition: An information processing approach.* New York: John Wiley & Sons.

Fowler, J. W., & Peterson, P. L. (1981). Increasing reading persistence and altering attributional style of learned helpless children. *Journal of Educational Psychology, 73,* 251–260.

Freud, S. (1925). Mourning and melancholia. In E. Jones (Ed.) & J. Riviere (Trans.), *Collected papers* (Vol. 4). London: Hogarth.

Golin, S., Sweeney, P. D., & Shaeffer, D. E. (1981). The causality of causal attributions in depression: A cross-lagged panel correlational analysis. *Journal of Abnormal Psychology, 90,* 14–22.

Gotlib, I. H., & Asarnow, R. F. (1979). Interpersonal and impersonal problem-solving skills in mildly and clinically depressed university students. *Journal of Consulting and Clinical Psychology, 47,* 86–95.

Hammen, C., & deMayo, R. (1982). Cognitive correlates of teacher stress and depressive symptoms: Implications for attributional models of depression. *Journal of Abnormal Psychology, 91,* 96–101.

Harvey, D. M. (1981). Depression and attributional style: Interpretations of important personal events. *Journal of Abnormal Psychology, 90,* 134–142.

Heider, F. (1958). *The psychology of interpersonal relations.* New York: John Wiley & Sons.

Horowitz, L. M. (1979). On the cognitive structure of interpersonal problems treated in psychotherapy. *Journal of Consulting and Clinical Psychology, 47,* 5–15.

Horowitz, L. M., French, R., & Anderson, C. A. (1982). The prototype of a lonely person. In L. Peplau & D. Perlman (Eds.), *Loneliness: A sourcebook of current theory, research, and therapy.* New York: John Wiley & Sons.

Horowitz, L. M., Weckler, D. A., & Doren, R. (1983). Interpersonal problems and symptoms: A cognitive approach. *Advances in Cognitive-Behavioral Research and Therapy, 2,* 81–125.

Jennings, D. L. (1980). Effects of attributing failures to ineffective strategies (Doctoral dissertation, Stanford University, 1979). *Dissertation Abstracts International, 40B,* 5461b. (University Microfilms No. 80-11, 654).

Johnson, J. E., Petzel, T. P., & Sperduto, V. W. (1983). An evaluation of the scale of attributional style using college students preselected on level of depression. *Journal of Social and Clinical Psychology, 1,* 140–145.

Jones, E. E., & Davis, K. E. (1965). From acts to dispositions: The attribution process in person perception. In L. Berkowitz (Ed.), *Advances in experimental social psychology,* 2. New York: Academic Press.

Jones, E. E., & Goethals, G. R. (1971). Order effects in impression formation: Attribution context and the nature of the entity. In E. E. Jones (Eds.) *Attribution: Perceiving the causes of behavior.* Morristown, NJ: General Learning Press.

Jones, E. E., & Nisbett, R. E. (1971). The actor and the observer: Divergent perceptions of the causes of behavior. In E. E. Jones (Eds.), *Attribution: Perceiving the causes of behavior*. Morristown, NJ: General Learning Press.

Jones, W. H. (1982). Loneliness and social behavior. In L. A. Peplau & D. Perlman (Eds.), *Loneliness: A sourcebook of current theory, research, and therapy*. New York: John Wiley & Sons.

Jones, W. H., Hobbs, S. A., & Hockenbury, D. (1982). Loneliness and social deficits. *Journal of Personality and Social Psychology, 42,* 682–689.

Kelley, H. H. (1967). Attribution theory in social psychology. In D. Levine (Ed.), *Nebraska symposium on motivation* (Vol. 15). Lincoln: University of Nebraska Press.

Kelley, H. H. (1973). The process of causal attribution. *American Psychologist, 28,* 107–128.

Kruglanski, A. W. (1980). Lay epistemo-logic—process and contents: Another look at attribution theory. *Psychological Review, 87,* 70–87.

Kuiper, N. A., Olinger, L. J., & MacDonald, M. R. (in press). Depressive schemata and the processing of personal and social information. In L. B. Alloy (Ed.), *Cognitive processes in depression*. New York: Guilford Press.

Layden, M. A. (1982). Attributional style therapy. In C. Antaki & C. Brewin (Eds.), *Attributions and psychological change*. New York: Academic Press.

Lazarus, A. A. (1968). Learning theory and the treatment of depression. *Behavior Research and Therapy, 6,* 83–89.

Lazarus, R. S. (1966). *Psychological stress and the coping process*. New York: McGraw-Hill.

Lewinsohn, P. M. (1974). Clinical and theoretical aspects of depression. In K. S. Calhoun, H. E. Adams, & K. M. Mitchell (Eds.), *Innovative treatment methods in psychopathology*. New York: John Wiley & Sons.

Lewinsohn, P. M., Mischel, W., Chaplin, W., & Barton, R. (1980). Social competence and depression: The role of illusory self-perceptions? *Journal of Abnormal Psychology, 89,* 203–212.

Lewinsohn, P. M., Steinmetz, J. L., Larson, D. W., & Franklin, J. (1981). Depression-related cognitions: Antecedent or consequence? *Journal of Abnormal Psychology, 90,* 213–219.

Lewinsohn, P. M., Youngren, M. A., & Grosscup, S. J. (1979). Reinforcement and depression. In R. A. Depue (Ed.), *The psychobiology of depressive disorders: Implications for the effects of stress*. New York: Academic Press.

Mahoney, M. J. (1974). *Cognition and behavior modification*. Cambridge, MA: Ballinger.

Manly, P. C., McMahon, R. J., Bradley, C. F., & Davidson, P. O. (1982). Depressive attributional style and depression following childbirth. *Journal of Abnormal Psychology, 91,* 245–254.

Meichenbaum, D. (1977). *Cognitive-behavior modification*. New York: Plenum.

Metlasky, G. I., Abramson, L. Y., Seligman, M. E. P., Semmel, A., & Peterson, C. (1982). Attributional styles and life events in the classroom: Vulnerability and invulnerability to depressive mood reactions. *Journal of Personality and Social Psychology, 43,* 612–617.

Monson, T. C., & Snyder, M. (1977). Actors, observers, and the attribution process. *Journal of Experimental Social Psychology, 13,* 89–111.

O'Hara, M. W., Rehm, L. P., & Campbell, S. B. (1982). Predicting depressive symptomatology: Cognitive-behavioral models and postpartum depression. *Journal of Abnormal Psychology, 91,* 457–461.

Paykel, E. S. (1974). Recent life events and clinical depression. In E. K. Gunderson and R. H. Rahe (Eds.), *Life stress and illness*. Springfield, IL: Charles C. Thomas.

Paykel, E. S., Myers, J. K., Dienelt, M. N., Klerman, G. L., Lindenthal, J. A., & Pepper, M. P. (1969). Life events and depression: A controlled study. *Archives of General Psychiatry, 21,* 753–760.

Peplau, L. A., Russell, D. & Heim, M. (1979). The experience of loneliness. In I. Frieze, D. Bar-Tal, & J. Carroll (Eds.), *New approaches to social problems*. San Francisco: Jossey-Bass.

Peterson, C., Schwartz, S. M., & Seligman, M. E. P. (1981). Self-blame and depressive symptoms. *Journal of Personality and Social Psychology, 41*, 253–259.

Pilkonis, P. A. (1977). The behavioral consequences of shyness. *Journal of Personality, 45*, 596–611.

Pyszczynski, T. A., & Greenberg, J. (1981). Role of disconfirmed expectancies in the instigation of attributional processing. *Journal of Personality and Social Psychology, 40*, 31–38.

Raps, C. S., Peterson, C., Reinhard, K. E., Abramson, L. Y., & Seligman, M. E. P. (1982). Attributional style among depressed patients. *Journal of Abnormal Psychology, 91*, 102–108.

Rehm, L. P. (1977). A self-control model of depression. *Behavior Therapy, 8*, 787–804.

Rehm, L. P. (1982). Self-management in depression. In P. Karoly & F. H. Kanfer (Eds.), *The psychology of self-management: From theory to practice*. New York: Pergamon Press.

Rehm, L. P., & O'Hara, M. W. (1979). Understanding depression. In I. Frieze, D. Bar-Tal, & J. Carroll (Eds.), *New approaches to social problems*. San Francisco: Jossey-Bass.

Rosch, E., Mervis, C. B., Gray, W. D., Johnson, D. M., & Boyes-Braem, P. B. (1976). Basic objects in natural categories. *Cognitive Psychology, 8*, 382–439.

Russell, D., Peplau, L. A., & Cutrona, C. E. (1980). The revised UCLA Loneliness Scale: Concurrent and discriminant validity evidence. *Journal of Personality and Social Psychology, 39*, 472–480.

Russell, D., Peplau, L. A., & Ferguson, M. L. (1978). Developing a measure of loneliness. *Journal of Personality Assessment, 42*, 290–294.

Secunda, S. K. (1973). Special report, 1973: The depressive disorders. Washington, D. C.: National Institute of Mental Health.

Seligman, M. E. P. (1975). *Helplessness: On depression, development, and death*. San Francisco: W. H. Freeman & Co.

Seligman, M. E. P., Abramson, L. Y., Semmel, A., & von Baeyer, C. (1979). Depressive attributional style. *Journal of Abnormal Psychology, 88*, 242–247.

Sisenwein, R. J. (1965). Loneliness and the individual as viewed by himself and others. (Doctoral dissertation. Columbia University, 1964). *Dissertation Abstracts International, 25*, 5379. (University Microfilms No. 65–4768).

Sweeney, P. D., Shaeffer, D., & Golin, S. (1982). Attributions about self and others in depression. *Personality and Social Psychology Bulletin, 8*, 37–42.

Taylor, S. E., & Fiske, S. T. (1978). Salience, attention, and attribution: Top of the head phenomena. In L. Berkowitz (Ed.), *Advances in experimental social psychology* (Vol. 11) New York: Academic Press.

Teglasi, H., & Hoffman, M. A. (1982). Causal attributions of shy subjects. *Journal of Research in Personality, 16*, 376–385.

Weiner, B. (1972). *Theories of motivation: From mechanism to cognition*. Chicago: Rand McNally.

Weiner, B. (Ed.). (1974). *Achievement motivation and attribution theory*. Morristown, NJ: General Learning Press.

Weiner, B. (1979). A theory of motivation for some classroom experiences. *Journal of Educational Psychology, 71*, 3–25.

Weiner, B., Russell, D., & Lerman, D. (1979). The cognition-emotion process in achievement-related contexts. *Journal of Personality and Social Psychology, 37*, 1211–1220.

Weiner, B. & Litman-Adizes, T. (1980). An attributional, expectancy-value analysis of learned helplessness and depression. In J. Garber & M. E. P. Seligman (Eds.), *Human helplessness: Theory and applications*. New York: Academic Press.

Wetzel, C. G. (1982). Self-serving biases in attribution: A Bayesian analysis. *Journal of Personality and Social Psychology, 43,* 197–209.

Wong, P. T. P., & Weiner, B. (1981). When people ask ''why'' questions, and the heuristics of attributional search. *Journal of Personality and Social Psychology, 40,* 650–663.

Wortman, C. B. & Dintzer, L. (1978). Is an attributional analysis of the learned helplessness phenomenon viable?: A critique of the Abramson-Seligman-Teasdale reformulation. *Journal of Abnormal Psychology, 87,* 75–90.

Zimbardo, P. G., Pilkonis, P. A., & Norwood, R. M. (1974). *The silent prison of shyness* (ONR Tech. Rep. No. Z–17). Stanford, CA: Stanford University.

Zuckerman, M., Lubin, B., Vogel, L., & Valerius, E. (1964). Measurement of experimentally induced affects. *Journal of Consulting and Clinical Psychology, 28,* 418–425.

PART III

CONCLUDING COMMENTS

In the final chapter, Olson and Ross place the current volume within the broader historical context of attribution theory and research. Their historical review, of course, begins with Heider's (1944) early theoretical work on social perception and phenomenal causality and highlights the systematic development of this domain of inquiry through 1980. Olson and Ross conclude their review by noting recent dissatisfaction with attribution research. This dissatisfaction, expressed by some critics as well as proponents of attributional perspectives, does not, they argue, foretell the end of work on attributional phenomena. Rather, it marks a transition point. Within this perspective, Olson and Ross take a critical look at each of the chapters in this volume. They note possible strengths and weaknesses of each contribution and suggest directions for future research. More importantly, Olson and Ross identify a number of themes that emerge from several of the chapters and that may provide the foundation for a new era of attribution theory and research.

CHAPTER **10**

Attribution Research: Past Contributions, Current Trends, and Future Prospects*

James M. Olson and Michael Ross

INTRODUCTION

The diversity of topics encompassed by the chapters in this volume attests to the continuing productivity of attribution theory. These topics range from getting back to the "basics" to applying attribution theory to close relationships and depression. Whereas this range has favorable implications for the future of attribution research, it makes the task of summarizing and evaluating the contributions rather formidable. To provide some structure to our analysis, we begin the chapter with a brief history and review of attribution research in social psychology. We then comment on each of the chapters, noting some of their highlights and problems and suggesting possible directions for future research. We close the chapter by listing several themes that emerge from the diverse topics in the volume. Our goal in this chapter is to discuss the current contributions in the context of where attribution research has been and where it appears to be going.

A SELECTIVE REVIEW OF ATTRIBUTION RESEARCH

The origins of attribution theory in social psychology are usually traced to Heider (1944, 1958), whose account of commonsense causal reasoning has exerted a tremendous influence over subsequent theorizing and research. Heider asserted that people are not content simply to observe

*This chapter was prepared while both authors were supported by research grants from the Social Sciences and Humanities Research Council of Canada.

events around them, but strive to understand the causes of these events. He proposed that perceivers are inclined to attribute actions to stable or enduring causes (e.g., personality traits) rather than transitory or variable causes (e.g., moods). Further, factors within the person and factors within the environment stand in an inverse relation to each other: The more the person is seen as causing the action, the less influence the environment will be perceived to exert, and vice versa. Another important aspect of Heider's theorizing was his emphasis on covariation as the major determinant of causal perception. An effect is attributed to a cause that is present when the effect is present and absent when the effect is absent.

In the appendix, we provide a bibliography of articles relevant to attribution theory, beginning with Heider's 1944 paper and continuing through 1980. Despite its length, this bibliography is by no means exhaustive. First, we have attempted to include only publications that have had a significant impact on the field. Our definition of impact is based on the extent to which the work has generated subsequent research or has been cited in articles and textbooks. Second, we limited our choices to papers that fall within the "traditional" domain of attribution theory, which resulted in the exclusion of many excellent publications on related topics (e.g., impression formation, stereotyping, self-fulfilling prophesies, and social cognition). Although the distinctions among these topics are somewhat arbitrary, we focused on articles that examined the effects of causal reasoning on self or social perception. Finally, we readily confess that our own prejudices and biases have guided at least some of the selections and omissions. The purpose of the list is heuristic rather than evaluative; it is intended to illustrate the systematic evolution of attribution research. We stopped at 1980 because it is difficult to assess the impact of more recent work.

Let us now review the bibliography. The 1950s was the era of consistency theories in social psychology, and there was relatively little work directly related to attribution theory. The experiments by Thibaut and Riecken (1955) and by Strickland (1958) were major exceptions. Both studies examined subjects' perceptions of the determinants of compliance.

In the early 1960s, Schachter and Singer (1962) added a new dimension to attributional thinking with their analysis of emotional experience. Their research suggested that individuals could be induced to attribute internal arousal, elicited by an injection of epinephrine, to plausible and salient features of the environment (e.g., an anger-inducing questionnaire). Subsequent interest in misattribution effects can be traced to this work.

The next major event in attribution theory, Jones and Davis's (1965) theory of correspondent inferences, provided a systematized and expanded version of some of Heider's ideas. Jones and Davis described how an "alert perceiver" might infer others' personal dispositions from their behavior. They proposed that observers attribute only intentional behavior to personal dispositions. In addition, they reasoned that nonnormative behaviors are more informative about personal dispositions than are normative behaviors. For example, a target is seen as helpful only if his or her helpfulness exceeds that expected of the average person.

Meanwhile, Bem (1965) was swinging into action with his alternative interpretation of cognitive dissonance phenomena. Using curious terms borrowed from Skinner such as mands and tacts, Bem provided a nonmotivational account of various dissonance findings. Like a lone gunslinger, Bem was taking on hordes of dissonance researchers and, in some eyes at least, winning.

In 1966, there were a number of intriguing empirical publications. Nisbett and Schachter reported a fear misattribution study that established the paradigm for later misattribution research. Valins explored the self-attributional implications of false heart-rate feedback. Walster's analysis of attributions of responsibility for an accident and Lerner and Simmons's examination of observers' reactions to innocent victims initiated important lines of research on the role of motivational factors in person perception.

In 1967, the second major theoretical extension of Heider's work appeared: Kelley's model of the attribution process. Kelley focused on how people establish the validity of their own or another's impressions of an object. He suggested that perceivers seek and examine three different kinds of information: (1) consensus information (Do other people respond to the object in the same way as the target person?), (2) distinctiveness information (Does the target person respond in the same way to other, similar stimuli?), and (3) consistency information (Does the target person always respond in the same way to this object?).

Perhaps the most important aspect of Kelley's paper was his insistence that self-perception as well as social perception is a proper domain for attribution theory. Although this was implicit in Heider's analysis, Jones and Davis (1965) had restricted their discussion to perceptions of others. Kelley expanded Heider's treatment by incorporating Bem's analysis of self-persuasion into the attribution framework. Kelley discarded Bem's Skinnerian terms and developed a general theory of attribution in which the rules governing self-perception were essentially identical to those governing social perception.

The late 1960s and the 1970s produced an outburst of attribution re-search. Some researchers explicitly tested the attribution models of Jones and Davis or Kelley; others utilized the misattribution paradigm of Nisbett and Schachter; and still others followed up the work on motivational factors initiated by Walster and Lerner. Important lines of research included:

1. Jones and Harris's (1967) work on the attribution of attitude, which served as a springboard for several additional developments, such as Jones and Nisbett's statement of the actor–observer hypothesis (in Jones, Kanouse, Kelly, Nisbett, Valins, & Weiner, 1972), L. Ross's (1977) analysis of the fundamental attribution error, and research on the effects of salience on the attribution process (e.g., McArthur & Post, 1977; Pryor & Kriss, 1977; Taylor & Fiske, 1975).

2. Analyses of the layperson's awareness of his or her mental processes. Schachter and Singer (1962) challenged the commonsense view that emotions are directly accessible to consciousness. Similarly, Bem (1967, 1972) argued against the naive view that individuals can access their attitudes on demand. Nisbett and Wilson (1977), however, provided perhaps the greatest blow to the naive view that perceivers have introspective access to their experiences and mental events, proposing that we have little or no direct awareness of the causes of our behavior. This contention has resulted in a lively debate that continues today (see Nisbett & L. Ross, 1980, and M. Ross & Fletcher, in press, for summaries).

3. Work on misattribution. This research typically had two goals. First, it provided empirical tests of the attribution formulations of Schachter and Singer, Kelley, and so forth. Second, it made the case that attribution theory had significant therapeutic implications (e.g., Davison & Valins, 1969; L. Ross, Rodin, & Zimbardo, 1969; Storms & Nisbett, 1970; Valins & Ray, 1967; see M. Ross & Olson, 1981, for a review).

4. Attempts to analyze everyday situations and/or social problems in terms of attribution concepts. This list is almost endless and encompasses such topics as intrinsic motivation (e.g., Deci, 1971; Lepper, Greene, & Nisbett, 1973), learned helplessness (e.g., Abramson, Seligman, & Teasdale, 1978; Diener & Dweck, 1978), and attitude change (e.g., Bem & McConnell, 1970).

There were also theoretical advances, in particular Kelley's (1972, in Jones et al., 1972; Kelley, 1973) and Reeder and Brewer's (1979) elaborations of causal schemata. Kelley's earlier theorizing implied that causal analyses follow a set of formal guidelines and essentially occur anew in each situation. The more recent formulations are based on the plausible assumption that people have preconceptions about causality. This stored knowledge permits the individual to dispense with the formal guidelines and take shortcuts.

A glance at our bibliography indicates that the amount of attribution-related research grew steadily over the 26 years. For a field known for its fads, such sustained growth is impressive. Currently, though, one senses a certain ennui. There are mutterings that we have entered a "postattribution" era. For example, the burgeoning area of social cognition relies heavily on theories imported from cognitive psychology, rather than on our homegrown theories of attribution.

There are some good reasons for the dissatisfaction with research on attributions per se. Studies aimed at testing derivations from the various theories have provided general support but almost always used a paper-and-pencil methodology and a limited range of dependent measures. For example, many researchers assessed only the person–environment dimension of causality. The internal validity of this research was strong; its external validity was questionable. Moreover, one experiment looked pretty much like the next. The area had grown stale.

As a result, we enter the 1980s with at least some of the excitement gone. But although the candle may be flickering, it has certainly not gone out. The 1980s can be a time for renewal. As this volume demonstrates, there are many new issues to be explored, many new applications to be tested. The problem with the attribution area has not been that we answered all of the interesting questions, but rather that we kept addressing the same limited set of issues. Let us now consider how the present volume offers some new perspectives on attributional phenomena.

BASIC PROCESSES

A distinction often made in the attribution literature (e.g., Harvey & Weary, 1984) is between research on the "basic processes" of attributions and research on the "consequences" of attributions. The first category examines such issues as how people combine information to make causal judgments, when attributional processing will occur, and whether judgmental biases can distort causal conclusions. In other words, this research is concerned with the antecedents and concomitants of attributional reasoning. The second category of research examines the consequences of attributions for perceivers' thoughts, emotions, and behaviors. These studies address the effects of attributions once they have been made, rather than the processes underlying the attributions themselves.

In the current volume, Wilson (Chapter 1), Kassin and Baron (Chapter 2), Hansen (Chapter 3), and Reeder (Chapter 4) are primarily concerned with the basic processes of attributions. We will begin our commentary by discussing some of the strengths and limitations of these contributions.

Wilson's chapter (Chapter 1) has its roots in his earlier work with Nisbett on people's awareness of mental processes (Nisbett & Wilson, 1977). Nisbett and Wilson argued that people do not have direct access to the causes of their behavior. Although the research they presented to buttress their argument has been heavily criticized, their major conceptual point should come as no surprise to anyone who accepts the Humean view of causality. It is logically impossible to observe causal processes per se. We can merely observe correlations between events. All causal judgments are just that—judgments based on causal theories and empirical observations. If the true causal determinants conflict with our preconceptions or are nonsalient, we may well make an error in judgment.

In the present volume, Wilson takes what is perhaps a more controversial position: We may lack direct access not only to the causes of behavior but, on occasion, to mental states in general. Wilson suggests that we possess two independent cognitive systems. One is largely unconscious and mediates behavior. The second is largely conscious, and its function is to verbalize and explain mental states. The verbal system often has direct access to mental states and can make accurate reports. When there is indirect access, however, the verbal system makes inferences about these states. An implicit but unstated assumption underlying Wilson's analysis is that people cannot tell when their verbal system is directly reporting versus guessing. It is possible to imagine a model of mind in which individuals have a meta-cognitive awareness of the basis of the verbal system's reports.

Wilson justifies his claim of the verbal system's occasional lack of direct access to mental states in a variety of ways. He begins by attempting to show that self-reports of mental states can be inaccurate. The conundrum, of course, is how to assess accuracy. Self-reports of mental states are defined as accurate when there is a correspondence between these reports and overt behavior which has been shown to be diagnostic of the state in question. Stated thus baldly, Wilson's thesis appears naive. There are numerous pitfalls facing a researcher who declares by fiat that one set of indicants of mental states, namely overt behaviors, is more valid than a second set, namely self-reports. Wilson is sensitive to such issues and deals with them as best he can while acknowledging the difficulties inherent in his analysis.

We take issue, though, with Wilson's review of the overjustification literature where he claims support for the view that overt behaviors provide a better indication of mental states than do self-reports. He adduces support for this conclusion from the finding that the experimental manipulations generally had a greater impact on behavioral measures of intrinsic motivation (e.g., free play with the target activity) than on self-report measures. But the review is oddly one-sided. Studies were included only if they incorporated both sets of measures *and* obtained significant results on the behavioral measure. However, a review that included only studies showing significant effects on self-report measures might well have yielded the opposite conclusion.

Wilson then describes the results of several intriguing studies of his own in which the verbal system was primed experimentally. He presents evidence that certain independent variables can affect one system but not the other, and that priming the verbal system in the domain of attitudes reduces attitude–behavior consistency. These findings are generally compatible with Wilson's analysis, and his speculations about their causes seem plausible. One point that remains unclear, however, is Wilson's suggestion that priming the verbal system somehow alters subjects' attitudes. Yet, he presents data that seem to argue for the essential similarity of attitudes reported with or without priming of the verbal system (equivalent means and variances, etc.). It is difficult to interpret the data without knowing what quality of the attitude is affected by the priming manipulation. Wilson concludes his chapter by describing some of the factors that inhibit direct access to mental states. These ideas are interesting and deserve research attention, although they are methodologically difficult to test.

Kassin and Baron (Chapter 2) call for a reexamination of the basic determinants of attribution. *Basic determinants* are defined as those that activate perceptual rather than inferential attribution processes. Kassin and Baron acknowledge that this distinction is not clear-cut, but they argue persuasively that at least some of our social and causal perception involves automatic processing, including the assessment of emotions from facial configurations and the attribution of personality traits from physical features. Kassin and Baron's thesis is consistent with an emerging recognition in the attribution literature that we need to deemphasize information processing and incorporate perceptual factors into analyses of attributional judgments (e.g., McArthur & Baron, 1983; McArthur & Post, 1977; Nisbett & L. Ross, 1980).

Kassin and Baron review several diverse literatures, including a number of intriguing studies that we, at least, were unfamiliar with. We agree with the general thrust of the chapter and will comment only on their

discussion of perceptions of causality and the role of salience in the attribution process.

The section on perceiving causality should probably be entitled "perceiving physical (inanimate) causality." The analysis refers primarily to
simple, billiard-ball situations. In such contexts, an event is seen as a
cause if it temporally precedes and is spatially and temporally contiguous with an effect. Matters become more complex, however, in the
domain of social perception. Perceivers may recognize that effects can
have proximal and distal causes. For example, behavior can be attributed
to personality dispositions, which in turn might be attributed to one's
upbringing, which in turn might be attributed to the personality of one's
parents, and so on. In short, perceivers can often choose an explanation
from an array of plausible proximal and distal causes to suit their own
needs and goals. In many contexts, causal perception does not seem
particularly automatic or basic.

Kassin and Baron argue that perceptual salience guides perceivers'
selection of a cause from among the various antecedent events: People
tend to attribute effects to salient events. Nisbett and L. Ross (1980)
added a second perceptual characteristic that guides this choice: Events
that resemble the effect tend to be selected as causes (e.g., big effects
need big causes).

It should be emphasized, however, that salience and resemblance are
not simply perceptual dimensions. Factors can be salient because we are
primed to look for certain causes and not others on the basis of past
experience or knowledge. For example, where the personality psychologist sees behavior as caused by personal dispositions, the social psychologist sees it as caused by situational factors. Similarly, consider the
factors that contribute to resemblance. Whether x appears to resemble
y often depends on prior experience and knowledge. For instance, part
of Freud's genius was to spot resemblances where others did not. Like
salience, resemblance is perhaps more conceptual than perceptual.

One of the intriguing claims made by Kassin and Baron is that temporal contiguity is a more basic determinant of causal perception than
is covariation. Both Heider (1958) and Kelley (1967), as well as philosophers such as Hume and John Stuart Mill, emphasized that covariation
is the sine qua non of causal inference. Kassin and Baron base their claim
on the finding that young children appear to attribute an effect to a temporally contiguous event even when the two do not covary across trials.
It is important to distinguish, however, between objective covariation
and perceptions of covariation. We now know that both adults and children see covariation where none exists or overlook covariations that do
occur (Crocker, 1981; Nisbett & L. Ross, 1980). That people may be poor

detectors of "objective covariation" does not necessarily undermine the psychological validity of the covariation principle.

Kassin and Baron provide evidence that objective covariation may not always mediate causal attribution. Nonetheless, the perception of covariation may be critical to the perception of causation. Temporal contiguity may be important because it contributes to the perception of covariation. But will temporally contiguous events that are not seen to covary with the effect be viewed as causes, even by young children? We suspect not. Will people, even young children, see a causal connection when temporal contiguity is violated, but an event is perceived to covary with an effect? We suspect that the answer to this question is "yes."

These comments notwithstanding, we welcome Kassin and Baron's call to examine attribution in new contexts and using dependent measures other than self-reports. We agree that there is a need to examine more basic attributions. But we also welcome the move, illustrated by several other chapters in the current volume, toward examining the highly inferential attributions involved in everyday life (e.g., within close relationships—see Fincham, Chapter 8). To this point, most attribution research has occupied a middle-ground between the basic research called for by Kassin and Baron and research on attributions occurring in more naturalistic settings. By all means, let us venture out in both directions. Our own suspicion is that the process of making attributions may well be simpler than many attribution theorists have implied, often being influenced by such factors as perceptual salience, whereas the content of causal explanations resulting from this process may well be more diverse than is commonly assumed, incorporating causal factors that are unique to the behavioral domain and recognizing multiple causation. This "process simplicity" versus "content complexity" idea is reflected in the contrasting perspectives taken in the next two chapters to be discussed.

Hansen (Chapter 3) argues that causal thought is economic and that its goal is to establish a "reasonable" rather than an accurate view of causal reality. According to this perspective, attribution theorists like Kelley (1967) or Jones and Davis (1965), with their emphasis on causal precision, fail to capture commonsense causal logic.

Perhaps the most interesting aspect of Hansen's chapter is his attempt to make Kelley's ANOVA model more consistent with commonsense causal analyses. According to Hansen, perceivers may make use of consensus, consistency, and distinctiveness information even though they do not systematically sample from all three dimensions before venturing a causal attribution. Hansen suggests that perceivers begin with a causal guess. If the guess suggests a person attribution, they then search for distinctiveness information to assess the accuracy of their hunch. If the causal guess implies a stimulus attribution, then perceivers search for consensus information.

Of course, people may not recognize that their attribution is a guess or hypothesis. As Heider (1958) noted, observers tend to attribute their own reactions to the object world. When I enjoy a movie, I assume that it is a good movie (stimulus attribution). If I bother to think about others at all, I assume that consensus would obtain. Perceivers are likely to engage in information search only when they lack confidence in their attributions. If I know that my preferences in movies are often not shared by others, I may appreciate that such judgments reflect personal tastes. I may then hesitate to make a stimulus attribution in the absence of consensus information. It is possible that Hansen's discussions of "minimal causal processing" and "causal schemas" address these sorts of situations; we found the latter portions of his chapter difficult to understand.

Finally, the major thrust of Hansen's chapter, its proposed marriage of attribution and social cognition research, deserves comment. We agree that these literatures have much to offer one another. But whether the directions suggested by Hansen constitute the most productive avenues for integrative work is debateable. Hansen calls for "molecular" models of attribution, focusing on event schemas and other cognitive structures relevant to the perceiver's causal understanding. But the roles of more social factors, such as motivation and interpersonal dynamics, are generally ignored. We are more optimistic about the value of attribution research than Hansen appears to be in his concluding comments.

Almost alone in social psychology, Reeder and his colleagues (e.g., Reeder & Brewer, 1979) have stressed that the content of dispositional attributions is important. Other theorists have generally ignored distinctions among the different kinds of dispositions (attitudes, abilities, personality characteristics, etc.) in their analyses of when and how perceivers infer personal dispositions from behaviors. In the present volume (Chapter 4), Reeder discusses this content specificity theme with regard to Kelley's (1972) discounting principle. The discounting principle states that attributors will perceive a given cause as contributing less to an effect if other plausible causes are also present. Reeder notes that there is a voluminous literature relevant to the discounting hypothesis, and the data are rather mixed. Reeder attempts to make sense of the apparently inconsistent results by pointing out that people's inferences are affected by the content of the behavior and the trait in question.

The typical experiment assesses subjects' propensity to attribute a target's actions to personal dispositions when strong external constraints on the behavior are either present or absent. Theoretically, the contribution of personal dispositions should be discounted in the presence of external constraints. Reeder suggests that discounting is less likely to occur in some contexts, for example, when the behavior is nonnormative in that it is extreme, immoral, or reflects a high degree of social skills or ability.

Perhaps the most intriguing implication of Reeder's chapter, in our opinion, is that there may be a discrepancy between self- and social perception in the application of the discounting principle. Most of the chapter is focused on social perception, but Reeder describes several studies that use self-reports of attitude as a criterion for assessing the accuracy of observers' attributions. These data suggest that actors are more likely to apply the discounting principle than are observers. More generally, we wonder whether the schematic implications of behavior are sometimes reversed in the context of self-perception.

A reversal could occur because actors and observers frequently judge a behavior against different reference scales. An observer tends to compare the actor's behavior with that of other actors. In contrast, actors typically use an idiographic reference scale: They assess their behavior in light of their own previous actions (Jones & Nisbett, 1972). Discounting should occur in self-perception when external factors are available to explain behaviors discrepant from past actions. Suppose actors behave in an extreme fashion relative to their own previous actions, for example, say nicer things about Castro than they ever said before. They should then quite readily attribute the behavior to plausible external factors. Observers, on the other hand, would probably view the same behavior as nonnormative with respect to the actions of other targets. As a consequence, observers may be unlikely to apply the discounting principle, instead inferring a personal disposition. Using the same logic, let us consider judgments of morality. Most people probably see themselves as moral. Thus, for actors' self-attributions, external constraints should lead to discounting when a behavior is immoral but not when a behavior is moral. Again, observers who use others' actions as the normative standard may show the opposite pattern, discounting moral but not immoral behavior.

Note that we are not arguing that the attribution process is fundamentally different in self- and social perception. Actors and observers may simply base their inferences on different data. When observers reckon a behavior to be nonnormative, they see it as diagnostic of personal dispositions even when the behavior occurs in the presence of external constraints. If actors view the same behavior as discrepant from their past actions, they apply the discounting principle in the presence of the external constraints.

Finally, we hope that Reeder's general concern with the content of dispositional attributions will be incorporated into other attribution models. It has important implications for attributional phenomena beyond the discounting principle and promises to increase the ecological validity of our theoretical formulations.

CONSEQUENCES OF ATTRIBUTIONS

An increasing trend in the attribution literature has been the investigation of the *consequences* of attributions, that is, the effects of attributions on perceivers' subsequent thoughts, emotions, and behaviors. Of course, the importance of these topics was recognized even in the earliest statements of attribution theory. Heider (1958) argued that perceivers make attributions in order to predict and control the world around them; Kelley (1967) proposed that attributions for our own and others' actions allow us to respond effectively in the social environment. Indeed, if attributions did not have direct consequences for emotions or behavior, then the concept would lose much of its appeal for social psychologists—attributions would be relegated to the status of an "epiphenomenon," perhaps interesting insofar as they reflect individuals' naive theories about causality, but lacking explanatory power for social behavior.

Fortunately, researchers have documented numerous consequences of attributions, encompassing a wide variety of dependent measures. These studies can be grouped into two major categories, although some research straddles our distinction. One approach has been to investigate the everyday consequences of attributional inferences within common, nonpathological domains. These researchers have identified many important, practical implications of everyday attributions. Early, well-known examples of this approach include Lepper et al.'s (1973) demonstration of the effects of extrinsic rewards on the perception of intrinsic motivation, the research by Weiner and his colleagues (e.g., Weiner, Frieze, Kukla, Reed, Rest, & Rosenbaum, 1972) on the cognitive, affective, and behavioral consequences of attributions in achievement settings, and research following from Schachter's (1964) attributional analysis of emotions, which has focused on the emotional and behavioral consequences of misattributing arousal symptoms to an erroneous cause. An interesting observation is that research on the everyday consequences of attributions has focused on self-attributions, rather than attributions about others' actions. Although self-attributions have not been the exclusive target of this approach (e.g., see Regan's 1978 attributional analysis of interpersonal attraction), they have certainly dominated theorists' attention. We are uncertain why this emphasis has occurred, particularly since the original statements of attribution theory were primarily concerned with causal judgments about the behavior of others (and most research on the basic processes of attribution has continued to be other-focused). One possibility is that the consequences of self-attributions are easier to study. Another reason may be that self-attribution topics (intrinsic motivation, misattribution, etc.) have generally been more interesting, surprising, and practically important than social perception questions, which have tended to revolve around how observers apply logical principles to infer others' dispositions. In this context, recent work on social perception is moving toward a more dynamic, interactive approach to interpersonal attributions; this integration of self and social perception promises to reduce the dominance of research on the consequences of self-attributions per se. Nevertheless, at the current time, there is relatively little evidence that our attributions about others' actions have important consequences, especially for our behavior in interpersonal settings.

The second major approach to investigating the consequences of attributions has applied attributional principles to important social problems. Researchers have provided novel perspectives on social problems that were previously interpreted in nonattributional ways, most often in terms of environmental or personality factors. Well-known examples of this approach include the work by Seligman and his colleagues who applied attributional principles to the understanding of learned helplessness and depression (e.g., Abramson et al., 1978), attributional analyses of helping behavior (e.g., Ickes & Kidd, 1976), and the investigation of the role of attributions in conflict and distress within close relationships (e.g., Harvey, Wells, & Alvarez, 1978; Orvis, Kelley, & Butler, 1976). The diversity of possible applications of attribution principles to social problems is illustrated by the recent volume edited by Frieze, Bar-Tal, and Carroll (1979).

Although they do not all fit neatly within our distinction between the two major approaches to studying the consequences of attributions, it seems that Pittman and D'Agostino (Chapter 5), Hill, Weary, Hildebrand-Saints, and Elbin (Chapter 6), and Arkin and Baumgardner (Chapter 7), reflect the tradition of investigating the everyday consequences of attributional inferences within a particular domain. Fincham (Chapter 8) and Anderson and Arnoult (Chapter 9), on the other hand, clearly illustrate the application of attributional principles to social problems.

Pittman and D'Agostino (Chapter 5) describe the effects of "control

deprivation." They suggest that being exposed to an uncontrollable situation threatens the assumption that one's understanding of the environment is satisfactory. This occurrence arouses a motivation to
reestablish control and increases the efficiency of subsequent information processing. Pittman and D'Agostino present a series of experiments
that test the implications of this hypothesis, ranging from the specific
consequences of control deprivation for the accuracy of attributional
judgments to the limits of the phenomenon in terms of prior expectations of control. Taken together, these studies provide convincing evidence that control motivation results from exposure to uncontrollable
situations and that this motivation is an important determinant of perceivers' spontaneous utilization of relevant information in their attributional judgments.

Pittman and D'Agostino's suggestion that chronic individual differences in control motivation may exist is intriguing. The possible link
between control deprivation and depression noted by the authors is one
potential avenue for such research, but numerous other personality factors may also be relevant (e.g., locus of control, self-esteem, and achievement motivation).

We found one aspect of Pittman and D'Agostino's chapter confusing.
They point out that certain attributional biases may reflect a desire for
control, such as the self-serving bias, the overestimation of control over
random events, and the belief in a controllable or just world. Then they
ask how control motivation will affect such biases; rather than its typical
effect of increasing the accuracy of attributional inferences, perhaps control motivation will exacerbate these control-relevant biases. This is indeed an interesting hypothesis. We do not believe, however, that the
experiment reported by Pittman, Quattrone, and Jones (1983) fully tested
it. Pittman et al. showed that control deprivation reduced the *attitude
attribution bias*, that is, the tendency to attribute attitudes to a target person that are consistent with an essay he or she wrote under no-choice
conditions. Presumably, control deprivation motivated careful processing of the no-choice information. But this attitude attribution error seems
unlikely to be motivated by a desire for control; instead, it is generally
interpreted in cognitive terms, such as focus of attention or implicational
schemas (see Reeder, Chapter 4). Although motivational interpretations
are possible, they are not as compelling for this bias as for others (e.g.,
the self-serving and overestimation of control biases). Thus, the question of how control deprivation will affect attributional biases that are
themselves motivated by a desire for control is not directly addressed
by Pittman et al.'s data. Will control deprivation decrease such biases
by producing careful monitoring of relevant information, or will it exacerbate such biases by increasing the desire for control?

In their chapter on the social comparison of causal understandings (Chapter 6), Hill, Weary, Hildebrand-Saints, and Elbin examine the effects of similar versus dissimilar attributions for a target's behavior on attraction between two observers. This work provides an intriguing integration of several disparate research areas, including the attribution, social comparison, self-presentation, and similarity-liking literatures. The reported studies are interesting, although the hypothesized processes underlying the obtained findings remain speculative. For example, the authors distinguish between social comparison and consensual validation motives for comparisons with others. It should be possible to collect evidence on which of these motives are operative in a given setting by measuring such variables as individuals' confidence in their attributions and their affective states following comparison with agreeing or disagreeing others. Yet, Hill et al. focused only on subjects' liking for the comparison person; it is questionable whether the attraction findings necessarily reflected the assumed psychological mechanisms.

Numerous ideas for future research can be derived from Hill et al.'s work. Some of the more straightforward possibilities are investigations of the consequences of comparisons by actors, comparing their self-attributions for their own behavior with the attributions made by observers (rather than the two-observers paradigm utilized by Hill et al.) and investigations of the effects of social comparison processes on perceivers' *confidence* in their attributions, a variable that has received a lot of attention in the literature on comparisons of abilities and opinions. Another issue concerns individuals' spontaneous desires to engage in social comparisons of attributions. Hill et al. forced subjects to compare their judgments with that of another person; future research should examine whether such processes will occur in the absence of external pressures. We also see some intriguing possibilities for research on how similarity along related attributes (e.g., attitudes and values) affects perceivers' selection of comparison others. Individuals who are seeking only consensual validation may prefer similar comparison persons, since such persons are most likely to agree with their original attributions. To the extent that perceivers want to establish the accuracy or validity of their attributions, however, they may prefer dissimilar comparison persons, who do not share their biases or idiosyncracies (Goethals & Nelson, 1973). Note that we are using *similarity* in this context to refer to similarity along nonattributional dimensions, whereas Hill et al. use the term as a synonym for attributional agreement. Our use of the term coincides with its general meaning in the social comparison literature, so it would probably clarify matters to label Hill et al.'s concept of similarity of attributions as "agreement."

Arkin and Baumgardner (Chapter 7) provide a cogent analysis of *self-*

handicapping strategies, whereby individuals seek or create inhibitory factors that interfere with success and thus provide a reasonable explanation for potential failure. Their organizational scheme of internal–external × acquired–claimed impediments is valuable, as is their analysis of possible motives underlying self-handicapping, that is, protective–acquisitive × public–private motivations. The authors conclude that self-handicapping phenomena illustrate the potent effects of ability attributions on individuals' self-esteem; self-handicappers are willing both to increase their objective probability of failure and to accept such undesirable labels as "drunk" and "test anxious" in order to avoid the even more threatening label of "low ability."

One interesting issue that is raised in the chapter concerns individuals' selection of a particular impediment from the range of possible choices. The authors discuss some of the advantages and disadvantages of different strategies (e.g., "external" impediments may have fewer negative implications for the self-handicapper, but may also provide less convincing explanations for failure than "internal" impediments); it should be possible to derive from this analysis some predictions concerning subjects' choices of strategies under various conditions and/or individual differences that will be associated with the selection of a particular strategy.

Perhaps not surprisingly, the least satisfying section of Arkin and Baumgardner's chapter concerns the effectiveness of self-handicapping strategies. This issue is difficult to investigate and is a relatively recent topic in the literature. Nevertheless, it is an important aspect of the phenomenon, and there are data that pertain to it. In a recent study by McFarland and M. Ross (1982), internal ability attributions for failure produced more negative affect and lower feelings of self-esteem than did similar attributions for success, whereas the affective consequences of outcome were eliminated by external, task difficulty attributions. These data suggest that, assuming the existence of "private" self-handicapping, the presence of an inhibitory factor (the impediment) will protect the individual's self-esteem should failure occur. In terms of ego-protection, self-handicapping may indeed be effective. A second possible reason for self-handicapping, perhaps the more common one, is to maintain a positive public image. This self-presentational goal, according to Arkin and Baumgardner, is likely to be achieved only for a minority of observers; namely, those who view effort and ability as inversely related. Thus, Arkin and Baumgardner conclude that self-handicapping is probably less effective as an impression-management strategy than most self-handicappers realize. We would feel more confident about the validity of their analysis if there were direct data on observers' reactions to self-handicapping. Also, lack of effort is only one impediment that self-handicappers may select; Arkin and Baumgardner's reasoning does not seem to apply to other strategies, such as the creation of external impediments.

We are intrigued by Arkin and Baumgardner's observation that self-handicapping can be viewed, ironically, as a strategy for maintaining one's sense of control. In reality, of course, self-handicapping reduces control by interfering with performance. Nevertheless, individuals may decide to risk failure in order to maintain an illusion of control and to avoid the costs associated with unambiguous evidence of incompetence. In this context, the adaptiveness of self-handicapping becomes an interesting question. If failure seems likely irrespective of one's efforts, then self-handicapping may not be a maladaptive strategy in that it is not increasing the chances of failure. The problem confronting the potential self-handicapper is to assess the objective probabilities of success and failure, the conditional probabilities of success and failure given the creation of an impediment, and the costs and benefits of success and failure in these two situations. This analysis suggests that models of decision making under uncertainty may provide a heuristically valuable perspective on self-handicapping (see Fischhoff, 1976, for a related discussion of possible integrations of decision-making and attribution research).

Finally, there appear to be some important parallels between control motivation and self-handicapping strategies. In a sense, these phenomena reflect differing responses to the same threat, namely the threat of attributions of low ability. Self-handicapping occurs when failure seems likely; this strategy allows the individual to avoid diagnostic information, sometimes via effort reduction, thereby eliminating the possibility of unambiguous evidence of incompetence. Control motivation results from brief exposure to an uncontrollable situation. It produces an eagerness for diagnostic information—the individual increases effort expenditure and actively seeks to test his or her ability to control the environment. Thus, self-handicapping reflects individuals' desire to avoid an attribution of low ability, whereas control motivation reflects individuals' need to reestablish their self-attribution of high ability. This comparison suggests that an integration of these literatures may be possible. For example, control motivation should reduce self-handicapping when the perceived chances of success are reasonable, and chronic individual differences in control motivation may be inversely related to chronic tendencies to self-handicap.

Fincham (Chapter 8) applies attribution theory to the understanding of close relationships and the treatment of relationship problems. He reports data showing that distressed couples seem to make maladaptive attributions for their spouse's behaviors, which accentuate negative actions and undermine positive actions by the spouse. His argument that the traditional dimensions of causality examined in attribution research (internal–external, stable–unstable, etc.) are inadequate for describing attributions within close relationships is quite convincing. For example, the content of causal explanations for spouse behaviors appear to reflect such categories as internal and external causes unrelated to the dyad, internal causes within the perceiver or the spouse, and relationship causes (properties unique to the dyad). Fincham's analysis of different types of relationships is also illuminating. For example, he suggests that "exchange" versus "communal" relationships may differ in their tendency to evoke causal explanations for a partner's behaviors.

Fincham admits the limitations of his cross-sectional data: It is impossible to know whether maladaptive attributions cause relationship distress or relationship problems lead to maladaptive attribution styles (or, indeed, whether other personal or relationship characteristics cause both of these symptoms). Of course, it seems quite reasonable to expect that attributions and distress in close relationships are reciprocally interdependent. Nevertheless, it is important that clearer causal data be obtained. Since experimental approaches are difficult in this domain (although some experiments have been conducted, e.g., Seligman, Fazio, & Zanna, 1980), longitudinal studies of the relation between attribution styles and relationship satisfaction appear to hold the most promise. The second important goal of future research should be to document the overt, behavioral consequences of attributions in close relationships. Fincham's studies measured only behavioral intentions; researchers must observe overt actions between relationship partners in order to understand how various attributions impact on the interaction process.

One section of Fincham's chapter that especially piqued our interest was his suggestion that relationship phases moderate the attribution process. The idea that attributions will be more salient and more frequent during the formation and/or dissolution of a relationship than during the intervening maintenance phase seems plausible (see Harvey et al., 1978, for a related discussion of the intense attributional activity during marital breakdown). We suspect, however, that relationship phases have wider-ranging effects on the attribution process than simply affecting its salience or frequency of activation. For example, it seems likely that individuals are concerned about different attributional questions during the various phases of their relationship. In the formative stage, attributions about the partner, such as his or her traits, needs, or goals, probably dominate. During the maintenance phase, it seems possible that relationship attributions dominate; the dyad may be viewed as a psychological unit, and events within the relationship may therefore be understood primarily in terms of the norms, agreements, and so on, that have developed. During the dissolution phase, attributions about the partner may again dominate, although factors external to the dyad also seem likely to become salient. The formative and dissolution phases may also increase the frequency of self-attributions, relative to the maintenance phase, again reflecting the "individual" versus "group" perspectives that may be salient during the different phases.

Anderson and Arnoult (Chapter 9) apply attribution principles to the problems of depression, loneliness, and shyness. They present an attributional model of these problems, based on the notion that maladaptive attributions reduce individuals' expectations of success, which then reduce their motivation and subsequent performance. The resultant failure perpetuates the problem. Anderson and Arnoult's work builds upon Weiner's (Weiner et al., 1972) research on achievement attributions and Seligman's (e.g., Abramson, Seligman, & Teasdale, 1978) theorizing about learned helplessness and depression. The present authors argue, however, that the most important dimension underlying maladaptive attributions is a controllable–uncontrollable factor (rather than the more widely discussed dimensions of internal–external, stable–unstable, and global–specific). They provide data which show that the various dimensions of causality are confounded and that the controllability dimension is central in attributional styles associated with the social problems, although the absolute sizes of the relations are modest. Further, by measuring subjects' attributional styles within both interpersonal and noninterpersonal domains, they demonstrate that loneliness and shyness are related to attributions of uncontrollability in the interpersonal domain only, whereas depression is also associated with non-interpersonal attributions of uncontrollability. Finally, in their "correlational experiment," the authors provide evidence that attributional manipulations can eliminate the effects of chronic attributional styles, either facilitating or impairing performance in the manner predicted by their theoretical model. Overall, this chapter makes a strong case for the role of attributions in depression, loneliness, and shyness, and serves as a useful counterpoint to recent criticisms of cognitive models of these problems (e.g., Coyne & Gotlib, 1983).

Although Anderson and Arnoult's correlational experiment showed that attribution manipulations can affect performance, the effects of such manipulations on feelings of depression, and so on, were not assessed. Data showing that changes in attributional styles are associated with changes in the social problems would provide more compelling support for the postulated model. Another issue that requires attention is the role of affect in the hypothesized process. As Anderson and Arnoult point out, it is unclear whether affect results from individuals' attributions, performance outcomes, or some other element in the sequence. Indeed, it is even unclear whether affect plays any causal role in the development of the social problems. We hope that future research will examine the role of affect directly.

Finally, the conceptual overlap between Anderson and Arnoult's analysis of social problems, Pittman and D'Agostino's work on control motivation, and Arkin and Baumgardner's model of self-handicapping is worth noting. All three chapters assume that the perception of control is important for attributional phenomena. Pittman and D'Agostino show that brief exposure to an uncontrollable situation motivates greater effort toward careful processing of subsequent information. Anderson and Arnoult demonstrate that chronic tendencies to attribute outcomes to uncontrollable factors are associated with social problems, which may be exacerbated by a lack of effort or motivation to improve one's fortunes. Arkin and Baumgardner show that individuals may withdraw effort, or create some other impediment to success, prior to engaging in a task where failure seems likely. Thus, these contributions share some important features, and the overlap between their target behaviors suggests that a theoretical integration might be profitable. For example, previous and anticipated success–failure may contribute to these phenomena. Perhaps exposure to an uncontrollable situation arouses control motivation when future success (control) seems possible, but produces self-handicapping when failure seems likely. Control motivation may also be more likely when previous outcomes were ambiguous, whereas self-handicapping may occur when the individual experienced apparently random success. Depression, on the other hand, may result from unambiguous evidence of previous failure, producing both self-denigration and a sense of hopelessness about the future. Prolonged lack of control may also be necessary for depression, unlike the brief exposures that produce control motivation. Of course, the mediating factors that influence both perceptions of previous outcomes and expectations about the future are complex (e.g., personality characteristics, past experiences, etc.) and would need to be specified in an integrative model.

CONCLUSIONS

As we stated at the outset of our commentary, the chapters in the present volume encompass a broad spectrum of work on attribution processes. They include both basic and applied attribution topics and explore both the antecedents and consequences of attributional inferences. As such, they illustrate that attribution processes are important for understanding a variety of social phenomena and that the 1980s can, indeed, be a time for renewal in the attribution literature. We hope that our comments have indicated the merits of the present contributions, as well as some of their limitations and some remaining gaps in our knowledge. We are confident that attribution research has more to add to our understanding of social behavior; some of the existing gaps will soon be closed.

Despite the diversity of the present contributions, it is possible to identify a number of themes in the volume beyond such basic ones as a common interest in attributions. We have identified nine themes; other readers might come up with more. Each of these themes is reflected in several chapters, and each represents, we believe, an emerging trend in the attribution literature. Let us close our chapter by listing these nine themes.

1. *Control.* The perception of control is emerging as an important element in attribution models. Research on learned helplessness and depression, control motivation, self-handicapping, and self-serving attributional biases all reflect this trend. Control may become a major integrative theme in the attribution literature.

2. *Individual differences.* Another theme in the present volume is the concern with individual differences in attributions. Attributional styles have become an important element in many applications of attribution theory to social problems, and personality factors are receiving increased attention from attribution researchers. Besides increasing our predictive power, this trend promises to clarify the psychological mechanisms underlying attributions.

3. *Etiology of attributions.* Several authors in this volume comment on environmental or historical factors that may produce a particular attributional phenomenon. There seems to be an increasing interest in the development or etiology of attributions, especially in the context of social problems.

4. *Basic processes of attribution.* Research on so-called "basic processes" of attribution also continues apace, despite the increasing trend toward applications of attribution principles to everyday problems and situations. As indicated by several chapters in the present volume, our understanding of the attribution process is becoming more sophisticated (although "more sophisticated" sometimes means becoming conceptually simpler; see Chapter 2, Kassin and Baron and Chapter 3, Hansen).

5. *Dimensions of causality.* A recurring observation in the current volume is that the traditional dimensions presumed to underlie causal ex-

planations (internal–external and stable–unstable) are inadequate to describe the diversity of attributions in everyday life. This recognition of the complexity and multidimensionality of causal explanations has occurred, in part, as a result of moving attribution research into real-life settings.

6. *Domain specificity.* A related theme in this volume is that characteristics of particular content domains can modify the nature and/or the process of attributional inferences. One consequence has been the development of attributional "mini-theories"—models that apply only to a specific problem or context. This trend may have reduced the integrativeness of the attribution literature, but it has also increased the ecological validity of the models themselves.

7. *Motivational factors.* Historically, attribution researchers have paid little attention to affective and motivational factors, instead emphasizing the cognitive and rational aspects of causal judgments. Motivation is becoming important, though, as topics like control motivation and depression appear in the attribution literature. Attributional inferences may be guided by rational thinking, but they are probably instigated and biased by a variety of motivational forces. Also, there has been a tendency for social psychologists to view cognition and motivation as mutually exclusive; either one or the other is presumed to underlie a particular phenomenon. Recent attribution work, however, reflects the more reasonable and productive position that these factors interact. Both cognitive and motivational processes influence causal perceptions, often simultaneously.

8. *Self-presentation factors.* A related trend is the increasing attention being paid in the attribution literature to self-presentation or impression-management factors. Several authors in the present volume, for example, show that attributions in public settings can be conceptualized, at least in part, as attempts to create a favorable impression of oneself. This recognition that attributions may serve goals other than causal understanding is important because it underscores the social context of attributional statements.

9. *Interpersonal consequences.* Finally, a theme of several chapters in the present volume is that attributions have important consequences for interpersonal behavior. As social psychologists interested in understanding social behavior, we hope that this trend will grow stronger as the attribution literature matures.

In closing, we believe that the trends in the attribution literature discussed above are helping to rekindle excitement in attribution theory. Recent developments have also given the attribution literature an identity quite distinct from the growing social cognition area. Some authors (e.g., Hansen, Chapter 3) call for an integration of the attribution and social cognition literatures. We agree that fruitful collaborative work is possible. At the same time, though, we value the unique qualities of the attribution approach. Social cognition researchers have, for the most part, restricted their attention to cognitive phenomena, staying "within the head" of the perceiver. In contrast, attribution researchers have increasingly incorporated affective and behavioral measures into their studies and have moved their research into dynamic, interpersonal settings. As a consequence, we believe that the attribution literature holds promise for becoming a true "*social* psychology of interpersonal cognition," both distinct from and complementary to social cognition's cognitive emphasis.

APPENDIX: BIBLIOGRAPHY OF SELECTED HIGHLIGHTS OF ATTRIBUTION THEORY AND RESEARCH, 1944–1980

1944
Heider, F. Social perception and phenomenal causality. *Psychological Review, 51*, 358–374.
1955
Thibaut, J. W., & Riecken, H. W. Some determinants and consequences of the perception of social causality. *Journal of Personality, 24*, 113–133.
1958
Heider, F. *The psychology of interpersonal relations.* New York: Wiley.
Jones, E. E., & Thibaut, J. W. Interaction goals as bases of inference in interpersonal perception. In R. Tagiuri & L. Petrullo (Eds.), *Person perception and interpersonal behavior.* Stanford, CA: Stanford University Press.
Strickland, L. H. Surveillance and trust. *Journal of Personality, 26*, 200–215.
1961
Jones, E. E., Davis, K. E., & Gergen, K. J. Role playing variations and their informational value for person perception. *Journal of Abnormal and Social Psychology, 63*, 302–310.
1962
Schachter, S., & Singer, J. E. Cognitive, social, and physiological determinants of emotional state. *Psychological Review, 69*, 379–399.
1964
Schachter, S. The interaction of cognitive and physiological determinants of emotional state. In L. Berkowitz (Ed.), *Advances in experimental social psychology* (Vol. 1). New York: Academic Press.
1965
Bem, D. J. An experimental analysis of self-persuasion. *Journal of Experimental Social Psychology, 1*, 199–218.
Jones, E. E., & Davis, K. E. From acts to dispositions: The attribution process in person perception. In L. Berkowitz (Ed.), *Advances in experimental social psychology* (Vol. 2). New York: Academic Press.

1966

Bem, D. J. Inducing belief in false confessions. *Journal of Personality and Social Psychology,* 3, 707–710.

Lerner, M. J., & Simmons, C. H. Observer's reaction to the innocent victim: Compassion or rejection? *Journal of Personality and Social Psychology,* 4, 203–210.

Nisbett, R. E., & Schachter, S. Cognitive manipulation of pain. *Journal of Experimental Social Psychology,* 2, 227–236.

Rotter, J. B. Generalized expectancies for internal versus external control of reinforcement. *Psychological Monographs, 80* (Whole No. 609).

Valins, S. Cognitive effects of false heart-rate feedback. *Journal of Personality and Social Psychology,* 4, 400–408.

Walster, E. The assignment of responsibility for an accident. *Journal of Personality and Social Psychology,* 3, 73–79.

1967

Bem, D. J. Self-perception: An alternative interpretation of cognitive dissonance phenomena. *Psychological Review, 74,* 183–200.

Jones, E.E., & Harris, V. A. The attribution of attitudes. *Journal of Experimental Social Psychology,* 3, 1–24.

Kelley, H. H. Attribution theory in social psychology. In D. Levine (Ed.), *Nebraska symposium on motivation* (Vol. 15). Lincoln: University of Nebraska Press.

Valins, S., & Ray, A. Effects of cognitive desensitization on avoidance behavior. *Journal of Personality and Social Psychology, 20,* 239–250.

1968

Bandler, R. J., Madaras, G. R., & Bem, D. J. Self-observation as a source of pain perception. *Journal of Pesonality and Social Psychology,* 9, 205–209.

deCharms, R. *Personal causation.* New York: Academic Press.

Jones, E. E., Rock, L., Shaver, K. G., Goethals, G. R., & Ward, L. M. Pattern of performance and ability attribution: An unexpected primacy effect. *Journal of Personality and Social Psychology, 10,* 317–340.

1969

Davison, G., & Valins, S. Maintenance of self-attributed and drug-attributed behavior change. *Journal of Personality and Social Psychology, 11,* 25–33.

Kiesler, C. A., Nisbett, R. E., & Zanna, M. P. On inferring one's beliefs from one's behavior. *Journal of Personality and Social Psychology, 11,* 321–327.

Ross, L., Rodin, J., & Zimbardo, P. G. Toward an attribution therapy: The reduction of fear through induced cognitive-emotional misattribution. *Journal of Personality and Social Psychology, 12,* 279–288.

1970

Bem, D. J., & McConnell, H. K. Testing the self-perception explanation of dissonance phenomena: On the salience of premanipulation attitudes. *Journal of Personality and Social Psychology, 14,* 23–31.

Storms, M., & Nisbett, R. E. Insomnia and the attribution process. *Journal of Personality and Social Psychology, 16,* 319–328.

Weiner, B., & Kukla, A. An attributional analysis of achievement motivation. *Journal of Personality and Social Psychology, 15,* 1–20.

1971

Deci, E. L. Effects of externally mediated rewards on intrinsic motivation. *Journal of Personality and Social Psychology, 18,* 105–115.

Dienstbier, R. A., & Munter, P. C. Cheating as a function of the labeling of natural arousal. *Journal of Personality and Social Psychology, 17,* 208–213.

1972

Bem, D. J. Self-perception theory. In L. Berkowitz (Ed.), *Advances in experimental social psychology* (Vol. 6). New York: Academic Press.

Dion, K., Berscheid, E., & Walster, E. What is beautiful is good. *Journal of Personality and Social Psychology, 24,* 285–290.

Jones, E. E., Kanouse, D. E., Kelley, H. H., Nisbett, R. E., Valins, S., & Weiner, B. (Eds.). *Attribution: Perceiving the causes of behavior.* Morristown, NJ: General Learning Press.

McArthur, L. A. The how and what of why: Some determinants and consequences of causal attribution. *Journal of Personality and Social Psychology, 22,* 171–193.

1973

Chaikin, A. L., & Darley, J. M. Victim or perpetrator?: Defensive attribution of responsibility and the need for order and justice. *Journal of Personality and Social Psychology, 25,* 268–275.

Goethals, G. R., & Reckman, R. F. The perception of consistency in attitudes. *Journal of Experimental Social Psychology, 9,* 491–501.

Jones, E. E., & Wortman, C. *Ingratiation: An attributional approach.* Morristown, NJ: General Learning Press.

Kelley, H. H. The process of causal attribution. *American Psychologist, 28,* 107–128.

Lepper, M. R. Dissonance, self-perception, and honesty in children. *Journal of Personality and Social Psychology, 25,* 65–74.

Lepper, M. R., Greene, D., & Nisbett, R. E. Undermining children's intrinsic interest with extrinsic reward: A test of the "overjustification" hypothesis. *Journal of Personality and Social Psychology, 28,* 129–137.

Nisbett, R. E., Caputo, C., Legant, P., & Marecek, J. Behavior as seen by the actor and as seen by the observer. *Journal of Personality and Social Psychology, 27,* 154–165.

Storms, M. D. Videotape and the attribution process: Reversing actors' and observers' points of view. *Journal of Personality and Social Psychology, 27,* 165–175.

1974

Laird, J. D. Self-attribution of emotion: The effects of expressive behavior on the quality of emotional experience. *Journal of Personality and Social Psychology, 29,* 475–486.

Tversky, A., & Kahneman, D. Judgment under uncertainty: Heuristics and biases. *Science, 185,* 1124–1131.

Zadney, J., & Gerard, H. B. Attributed intentions and informational selectivity. *Journal of Experimental Social Psychology, 10,* 34–52.

Zanna, M. P., & Cooper, J. Dissonance and the pill: An attributional approach to studying the arousal properties of dissonance. *Journal of Personality and Social Psychology, 29,* 703–709.

Zillman, D., Johnson, R. C., & Day, K. D. Attribution of apparent arousal and proficiency of recovery from sympathetic activation affecting excitation transfer to aggressive behavior. *Journal of Experimental Social Psychology, 10,* 503–515.

1975

Brickman, P., Ryan, K., & Wortman, C. Causal chains: Attribution of responsibility as a function of immediate and prior causes. *Journal of Personality and Social Psychology, 32,* 1060–1067.

Comer, R., & Laird, J. D. Choosing to suffer as a consequence of expecting to suffer: Why do people do it? *Journal of Personality and Social Psychology, 32,* 92–101.

Dweck, C. S. The role of expectations and attributions in the alleviation of learned helplessness. *Journal of Personality and Social Psychology, 31,* 674–685.

Kruglanski, A. W. The endogenous–exogenous partition in attribution theory. *Psychological Review, 82,* 387–406.

Langer, E J. The illusion of control. *Journal of Personality and Social Psychology, 32,* 311–328.

Miller, D. T., & Ross, M. Self-serving biases in the attribution of causality: Fact or fiction? *Psychological Bulletin, 82,* 213–225.

Miller, R., Brickman, P., & Bolen, D. Attribution versus persuasion as a means for modifying behavior. *Journal of Personality and Social Psychology, 31,* 430–441.

Orvis, B. R., Cunningham, J. D., & Kelley, H. H. A closer examination of causal inference: The roles of consensus, distinctiveness, and consistency information. *Journal of Personality and Social Psychology, 32,* 605–616.

Ross, L., Lepper, M. R., & Hubbard, M. Perseverance in self-perception and social perception: Biased attribution processes in the debriefing paradigm. *Journal of Personality and Social Psychology, 32,* 880–892.

Taylor, S. E., & Fiske, S. T. Point of view and perceptions of causality. *Journal of Personality and Social Psychology, 32,* 439–445.

1976

Harvey, J. H., Ickes, W. J., & Kidd, R. F. (Eds.). *New directions in attribution research* (Vol. 1). Hillsdale, NJ: Erlbaum.

McGuire, W. J., & Padawer-Singer, A. Trait salience in the spontaneous self-concept. *Journal of Personality and Social Psychology, 33,* 743–754.

Nisbett, R. E., Borgida, E., Crandall, R., & Reed, H. Popular induction: Information is not necessarily informative. In J. S. Carroll & J. W. Payne (Eds.), *Cognition and social behavior.* Hillsdale, NJ: Erlbaum.

1977

Ajzen, I. Intuitive theories of events and the effects of base-rate information on prediction. *Journal of Personality and Social Psychology, 35,* 303–314.

Bulman, R. J., & Wortman, C. Attributions of blame and coping in the "real world": Severe accident victims react to their lot. *Journal of Personality and Social Psychology, 35,* 351–363.

McArthur, L. Z., & Post, D. L. Figural emphasis and person perception. *Journal of Experimental Social Psychology, 13,* 520–535.

Monson, T. C., & Snyder, M. Actors, observers, and the attribution process: Toward a reconceptualization. *Journal of Experimental Social Psychology, 13,* 89–111.

Nisbett, R. E., & Wilson, T. D. Telling more than we can know: Verbal reports on mental processes. *Psychological Review, 84,* 231–259.

Pryor, J. B., & Kriss, M. The cognitive dynamics of salience in the attribution process. *Journal of Personality and Social Psychology, 35,* 49–55.

Ross, L. The intuitive psychologist and his shortcomings: Distortions in the attribution process. In L. Berkowitz (Ed.), *Advances in experimental social psychology* (Vol. 10). New York: Academic Press.

Ross, L., Amabile, T. M., & Steinmetz, J. L. Social roles, social control, and biases in social perception processes. *Journal of Personality and Social Psychology, 35,* 817–829.

Ross, L., Greene, D., & House, P. The "false consensus effect": An egocentric bias in social perception and attribution processes. *Journal of Experimental Social Psychology, 13,* 279–301.

Shweder, R. A. Likeness and likelihood in everyday thought: Magical thinking in judgments about personality. *Current Anthropology, 18,* 637–648.

Snyder, M., Tanke, E. D., & Berscheid, E. Social perception and interpersonal behavior: On the self-fulfilling nature of social stereotypes. *Journal of Personality and Social Psychology, 35,* 656–666.

Wells, G. L., & Harvey, J. H. Do people use consensus information in making causal attributions? *Journal of Personality and Social Psychology, 35,* 279–293.

1978

Abramson, L. Y., Seligman, M. E. P., & Teasdale, J. D. Learned helplessness in humans: Critique and reformulation. *Journal of Abnormal Psychology, 87,* 49–74.

Diener, C. I., & Dweck, C. S. An analysis of learned helplessness: Continuous changes in performance, strategy, and achievement cognitions following failure. *Journal of Personality and Social Psychology, 36,* 451–462.

Dweck, C. S., Davidson, W., Nelson, S., & Enna, B. Sex differences in learned helplessness: II. The contingencies of evaluative feedback in the classroom and III. An experimental analysis. *Developmental Psychology, 14,* 268–276.

Harvey, J. H., Ickes, W. J., & Kidd, R. F. (Eds.). *New directions in attribution research* (Vol. 2). Hillsdale, NJ: Erlbaum.

Jones, E. E., & Berglas, S. Control of attributions about the self through self-handicapping strategies: The appeal of alcohol and the role of under-achievement. *Personality and Social Psychology Bulletin, 4,* 200–206.

Langer, E. J., & Benevento, A. Self-induced dependence. *Journal of Personality and Social Psychology, 36,* 886–893.

Snyder, M., & Swann, W. B. Behavioral confirmation in social interaction: From social perception to social reality. *Journal of Experimental Social Psychology, 14,* 148–162.

Taylor, S. E., & Fiske, S. T. Salience, attention, and attribution: Top of the head phenomena. In L. Berkowitz (Ed.), *Advances in experimental social psychology* (Vol. 11). New York: Academic Press.

Weary Bradley, G. Self-serving biases in the attribution process: A re-examination of the fact or fiction question. *Journal of Personality and Social Psychology, 36,* 56–71.

1979

Alloy, L. B., & Abramson, L. Y. Judgment of contingency in depressed and nondepressed students: Sadder but wiser? *Journal of Experimental Psychology: General, 108,* 441–485.

Elig, T., & Frieze, I. H. Measuring causal attributions for success and failure. *Journal of Personality and Social Psychology, 37,* 621–634.

Frieze, I. H., Bar-Tal, D., & Carroll, J. S. (Eds.). *New approaches to social problems.* San Francisco: Jossey-Bass.

Janoff-Bulman, R. Characterological versus behavioral self-blame: Inquiries into depression and rape. *Journal of Personality and Social Psychology, 37,* 1798–1809.

Kassin, S. M. Consensus information, prediction, and causal attribution: A review of the literature and issues. *Journal of Personality and Social Psychology, 37,* 1966–1981.

Marshall, G. D., & Zimbardo, P. G. Affective consequences of inadequately explained physiological arousal. *Journal of Personality and Social Psychology, 37,* 970–988.

Maslach, C. Negative emotional biasing of unexplained arousal. *Journal of Personality and Social Psychology, 37,* 953–969.

Reeder, G. D., & Brewer, M. B. A schematic model of dispositional attribution in interpersonal perception. *Psychological Review, 86,* 61–79.

Ross, M., & Sicoly, F. Egocentric biases in availability and attribution. *Journal of Personality and Social Psychology, 37,* 322–336.

Schneider, D. J., Hastorf, A. M., & Ellsworth, P. C. *Person perception.* Reading, MA: Addison-Wesley.

Snyder, M. L., Kleck, R. E., Stenta, A., & Mentzer, S. J. Avoidance of the handicapped: An attributional ambiguity analysis. *Journal of Personality and Social Psychology, 37,* 2297–2306.

1980

Darley, J. M., & Goethals, G. R. People's analyses of the causes of ability-linked performances. In L. Berkowitz (Ed.), *Advances in experimental social psychology* (Vol. 13). New York: Academic Press.

Fincham, F. D., & Jaspars, J. M. Attribution of responsibility: From man the scientist to man as lawyer. In L. Berkowitz (Ed.), *Advances in experimental social psychology* (Vol. 13). New York: Academic Press.

Greenwald, A. G. The totalitarian ego: Fabrication and revision of personal history. *American Psychologist, 35,* 603–618.

Hansen, R. D. Commensense attribution. *Journal of Personality and Social Psychology, 39,* 996–1009.

Harvey, J. H., Yarkin, K. L., Lightner, J. M., & Town, J. P. Unsolicited interpretation and recall of interpersonal events. *Journal of Personality and Social Psychology, 38,* 551–568.

Kelley, H. H., & Michela, J. L. Attribution theory and research. *Annual Review of Psychology, 31,* 457–501.

Lerner, M. J. *The belief in a just world: A fundamental delusion.* New York: Plenum.

Major, B. Information acquisition and attribution processes. *Journal of Personality and Social Psychology, 39,* 1010–1023.

Nisbett, R. E., & Ross, L. *Human inference: Strategies and shortcomings of social judgment.* Englewood Cliffs, NJ: Prentice-Hall.

REFERENCES

Note: References listed in the Appendix are excluded.

Coyne, J. C., & Gotlib, I. H. (1983). The role of cognition in depression: A critical appraisal. *Psychological Bulletin, 94,* 472–505.

Crocker, J. (1981). Judgment of covariation by social perceivers. *Psychological Bulletin, 90,* 272–292.

Fischhoff, B. (1976). Attribution theory and judgment under uncertainty. In J. H. Harvey, W. J. Ickes, & R. F. Kidd (Eds.), *New directions in attribution research* (Vol. 1). Hillsdale, NJ: Erlbaum.

Goethals, G. R., & Nelson, R. E. (1973). Similarity in the influence process: The belief-value distinction. *Journal of Personality and Social Psychology, 25,* 117–122.

Harvey, J. H., & Weary, G. (1984). Current issues in attribution theory and research. *Annual Review of Psychology, 35,* 427–459.

Harvey, J. H., Wells, G. L., & Alvarez, M. D. (1978). Attribution in the context of conflict and separation in close relationships. In J. H. Harvey, W. J. Ickes, & R. F. Kidd (Eds.), *New directions in attribution research* (Vol. 2). Hillsdale, NJ: Erlbaum.

Ickes, W. J., & Kidd, R. F. (1976). An attributional analysis of helping behavior. In J. H. Harvey, W. J. Ickes, & R. F. Kidd (Eds.), *New directions in attribution research* (Vol. 1). Hillsdale, NJ: Erlbaum.

Jones, E. E., & Nisbett, R. E. (1972). The actor and the observer: Divergent perceptions of the causes of behavior. In E. E. Jones, D. E. Kanouse, H. H. Kelley, R. E. Nisbett, S. Valins, & B. Weiner (Eds.), *Attribution: Perceiving the causes of behavior.* Morristown, NJ: General Learning Press.

Kelley, H. H. (1972). Causal schemata and the attribution process. In E. E. Jones, D. E. Kanouse, H. H. Kelley, R. E. Nisbett, S. Valins, & B. Weiner (Eds.), *Attribution: Perceiving the causes of behavior.* Morristown, NJ: General Learning Press.

McArthur, L. Z., & Baron, R. M. (1983). Toward an ecological theory of social perception. *Psychological Review, 90,* 215–238.

McFarland, C., & Ross, M. (1982). Impact of causal attributions on affective reactions to success and failure. *Journal of Personality and Social Psychology, 43,* 937–946.

Orvis, B. R., Kelley, H. H., & Butler, D. (1976). Attributional conflict in young couples. In J. H. Harvey, W. J. Ickes, & R. F. Kidd (Eds.), *New directions in attribution research* (Vol. 1). Hillsdale, NJ: Erlbaum.

Pittman, T. S., Quattrone, G., & Jones, E. E. (1983). *Control deprivation and the accuracy of attributional inferences.* Unpublished manuscript, Gettysburg College, Gettysburg, PA.

Regan, D. T. (1978). Attributional aspects of interpersonal attraction. In J. H. Harvey, W. J. Ickes, & R. F. Kidd (Eds.), *New directions in attribution research* (Vol. 2). Hillsdale, NJ: Erlbaum.

Ross, M., & Fletcher, G. J. O. (in press). Attribution and social perception. In G. Lindzey & E. Aronson (Eds.), *Handbook of social psychology* (3rd ed.). Reading, MA: Addison-Wesley.

Ross, M., & Olson, J. M. (1981). An expectancy-attribution model of the effects of placebos. *Psychological Review, 88,* 408–437.

Seligman, C., Fazio, R. H., & Zanna, M. P. (1980). Effects of salience of extrinsic rewards on liking and loving. *Journal of Personality and Social Psychology, 38,* 453–460.

Weiner, B., Frieze, I., Kukla, A., Reed, L., Rest, S., & Rosenbaum, R. M. (1972). Perceiving the causes of success and failure. In E. E. Jones, D. E. Kanouse, H. H. Kelley, R. E. Nisbett, S. Valins, & B. Weiner (Eds.), *Attribution: Perceiving the causes of behavior.* Morristown, NJ: General Learning Press.

Author Index

Numbers in italics refer to the pages on which the complete references are cited.

Subject Index

A

Ability, effort trade-off in social perception, 195–197
  implicit assumptions, 103–104
Attitudes, accessibility of processing preceding, 28–29
Attribution, and control motivation, 119–138
  covariation, 53–54
  developmental priority, 40–42
  salience determinant, 48–50
  selective review of research, 283–287
Attributional style, models and data, 244–272
Attributions, affect and behavior in relationships, 226–228
  basic processes, 287–294
  communicative role, 144–145
  consequences, 294–302
  content of attributions in relationships, 224–225
  level of attributions in relationships, 223–224
  observers' reactions to individuals', 145–147
  trait, 50–53

C

Causal processing, 75–81
  beyond minimal causation, 78–79
  minimal, 76–78
Causal schema, 80–81
Clinical psychology, implications for work on attributions in relationships, 217–228
  research on attributions in relationships, 208–212
Cognitive economy to inference economy, 66–67

Commonsense inference economy, 73–75
Consensus, 71–72
Control deprivation, information processing, 122–138
Controllability as an attributional dimension, 250–257
Covariation psychologic, 68–70

D

Depression, loneliness, and shyness, causality issue, 264–272
  causes, 240–244
  measuring, 238–239
Discounting, and augmentation psychologic, 70–71
  partial or insufficient, 94–96
Disposition, concept of, 108–111
Dispositional attribution, asymmetrical discounting in moral attribution, 105–108
  of ability, 104–108
  schematic model, 87–112
Distinctiveness, 71

E

Explanatory system, verbal, 16–20

I

Implicational relations, 89–94
Implicit central tendency assumptions, 91–93
Implicit social desirability assumptions, 98–100

L

Learned helplessness, 248–250

325